JOHN BOGLE
ON
INVESTING

JOHN BOGLE ON INVESTING

The First 50 Years

John C. Bogle

MCGRAW-HILL

New York San Francisco Washington, D.C. Auckland Bogotá
Caracas Lisbon London Madrid Mexico City Milan Montreal
New Delhi San Juan Singapore Sydney Tokyo Toronto

Library of Congress Cataloging-in-Publication Data

Bogle, John C.
    John Bogle on investing: the first 50 years / by John C. Bogle.
      p. cm.
    ISBN 0-07-136438-2
    1. Investments.   2. Securities.   3. Mutual funds.   4. Portfolio management.
  5. Vanguard Group of Investment Companies.   I. Title.

HG4521.B575 2000
332.6—dc21   00-041875

McGraw-Hill

A Division of The **McGraw·Hill** Companies

Chapter 8, "Selecting Equity Mutual Funds," is reprinted with permission of Institutional Investor, Inc.

  2 3 4 5 6 7 8 9 0   AGM/AGM   0 9 8 7 6 5 4 3 2 1 0

ISBN 0-07-136438-2

Printed and bound by Quebecor World/Martinsburg.

McGraw-Hill books are available at special quantity discounts to use as premiums and sales promotions, or for use in corporate training programs. For more information, please write to the Director of Special Sales, Professional Publishing, McGraw-Hill, Two Penn Plaza, New York, NY 10121-2298. Or contact your local bookstore.

This publication is designed to provide accurate and authoritative information in regard to the subject matter covered. It is sold with the understanding that neither the author nor the publisher is engaged in rendering legal, accounting, or other professional service. If legal advice or other expert assistance is required, the services of a competent professional person should be sought.
—*From a Declaration of Principles jointly adopted by a Committee of the American Bar Association and a Committee of Publishers.*

This book is printed on acid-free paper.

GREAT IDEAS

Dedicated to all of the human beings
who have meant so much to me
during the first 50 years of my career:
those loyal and steadfast members of the Vanguard crew
who together have made me look so much better than I am;
those millions of intelligent investors
who own the Vanguard Funds and The Vanguard Group,
and who have been willing to pay me a salary
for all the fun I've had and all the challenges I've faced;
and especially those "Bogleheads" of the Internet,
that dedicated and loyal cadre of Vanguard Diehards
who give me strength to carry on my mission.

CONTENTS

Part III
ECONOMICS AND IDEALISM: THE VANGUARD EXPERIMENT

Part IV
PERSONAL PERSPECTIVES

Part V
THE PRINCETON THESIS

FOREWORD

FIDUCIARY RESPONSIBILITY, OBJECTIVITY OF ANALYSIS, AND WILLINGNESS TO TAKE A STAND

*I*F A MODERN DAY Rip van Winkle were to wake up after a sleep of 50 years, he'd have a lot of trouble understanding today's financial markets or recognizing the names of the major participants. But if Rip happened to be, say, a Princeton professor who had monitored or read John Bogle's senior thesis, he wouldn't be at all surprised about one of the most significant developments in the world of the stock market and money management.

John Bogle didn't invent the business of mutual investment funds. They had started before he went to college, but were barely visible. His curiosity about the business was piqued by an article in a magazine as he was ruminating about a thesis topic. That bit of serendipity led not only to an honors thesis but to a lifelong vocation.

Today, mutual funds are the dominant investment medium for American families. They directly own a large fraction of all traded stock and a sizable share of bonds and liquid assets as well.

The success of the industry is built on a solid base—the demonstrable value of diversifying risk and spreading costs by collective investment. Those were concepts intuitively recognized and emphasized by the Princeton senior.

John Bogle has not, of course, been alone in seeing the basic merit of mutual funds, now counted in the thousands. His great contribution—his single-minded mission—has been to insist that those funds should be managed, first and foremost, in a way truly to serve the interests of the investing public.

That has meant strong emphasis on minimizing conflicts of interest and operating at the lowest possible cost. To those ends, the family of funds which John Bogle established a quarter of a century ago—The

Vanguard Group—has remained independent of ties to other businesses. It has long led the industry in operating without sales charges and with minimal operating costs.

Early in its life, Vanguard established the industry's first index fund. Over time, the stress on the value of index funds responded to the clear logic—a logic fully supported by the plain evidence—that most "active" money managers most of the time will not be able to "beat" the market. These days, after all, mutual funds largely are the market. On the average, they couldn't do better, even if they had no costs, operated with perfect efficiency, and incurred no taxes. With those hurdles to jump, very few funds can consistently outperform the averages.

That's not an easy conclusion for money managers to accept. John Bogle has not won many popularity contests among his professional colleagues. Moreover, he himself would readily confess that the unique form of governance and style of management that he instilled in Vanguard is not easy to replicate.

But from a distance, I along with many others have enormously admired the force and eloquence with which he has set forth his thinking. It is thinking that I find fully persuasive as an analytic matter and entirely consistent with the public interest. John Bogle's basic conviction that the mutual fund investor is entitled, in his words, to a "fair shake" should serve as the motto of every mutual fund.

This new volume happily makes that thinking easily available to a wider audience. John Bogle writes with unusual clarity and simplicity, clarity of the vision and simplicity of the written word. He has a rare ability to set out concisely and effectively the evidence to support his argument. A wry sense of humor can't quite disguise, and shouldn't disguise, his sense of frustration—even outrage—about some practices that permeate the industry that has been his life's work and personal passion.

All of us dependent on mutual funds or other collective investment institutions to manage our savings, and that is most of us, owe thanks to John Bogle for insisting that our interests be placed front and center.

Even more broadly, the strong sense of fiduciary responsibility, the objectivity of analysis, and the willingness to take a stand—qualities that permeate all his writings—set high standards for all those concerned with the growth and integrity of our open and competitive financial system.

Paul A. Volcker
May 1, 2000

INTRODUCTION

VISION AND CHARACTER

*L*ET ME INTRODUCE the great ideas in finance presented in this book by focusing on the author of them.

Virtue is a word that tends to embarrass us today. Perhaps we have lost a bit of the easy confidence that permitted earlier ages to believe in a fixed universe of good and evil. We are now very sensitive to the fact that in a diverse society we may not agree on the characteristics that constitute virtue, and today we may be on guard lest we be thought to impose our own contestable views of goodness on others who don't share them.

Yet in introducing the collected speeches of John Clifton Bogle I can start with no word other than virtuous to describe the author of these pieces, even if that word seems quaint to our ear. For John Bogle's life reflects such a deep commitment to the concepts of duty, honor, candor, diligence, and service to others that the most complete summarization of the man is to say that he is a man of high virtue. In an age that sometimes seems to have tried to raise gratification of the self to the status of a virtue, his life reminds us that the value of a life is measured by how one affects the lives of others, not by either celebrity or by balance sheet.

The power to affect the welfare of others positively is the aspect of business that gives it nobility. Bill Gates—arguably our most success-ful businessman—is, I suggest, not a great man because he is worth an astronomical sum. On that, I trust, we would all agree. If he is great, it is because, along with a team of others, he has done a great deal to bring the benefits of computers to millions of American homes. And in doing so has empowered others to achieve their various goals. His efforts have improved human welfare. The world is a noticeably better place because of his efforts.

Jack Bogle is a great businessman because he has changed the world in a way that confers huge benefits upon countless citizens, allowing them to better achieve their goals. He envisioned a firm that would be different from all those that had gone before and indeed is different still in a fundamental way. He worked with his team—his crew—to build that business into a great enterprise. He is a great man because of the content of his vision and the impact it has had on others.

Vanguard is not simply a successful company. It is an idea of service which, while not selfless, is deeply committed to fairness and the delivery of value. It is a cliché for business to be committed to delivery of value to customers in order to deliver value to shareholders. But in the mutual fund business at any rate, the best evidence suggested to Jack Bogle that an unconscionable share of value was being sidetracked from investors by excess costs. Of course neither Jack Bogle nor those who worked with him wear sackcloth. In creating a successful enterprise, Jack and his team created value that compensated them for their efforts. But his vision was from the beginning radically inconsistent with maximizing returns for the managers of the fund. The public was the principal beneficiary of his vision.

During decades in which average mutual funds charged fees of 150 basis points or considerably more, Vanguard's structure allowed it to offer comparable—actually superior—service for far less than a quarter as much. Today Vanguard manages about $500 billion in retirement and other savings. Thus, this year it will return some $4 billion more to its investors than they would have had if Jack Bogle had not had the vision to build this enterprise. But this estimated number *underestimates* Vanguard's annual impact upon the savings and retirement portfolio of Americans. There is every reason to suppose that, had Vanguard never been founded, the average costs of management of mutual funds would remain as high as they were in 1970. Considering that the existence of the Vanguard philosophy has forced other funds to reduce their fees and costs materially, it would be difficult indeed to estimate how many billions of dollars of savings go into the retirement savings of working men and women across this country today as a result of Mr. Bogle's vision.

An interesting fact about this unique enterprise is that it reflects an academic theory. When Jack Bogle encountered the efficient market hypothesis, he understood it and its implications quickly and intuitively.

His years of pupilage with Walter Morgan in Philadelphia had trained him to understand that in the long term it would be exceedingly difficult for any investment adviser to produce substantial excess returns over the returns of the market itself. Thus his famously successful business plan was simply to reduce costs and diversify risks. He applied theory to practice, inventing the index mutual fund as a commercial alternative to savings. The idea of course is simple, not fancy; in that it reflects the character of the man. For Vanguard's founder is, like his company, world class in performance and straightforward and unaffected in manner.

Perhaps these characteristics were inculcated in the young man at the Blair Academy or at Princeton University. Perhaps he learned them at the side of his older brother and his twin brother, who is now gone. Certainly the idea of fair sharing and of duty to another are concepts that brothers share. Almost certainly the boys learned at home the characteristics that shine in the man today. Strength of character, belief in candor rather than artifice, in substance rather than in form, and in performance not promises.

Jack Bogle's life has not been without its moments of drama and tension and not without its keen and painful losses. The story of Vanguard's founding is an arresting business drama in which, at the beginning at least, the outcome did not seem foreordained. But Vanguard's rise to eminence in the world of finance attests to the soundness of its principles. The speeches that are collected in this volume capture in vivid outline the core concepts of Jack's vision and inevitably disclose as well the outstanding character of the man. That these two elements—vision and character—are inextricably linked is possibly the most fundamental and basic lesson that Jack Bogle's career teaches those of us interested in finance and investing.

William T. Allen
Professor of Law and Finance
Director, Center for Law and Business
New York University
Former Chancellor, Court of Chancery,
The State of Delaware

Abridgment of remarks delivered on the occasion of the awarding of the honorary degree Doctor of Laws upon John Clifton Bogle by the University of Delaware, October 22, 1999.

PREFACE

*T*HOUGH IT HAPPENED more than a half-century ago, it seems like only yesterday that I was a junior at Princeton University, barely out of my teenage years, an insecure but determined young man with a crew cut, majoring in economics. Seated in the reading room of the newly opened Firestone Library, I was reading current business literature as I considered a topic for my forthcoming senior thesis. As the sun poured into the reading room, I paged through the December 1949 issue of *Fortune* magazine. Fate must have been looking on me with favor, for, as I came to page 116, my eye caught an article entitled, "Big Money in Boston." It appraised a business of which I was totally ignorant: The mutual fund industry. I guess it's fair to say that the rest is history.

After reading and re-reading the article, I quickly decided that, for a whole variety of reasons, the fund industry would be the perfect topic for my thesis. First, because I had long since decided I would write my thesis on a subject no previous thesis had ever tackled; there, by the process of elimination, went Adam Smith, Karl Marx, John Maynard Keynes, and a score of other noted economists. Second, because it was a subject on which little had been written, and thus represented a wonderful opportunity for original research. Indeed when I'd finished my research, the *Fortune* article turned out to be the *only* substantive mutual fund article in a major magazine that I ever found. And third, because the article described the industry as "tiny . . . but contentious." To me, *tiny* suggested an opportunity for growth, and *contentious* appealed to the argumentative, stubborn, and contrarian side of my persona.

It all seemed too good to be true. Within a few months, in a tiny carrel in Firestone, I began the arduous task of researching and writing my thesis. In the course of my work, I read scores of articles from *The Wall Street Journal, The New York Times,* and the trade press; three *Investment Companies* manuals, published annually by Arthur Weisenberger & Company; and the entire 4217-page report of the Securities and Exchange Commission to the Congress, a report that led to the passage of the Investment Company Act of 1940. I also interviewed a half-dozen fund industry executives, and evaluated the limited data made available by the fund industry's trade association (predecessor to today's Investment Company Institute), then with a one-man staff. (It took John Sheffey, that doubtless overburdened executive director, four months merely to acknowledge my request for information.) It was hard work, but it was a thrilling project. And in March 1951, I completed my hunt-and-peck typing and my hand-drawn charts, had the 140-page document bound in hard cover, and, right on deadline, handed my adviser the finished copy: "The Economic Role of the Investment Company."

It seems problematic, as some have generously alleged, that my thesis laid out the design for what Vanguard would become. But whatever the case, many of the practices I specified then would, 50 years later, prove to lie at the very core of the firm's success. "The principal function of mutual funds is the management of their investment portfolios. Everything else is incidental. . . . Future industry growth can be maximized by a reduction of sales loads and management fees. . . . Mutual funds can make no claim to superiority over the market averages. . . . The industry's tremendous growth potential rests on its ability to serve the needs of both individual and institutional investors." And, with a final rhetorical flourish, funds should operate "in the most efficient, honest, and economical way possible." Were those words of mine merely callow, even sophomoric, idealism? Or were they the early design for a sound enterprise? I'll leave it to you to decide. But whatever was truly in my mind all those years ago, the thesis clearly put forth the proposition that mutual fund shareholders must be given a fair shake.

Three Surprising Turnarounds

As it happened, the thesis brought my collegiate career to a wonderful and surprising climax. During my early years at Princeton, I had struggled to produce satisfactory grades. My lack of intellectual brilliance, the tough academic environment, the long hours I spent on campus jobs to earn the money I needed beyond the full scholarship the university had generously provided me, and perhaps my slow maturation—all combined to limit my scholastic achievements. Indeed, my midterm grade in the first economics course I took was a scholarship-threatening 4+ (D+ in today's terms), which endangered my very continuance at Princeton. But it may have been that early scholastic shock that led to the pinnacle of my collegiate career. My grades steadily improved, into the threes, then into the twos, and finally into the ones. With the coveted 1+ that I earned on my thesis, my diploma would read: *magna cum laude.*

A second surprising turnaround was in my relationship with Professor Paul M. Samuelson of the Massachusetts Institute of Technology. It was the first edition of his *Economics: An Introductory Analysis* that I had struggled with in Economics 101 in the autumn of 1948. But my baneful introduction to economics came to a blessed conclusion a half-century later, when Dr. Samuelson, by then a Nobel Laureate in Economics, wrote the foreword to my 1993 book, *Bogle on Mutual Funds*, and then endorsed my 1999 book, *Common Sense on Mutual Funds.*

The final turnaround in the series also required a full half-century. After I graduated from Princeton, I sent a copy of my thesis to Paul Johnston, the mutual fund editor of *Barron's.* To my amazement, he urged me to edit it for publication by Dow Jones & Company, owner of *Barron's.* Inspired and delighted, I did just that. Alas, they decided not to go forward. So it must be some form of poetic justice that, exactly a half-century after I sat down in the reading room of Firestone Library in December 1949, McGraw-Hill came to me with a proposal that my writings on investment philosophy and strategy over the years constitute the first volume of its new series, *Great Ideas in Finance,* using as its centerpiece that ancient thesis that began my career all those years ago. Just 50 years after I began to write it, my thesis is at last published! As John Milton reminded us: "They also serve who only stand and wait."

Great Ideas in Finance

The storybook career that followed my graduation, recounted in various sections of this book, requires no further mention here. Suffice it to say that in 1965, at the tender age of 36, I was put in charge of the mutual fund organization I had joined immediately following my graduation, and promptly arranged an unwise merger that came back to haunt me. I was fired in January 1974, and founded Vanguard in September of that year. By the mid-1960s I began to speak out publicly on industry affairs, first as the consummate insider and later, after the novel road taken by Vanguard—with our unique governance structure, unusual economics, singular investment philosophy, and enlightened approach to human values—as a maverick, regarded (generously put) as a heretic in the mutual fund temple.

In my speeches over the years, I've presented a chain of interlinked ideas that I hope merit inclusion as great ideas in finance. Together, they constitute a philosophy whose bedrock principle is that, because of the heavy frictional costs of investing, the odds against any investor's outpacing the market over the long pull are stunning—perhaps less than one chance out of 30. That being the case, the most effective means of building wealth is simply to emulate the annual returns provided by the financial markets, and reap the benefits of long-term compounding.

This goal, as it turns out, can best be achieved by minimizing the costs of investing—sales commissions, advisory fees, taxes, and the like—and seeking to earn the highest possible portion of the annual return earned in each sector of the financial markets in which you invest, *recognizing, and accepting, that that portion will be less than 100%*. To achieve this goal, the ideal investment program includes four elements:

1. *Simplicity: Matching*, not *beating*, the markets; asset allocation that is *strategic*, not *tactical*.
2. *Focus:* Maximizing the *productive economics* (earnings and dividends, interest yields) of investing; minimizing the *counterproductive emotions* of investing (changing price-earnings ratios).
3. *Efficiency:* Economical operations; minimization of the frictional costs of fees and commissions and taxes.
4. *Stewardship:* Placing the interest of the client first; unyielding emphasis on human beings and eternal values—integrity, honesty, candor.

"The majesty of simplicity in an empire of parsimony," pretty well sums it all up. And over the years, practice has confirmed theory. *In the real world, investment experience has confirmed that these principles work.*

In important measure, Vanguard's corporate structure, focus on cost and service to clients, and pioneering implementation of index (and index-like) mutual funds have combined to become a classic example of the link that I've long observed between idealism and economics: *Enlightened idealism is sound economics.* Even a casual reading of my ancient Princeton thesis would, I think, reflect that pervasive idealism. To this day, I use quotations from it to define the genesis of my views, from the forces that move financial markets (both *enterprise* and *speculation,* in Lord Keynes' timeless formulation), to the forces that *fail* to move fund managers to behave as responsible corporate citizens (Chapter 14, "The Silence of the Funds"). But the highest manifestation of this idealism comes in my long-standing view that the central principle of the mutual fund business should be, *not the marketing of financial products to customers, but the stewardship of investment services for clients.*

The fund industry, however, has moved in just the opposite direction. As striking as has been the rise of mutual funds to become the investment of choice of American families, the Great Bull Market that has fostered that growth, and the reversal of the role of stocks from engines of income to engines of capital growth, the change in the character of the industry has been equally dramatic. Marketing has displaced management as the industry's chief principle, and expenditures on investment advisory services are today dwarfed by expenditures on advertising and sales promotion, with boxcar past returns advertised—contrary to the vision in my thesis—as if they would recur into eternity. It is fund investors who pay all of these costs. Despite the exponential growth in industry assets, fund *unit* costs have actually *risen,* and the *dollar* costs paid directly by fund shareholders have leaped from $18 *million* in 1950 to an estimated $62 *billion* in 2000! ($125-plus billion if we include indirect costs such as those incurred in the execution of fund portfolio transactions.)

Not only has the industry become a "cash cow" for fund sponsors and managers as well as Wall Street brokers and bankers, it has increasingly become a vehicle for short-term speculation, a trend fostered in part by the industry's focus on marketing. Today, the average *fund* holds the average stock for about 400 *days,* compared with six years when I wrote my thesis. And the average fund *shareholder* holds each of his or her mutual funds for about three years, compared with 15 years a half-century ago. What a sad interregnum—and I'm confident it is no more than that—in the history of what should be the finest medium ever designed for the long-term investor.

How the Book Is Organized

This book is divided into five sections. The first four parts include the texts of 25 speeches, delivered over the past 30 years, that articulate my philosophy of sound investing.

- Part I, "Investment Strategies for the Intelligent Investor," deals with equity fund selection and index funds ("The Bagel and the Doughnut" and "The Needle or the Haystack"); the relative merits of complexity and simplicity; the risks of investing as they appeared in year 2000 and in 1988 ("Buy Stocks? No Way"), and bond fund selection.

- Part II, "Taking on the Mutual Fund Industry," describes past and future trends driving the fund industry ("Mutual Funds: The Paradox of Light and Darkness"); information about how the mutual fund business is conducted ("Economics 101: For Mutual Fund Investors . . . For Mutual Fund Managers"); and reflections on corporate governance, including the role played by mutual funds as investors, as well as fund governance itself ("Where Are the Independent Directors?").

- Part III, "Economics and Idealism: The Vanguard Experiment," touches on the investment philosophy and human values that I've done my best to inculcate into our enterprise. This section includes "The Winds of Change: The Vanguard Experiment in Internalized Management," explaining our mission to industry executives six months after our 1974 founding; and one speech ("Deliverance") given in 1971, more than three years *before* our founding, that comes surprisingly close to describing the structure and the philosophy the yet-unborn Vanguard would adopt.

- Part IV, "Personal Perspectives," presents five speeches to general audiences, including a lecture at Princeton University, where I received the Woodrow Wilson Award for "Princeton in the Nation's Service" in early 1999 ("The Hedgehog and the Fox"); and, later in 1999, an address to a high school graduating class on the theme, "The Things by Which One Measures One's Life"; and an appreciation of organ donation ("Telltale Hearts"), delivered in May 2000. This section concludes with a commencement speech to new masters of business administration at Vanderbilt University in 1992 ("Press On Regardless").

- Part V, "The Princeton Thesis," includes the entire text, reset in type but unedited from the 1951 original that I typed by hand on my ancient Smith-Corona.

In publishing this compilation of speeches, we had to choose between two alternatives: (1) printing each speech in its entirety so it would stand completely on its own, at the cost of an inevitable repetition of data and themes; and (2) editing each speech to eliminate any repetition, at the cost of making the reader's course through the book somewhat bumpy and discontinuous. We chose the first alternative, though I did some minor editing to remove a few obvious overlaps. Even as Sunday after Sunday the minister in the pulpit speaks of God, the Golden Rule, and the Ten Commandments, so perhaps will my own repetition—in a far more parochial calling—serve the useful purpose of reinforcing my principles.

While none of my most basic ideas has changed over the years, I suspect you will note that I have become more assured, confident, and even strident in my expression of the validity of these bedrock principles. Nonetheless, when the passage of years proved some of my ideas misguided or wrongheaded, I did not change the original text. For I believe it is important to maintain the integrity of the speeches as they were written at the time. To the extent my views have been altered, I fall back on the words of Supreme Court Justice Felix Frankfurter. Explaining his change of heart on a legal matter, he said, "Wisdom too often never comes, and so one ought not to reject it just because it comes late."

Two Careers

In a sense, my long business career has been paralleled by a long writing career. I can fairly date the beginning of my major concern with the written word to the autumn of 1945, when, in my junior year at Blair Academy, I studied under my first truly challenging master of English by the name of, believe it or not, Henry Adams. He was an inspiring teacher, who in my senior year was succeeded by Marvin Garfield Mason, an even more memorable character. Mr. Mason seemed somehow to sense a grain of writing potential within me, for he marked my weekly themes with the enthusiasm of the devil himself, his red pencil flying across my every phrase, or so I recall it today. What he drummed into me, most of all, was what Macaulay wrote about Dr. Johnson: "The force of his mind overcame his every impediment."

Thanks to those two masters, I was well prepared for the extensive writing of themes and papers and examinations required at Princeton. During my first two years there, I became a passable—no more than that!—writer of expository prose. But it was the writing of my senior thesis that became the first *magnum opus* of my writing career. When you read my thesis, I imagine you will be bowled over neither by the grace of my prose nor the power of my arguments. But in my defense, I have done my best to recognize my inadequacies, striving for improvement in both areas ever since. I hope the demanding reader will recognize a gradual increase in the quality of my writing and the focus of my ideas during the half-century.

I love the English language. I check my set of the 20-volume second edition of the Oxford English Dictionary virtually every day, not only to make sure I get my words just right, but to enjoy learning from whence all those words come. *Every word comes from somewhere!* And words have power. As I wrote in the chapter "On Leadership" in my second book, *Common Sense on Mutual Funds,* the right words have the power to "shape the way investors look at us, and the way we look at ourselves." *Employee,* for example, is banned at Vanguard in favor of *crewmember, customer* is banned in favor of *client;* and *product* is banned in favor of *mutual fund.* I have a passion for the words of our splendid mother tongue, a passion that I hope is reflected in my writing.

As I have become a virtual missionary for the philosophy reflected in this book, it occurs to me that, after the huge output of writing I've produced over the years, there is a close link between my twin careers as investment executive and financial writer: *The power of the word and the power of the book have played a major role in turning my vision of 1949 into the reality of year 2000.* It is the power of words and books—explaining and dramatizing great ideas and articulating high ideals—that is the greatest weapon in the missionary's arsenal. And so it has been for this mundane advocate of the great ideas in finance that are set forth in this book—deceptively simple ideas that are gradually changing the way Americans invest. The gospel continues to spread, and the best is yet to be.

Valley Forge, PA   John C. Bogle
April 4, 2000

SOME WORDS OF
APPRECIATION

IT SEEMS LIKE ONLY yesterday
when Jeffrey A. Krames, publisher at The McGraw-Hill Companies,
visited me in my Vanguard offices to propose a new book: selections
from the 100-plus formal speeches that I've delivered over the past
30 years. Actually, it was on November 1, 1999, close to the 50th
anniversary, as it were, of my fortuitous reading of an article in the
December 1949 issue of *Fortune* magazine. The subject of the story
intrigued me, and I decided to write my Princeton thesis on it: *the
mutual fund industry.* On that random event of a half-century ago
depended everything that followed in my long career in this business.
When Jeff suggested that my ancient thesis be one of the center-
pieces of the book, I quickly succumbed to the obvious temptation
and agreed to his proposal.

So, first, I thank Jeff for his initiative. I also thank both him and
McGraw-Hill editor Stephen Isaacs for their constructive support in
helping me select the most significant speeches, in reviewing my new
text that places the thesis and the speeches in context, and in bringing
the publication of my third book to a happy conclusion. I also express
my special appreciation to my associates who comprise the staff of
Vanguard's Bogle Financial Markets Research Center: My good right
arm Kevin P. Laughlin provided tireless assistance, not only in preparing this manuscript for publication, but also in the yeoman's work he's
done for me in research and editorial support during his first year at
my side. Emily A. Snyder, my ever-loyal assistant, gave me the same
high level of secretarial assistance, constructive suggestions, and Job-
like patience that she's offered me for more than a decade. Denise
Diefenderfer, our newest aide, also played a supportive role. With

their help, and with the special insights of Vanguard's Craig M. Stock, we have a book!

I also want to thank two of America's titans for their willingness to write a foreword and an introduction, respectively: Paul A. Volcker, international statesman *extraordinaire* and distinguished chairman of the Federal Reserve Board from 1979 to 1987 (and member of Princeton's Class of 1949); and William T. Allen, eminent jurist, Chancellor of the Court of Chancery of the State of Delaware from 1985 to 1997, and now Chairman of the Independence Standards Board. That their words are generous beyond measure is gratifying. But that these two brilliant leaders—in fields as varied as banking and jurisprudence—are firm believers in the core investment ideas of my career is an endorsement beyond compare.

JCB

Part I

INVESTMENT STRATEGIES FOR THE INTELLIGENT INVESTOR

I N MY MISSION to bring the simplicity of investing to American families—the wisdom of focusing on the long term, the futility of trying to outguess the market, and the powerful burden that the high cost of investing places on investment success—I've constantly strived to translate abstract financial ideas into down-to-earth terms to which ordinary human beings can relate. Perhaps my efforts to do so will be obvious in the opening three chapters of this book. Chapter 1, "Investing in the New Millennium: The Bagel and the Doughnut," was inspired by an essay by *New York Times* journalist William Safire. While he was writing about, well, bagels and doughnuts, I use these baked goods as an analogy for both the stock market (the hard-crusted nutrition of corporate earnings and dividends versus the tempting but transitory sweetness of price-earnings multiples) and the mutual fund industry (the solid, patient index fund versus the frenetic, but finally undernourishing, actively managed mutual fund).

The next two chapters pursue the same theme in different ways, with "The Clash of the Cultures in Investing" describing the disappointing records achieved by four groups of money managers and financial advisers following traditional active strategies. These approaches face long odds, I conclude, so gamblers should use them only for their "funny money account." I contrast them with passive strategies such as indexing, my preferred choice for the "serious money account." Perhaps unsurprisingly, I recommend that no more than 5% of the investor's assets be allocated to funny money. Next, in "Equity Fund Selection: The Needle or the Haystack," I rely on Cervantes' timeless warning against looking for a needle in a haystack. The odds against finding the winning mutual fund in the stock market haystack are demonstrably long, so I conclude: *Don't bother looking. Just buy the all-market haystack.*

In these heady market days at the turn of the century, I thought it would prove wise—perhaps even prescient—to remind investors about the importance of risk and risk control, the subject of Chapter 4. When the day comes that the stock market falls flat on its face, as it does periodically, investors will need to keep their perspective. So, in Chapter 5 I present a speech delivered in 1988, with the stock market still pale, sickly, and, well, hungover, after the abrupt 35% market decline that took place in September–October 1987. My title, "Buy Stocks? No Way!," was a quotation from a cover story in *Time* magazine in September 1988 that warned investors to stay away from the stock market: ". . . one of the sleaziest enterprises in the world . . . a dangerous game . . . a crapshoot." Even then I was beating the index fund drum, urging "low cost, unmanaged index-oriented investing as a core portion of the equity portfolios of most investors." Ever the contrarian, I took the *Time* story as a sign that investors "should avoid liquidating equity holdings at prices that reflect fear and pessimism, (hold) common stocks as the centerpiece of their financial programs," and stay the course. It may well be that not too far down the road, the long bull market of 1982–2000 will face its own Waterloo, and I'll have to dust off that perspective and once again air some consummate good sense. Who really knows?

I've also talked often to professional audiences about, not only the remarkable value of stock market indexing, but the critical need for the managers and marketers of index funds to face up to the limitations of indexing and the risks in dragging this inherently simple concept too far from its roots: Owning a passive portfolio that represents the entire U.S. stock market. The speeches in Chapters 6 and 7, delivered at The Superbowl of Indexing in 1998 and 1999, respectively, present some of these issues. The former talk challenges the essay published by a deservedly respected investment banking firm entitled "The Death Rattle of Indexing" and concludes, Macbeth-like, that "the knell that summons thee to heaven or hell" was in fact tolling for the death, not of indexing, but of active managers. The latter talk celebrates the growth of the assets of Vanguard's 500 Index Fund to $100 billion, a milestone that serves to mark "the moment that heresy (the idea of market indexing) finally turned to dogma." Even so, I express concerns about overmarketing the index concept, cautioning that "there is a difference between designing a product that sells, and creating an investment that serves."

Chapters 8 and 9, both dating back nearly a decade, present my ideas on the successful selection of equity funds and bond funds. In both cases, I stress the need for careful analysis of past returns and risks, consistency of investment policies, emphasis on high quality and broad diversification, avoidance of strategic gimmickry, and focus on funds with the lowest sales charges (or, even better, *none*) and the lowest management fees and operating expenses. Most of these ideas date to my Princeton thesis.

1

INVESTING IN THE NEW MILLENNIUM: THE BAGEL AND THE DOUGHNUT

Sunday Breakfast Club of Philadelphia
January 5, 2000

MY TITLE IS INSPIRED by William Safire's essay, "Bagels vs. Doughnuts," published just a few months ago in *The New York Times*. These baked goods, Safire tells us, are similar in shape but different in character: Bagels are "serious, ethnic, and hard to digest. Doughnuts are fun, crumbly, sweet, and fattening. . . . The triumph of bagelism in the 1980s and early 1990s meant that tough munching was ascendant; the decline of doughnutism meant that soft sweetness was in trouble." But, Safire commiserates, the doughnut is coming back into the mainstream. Why? Because, with the advent of—Heaven forbid!—the *blueberry* bagel and the bagel *sandwich*, "the bagel has moved toward the center, its crust going soft and spongy, and lost its distinctive hard-boiled nature."

Well, surprising as it may seem, in all of this food for thought (pun *intended*), I find a message about bagels and doughnuts in each of the three subjects on which I'd like to reflect with you this evening, a year before the start of the new millennium, which, as only a killjoy would point out, doesn't begin until January 1, 2001: (1) The outlook for the stock market; (2) the coming change in the mutual fund industry; and (3) the challenges faced by Vanguard—the enterprise I founded on September 24, 1974, just over a quarter-century ago—as the new century begins.

5

1. The Bagel and the Doughnut in the Stock Market

During the final two decades of the 20th century, the U.S. stock market has provided the highest returns ever recorded in its 200-year history—17.7% per year, as stock prices have doubled every four years. What have been the sources of this unparalleled growth? Well, complex and mysterious as the stock market may seem, its returns are determined by the simple interaction of just *two* elements: *investment returns,* represented by dividend yields and earnings growth; and *speculative returns,* represented by changes in the price that investors are willing pay for each dollar of earnings. It's that simple. It really is!

It is hardly farfetched to consider that investment return is the bagel of the stock market. The investment returns on stocks reflect their underlying character, nutritious, crusty and hard-boiled. By the same token, *speculative* return is the spongy doughnut of the market. The speculative returns on stocks represent the impact of changing public opinion about stock valuations, from the soft sweetness of optimism to the acid sourness of pessimism. The bagel-like *economics of investing* are almost inevitably productive. Corporate earnings and dividends have provided a steady underlying return over the long pull, the result of the long-term growth of productivity and prosperity in our resilient American economy. But the flaky, doughnut-like *emotions of investors* are anything but steady—sometimes productive, sometimes counterproductive. Price-earnings ratios may soar or they may plummet, reflecting wide swings in investor valuations of the economy's future prospects.

Over the past two decades, the investment returns on stocks have been solid. The initial dividend yield contributed a generous 4.5% to returns, and earnings growth set a good, but hardly remarkable, pace of 5.9% annually. Combining the two produced a fundamental return of 10.4%, closely in line with the 11% nominal return on stocks over the long term. But the speculative return was larger than *either* of those two fundamental elements of investment return. The market's price-earnings ratio rose from 7.3 times as 1980 began to 30 times as year 2000 begins, a rise that, spread over two decades, has contributed another 7.3% per year, the laboring oar in carrying the *total* return of the market to 17.7% annually. (See Table 1.1.)

If we cumulate these figures, the twenty-year return on the Standard & Poor's 500 Index came to +2500%. Just 600 points—one-fourth of this gain—were accounted for by investment fundamentals;

TABLE 1.1 Annual Rates of Return on U.S. Stocks

COMPONENTS OF RETURN	ACTUAL 1969–1979	ACTUAL 1979–1999	POSSIBLE 1999–2009
Initial dividend yield	3.4%	4.5%	1.2%
Earnings growth	9.9	5.9	8.0
Investment return	13.3%	10.4%	9.2%
Speculative return*	−7.5%	7.3%	−4.0%
Total return	5.8%	17.7%	5.2%
Initial earnings	$5.78	$14.90	$47.00
Initial P/E ratio	15.9x	7.3x	30.0x
Final earnings	$14.90	$47.00	$101.50
Final P/E ratio	7.3x	30.0x	20.0x

*Impact of P/E change.

the other 1900 points represented the pendular swing from pervasive pessimism to overpowering optimism on the part of investors. Put another way, more than three-quarters of the cumulative increase in stock prices during this great bull market has simply reflected a sea change in public opinion about the future prospects for common stock returns, as price-earnings ratios more than *quadrupled.*

Now of course both history and common sense tell us that price-earnings ratios cannot rise forever. In the decade of the 1970s, for example, the price-earnings ratio *fell* by more than 50%, from 16 times to 7.3 times, an annual drag of −7.5% that *reduced* the 13.3% fundamental return generated by earnings and dividends to just 5.8% per year. Yet ironically, that bagel of investment fundamentals—dividend yield of 3.4% and annual earnings growth of 9.9%—produced almost 30% more nutrition than the 10.4% investment return of the next two decades of soaring stock prices. The overriding difference between the inadequate 1970s and the golden 1980s and 1990s, then, was not better bagelism, but the swing of doughnutry from the sweetness of optimism to the sourness of pessimism in the 70s, and then back again in the 80s and 90s, to the greatest sweetness the market has ever recorded.

As we come to consider the outlook for the stock market in the first decade of the new millennium, we need answer on only two questions: Will the bagel of investment fundamentals give us its usual sustenance? And will the doughnut of speculation get even sweeter than it is today, or will it finally sour again? As to the fundamentals, please realize that we begin the decade with far less sustenance than when the bull market began. For the dividend yield on stocks is at an all-time low of just over 1%, meaning that it will take earnings growth of more than 9% to provide a fundamental return equal to the 10.4% total of the past two decades. I think that's too optimistic. But 8% growth maybe possible, given the revolution—and it is indeed no less than that—now taking place in global technology, communications, and productivity. We are clearly in a New Era for the *economy*.

Whether we are in a New Era for *investing*, however, is a far different question. If we are to have a continuation of 17%-plus returns—which, polls tell us, represent the public expectation—the doughnut of speculation will have to soar even beyond today's unprecedented peak of sweetness. To get there, assuming a fundamental return of 9.2% (1.2% yield and 8% earnings growth), the market's price-earnings ratio would have to rise from 30 times today to 67 times a decade from now. I simply can't imagine that happening.

Confession being good for the soul, however, I admit that a decade ago, I made a similar analysis of the market, and I was wrong. My fundamentals were about right—my projection of an investment return of 9.7% per year for the 1990s was remarkably close to the actual figure of 10.5%. But I guessed that the price-earnings ratio might ease back from 15.5 times to its then-historic-norm of 14 times. While, happily, I urged investors to maintain their equity positions, I waited and watched the price-earnings ratio rise, as we now know, to 30 times, more than double that figure, making my midrange projection of 9% stock returns—and even my optimistic projection of 13%—seem stodgy. Clearly history doesn't always repeat! And even if one believes that reversion to the mean in market returns will inevitably take place, it can take a long, long time to do so. As I reminded investors then—and I remind you tonight—be leery of projections, whether founded in reasonable expectations or just picked out of the proverbial hat. *Anything can happen in the stock market.*

But with that caution in mind, I'll nevertheless combine my (decidedly optimistic) fundamental forecast of 9.2% with a forecast that today's speculation will retreat from the market's heady optimism to something considerably less exuberant. Should the current price-earnings ratio ease back to 20 times—hardly bearish—the fundamental return would be reduced by −4.0% annually to bring the market return to 5.2% per year—well short of the 7.5% to 8% available on a high-grade bond portfolio today. That scenario would be a rare one, for bonds have outpaced stocks in but one of every six past decades. But it could easily happen in the coming decade. Only time will tell.

For whatever comfort—or discomfort—it's worth, my views are very close to those of the estimable Warren Buffett. In October's *Fortune* magazine, using a somewhat different methodology, he suggested 6% as a reasonable expectation for stock returns over the next decade. It's nice to find myself in such good company. But I hardly need warn you that the fact that Mr. Bogle and Mr. Buffett agree doesn't prove *anything*. Nonetheless, following two decades of record-setting market returns, it would be hard to be shocked by—*or even dissatisfied with*—a third decade that witnesses some consolidation of past gains. And if we face a decade in which we enjoy a continuation of the solid sustenance of the bagel, but without the added sweetness of the doughnut, I, for one, would count my blessings.

2. The Bagel and the Doughnut in the Mutual Fund Industry

In an environment of lower equity market returns, however, the mutual fund industry will not count *its* blessings. For lower market returns are the industry's bane. The extraordinarily high stock returns generated in the great bull market that has happily persisted for close to two full decades have blessed this market-sensitive industry, which is among the fastest growing of all American industries during the past twenty years. Since 1980 began, fund assets have risen nearly 70-fold, from less than $100 billion to some *$6.5 trillion*. Assets of stock funds alone, now almost $4.0 trillion of the total, have risen 120-fold.

While the rising market tide has lifted *nearly* all mutual fund boats, very few equity funds have provided their shareholders with anything like the generous returns offered by the market. Indeed of the 426 fund boats that began the voyage 15 years ago, 113—nearly one of every four—have sunk along the way, despite the absence of even one protracted market storm. Fair weather for the market, yes, but foul weather for most funds. Still, the average diversified stock fund that survived the period—obviously excluding the poorer performers— provided an after-tax return of just 12.3%, compared to the 17.7% return of the stock market itself. Final value of $10,000 invested at the outset: total stock market, $115,000; average mutual fund, $57,000.

What was the problem? Simply this: in their frenetic search for sweet, fattening returns, the mutual fund doughnuts levied heavy sales charges, charged excessive fees, spent too much on marketing, and failed to share the economies of scale with the investors they were responsible to serve. On average, equity fund operating expenses and management fees cost some 1.2% of assets annually (they're now more than 1.5%); sales charges cost some 0.5%; and funds paid an opportunity cost of 0.6%, simply because funds were not fully invested in stocks as the market rose. That's a total hit to return of 2.3%.

But that's only the beginning. The doughnut-like mutual funds, ever-searching for the market's sweet spots, turn over their portfolios at an astonishing rate of 90% per year—clearly short-term speculation, not long-term investing. The cost of executing these transactions came to an estimated 0.7% per year. (Funds don't disclose this hidden cost.) And while all of that turnover has failed to add any value whatsoever to the returns of fund shareholders as a group, it has surely enriched the federal government, as taxes cost fund investors an estimated 2.7% of return per year. The combined transaction and tax costs: 3.4% per year. Hardly surprisingly, the *surviving* funds as a group appeared to be slightly above-average stock pickers, earning an estimated return of 18.0%. However, because of all-in annual costs of 5.7%, their return crumbled to just 12.3% for their owners. Contrary to the entirely reasonable expectations of their shareholders, the sinfully sweet and apparently addictive fund doughnuts failed abjectly to fatten their returns. (See Table 1.2.)

TABLE 1.2   Annual Investment Returns, 1984–1999

	AVERAGE MUTUAL FUND*	WILSHIRE 5000 INDEX FUND
Equity return	18.0%	17.7%
Sales commission, 6% (annual impact)	−0.5	—
Cash drag	−0.6	—
Fund return	16.9%	17.7%
Transaction costs	−0.7	—
Expense ratio	−1.2	−0.2
Investor return	15.0%	17.5%
Tax	−2.7	−0.9
Investor return (after tax)	12.3%	16.6%
Reduction in equity return	−5.7%	−1.1%

*Surviving funds only, 15 years ended 11/30/1999.

But this industry is not composed solely of doughnuts. There are some—but very few—fund bagels, maintaining the hard-crusted, long-term-focused, low-cost character that was in fact this industry's hallmark when I first analyzed it 50 years ago in my senior thesis at Princeton University. In its purest manifestation—no blueberry here!—the fund bagel is the market index fund. Stripped of all the proffered sweetness of mutual fund doughnutry, the index fund offers the ultimate in character—the broadest possible diversification, the lowest possible cost, the longest time horizon, and the highest possible tax efficiency. Simplicity writ large!

At the outset of the great bull market, there was but a single one of these hard bagels in the entire soft doughnut-filled fund bakery. The first index mutual fund was founded in 1975, designed simply to own the 500 stocks in the Standard & Poor's 500 Index, and hold them as long as they remain there. The second index fund wasn't introduced until 1984, after the lapse of nine years. But the idea behind this bagel-like manifestation of fund investment strategy—own the market and hold it forever—has finally moved from heresy to dogma.

That idea, simply put, is to capture *almost* 100% of the market's annual return simply by owning all of the stocks in the market and holding them forever, all the while operating at rock-bottom cost. Since the 500 giant corporations of the Standard & Poor's 500 constitute more than three-quarters of the market's total capitalization, the first index fund substantially captured this concept. Recognizing that the remaining one-quarter of the stock market includes corporations with medium-sized and small market capitalizations, and that owning the entire market is an even better idea, the first *total* stock market index fund was founded in 1992. It is modeled on the Wilshire 5000 Index, now encompassing the more-than-8000 publicly held corporations in the United States.

I recognize, of course, the irony that the all-market index fund delivers so much but appears to offer so little. It can be accurately described as a fund that, because of its expenses—tiny as they are— *rises slightly less* than the market in good times, *declines slightly more* in bad times, and will *never* quite capture 100% of the market's long-term return. *But it works.* Before taxes, the all-market index fund provided 99% of the market's annual 17.7% annual return during the past 15 years, while the average fund captured just 85%. After taxes, the investor selecting a diversified stock fund at the outset in 1984 proved to have just one chance in 33 of outpacing the all-market fund by as little as a single percentage point on an annual basis. Like looking for a needle in a haystack, you say? Of course. So what is the alternative? *Just buy the entire market haystack.*

The all-market index mutual fund is the industry's consummate bagel, tough and crusty, serious and, above all, a blessing to the investor's wealth. The traditional managed mutual fund is the industry doughnut, fun, sweet, and crumbly to be sure, and looking swell in all of those chocolate-covered, as it were, mutual fund advertisements you see (and pay for) on television. But it has proved to be anything but fattening to investors' wallets. In fact—bereft of the kind of mandatory federal health warning-label carried on cigarette packs and liquor bottles—the typical equity mutual fund has proved dangerous to the wealth of investors who succumbed to its sugary smiles. Over the past 15 years, remember, *after* all expenses and federal taxes, $10,000 invested in the average mutual fund doughnut has grown to $57,000. By contrast, the all-market fund bagel has grown to $100,000. The bagel rewarded the investor with nearly *double* the reward of the doughnut. Looked at another way, the all-market bagel provided 87% of the stock market's return after all costs and taxes, compared to just 48% for the average stock fund. (See Figure 1.1.)

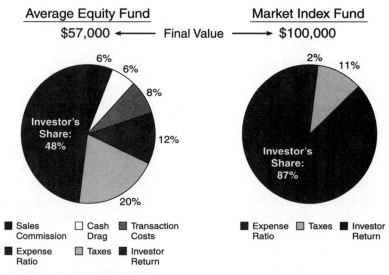

FIGURE 1.1 Cumulative investment returns, 1984–1999.

It takes no brilliance to recognize that many fund investors are delighted to have made a $47,000 profit on their $10,000 stake. They don't realize they might have made a $90,000 profit simply by investing in the market and then doing absolutely nothing. But if I'm correct that the doughnut of market speculation that has driven returns upward in the past two decades will lose some of the sweetness in the years ahead, the mutual fund doughnuts will find themselves in a bad spot. For the lower the market return, the bigger the bite taken by fund costs. If the annual stock market return falls to 5.2%, fund all-in costs of even 2.5% would confiscate nearly *one-half* of the market's return, reducing the fund investor's return to 2.7%. While the fund bagels would hardly shine in this environment, they would at least produce a 5% return, generous by comparison.

3. *Vanguard in the New Millennium: The Bagel in a Doughnut-Dominated Industry*

I'm sure this audience of investment-savvy citizens of the Greater Philadelphia region is well aware that the great bagel in the doughnut-dominated mutual fund industry is Vanguard. While Mr. Safire was taking some literary license when he described the bagel-doughnut war as a test of America's national character, it is hardly hyperbole to describe Vanguard's pioneering of bagel-like, market-indexing-type, low-cost investing as a test of the character of a mutual fund industry, an industry heretofore slavishly devoted to the easy—but undeliverable—promise of doughnut-like sweetness in returns.

Safire is appalled by the bakery bagel's attempt at self-destruction—moving toward the center, reaching for an ever-wider audience by compromising its values. Sure, he concedes, sourdough and caraway (may I throw in an "everything?") are permissible variations, but the blueberry bagel—sweet and soft—reduces a bagel to the level of a stale doughnut. At the same time, the rival doughnut is defiantly reasserting its fattening identity, adding an excess of sweetness and slickness, exemplified by the soon-to-come frosted chocolate "Krispy Kreme," so Safire tells us. "The bagel, devoid of character and becoming half-baked, seeking to be all pastry to all men, reflects what is wrong with America at the *fin de millenaire*."

But the momentum in the fund industry, so far at least, lies with the bagelism of indexing. (Or is it the Bogleism of Vanguard?) While it took years for our rivals to copy our pioneer 500 Index Fund of 1975 and our pioneer Total Stock Market Index Fund of 1992, there are now 332 index mutual funds. While they represent but 10% of equity fund assets, index funds accounted for fully 35% of cash flow in 1999. I, for one, welcome these converts. For if we are to maintain our competitive edge, we need strong rivals who compete with us on the grounds of low investment cost, high-quality service, and giving the investor a fair shake. For while indexing comes at the direct expense, dollar-for-dollar, of the return on capital of the *manager*, it commensurately enhances the return on capital of the *investor*.

While our index pioneering was motivated by conviction and missionary zeal, our rivals have been motivated only by the growing public demand for index funds, and dragged kicking and screaming into the fray. Most other index funds, however, are fatally flawed by excessive expense ratios, although some waive their fees for "a temporary period of time," so as to appear to match Vanguard's low cost. This sort of "bait and switch" strategy (bait the investor, then switch to a higher fee later) may deceive gullible investors for a time, but will not, finally, stand public scrutiny. Emulating a market index is essentially a commodity-like strategy, with the expense ratio the major differentiator. Low costs, simply put, are better than high costs! What is more, the missionary zeal to offer *an investment that serves* has proven more successful than the reluctant decision to offer *a product that sells*.

How successful? Today, nearly $250 billion of Vanguard's assets are represented by pure index funds, with another $150 billion invested in high-quality, low-cost, defined asset-class bond and money market funds—$400 billion of our $535 billion total that is clearly dedicated to the bagel mandate. And most of our remaining funds are also bagel-like; that is, they offer clearly specified strategies, exceptionally low costs, and portfolio turnover that is modest by industry standards. To be fair, we have some—albeit far too few—competitors that can fairly be characterized as bagel-like in nature. But the overwhelming majority of mutual funds clearly meet the doughnut definition. And so the great bakery confrontation is joined. May the concept that provides the most financial nutrition for investors win!

In that confrontation, I remain, not on the sidelines, but in the heat of the battle. I begin the year 2000 just as I have begun every year since 1975: Ready to serve the Vanguard shareholders—now eight million in number—arm-in-arm with my fellow crewmembers—now 10,500 strong. In my role as Vanguard's Founder, I continue to act as ambassador to our crew and our owners; in my role as President of

Vanguard's newly created Bogle Financial Markets Research Center, I continue to pursue my career-long mission with the enthusiasm and energy that only a now-29-year-old heart could muster. ("Thanks," to my guardian angels at Hahnemann Hospital!) My research, writing, and speaking come from a perspective that is without parallel in this industry, and my first two books, published in 1993 and 1999, will be followed by two more in 2000, with at least three more on the drawing board.

Many shareholders have asked: "What about Vanguard post-Bogle?" I can only answer: "Don't worry." First, I expect to be around Vanguard in *body* for as far ahead as I can see today, energetically pursuing my work. Second, I also expect to be around my firm in *soul* for as long as the simple investment principles and basic human values that I've invested in Vanguard make sense. As I said to our shareholders in my message in this year's fund annual reports, those principles and those values are not only enduring, but eternal.

Recently, a management consultant applied Emerson's aphorism, "an institution is the lengthened shadow of one man," to Vanguard. I simply don't believe it. None of what we have accomplished is one man's work; all is the result of a dedicated crew working together for the common good. Our managers and crew are strong; with each passing day, they are gaining experience and, I hope, wisdom. What is more, each passing day reaffirms the worthiness of the principles and values that are so much a part of my very spirit.

Happily, what I have strived for with missionary zeal all of these years has also proved to be a winning *business* formula. Not only has our strategy been singled out for praise by academics such as Harvard Business School strategic guru Michael Porter, it has also won for Vanguard an ever-growing market share in an industry that "just doesn't get it" when the job is to give mutual fund investors a fair shake. Responding to our challenge as the 2000s begin, some of our rivals are finally starting to get the *business* side of it right. But they won't capture the *real* message until they have, well, a change of heart, placing above all other values, not the marketing of financial products, which is what doughnutry is all about, but the stewardship of investor assets, the central principle of bagelism.

HMS Vanguard will flourish so long as we stay the basic course we have set for ourselves—not, to be sure, blindly or complacently, but open always to midcourse corrections in the face of the sea changes now occurring in every activity on the globe in this truly new era of information, technology, and communications. Nonetheless, having stripped the mystery from investing, exposed the importance of cost, *earned* rather than *bought* our market share, propounded the essentially long-term character of successful investing, and held high the mission of stewardship, Vanguard must avoid at all costs emulating the periodic attempts of our rivals to pander to the fads and fashions of the day, even if it causes our vaunted market share—Heaven forfend!—to slip for a while. In the long run, staying the course will carry the day.

In that light, after I read Mr. Safire's October essay, I dispatched copies of it to each of Vanguard's 200 officers, with the hope and expectation that it would be circulated widely among our crew members. My aim was to warn them of the dangers of adopting even a hint of the doughnut's lightness, softness, and sweetness, and to remind them of our commitment to the bagel's hard-hitting and uncompromising standards, its crusty and nutritious character. The three lessons Safire cites in "Bagels vs. Doughnuts" are poignant for any enterprise, and remarkably relevant for Vanguard.

1. **When you score a breakthrough and surge far ahead, never forget the reason for your success. In the bagel's case, that reason was a certain quality of tasty toughness against a crumbling opposition of sustained sweetness.**
2. **When you open up a long lead against the competition, never let up and freeze the case, lest hungry runners-up eat your lunch.**
3. **When greed for an ever-growing market share causes you to sacrifice your authenticity and compromise core principles, repent and take a stand—or your flavor will disappear into the mealy maw of moderation.**

Put another way, Vanguard must—and we will—protect our *brand* name with our actions, and let our rivals use their own *bland* names to seek their own destinies in their own ways. Quoting Safire for the final time, "Let doughnuts be doughnuts, let bagels be bagels. Character counts. Authenticity attracts." I have not the slightest doubt that Vanguard—not only while I live here on earth, yes, but when I live beyond some far horizon, too—will maintain its *character.* The stamp of *authenticity* that Vanguard investors have come to rely on is here to stay.

2

THE CLASH OF THE CULTURES IN INVESTING: COMPLEXITY VS. SIMPLICITY

Keynote Speech
The Money Show
Disney Coronado Springs Resort, Florida
February 3, 1999

I'M DELIGHTED to have the opportunity to present this keynote address to this awesome throng of 9,000 individual investors. Given the opportunity to do so in this landmark centennial year, I want to focus your attention on a landmark theme: *The clash of two cultures in investing: complexity and simplicity.* As the creator of a mutual fund firm that has, since its inception almost 25 years ago, been the apostle of simplicity, I'm confident that you will be less than astonished at which side I shall take in this debate.

Now, I am well aware that much of The Money Show's appeal is based on complexity. Essentially, the thesis presented here is that there are various kinds of complex financial strategies, systems, and investments that will enable you to overcome the awesome odds against beating the market, and that there are various individuals who have clear insights into what the future—be it a new era or the apocalypse—will hold for financial assets.

I count that you'll have the opportunity to attend roughly 130 different seminars, masterminded by more than 100 speakers. Remarkable! It looks to me as if the great preponderance of them will offer you their secrets for success in the new millennium (which, not to be a purist, but facts are facts, will begin not on January 1, 2000, but on January 1,

2001). Many speakers will offer you tempting solutions involving at best complexity, and at worst financial legerdemain and witchcraft.

I must confess that (no offense intended to the presenters) I wince when I see so many subjects that seem to offer easy roads for you to build your capital: "Wealth Creation and Preservation: Increasing Yields to 15–20%," "The Possible Trillion Dollar Opportunity of the Internet," "Finding Your Future Wealth in Diamond Mines," "High-Profit Low-Risk Strategies," "The 10 Top Funds of 1999," "Finding the Next Super Stock," "Index Funds: Making Handsome Returns in Bull and Bear Markets," and "Five Ways to Beat the Standard & Poor's 500." (Just for the record, presented by a newsletter which, *since its inception seven years ago, has lagged the S&P 500 by the awesome margin of 64 percentage points!*)

I assume from the titles that these speakers will offer you the secrets of success. Let me offer mine: *the one great secret of investment success is that there is no secret.* My judgment and my long experience have persuaded me that complex investment strategies are, finally, doomed to failure. Investment success, it turns out, lies in simplicity as basic as the virtues of thrift, independence of thought, financial discipline, realistic expectations, and common sense. And I am heartened by the fact that at least one panel may be operating on my wavelength. So I endorse without reservation: "Investing Made Simple: How to Simplify your Life and Increase your Return."

Let's now examine the issue of complexity. I'll begin with some quotes from a man whom I have never met, but for whom I have great respect. Warren Buffett's esteemed and acute partner at Berkshire Hathaway Inc., Charles T. Munger, puts the case against complexity this way:

> **Complexity is the direction taken . . . by many large foundations and college endowment funds, with not few but many investment counselors, chosen by an additional layer of consultants to decide which are best, relying on security analysts paid seven-figure salaries by investment banks, and including foreign securities in their portfolios, . . . trying to emulate Bernie Cornfeld's fund-of-funds. There is one sure thing about all this complexity . . . the total cost can easily reach 3% of assets. People are ridiculously over-optimistic [if they expect that they can make up] what these croupiers take.**

Mr. Munger goes on to point out the devastating impact of the cost of all of this complexity on the returns of foundations and endowments in a stock market with lower returns: Market return, 5%; total cost, 3%; net return, 2%. Payout to beneficiaries, 5%; net annual loss of capital, 3%. If we extend this analysis out for a decade, the capital wealth of the endowment falls by 26%; over two decades by 46%; after three decades by 60%. (Please don't scoff at the use of the 5% return on stocks. The long-term *real* return on stocks has been 7%, so Mr. Munger's hypothetical future figure is far from apocalyptic.)

The investor who owns a portfolio of mutual funds would, I hasten to add, be in precisely the same boat. Once retirement comes, you will depend on your accumulated capital to provide you with monthly income, indeed income that must grow in an amount sufficient to protect you against rising living costs. In today's financial markets, with common stocks yielding less than 1½% and high-grade corporate bonds yielding but 6%, make no mistake about it: Income *alone,* with all of its stability and predictability, will not do the job. Capital, with all of its volatility and unpredictability, will have to help create your returns. What is more, mutual funds will make the job tougher for you. For funds, or at least most of them, are among the most income-unfriendly investment vehicles ever created. Today, the average stock fund has a yield of only 4/10ths of 1%, and the average corporate bond fund must now have a true yield of only 5%.

What does the past tell us about the complex investment strategies that entail selecting winning mutual funds? Over and over again, it sends the same message: *Don't go there.* (Why? Because using Gertrude Stein's inspired phrase, "there is no there there.") No matter where we look, the message of history is clear. Selecting funds that will significantly exceed market returns, a search in which hope springs eternal and in which past performance has proven of virtually no predictive value, is a loser's game. To make the point, let's consider five examples of funds selected by professionals seeking investment superiority:

- First, the past records of fund managers compared to the stock market.
- Second, the records of investment newsletters, many of which are represented at this Money Show.
- Third, the records of fund advisers chosen by *The New York Times.*
- Fourth, the record of the "Managers of the Year" selected by Morningstar.

- Fifth, and most dismal of all in this (as it turns out uninspiring) universe, the record of funds-of-funds, which preen about their ability to choose a portfolio of the best funds for you. (The original fund-of-funds, of course, was formed by the aforementioned Bernie Cornfeld. It did not have a pretty burial.)

Successful Fund Managers Fail

Fund managers, of course, are following what is a complex methodology. They decide on their investment strategy, evaluate individual stocks, try to determine the extent to which a company's stock price may discount its future prospects, and turn their portfolios over with a passion. All of this complexity, however, has failed to produce market-beating returns. In recent years, that fact has become well accepted. Not merely by academics and financial analysts who have been proving that elemental fact since time immemorial, but by the fund industry itself. In the past 15 years, for example, only 42 of the 287 funds *that succeed in surviving the period*—one out of seven—outpaced the all-market Wilshire 5000 Equity Index (a much less demanding standard during this period than the Standard & Poor's 500 Stock Index). Fully 245 funds failed to do so. What is more, only 10 of the top funds—one out of 29—did so by what the experts describe as a "statistically significant amount"—an amount sufficient to justify their greater volatility. The annual return on the market was 16.7%, for the average fund, 13.9%. So, the funds provided 83% of the market's annual return. During the full period, an investment of $10,000 in the average fund would have grown to $70,400; the stock market itself to $101,400. The added capital accumulated by the funds was but 59% of the market's accumulation. *The fund industry itself consumed 41% of its shareholders' potential capital.* It must have been figures like these that persuaded one former fund chief executive to concede recently that equity mutual funds can "never" (his word) beat the market, and Peter Lynch to admit that "most investors would be better off in an index fund." (See Table 2.1.)

Newsletters Do Even Worse

Investment newsletters reinforce the same message, even as they add their own layer of complexity to that of the funds they select. A new study by the *Hulbert Financial Digest*—and bless Mark Hulbert for his pioneering work—finds that, from the market high in August 1987

TABLE 2.1   The Cost of Complexity, Managers versus the Market ($10,000 Investment–15 Years)

	ANNUAL RETURN	% OF MARKET RETURN	ENDING VALUE	% OF CAPITAL INCREASE
Average equity fund	13.9%	83%	$ 70,400	59%
Index°	16.7	100	101,400	100
Index advantage	2.8%	17%	$ 27,700	41%

°Wilshire 5000.

through the end of 1998—a fine period for analysis, including as it does both bull and (a few) bear markets—the average fund newsletter provided an annual return of 7.3%, *only one-half of the 14.1% return on the Wilshire 5000 Index*. Based on $10,000 invested at the 1987 market high, the increase in the value of the index investment would have been $34,100, the increase in the value of the newsletter picks, $10,000— only 29%. The fund managers collected an estimated $2,900 from the funds for their failure, and just a single newsletter cost a cumulative $2,100. Clearly these two sets of croupiers collected $5,000 of the average $15,000 value of the account, or about the apparently customary 3% per year cited by Mr. Munger. The gurus were better rewarded by the market's return than were their subscribers. Only six out of 55 advisers did better than the market; only three—*three out of 55*—did so when risk was taken into account. All claim, at least implicitly, to provide market-beating returns with their complex multilayered approaches, but precious few delivered on that promise. It would take more confidence than I can muster to even dream that those few will repeat their success in the next long cycle of the market. (See Table 2.2.)

TABLE 2.2   The Cost of Complexity, Newsletters versus the Market ($10,000 Investment: 8/87–11/98)

	ANNUAL RETURN	% OF MARKET RETURN	ENDING VALUE	% OF CAPITAL INCREASE
Average newsletter	7.3%	52%	$20,000	29%
Index°	14.1	100	44,100	100
Index advantage	6.8%	48%	$22,000	71%

°Wilshire 5000.

"All the News That's Fit to Print"

The record hardly improves when we consider the accomplishments, published each quarter, of five investment advisers who, five and one-half years ago, were asked to select and manage hypothetical portfolios for *The New York Times* based on their own complex methods of evaluation. Since then, the $50,000 that each adviser initially invested has grown, on average, to $103,500. Not bad? Not bad until you realize that the measurement standard set by the *Times* (the largest S&P 500 Index Fund) grew to $156,100. (With an uncharacteristic lack of candor, the *Times* did not see fit to print that figure, so I have now done it for them.) Thus, the investor who chose *not* to use the pros gained an *extra* $53,000 on his $50,000 initial stake. The advisers earned just 61% of the market's *annual* return (14% vs. 23%), resulting in only 50% of the extra capital accumulated by the index fund. (See Table 2.3.)

"Manager of the Year"

I bow to no man in my respect and admiration for Morningstar Mutual Funds, and, I add hastily, for their courage in having selected, each year since 1987, the equity fund "Manager of the Year" (equivalent, I suppose, to the "superstars" with whom those of you with $49 will be taking an intimate lunch tomorrow). It is a complex task, and the Morningstar editors obviously add a healthy dollop of judgment when they consider the chosen fund's inevitably superior record of past performance. Alas, in investing, such courage is rarely rewarded, and the managers selected through 1997 have, after admittedly brilliant records prior to their selections, quickly turned nondescript. *Not a single one* of these managers surpassed the S&P 500 Index in the years that followed his selection. The average cumulative annual

TABLE 2.3 The Cost of Complexity, *The New York Times* Test of Five Advisers ($50,000 Investment: July 1993–Dec. 1998)

	ANNUAL RETURN	% OF MARKET RETURN	ENDING VALUE	% OF S&P INDEX INCREASE
Advisers	14.1%	61%	$103,500	50%
Index°	23.1	99	156,100	99
Index advantage	9.0%	38%	$ 52,600	49%

°Vanguard 500 Index Fund.

TABLE 2.4   The Cost of Complexity, "Managers of the Year" versus the Market°

	ANNUAL RETURN	% OF MARKET RETURN
Managers of the Year	16.2%	66%
Index°°	24.3	100
Index advantage	8.1%	34%

°Managers who have not retired or changed funds.
°°S&P 500.

return for the managers through 1998 was 16.2% vs. 24.3% for the S&P Index. The "Managers of the Year" earned but 66% of the market's annual return. (See Table 2.4.) Let's hope that the "Time-Magazine-Cover-Jinx" doesn't strike the 1998 winner, whose past record, like those of his predecessors, has been truly extraordinary.

Bernie Cornfeld's Successors

I have just one more example: the sad record of funds-of-funds that charge an extra fee for the extra complexity they add to the issue of fund selection—picking advisers to pick advisers, precisely what Berkshire Hathaway's Mr. Munger warned us about. The idea of funds-of-funds is essentially this: given the market-beating returns of so few mutual funds, and the inability of investment newsletters, financial advisers, and even Morningstar to pick winning funds in advance, why not pay professional fund pickers a generous fee and let *them* do the heavy lifting purportedly involved in beating the market? It seems, on the face of it, a fine idea.

Alas, their record is probably the worst of the lot. The original fund-of-funds, an idea that began with Bernie Cornfeld and collapsed with his entire Swiss-headquartered fund empire, has now attracted some 120 U.S. emulators. Nearly all of them extract an exorbitant annual fee, *averaging* 1.6% of assets—just for picking funds! With the average fund expense ratio of 1.5%, this add-on more than doubled the direct cost of fund ownership, to a hefty 3.1% Funds-of-funds have failed in two ways. Not only have they failed to pick funds that can outpace the *market*, but they have failed even to pick funds that can outpace their *peers* (as we have already learned, a measurably lower standard of accomplishment). (See Table 2.5.)

TABLE 2.5 The Cost of Complexity, Funds-of-Funds versus Style (3 Years)

	ANNUAL RETURN 1995–1998	% OF MARKET RETURN
S&P 500	28.2%	100%
Large-cap funds	19.5	69
Large-cap funds-of-funds	17.9	63
Index advantage	10.3%	37%

On average, during the past three years in which their numbers have burgeoned, funds-of-funds that charge fees—there are but a handful that don't—have underperformed 77% of the mutual funds in the large-cap style group. That result suggests that the fund selections by these funds-of-funds are far below what mere random selection would have offered. As a result of the gap caused by both their extra layer of selection complexities and their extra layer of fees, large cap funds-of-funds have provided annual returns of just 17.9%, compared with 19.5% for large-cap mutual funds as a group, and 28.2% for the S&P 500 Index. Providing a mere 63% of the market's annual return is hardly a monument to the doubling of the complexity component that funds-of-funds offer.

Life Is Short. Enjoy! But Only Up to 5%

You must now be as exhausted as I am by the unremitting pounding of the theme that complexity simply doesn't work. What you are seeing at the Money Show, by and large, is also complexity writ large. I have no ability to tell you how it will work in the future, but I can assure you that it hasn't worked very well in the past. To be sure, you'll meet lots of smart, engaging, purposeful financial advisers here. It will be exciting and enticing, but, after all is said and done, you'll find no surefire solutions for investment success—wealth without risk, if you will. It's just not a realistic expectation. But being here is fun, and trying out modern remedies for age-old problems lets you exercise your animal spirits. Given the circumstances, I would encourage you to do exactly that. Life is short. If you want to enjoy the fun, *enjoy!*

But not with *all* of your hard-earned resources. Specifically, *not with one penny more than 5% of your investment assets*. At most!

Have the fun of gambling, but *not* with your rent money—and certainly not with your retirement assets nor with your funds for college education. Perhaps test two or three of the presenters' recommendations. They may teach you some valuable lessons, and probably won't hurt you too much in the short term. Fun, finally, may be a fair enough purpose for your Funny Money Account. But what, you ask, should you do with your Serious Money Account? How should you invest that 95% of your assets on which you now depend—or will one day depend—for your comforts of human existence?

Now . . . to the Serious Money Account

Rely on simplicity in setting and implementing strategy for your Serious Money Account. You need not believe me, though I've been at it for a long time. Rely instead on the wisdom of Charles Munger's more renowned partner at Berkshire Hathaway, the legendary Warren Buffett. Best known for his strategy of owning *businesses* that create long-term value, rather than *pieces of paper* that his friend "Mr. Market" comes by to bid on every day (to no avail), Mr. Buffett's buy-and-hold strategy is the essence of simplicity, evil complexity's angelic twin. Hear his words:

> **The art of investing in public companies is . . . simply to acquire, at a sensible price, a business with excellent economics and able, honest management. Thereafter, you need only monitor whether these qualities are being preserved. Most investors, both institutional and individual, will find that the best way to own common stocks is through an index fund that charges minimal fees. Those following this path are sure to beat the net results (after fees and expenses) delivered by the great majority of investment professionals. Seriously, costs matter. For example, equity mutual funds incur corporate expenses— largely payments to the funds' managers—that average about 100 basis points, a levy likely to cut the returns their investors earn by 10 percent or more over time.**

It will hardly surprise you that I wish to associate myself with each element of Mr. Buffett's position: investing in businesses; using an index fund to do so; and holding costs to bare-bones minimums. In a sense, I take the middle ground between the Munger anti-complexity philosophy (because its 3% cost would confiscate 30% of a 10% long-term stock return) and the Buffett pro-simplicity philosophy (because its 1% cost would confiscate 10% of the return). I believe that the annual cost of equity mutual funds today is upwards of 2% per year—an average annual expense ratio of 1.5% (which you can measure) and an average cost of from 0.5% to 1.0% or more incurred by portfolio turnover (which *you* can't measure; the fund's adviser can, but he won't tell). This hidden cost is the result of the absurd 85% average annual turnover of fund portfolios. This rate suggests an average holding period of only 1.1 years for the typical portfolio holding. Such short-term *speculation* is the antithesis of long-term *investing*—buying businesses, not pieces of paper—which is the cornerstone of the Buffett-Munger strategy.

Why do Mr. Buffett, Mr. Munger, and I all agree on the inherent value of a low-cost market index fund? Simply because of these two brutally obvious facts: (1) All investors as a group *must* match the market's return *before costs*. Therefore: (2) All investors as a group *must* fall short of the market's return *by the amount of their costs*. Conclusion: Nearly all investors—nearly every human being here in this audience tonight—will fall short of the market's return by an appreciable amount. Yes, it is true. But you can avoid this dire yet predictable fate if you will simply turn from complexity to simplicity. Simplicity in investing begins with setting this standard as your objective:

The realistic epitome of investment success is to realize the highest possible portion of the market returns earned in the financial asset class in which you invest—the stock market, the bond market, or the money market—recognizing, and accepting, that that portion will be less than 100 percent.

How close can you get to 100%? Your best chance is with an index fund. It is the embodiment of simplicity, investing in the entire stock market; diversified across almost every publicly held corporation in America; essentially untouched by human hands; nearly bereft of costly portfolio turnover; remarkably cost-efficient; and extraordinarily tax-effective. Such a fund will provide you with—indeed, virtually guarantee you—98% to 99% of the market's annual return over time, a vast improvement over the 85% or so that the typical mutual fund has provided.

An index fund based on the Wilshire 5000 Equity Index owns 100% of the market, so, in an environment of, say, 12% returns, such a fund, carrying an annual cost of 0.2 of 1%, will provide a return of 11.8%, or 98% plus. Another reasonable choice is an S&P 500 Index fund, which is based on an index that includes 75% of the value of all U.S. stocks.

Because of the powerful surge of the large-cap stocks in the Index, the 500 Index fund is the popular favorite of the day, but I do not believe that large-caps, important as they may be in the market's mix, are destined for permanent ascendancy. So a little caution is called for in projecting the past. Small- and mid-cap stocks, the dogs of recent years, will have their day. In the long-run, large- and small-cap stocks are apt to provide similar returns, so either fund should work out just fine. But over the short run, a total stock market index fund will obviously provide a closer tracking of the total market—the quintessential rationale for the theory of indexing.

Simplicity Works

Since I have earlier shown you five clear examples of the cost of complexity in investing, let me know show you, with equal clarity, the value of simplicity. The superiority of the passively managed S&P 500 Index has now prevailed for at least a half century. During the past 50 years, the return on the Index has averaged 13.6% per year, a 1.8% margin over the average large growth and income mutual fund. Thus, the average fund has earned 87% of the market's annual return. Given the powerful compounding of returns over this long period, the final value of an initial investment of $10,000 in the 500 Index would be $5,782,000. For the equity mutual fund, the final value would be $2,589,000. Result: The fund provided less than half—45%, to be precise—of the market's accumulation. Table 2.6 and Figure 2.1 show how these assets accumulated over time. (Taxes are ignored; if they were included, the Index advantage would be *substantially* larger.) The obvious fact: Simplicity works.

It would be easy, I suppose, to say "case closed" at this point. But I owe it to you to point out that the value of the simplicity that is mani-

TABLE 2.6 The Value of Simplicity

PAST PERIOD	S&P INDEX	EQUITY FUNDS	DIFFERENCE	FUNDS AS % OF INDEX
50 years	13.6%	11.8%	+1.8%	87%
40 years	12.0	10.5	+1.5	87
30 years	12.7	10.7	+2.0	84
20 years	17.7	15.1	+2.6	85
10 years	19.2	15.2	+4.0	79

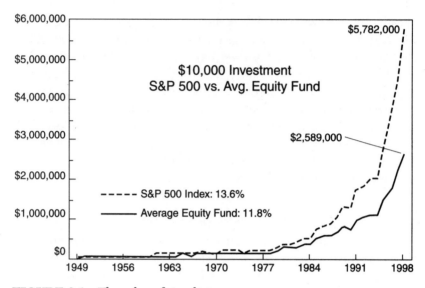

FIGURE 2.1 The value of simplicity.

fested in indexing seems to be growing. Why? Because the cost of owning mutual funds has been rising over the years.

I must quickly add a warning that the huge 4% positive annual margin of the S&P 500 Index during the past decade is unlikely to be repeated. Large-cap stocks have dominated their medium- and small-sized cousins during this period, and such trends, as I noted earlier, typically revert to the market mean over time. But even the 2% to 2½% *long-term* margin I would expect for the Index would provide another remarkable tribute to the virtue of low-cost simplicity.

In short, the simple—utterly, infinitely simple—concepts of indexing are of surpassing importance in investing your Serious Money Account. By focusing on the long term—always the long term—indexing holds the master key to your investment success. These three final charts beautifully exemplify how *time*—the fourth and crucial temporal dimension of investing—interacts with *reward, risk,* and *cost,* the three spatial dimensions. Do not fail to apply these three simple concepts to the simple idea of index investing.

The Reward Dimension

Reward is the first and most important dimension of investing. Time accelerates rewards. "The Magic of Compounding," encapsulated in

28

compound interest, is truly, as Einstein is said to have noted, the greatest mathematical discovery of all time. Use it to multiply your financial assets by emphasizing equities, but not to the exclusion of bonds. Despite, or perhaps because of the fact that we've enjoyed a sun-drenched environment for 16 years, stormy years have always punctuated the long two-century up-trend in U.S. stocks. But if we can assume future returns of stocks in the 10% range and of bonds in the 5% range, the difference in capital accumulation on a $10,000 initial investment is dramatic: after 40 years, stocks, $453,000; bonds, $70,400. Take advantage of the rewards available in equities, and multiply them by putting time on your side. (See Figure 2.2.)

The Risk Dimension

But don't ignore risk, the second dimension of investing. Stocks, especially today, carry high short-term risk. But time moderates risk. It does so in a manner that also seems like magic. We might call it "the moderation of compounding." The risk in stocks (we use a measure known as standard deviation, which measures the typical range of real returns on stocks), drops by fully 60% (from 18.1% to 7.5%) simply by extending the time horizon from one year to five years. After 10 years, 75% of the

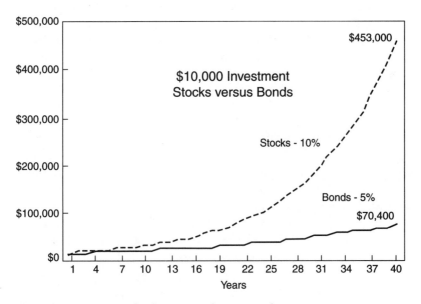

FIGURE 2.2 Reward: The magic of compounding.

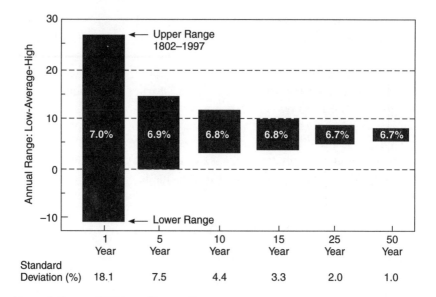

FIGURE 2.3 Risk: The moderation of compounding. (Range of real returns and standard deviations, 1802–1997)

risk (the risk measure is now down to 4.4%) has been eliminated. It continues to drop (to 2.0 by 25 years and to 1.0 by 50 years), but the most significant reduction has come within the first decade. No investor should forget, however, that odds should *never* be mistaken for certainties. Who is to say, really, that we are not facing a decade which will parallel the lowest decade in market history (1964–74), when the annual real return on stocks was −4.1%. (See Figure 2.3.)

The Cost Dimension

You may have thought a great deal about how time moderates risk and accelerates reward, but if you are like most investors, you haven't thought about the third dimension: Cost. Time magnifies the impact of cost. Almost without your noticing, the costs of investing nibble at your returns, gradually eroding them almost right before your unsuspecting eyes. As the years roll on, costs loom ever larger. We see the same principle at work that creates the magic of compounding, but it works in reverse. I call it "the tyranny of compounding." If we assume that the stock market provides a 10% long-term return, the average mutual fund will provide an 8% annual return, net of its 2% all-in

Fund Capital Accumulation as % of Market

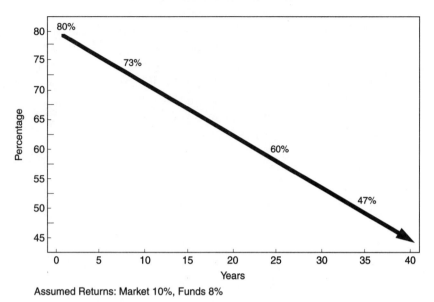

FIGURE 2.4   Cost: The tyranny of compounding.

costs. At the end of a single year, the investor will have accumulated
80% of the market's appreciation. But then cost tyranny rears its ugly
head. After five years, the fund accumulation is but 77% of the market's; by 10 years, 73%; and by 25 years, only 60%. And at the end of
today's typical 40-year time horizon for a beginning investor, the fund
accumulation has fallen to a mere 47% of the market's. (See Figure
2.4.) The mutual fund *industry*, without putting up a penny of the initial $10,000 investment in stocks, will have consumed more than half
of your capital that might have accumulated in the market, as its high
costs are extracted from the returns the market earned over the years.
Cost matters.

So there you have it. The case for complexity compels the conclusion that the game—fun though it may be—is hazardous to your
wealth. The case for simplicity seems, to me and to Charles Munger
and Warren Buffett at least, compelling. Low cost, marginal in its
annual impact, becomes overpowering as the years roll on. Indexing,

by eliminating the risks both of selecting an investment style and selecting a portfolio manager who fails, leaves the investor with the single risk that all investors must incur: market risk. A Funny Money Account, I suppose, has its place—provided it is a tiny place—in investing. We all must, or so it seems, learn by making our own mistakes. But the lesson we finally must, and will learn, is that, for your Serious Money Account, simplicity trumps complexity in the long run.

Clash there may be between the two cultures of investing, but I have no doubt about the final victor. Do you?

3

EQUITY FUND SELECTION: THE NEEDLE OR THE HAYSTACK?

The American Association of Individual Investors
Philadelphia Chapter
November 23, 1999

*I*T IS A VERY SPECIAL PRIVILEGE to be here with you tonight, all the more so because you have graciously agreed to let bygones be bygones and forgive me for the abrupt cancellation of my previously scheduled appearance on November 5, 1995, just four years ago. But since then I've had a change of heart. So here I am.

Some of you insiders may know that I really *have* had a change of heart. I entered Hahnemann Hospital in Philadelphia on October 18, 1995, to await a transplant, and, after a 128-day wait, received my new heart on February 21, 1996. I hope it will be obvious that my new heart, young and strong, has given me not only boundless energy, but a wonderful outlook on life . . . qualities that have enabled me to face adversity with a smile, and to put the problems of the past just where they belong—in the past. Given a second chance at life, I accept more enthusiastically than ever before the challenge Kipling laid down for those who "face both triumph and disaster: To treat those two imposters just the same." So I intend not to dwell on the past, but to look to the future, keeping an eagle eye on the interests of Vanguard, our crew, and our shareholders, and energetically continuing my mission to give mutual fund investors everywhere a fair shake. As I tell our Vanguard shareholders in this year's annual reports: ". . . I have promises to keep, and miles to go before I sleep. And miles to go before I sleep."

But it is not my *non-appearance* before you in 1995 that sets the stage for my remarks this evening, but my previous *appearance* before the Philadelphia Chapter of AAII. That speech took place on September 27, 1988, in an investment environment that is such a contrast from our current environment as to constitute the difference between day and night, or, more appropriately, between night and day. Since then, we have enjoyed one of the finest economic eras in America's long history, raising the question Cervantes asked 400 years ago: **Can we ever have too much of a good thing?**[1] To tip my hand, I'll tell you later that I think the answer to that question may be "yes."

Economics and Emotions

Twelve years ago, caution—or even worse—was the watchword for investors. The Dow Jones Industrial average had suddenly dipped by 35%—from 2700 in August 1987 to 1700 in October 1987—with 523 points of the 1000-point drop coming on Black Monday, October 19, 1987. A year later, when I talked to you, the market had retraced but half of the lost ground. It was at this point that *Time* magazine wrote a frighteningly bearish article (accompanied, of course, with the obligatory illustration of an enormous bear) that I used as the theme of my remarks to you. My talk had this lengthy title, which I pulled from the *Time* story:

> **Buy Stocks? No Way! It's a dangerous game. . . . It's a vote of confidence that things are getting worse. . . . The market has become a crapshoot. . . . The small investor has become an endangered species. . . . The stock market is one of the sleaziest enterprises in the world.**

Time reported that the percentage of individual investors with immediate plans to buy more shares had plummeted from 35% at the August 1987 market high to just 3.7% in September 1988. But, both as unshakable optimist and market contrarian, I assured you that, with the Dow at 2080, the article—along with many similar articles I'd read after that Great Crash—was "far more likely to be a sign of investment opportunity than a harbinger of Armageddon."

---

1. In *Don Quixote,* Cervantes gave us an astonishing variety of phrases that have enriched the lexicon of investors. I've used eight of his most familiar sayings in this talk, setting them apart in boldface type in the printed version of these remarks.

A nice prophesy! For that was nearly 9000 points ago. Today the Dow rests, seemingly comfortably, near the 11,000 mark, a mere 450% higher than when I spoke to you then. But, as *Time's* survey of investor's intentions suggested, few investors indeed took advantage of the fantastic investment opportunity that lay before them at that moment. Investors had *purchased* $25 billion of equity mutual fund shares when stock prices were high during the first seven months of 1987, but *liquidated* $4 billion of their fund holdings when stock prices were cheap during the first seven months of 1988.

I have spoken often of the clash between economics and emotions in investing. By economics, I refer to the strength of our U.S. economy, the nation's remarkable capacity for innovation and growth, and the resilience of our financial markets. By emotions, I refer to our all-too-human tendency to be frightened at market lows and then brimming with confidence at market highs. Emotions too often stand in the way of our making sensible economic decisions, a counterproductive element in investing that rarely has been more evident than in 1987–1988. That may seem like ancient history to you, but to me it was "only yesterday," and holds lessons for us this evening that are every bit as relevant as they were eleven years ago.

If the idea is to keep our counterproductive emotions out of the productive economics of investing, there are two key decisions on which investors must focus. One is, of course, the allocation of your investment assets, essentially between stocks and bonds. I can't do much more here than repeat what I said eleven years ago about the proper balance: "It all *depends*." It all depends on the magnitude of your accumulated assets, your financial liabilities, your investment goals, your tolerance for risk, your need for income, and your age . . . perhaps a 50/50 balance as the starting point, less in stocks for a cautious investor age 65 who's just retired; much more— perhaps even 100% in stocks—for a carefree younger investor just beginning with an IRA or corporate thrift plan. But I acknowledged then, and I reaffirm now, that if you think, as Cervantes did, "**it is good to keep your nest egg,**" you need to take into account not only the risk of investing, but the risk that your emotions may intrude even on the soundest of plans. I confessed then that I could not measure, "your psyche—your patience, your independence, your determination, in all, the strength of both your heart (There, I've said it again!) and your stomach to press on, no matter how compelling the immediate case for abandoning your plan." But, eleven years later, in a far more bullish environment, those factors remain critical considerations.

A Needle in a Haystack

The other key decision and my main focus tonight will be the selection of common stock mutual funds for your portfolio. And it is here I come to my title theme: "The Needle or the Haystack?" It was Cervantes who warned us, "**Look not for a needle in a haystack.**" While that phrase has become deeply imbedded in our language, however, it has yet to gain acceptance from most mutual fund investors. Most of us spend countless time and effort poring over fund records, getting information from news articles and television interviews and friends, from hyperbolic fund advertisements and well-intentioned fund rating services. In substance, all of these statistics describe the past returns of mutual funds with decimal-point precision, yet have no predictive power to forecast the future returns a fund may earn. As it turns out, we are looking for a very small needle in a very large haystack.

How likely is it that you will find that elusive needle in the now-3500 stock fund haystack? The chances of picking winning funds or managers are, well, awful. And not because there are a horde of charlatans out there, though there are some. It is because time and again, looking backward leaves us, as the kids would say, "clueless." And children don't mean that in a complimentary sense. Let me give you some anecdotal evidence.

First, let's take a long-term look at your chances of finding the needle. Following Cervantes' advice that "**honesty's the best policy,**" I'll go back thirty years, to the end of 1969, to provide a fair perspective that includes not only the past two golden decades, but the tin decade of the 1970s. There were 355 stock funds in the market haystack at the outset. Astonishingly, 186 of them—more than half—hit the hay, metaphorically speaking, going out of business during the period. Of the 169 funds that remained for our analysis (doubtless, the better performers), the average return was 11.5% per year, 2.1 percentage points behind the 13.6% annual return of the total stock market. (See Figure 3.1.)

Only nine funds beat the aggregate return on the U.S. stock market by more than 1% per year. We'll describe them as the winners. Another 18 beat the market return by less than 1%, and 29 fell short

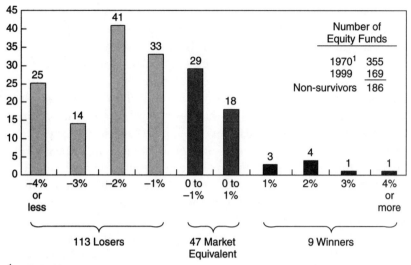

				Number of Equity Funds	
			1970[1]	355	
			1999	169	
			Non-survivors	186	

113 Losers   47 Market Equivalent   9 Winners

[1]SOURCE: Lipper.

FIGURE 3.1 The odds of success: Returns of surviving mutual funds, 1970–1999.

by less than 1%, a group of 47 funds that we can describe, more or less, as market-matchers. That left 113 funds that fell behind by more than 1% annually. We'll describe them as the losers. They include 39 funds which fell more than 3% a year behind the market—poor losers, as it were—including 25 that fell an utterly unacceptable 4% or more behind, and two that actually posted negative returns. (And they're both still in business!)

All told, your chances of owning a fund that survived were less than fifty-fifty. If you were one of the lucky ones whose fund made it through the period, the chances it was a loser were seven in ten; the chances it was a bomb, one in four, and the chances it was a winner but one in 19—if we count the number of funds that began the period, only one in forty! The odds of finding the winning needle in the fund haystack were fraught with peril; the odds of finding a losing needle rife; and the odds of losing the needle itself the largest of all.

Can an Expert Find the Needle?

But, you ask, can't the experts help us to pick the winners? The evidence is almost universally discouraging. Let me give you just two examples. One is the highly respected Morningstar Mutual Funds rating service, well-known for its award of "Morning-stars." They award five stars to the highest-rated funds, one star to the lowest-rated funds. So, playing on Warren Buffett's idea that investment managers should eat their own cooking, let's examine the funds Morningstar initially selected in 1991 as the investment options for the 401(k) Thrift Plan they offer to members of their own staff. Surely, this is where their expertise should find its proudest fulfillment. Indeed, they argue that, "we should know a thing or two about picking funds." They selected thirteen equity funds, a diverse group that included U.S. large-cap and small-cap funds, specialty and international funds alike—a wide range of choices that gave their employees "an expansive choice of top-rated funds."

But, alas, the past was not prologue. Despite Morningstar's unarguable expertise, nine of their 13 choices have lagged the market, and their selections have earned an average annual return of 15.3% since the outset—fully 2.8 percentage points per year behind the 18.1% return of the stock market, a cumulative shortfall in return of 80 percentage points (+172% versus +252%). (See Table 3.1.) That performance gap versus the market was even *worse* than the 2.1 point gap experienced by the fund survivors of the past three decades. Fund selection expertise, it seems, is not so easy to come by.

But if the experts of 1991 fell short of the market by an even larger amount than did the average fund chosen 30 years ago (although we have no way of knowing the results of the 186 funds that failed to survive), the experts of 1993 did even worse. In mid-1993, *The New York Times* asked five professional financial advisers to select and manage a $50,000 "paper portfolio" of mutual funds, with the goal of outpacing the target chosen by the *Times:* an index fund modeled on the Standard & Poor's 500 Stock Index. From personal experience, I can tell you that these were anything but fly-by-night advisers. They are com-

TABLE 3.1 Morningstar's 401(k) Funds vs. The Total Stock Market, 1991–1999

	ANNUAL RETURN	**CUMULATIVE RETURN**
Morningstar funds	15.3%	172%
Wilshire 5000	18.1%	252%
Funds' shortfall	−2.8%	−80%

petent and experienced, among the best in the field. Yet, by October 1999, some six years later, not a single adviser had provided a return that even came close to the 21% annual return achieved by the target index fund. The fund portfolio of the average adviser provided an annual return of just 13.8%, more than seven percentage points behind. The closing value of the initial $50,000 paper stake *The New York Times* provided each participant with at the outset: Average adviser, $112,000; Index fund, $164,000. Shortfall: $52,000. What an illuminating test of the challenge of equity fund selection! The experts, once again, proved utterly unable to find the needle in the haystack.

Why So Many Losing Needles? Costs!

What has caused those consistent and ghastly shortfalls of fund returns relative to the market? Fund costs. It turns out that the average fund manager simply matches the market return, before the deduction of costs, and, I should add, before taxes. We now have very good 15-year figures (from Morningstar Mutual Funds) on the impact of taxes, so to reinforce my point, I'm now going to evaluate mutual fund returns during the past 15 years and show you the combined toll that costs and taxes have taken on fund returns. During that period, the market's return was a generous 16.9% per year. Now, let's see the bite that costs took out of it:

- First, fund sales charge costs. Fifteen years ago, most funds were purchased on a "load" basis, with front-end sales commissions then averaging about 6%. Amortized over the period, that cost came to about 0.5 percentage points per year.
- Second, fund opportunity cost. Equity mutual funds typically held cash positions equal to about 7% of assets, earning the short-term interest rate rather than the higher returns available on stocks. Result: a return sacrifice of about 0.6 percentage points per year.
- Third, fund transaction costs. Portfolio turnover costs that funds incurred in buying and selling stocks amounted to at least 0.7 percentage points during the period. (These costs are not disclosed to investors.)
- Fourth, fund operating costs. Fund expense ratios—management fees and other operating expenses, all charged against fund returns—came to 1.2 percentage points per year.

39

Together, these costs come to 3.0 percentage points annually, exactly equal to the 3.0 point gap—13.9% between the average fund's reported return of 13.9% and the 16.9% return of the stock market. That gap is not materially different from the 2.1% gap over the past 30 years and the 2.8% gap of the Morningstar retirement plan, and less than one-half of the shortfall of *The New York Times*-selected advisers. So we're seeing some fairly consistent, if not conservative, data.[2]

The message: In a stock market in which prices are established by the interaction of smart buyers and smart sellers—fund managers, pension managers, financial advisers, stockbrokers, and certainly *most* individual investors—the average fund manager proves to have average stock-picking ability, a finding that falls well short of astonishing! Nonetheless, even the fund manager who beats the market by 3% per year *before* costs—no mean achievement—would end up, *after* costs, with only average returns. And, the manager who *wins* by 3% before costs must be counterbalanced by another manager who *loses* by 3%. So the loser ends up, *after* costs, falling behind the market by 6% per year. The appalling, yet unarguable, asymmetry of that example—that some of the biggest winners merely match the market and some of the biggest losers are left in the dust—helps to explain why, after all those costs, there are so few winning needles in the haystack.

To make matters worse, unlike the funds themselves, most fund *shareholders* incur yet another cost—a fifth deduction from returns—and it is large indeed: The taxes paid to the Federal government and to state and local governments on fund dividends and distributions. The heavy turnover of fund portfolios results in the realization of both long-term capital gains, now taxable at a maximum of 20%, and short-term capital gains, taxable at the full income tax rate of up to 40%. For funds held directly in taxable accounts by investors—the majority of fund investors—taxes reduced fund returns by 2.7 percentage points annually during the period, roughly *doubling* the costs of fund ownership that I showed you earlier. Fund *portfolio managers* by and large ignore the tax consequences of their decisions. But fund *investors* cannot afford to ignore taxes: You must *pay* them. With this extra reduction in the returns published by the funds, the average equity fund delivered a net annual return, after costs and taxes, of 11.2% to

---

2. NOTE: Like the 30-year analysis, the 15-year data includes only the 384 survivors of the period; 70 of the 454 funds that began the period failed to survive.

investors during the last 15 years, just two-thirds of the pre-tax market return of 16.9%. The odds of finding the needle in the haystack that represents the winning fund, then, are actually *worse*—far worse—than I've indicated.

Invest in the Haystack

If finding a needle in the fund haystack is so difficult, what sensible course of action is available to fund shareholders? The answer is as straightforward as it is simple: *Stop trying to find the needle. Invest in the haystack.* Own the entire U.S. stock market. Today, that is as easily said as done.

I'm speaking, of course, of the *all-market index fund.* A number of these funds are available today, targeted to the Wilshire 5000 Equity Index of all publicly held stocks in the U.S. (There are actually some 8000 such stocks, but these funds basically own the largest 2000 stocks, which account for about 98% of the $14 trillion market capitalization of the Index.) Visualize 75% of the assets of such a fund as being invested in the 500 large-cap stocks that constitute the Standard & Poor's 500 Stock Index, and 25% invested in the mid- and small-cap stocks that constitute the remainder of the market. A fund that tracks the 5000 Index truly *is* the U.S. stock market. The all-market index fund represents complete diversification, the ultimate response to Cervantes' warning: **"Do not venture all your eggs in one basket."** It is the haystack we ought to have been looking for all along rather than seeking out those impossibly few needles hidden deep within it.

Of course, the all-market fund would incur costs and taxes, so let's see how much of the return of the market itself it can capture. We'll compare its costs with those of the actively managed funds I've just described:

- First, no sales commissions. Most all-market funds are available on a no-load basis.
- Second, there is no opportunity cost. The fund is always 100% invested in stocks.
- Third, no (or only minimal) transaction costs, since stocks are bought and held, essentially forever.
- Fourth, low expenses. No advisory fee need be paid, since an investment manager is unnecessary. Operating expenses of 0.2% or less have proven to be feasible.

- Fifth, low taxes, estimated at 0.9% over the past 15 years, which consists primarily of taxes on net dividend income and, given the funds nominal turnover, on the minimal realized capital gains that result from corporate acquisition and mergers.

To make a long story short, the stock market's annual return averaged 16.9% during the past 15 years. The average fund, net of its costs and taxes, earned an annual return of just 11.2%. A no-load, low-turnover, low-cost all-market index fund, after *its* estimated costs and taxes, would have earned a return of 15.8%—a truly staggering enhancement of 4.6 percentage points per year.

This difference, compounded, has a staggering impact on capital accumulation. Assuming an initial investment of $10,000 in 1984, the value of the average equity fund in late 1999, after costs and taxes, was $49,000. The final value of the same investment in the all-market index fund would have been $90,000. Nearly twice as much capital accumulated. Therefore, twice as much retirement income and a more comfortable life. It would have been nice if the average fund had merely matched the market. And garnering the market's return shouldn't have been too much to ask.

Follow the Money

Now let's follow the money. In the active fund, the sales commission consumed 6% of your capital. Opportunity cost ate up 7%; transaction costs 8%; and management costs 12%. Taxes—largely unnecessary—confiscated 20%. All told, 53% of the market's return was consumed by our financial market and tax system, leaving but 47% for the investor—who, much more than incidentally, put up 100% of the capital and assumed 100% of the risk. It doesn't seem fair . . . and it isn't. And there *is* a better way. In an all-market index fund, the financial system consumed just 2%, and taxes 11% of your capital, leaving 87% for the investor—nearly twice as much as the 47% left by the average equity mutual fund.

Simply by cutting excessive equity fund costs to the bare-bones level, index fund investors (a) virtually assure themselves that the fund they select will *endure,* surviving the vagaries of time that have carried so many funds to an early grave; (b) substantially eliminate the huge risk of selecting a losing fund; (c) relinquish only the tiny opportunity of selecting a winning fund; and (d) assure themselves of nearly 100%

of the market's annual return. Given this balance of risk and return, it's hard to justify the search for a hard-to-find needle when, right before our very eyes, the huge haystack lies in full view.

What's To Be Done?

I imagine that most of you now own neither an all-market index fund nor its near-equivalent cousin, an S&P 500 index fund. (Their *long-term* returns have been nearly identical.) But it seems to me quite clear that most mutual fund investors—and nearly all *taxable* fund investors—should cease and desist from their efforts to find the needle in the haystack. Why bother seeking to select future fund winners when the odds against success are so awesome and the consequences of failure so grave? Sure, it may take a leap of faith to give up the traditional search for the needle in favor of an investment in the haystack. But, as Cervantes warned us, "**Faint heart ne'er won fair lady.**"

I quickly add even those with stout hearts must look carefully before they leap. The leap ought to be easy for *taxable* equity fund owners who want to use the index fund as a repository for new money; and those who own equity funds which they can sell and realize little or no capital gains. (Given some combination of poor fund performance and large taxable capital gains already realized and distributed, a misguided fund strategy the penalty for which their shareholders have already paid, there are many such funds.)

Stout-hearted investors who hold their fund shares in tax-deferred thrift plans and IRAs should also consider this great leap forward. While the clear tax advantage of index funds is of no special value to investors in tax-deferred programs, the other advantages of index investing remain; if they are *less* compelling, they are quite compelling enough on their own. For taxable investors who hold fund shares with substantial unrealized capital gains, however, a faint heart is an asset. Look before you leap. If your fund holding has a current value of $10,000 and a cost basis of $5,000, its liquidation would cost you $1,000 in taxes; fully 10% of your assets going directly to Uncle Sam. It would clearly take some years for the cost and tax advantages of index funds to compensate you for that loss.

But all investors should recognize the reality that a well-administered, no-load, low-cost, low-turnover, all-market index fund is the most sensible way to give up the search for the needle and own the haystack. In today's perhaps overly optimistic and highly volatile stock market, however, a second question quickly follows: Is it a good idea to invest in stocks today? Put another way, is today a wise time to own the haystack?

Owning the Haystack Today

Let me appraise the current level of the stock and bond markets by contrasting today's fundamentals with those that prevailed when I last spoke to you in September 1988. As for stocks, the Standard & Poor's Index was then at 270, a price that was equal to 12 times its earnings. The yield on the Index was 3.5%, and its earnings were to grow at 7.1% annually (from $23 per share in 1988 to $48 in 1999). Thus, the fundamental return on the Index—the portion of its annual return determined by earnings and dividends—totaled 10.6%, a measure that I call its *investment* return. Since 1988, its price has risen from 12 times earnings to 29 times, a change that measures what I call its *speculative* return. This increase in the price-earnings ratio—the change from post-1987 pessimism to pre-2000 optimism—has alone tacked an additional 8.3 percentage points per year onto the investment return, bringing the market's total rate of annual return to 18.9% during the period. (To illustrate the profound impact of this speculative return, had the price-earnings ratio merely remained at 12 times, the S&P Index today would be valued at 580, rather than at 1400—an 820 point difference. That is, the speculative return has accounted for nearly 75% of the 1130 point increase in the level of the Index.)

What might be a realistic expectation for the coming decade? We begin with today's 1.2% yield; then let's assume a solid earnings growth of 8% a year, even higher than the 7.1% growth since 1988. (Future earnings growth could be higher, or lower; in a heavy recession, earnings could even decline.) That's a 9.2% return, *before* we factor in the price-earnings multiple, which is at an all-time peak today. Let's assume it might ease back to 20 times. (It could remain unchanged; it could even rise. The long-term norm has been 15.5 times.) That change would knock 3.7 percentage points off the market's return, bringing it to 5.5%—even *less* than the plus-7% return available on high-grade bonds today. (I know that stocks have rarely provided lower returns than bonds over a decade; but I remind you that the stock market is not an actuarial table.) After all that we investors have been given in the fabulous bull market, it would be hard to feel crestfallen if such an economic return is all that the stock market gives us. However, if the economics of the fund industry remains intact, fund costs of 2.5% per year would cut the return of mutual fund investors to a measly 3.0%, a 45% slash in the return of the stock market—and before taxes at that—that would make future fund performance hard to swallow.

I've been around too long to describe that baneful forecast as a *prediction*. None of us is wise enough to be confident about the level of future market returns. But it *is* a *projection* of what the stock market *will* provide under a set of expectations that are far from irrational. The point is that market returns are determined by both *investment* factors—the fundamentals of the initial dividend yield on stocks plus the rate at which their earnings grow—and by *speculative* factors—the change in the price that investors will pay for each $1 of corporate earnings. If you disagree with my numbers, simply determine your own realistic expectations for earnings growth and for the final price-earnings ratio, and arrive at your own projection. But never forget that, while the parameters of the *investment* element of returns are set by the laws of economics, the parameters of the *speculative* element are bounded only by the whims of our emotions.

Bogle and Buffett Agree . . . But to What Avail?

For those who believe that, in Cervantes' words, "**there are no limits but the sky**," my projections will seem low. But at least recognize that I'm in good company. No less an investment icon than Warren Buffett, using an analysis similar in many respects to my own, recently cautioned that "investors in stocks these days are expecting far too much. . . . The fact is that (while) markets behave in ways that are not linked to value, sooner or later value counts." He sets "some reasonable expectations . . . GDP (the U.S. gross domestic product, a measure of how much the U.S. economy produces) grows at an average of 5% per year . . . interest rates (remain steady or rise) . . . the importance of dividends to total return is way down" and comes up with a future return on stocks of 7% per year. Mr. Buffett then reduces this return by one percentage point—an estimate "on the low side, of the frictional costs investors bear, which includes [just as I did earlier] a raft of expenses for the holders of equity funds," and concludes that "the most probable return would be 6%," soberly adding, "If it's wrong, I believe that the percentage is just as likely to be less as more." CAUTION: The fact that Buffett and Bogle agree is hardly proof positive that we know the answers. But perhaps our long experience, seasoned with some wisdom about realistic expectations for the stock market, may be worth factoring into your own thought process.

Let me turn now briefly to the bond market. (By the way, I happen to believe that the advantages of owning the haystack represented by a total *bond* market index fund vastly outweigh the long odds against finding the needle represented by a winning bond fund. The costs of owning most—but not quite all—bond funds is, well, unconscionable.) When I last spoke with you eleven years ago, the interest rate on a 10-year U.S. Treasury bond was 8%, indicating, net of the then-4¾% inflation rate, a real return of 3¼%. Today, the yield on a comparable bond is 6%, or, net of our present inflation rate of about 2%, a real return of 4%. Bonds were pretty good investments—though not as good as stocks—when I spoke to you then; they would appear to be even better investments now.

Why? Because the relationship between potential stock returns and potential bond returns has changed substantially since I talked to you in 1988. Then, the earnings yield on stocks (the inverse of the price-earnings ratio of 12 times) was about 8.4%, slightly more than 100% of the 8% yield of the 10-year Treasury. Today, the earnings yield on stocks is 3.4%, only 55% of the current 6% Treasury bond yield. This is essentially the relationship that has Federal Reserve Board Chairman Alan Greenspan worried about the stock market—though he has been wrong so far. But, given that stocks carry higher risk than bonds, this disparity suggests that today seems more a time for caution than for unbridled optimism.

In my 1988 speech to you, at a time of pessimism, I called your attention to, "the great paradox of the stock market: when stock prices are high [as they are now], everyone wants to jump on the bandwagon; when stocks are on the bargain counter [as they were then], it seems difficult to give them away." Just as I urged you then not to get carried away with pessimism, so I urge you now not to get carried away with optimism. The best strategy is to hold a sound balance of stocks and bonds, a balance that fits your own situation, the better to "stay the course" no matter what transpires in our ever uncertain and unpredictable financial markets. Cervantes, once again, had it right: "**Forewarned is forearmed.**"

4

RISK AND RISK CONTROL IN AN ERA OF CONFIDENCE (OR IS IT GREED?)

New England Pension Consultants' Client Conference
Boston, Massachusetts
April 6, 2000

*I*N THESE EXTRAORDINARY and volatile markets we are facing today, it's difficult for me to imagine more appropriate subjects than "Risk" and "Risk Control" to sound the keynote for an "Agenda for the Future"—the perennial theme, as I understand it, for this conference. It has been "Reward," of course, that has been the keynote of the past 18 years, and most particularly for the past six years, during which the longest and strongest bull market in the history of the world has taken a new lease on life. Even as "it is always darkest before the dawn," however, it may well always be brightest just before evening begins to fall. When *reward* is at its pinnacle, *risk* is near at hand.

Risk has been with us, well, forever. At the dawn of civilization in Rome during the second century B.C., for example, some of the characteristics of modern capitalism, financial markets, and speculation were already in place. Indeed, the term *speculator*—one who looks out for trouble—comes from ancient Rome. As Cato himself told us:

> **There must certainly be a vast Fund of Stupidity in Human Nature, else Men would not be caught as they are, a thousand times over, by the same Snare, and while they yet remember**

47

their past Misfortunes, go on to court and encourage the Causes to which they were owing, and which will again produce them.[1]

Although we cannot be certain whether our stock market today is the epitome of the same kind of speculative snare that has caught men a thousand times over, no investor today should forget those words. My point is not that we *are* now caught in one of those periodic snares set by the limitless supply of stupidity in human nature. Rather, my point is that we *might* be. Professional investors who ignore today's rife signs of market madness—of a bubble, if you will—are abrogating their fiduciary duty, and dishonoring their responsibility for the stewardship of their clients' assets.

Four Key Elements of Investing: Reward, Risk, Time, and Cost

How should that responsibility be honored? By recognizing that, for all of the projections and assumptions we make (and almost take for granted), there is one element of investing we cannot control: Reward. For future stock market returns are completely unpredictable in the short run and—unless we know more about the world 25 years from now then we do about the world today—may prove even less predictable over the long run. But we *can* control the other three primary determinants of investing: Risk, time, and cost, and we should focus on them. (See Figure 4.1.)

Risk, and risk control, will be my main theme today, but first just a few words on the roles that *Time* and *Cost* play in investing. We can control *Time* in two ways: First, by focusing on how much time will elapse from the date an individual investor or a corporate pension plan begins the accumulation of investment assets during the years of productivity and thrift until the investors will require the distribution of income, and even the drawdown of capital—essentially the liability on the balance sheet when retirement begins. We can control, after all, how many working years will pass before we retire, and we had best get as much time as we can on our side. Second, we can control the very time horizon over which we hold stocks. With our own free will, we have the power to choose whether we will be long-term

---

1. Cited in *Devil Take the Hindmost: A History of Speculation*, by Edward Chancellor (1999).

	Ability to Control	
	Yes	No
Risk	✔	
Time	✔	
Cost	✔	
Reward		✔

FIGURE 4.1   Four key elements of investing.

investors or short-term speculators. With its 90% portfolio turnover, the fund industry has chosen *short*. My own chips are on *long*.

And, lest we forget, we can also control *Cost*. In my remarks today, I'm not going to place my customary emphasis on the costs of investing, for my sense is that you money managers, clients, and consultants here assembled have already done your best to hold your investment costs to the reasonable minimum. In the industry in which I've plied by trade for a half-century, however, "money is no object." Alas, it is the shareholders' money which is no object, and mutual fund costs are completely out of control. Over the past 15 years, for example, mutual fund fees and operating expenses, sales charges and transaction costs, opportunity costs, and the horrendous tax costs—generated, in turn, by grossly excessive portfolio turnover—have consumed nearly six percentage points—one-third—of the stock market's return of 18% per year. (It would take a truly remarkable money manager to leap that six-point hurdle for 15 years in a row!) In the last year alone, all-industry costs absorbed an estimated $120 billion of the returns earned by mutual fund shareholders—an astonishing figure.

Reward: Out of Our Control

But what none of us can control is *Reward*. With few exceptions, generous investment rewards have been generated in the financial markets over the long run. But we have the ability to predict neither when the rewards will occur, nor when they will depart from past norms. Our markets are remarkable arbitrageurs that reconcile past realities with future expectations. The problem is that future expectations often lose touch with future reality. Sometimes hope rides in the saddle, sometimes greed, sometimes fear. No, there is no "new paradigm." Hope, greed, and fear make up the market's *eternal* paradigm.

The conventional wisdom is wrapped up in what we call "Efficient Market Theory," which holds that since the financial markets incorporate *all* knowledge of *all* investors about *all* things, they are by definition efficient, eternally priced to perfection. But I wonder, and no one has ever been able to explain to me why the market was perfectly priced on August 31, 1987, or January 2, 1973, or September 8, 1929, each of which was followed by a catastrophic market decline, ranging from 35% to 85%.

In this age of statistical abundance, to be sure, we see table after table of data showing annual returns in the U.S. stock and bond markets encompassing two full centuries. We quickly learn that stocks outpace bonds in **60%** of all **one-year periods**—well short of a sure thing. But the odds rise to **73%** when we go out **five years and 82%** when we go out **ten years.** And over **25-year periods,** stocks outpace bonds **more than 99%** of the time, about as close to zero risk as is imaginable here on earth. (I've deliberately committed the sin of using *outpace.* The correct phrase is: *have in the past outpaced.* Please join me expressing the idea correctly!)

Because we can never be certain of the *order* in which the annual returns will come, those kinds of cumulative data are period-dependent and therefore inevitably misleading. So, we try to rectify the problem by throwing each year's return into a sort of Waring blender, turn the dial to "puree," and pour out a fine potage. (Or is that a "mess of pottage," for which Esau traded his birthright?) At first glance this approach seems to provide more meaningful data. But the devil is in the details. So don't forget that this methodology goes under the title of a "Monte Carlo Simulation."

All of these statistics leave me apprehensive. Why? Because the future is not only unknown but unknowable. Yet with the acceptance of Modern Portfolio Theory; the ease of massaging data with the computer; and our existence (at least in the U.S.) in today's era of remarkable political stability combined with powerful economic growth, investors seem to have developed growing confidence that they can forecast future returns in the stock market. If you fall into that category, I send you this categorical warning: *The stock market is not an actuarial table.*

To which I add: When everyone assumes, at least implicitly, that the market *is* an actuarial table, that the past is inevitably prologue, and that common stocks, held over an extended period, will *always* produce higher returns than bonds—and at lower risk—then *stocks inevitably will be priced to reflect that certainty.* At that point, however, the certainty becomes that stocks will produce *lower* future returns, and at higher risk at that. It is impossible to escape the suspicion that such an actuarial mindset, if you will, is extraordinarily prevalent today among investment advisers, consultants, and economists—and, for that matter, the individual and institutional investors themselves. Forewarned is forearmed.

Risk in Today's Market

With all of the lip service we pay to the notions of risk and risk control, how do we explain that by almost any conventional measure of stock valuation, stocks have *never* been riskier than they are today. Looking back 70 years, major market highs were almost invariably signaled when the dividend yield on stocks fell below 3%, or the price-earnings ratio rose much above 20 times earnings, or when the aggregate market value of U.S. equities reached 80% of our nation's gross domestic product (GDP). Yet today, dividend yields have fallen to just over 1%, so far from the old "risk" threshold as to render it seemingly meaningless. What is more, stocks are now selling at something like 32 times last year's earnings. And, with our $9.4 trillion GDP and our $17 trillion stock market, that ratio has not quite reached 200%. (Just be patient!) Clearly, if past data mean anything, risk is the, well, forgotten man of this Great Bull Market.

Even as we talk about the stock market, furthermore, let's be clear that today, more than any time I can recall, there are really *two* U.S. stock markets. One exists on the New York Stock Exchange, along with a few smaller markets for listed stocks. The other exists on the Nasdaq (the "over-the-counter" market). The relationship between the market capitalizations of the two has changed radically. The value of Nasdaq ran about 10% of the value of listed U.S. common stocks in 1977, rose to 26% by 1995, to 53% in 1999, and then to an astounding 73% in mid-March 2000. (See Figure 4.2.) Since 1999 began, the capitalization of the listed market has remained roughly unchanged at $9 trillion, while the capitalization of the Nasdaq has soared from $2.5 trillion to $6.8 trillion, or by 172%. (Note: Since mid-March, the value of the Nasdaq has fallen to $5.6 trillion—$1.2 trillion of, well, water over the dam—and is now valued at 62% of the listed market.)

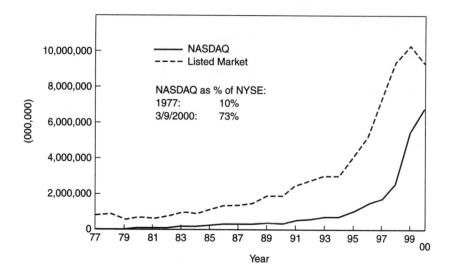

FIGURE 4.2 Market capitalization: NYSE/listed market vs. Nasdaq.

Old Economy, New Economy?

We can examine the nature of this dichotomy by comparing the stocks in the so-called *Old Economy,* which have been stagnant, with the stocks of the *New Economy,* which have been following a near-parabolic arc into the stratosphere. In a recent study of this dichotomy, Bernstein Research divided the market into two categories: The New, consisting of technology, telecommunications, and Internet commerce; the Old consisting of everything else.[2] Their analysis reflects an Old Economy valued at $10.6 trillion as 2000 began, and a New Economy valued at $6.7 trillion, respective totals that are remarkably close to the NYSE/Nasdaq split, though not with precisely the same stocks in each.

The past earnings growth of each Economy has almost been identical. During the expansion of earnings that Corporate America has enjoyed since 1995, earnings in the New Economy have grown at 8% annually, compared to 7% annual growth for Old Economy companies, meaning that the New Economy has provided no more than a remarkably steady share of about 16% of total corporate profits during the period. But, despite this similarity—and I *do* know that markets

---

2. Bernstein Disciplined Strategies Monitor, January 2000.

TABLE 4.1 New Economy vs. Old Economy*

	Year-end	
	1995	**1999**
Capitalization		
New	$ 1.1 T	$ 6.7 T
Old	5.5	10.6
Ratio	20%	64%
Reported earnings		
New	$ 49 B	$ 66 B
Old	314 B	412 B
Ratio	16%	16%
Trailing P/E		
New	23	102
Old	17	26
Ratio	1.3	4.0

*Sanford Bernstein & Co. Inc.

are valued less on the realities of past earnings than on the hopes and expectations of future earnings—the stocks in the New Economy were valued at 101.6 times earnings as 2000 began—compared to 25.6 times for the stocks in the Old Economy. (See Table 4.1.) Yes, the stock market is a wonderful arbitrage mechanism, but when it begins to discount not just the future, but the hereafter, watch out!

The Ultimate Test: Future Cash Flows

Why this note of caution? Because the theory you were taught in your finance classes is not only correct, but eternal. Sooner or later, the rewards of investing *must* be based on future cash flows. The purpose of any stock market, after all, is simply to provide liquidity for stocks in return for the promise of future cash flows, enabling investors to realize the present value of a future stream of income at any time. With current price-earnings ratios averaging more than 100 times, investors today clearly believe that the future streams of income in the New Economy will be enormous. How big must these cash flows be? Well, for the purpose of argument, let's assume that the investors who own the $6.7 trillion New Economy today expect these companies to provide a 15% after-tax return a decade hence. That's almost $1 trillion dollars . . . and that's a lot of money! Especially considering that these stocks earned just $66 billion last year. But who among us can be certain that, in this New Era in the economy, earnings *won't* grow at the 31% annual rate required to reach that total?

The Buffett Analysis

I, for one, don't believe these optimistic expectations will be realized. But don't mistake my word for the truth. If we use the kind of methodology that Warren Buffett uses to measure corporate value, we can at least put some sort of rule of reason on that kind of earning power. Mr. Buffett tells us that corporate profits after taxes have generally been slightly below 6% of the nation's gross domestic product (GDP), and presents good reasons to expect that a much higher ratio is unlikely to prevail over the long term. If we assume that our nation's economy grows at a 6% nominal rate, the GDP in 2010 would be about $16.5 trillion. If after-tax earnings in the Old Economy grow at that rate, they would rise from $412 billion to $740 billion. With the New Economy's $980 billion, we have total corporate profits of $1.7 trillion in 2010. At that level, projected corporate profits would be more than 10% of GDP, far above any share in history, and nearly double the fairly steady 5½% norm of the past. Nonetheless, that enormous share arguably represents the earnings expectations of today's investors. Their expectations are priced into the market, so the market, having discounted them once, will not discount them again. Put another way, unless that robust scenario comes true, market risk today is extremely high.

These historically high financial ratios and this crude economic analysis do not reflect my only concerns. Another is that the sheer mathematics of the market—*even assuming the continuation of boxcar growth rates that are by no means assured*—seem to defy reason. A recent analysis by Professor Jeremy Siegel (author of *Stocks for the Long-Run,* the source of virtually all of the data we use for long-term returns on financial assets) considered the nine large-cap companies that are currently priced at over 100 times 1999 earnings. Dr. Siegel accepted, for argument's sake, that the earnings of these companies would grow at their estimated average rate of 33% per year(!) over the coming decade—an even higher rate than I assumed earlier. Even so, for investors to earn a 15% annual return, they would have to sell at an average of 95 times their earnings five years from now, and 46½ times their earnings a decade hence. Based on his analysis of the nifty-50 era of the early 1970s, he reports "no stock that sold above a 50 p/e was

TABLE 4.2 Are Big-Cap Tech Stocks a "Sucker Bet"? (9 Large Tech Stocks vs. S&P 500)

	AVG. TECH STOCK	S&P 500
1999 P/E	257 x	35 x
Est. growth in EPS	33%	12.5%
2005 P/E*	95 x	30 x
2010 P/E*	46 x	27 x

*Required P/E assuming return of 15% for tech stocks and 10% for S&P 500.
SOURCE: Prof. Jeremy J. Siegel.

able to match the S&P 500 over the next quarter-century." His conclusion: "Big-Cap Tech Stocks Are a Sucker Bet." (See Table 4.2.)

As a veteran of the Go-Go era in the market during the mid-to-late 1960s, I observe disquieting similarities with today's tech-driven markets. During 1963–1968, based on their overheated records of past performance, the Go-Go funds drew ever larger portions of mutual fund cash flows. Five major funds turned in a total return of +344%, almost 3½ *times* the 99% gain of the S&P 500, and their assets promptly leaped 17 times over, from $200 million to $3.4 billion. Alas, retribution quickly came, and they posted negative returns averaging −45% through 1974, a period when the S&P was off just −19%. None of those Go-Go funds has prospered, and few have even survived.

Technology funds today are generating relative returns that are remarkably similar to those of the Go-Go era. Five of today's most successful funds have earned an average return of 403% during just the past three years, four times the 92% gain in the S&P 500. Their assets have soared seven times over, from $5.6 billion to $40 billion. And in another disquieting similarity, the records of both groups of funds are not without suspicion. In the Go-Go era, it was "letter stocks," private placements that funds bought from company insiders at large discounts and promptly marked-up to current value, that inflated fund returns. And in this era, it is hardly unreasonable to assume that hot IPOs may have inflated the records of the technology funds. Absent clear disclosure of the facts, investors would be foolish to consider such returns as a harbinger of the future. In any event, just as the Go-Go era of 35 years ago proved just another extraordinary popular delusion, so the Tech-Boom era of the turn of the millennium may prove just one more madness of crowds. (See Table 4.3.)

TABLE 4.3 Déjà Vu? (Comparison of Go-Go Era to Tech-Boom Era)

	5 LARGE GO-GO FUNDS			**5 LARGE TECH FUNDS**
1963–1968		1997–2000		
Fund return	344%	Fund return		403%
S&P return	99	S&P return		92
Ratio	3.4 x	Ratio		4.3 x
1963 assets	$200 M	1997 assets		$5.6 B
1968 assets	3.4 B	2000 assets		40 B
Increase	17 x	Increase		7 x
1969–1974		2000–2005		
Fund return	−45%	Fund return		?
S&P return	−19	S&P return		?
Ratio	2.4 x	Ratio		?

Yet another concern I have is today's high level of speculation. One of the best measures is, for me, a bittersweet one: the fascination of investors with market index funds that can be—and are—traded like individual stocks: Spiders, Webs (Cute! Just a fun game, or so it seems), Qubes, and iShares. A quarter-century ago, when I started the first index mutual fund, I viewed it as the ultimate in long-term investing—diversified, buy and hold, low-cost, and high tax efficiency—and it has worked marvelously. Ironically, these new index proxies are the ultimate in short-term speculation, and I cannot imagine that such speculation will serve investors well. Investors are now trading S&P-500-like Spiders at an annual turnover rate of nearly 2000%, and Nasdaq-like Qubes at a turnover rate of nearly 13,000%—average holding periods of just 18 days and 2.8 days, respectively. Their combined volume is staggering; if present volumes hold, some $1.5 trillion(!) of these shares will be traded this year. In the hectic market of April 4, 2000 alone, trading in these two listings totaled $10 billion! Welcome to the new millennium.

So, let me be clear: You can place me firmly in the camp of those who are deeply concerned that the stock market is all too likely to be riding for a painful fall—indeed a fall that may well have begun as I began to write this speech ten days ago. From Milton Friedman to Robert Schiller (author of the newly published *Irrational Exuberance*), to John Cassidy of *The New Yorker,* and Steven Leuthold,

Jeremy Grantham, Jeremy Siegel, Julian Robertson (who just threw in the towel), Gary Brinson (whose convictions may have cost him his job), and Alan Greenspan (whose conviction's haven't). Viewed a decade hence, today's stock market may just be one more chapter in "Extraordinary Popular Delusions and the Madness of Crowds."

Controlling Risk

All of us who serve as stewards of other people's money have a special responsibility, not only to consider the level of risk in the stock market today, but to control the risks to which our clients are exposed. There are three principal approaches to risk and risk control that I'll now discuss: (1) Ignoring equity risk; (2) Reducing risk by broadening diversification among sectors of the equity market; and (3) Reducing risk by reducing equity exposure.

The first approach, simply ignoring equity risk, is not as stupid as it may sound. Indeed, if the equity exposure of the portfolio is deemed appropriate to the client's time horizon and need for income (dividend yields and interest coupons, *not* capital gains), there are far worse strategies than simply "staying the course," a phrase which I have described as the single best piece of investment wisdom ever spoken. Such a solution implicitly assumes that the steward has *already* controlled the risk in the account, gradually reducing equities as, for example, the time for drawing down income or capital at retirement approaches, and probably having reduced equity exposure to (or at least toward) the account's norm as the Great Bull Market has carried the equity ratio ever upward. For example, a 60% equity position when the market rise began in mid-1982, untouched, would today have increased to 85%. (It should not go without saying that, taking no action whatsoever and letting the profits ride would have been a far more profitable strategy, so far at least. And continuing to bet the house's money is, after all, the conventional strategy of the gambler.)

Ignoring equity risk, to be sure, assumes that the client—or the client's investment committee—has both the financial resources and the emotional stability, indeed the courage (the guts, if you will), to stay the course. But make no mistake about it, even the best of intentions have a profound tendency to vanish when the stock market drops 50% (as in 1973–74) or even 35% (as in 1987). Panic is at best not a pretty emotion, and when panic is in the streets investors can turn ugly and act in ways that directly counter their own best interests. The counterproductive *emotions* of investing have had a way of eroding—and in some cases even destroying—the assets that have been created over the years by the productive *economics* of investing. Holding tight, moreover, means not engaging in market timing, which any intelligent investor must recognize is a *two-decision* process that requires not only *selling* right, but knowing when the day comes to reverse engines and *buying* right. It is not easy.

For me, staying the course implies owning a broad cross-section of the U.S. markets: growth stocks and value, large stocks and small, Old Economy stocks and New, listed stocks and Nasdaq. It's always tempting to make heavy sector bets, but betting is, well gambling, nowhere more obvious than in the (temporary to be sure) devastation wrought upon value investment strategies during the past five years (S&P Growth Index up 304%, Value Index up 157%). While the reversion to the mean that has been the eternal rule among market sectors strongly suggests that value's day is now in prospect, timing is hazardous duty, so my own view is that the optimal long-term strategy is to own a broad cross-section of the U.S. market. It will hardly surprise you that I'd realize that goal by owning the *broadest-possible* cross-section—a total stock market index fund. But for you who believe you can beat the market, be my guest. And good luck. (I *really* mean it!)

Ignoring equity risk, of course, in effect assumes that the economics of investing in U.S. stocks—the core portfolio for nearly all investors—will remain productive over the years ahead. I, for one, see no reason that this should not be the case. The powerful growth in our economy, our capacity for technological innovation, our global hegemony, the work ethic of our labor force, our rising productivity, all should be positive signals of future progress. And yet one can never be certain. Just a decade ago, each of those five factors—growth, innovation, global power, work ethic, productivity—defined the *Japanese* economy. (Remember "The Rising Sun"?) But for the better part of a full decade now, the Japanese economy has been a pallid shadow of its former self and the Tokyo market a near-perennial bear. (The Nikkei Index fell from a high of almost 40,000 in 1989 to a low of around 13,000 in 1998. It is now at about 20,000. Would most of today's U.S. investors have stayed the course through such rough seas? Not unless they were prepared to assume such risks.) So, we must never forget that "it *can* happen here." However far-removed that prospect may seem today, a lot can happen in a decade.

The second approach to risk control is broadening the conventional focus of an equity portfolio in marketable U.S. equities to encompass other equities that have *reliably* different correlations with the U.S. market, dominated as it is by large-cap growth and value stocks. I emphasize the word "reliably." While the returns on large-cap and small-cap stocks, and on growth and value stocks, have often had different correlations, they have been, and I assume will continue to be, spasmodic and mean-reverting. This brings us right to "Modern Portfolio Theory" (MPT), the cardinal principle of which is portfolio diversification: The broader the diversification, the lower the specific risk. In the ideal portfolio (the all-market index fund) *all* specific security risk is diversified away.

The classic example of broadened diversification, of course, is the addition of foreign stocks to U.S. equity portfolios. The record is crystal clear that, *if we accept standard deviation as our risk measure,* the use of foreign equities reduces risk. The problem is that I'm not at all sure that it is proper to use standard deviation as a proxy for risk, and even less sure that we should use risk-adjusted return as a proxy for investment success. After all, over-simplifying ever so slightly, the Sharpe ratio for calculating risk-adjusted return equates an extra percentage point of return with an extra percentage point of risk. But this much must be clear: *An extra percentage point of long-term return is priceless, and an extra percentage point of short-term standard deviation is meaningless.* So what *investment* purpose is served by dividing the meaningless into the priceless, weighting both equally? I'll leave it to you to answer that question, even as I applaud the Sharpe ratio for serving a useful *academic* purpose in objectively weighing returns earned against risks assumed.

The "Efficient Frontier"

When we consider the impact of international diversification on U.S. portfolios, we are led quickly to the famous "efficient frontier" of the financial academy. Clearly, the ultimate diversification would be to own the entire World portfolio, now about 50% U.S., 25% Europe, 15% Japan and Pacific, 10% emerging markets. But a decade ago, it was 50% Japan and Pacific, 30% U.S., 15% Europe, and 5% emerging markets. But I'm not at all convinced that a U.S. investor should have had 70% of assets outside the U.S. then, or even 50% of assets outside the U.S. now.

Most of the academic community rejects the full market-weight strategy but endorses a more sophisticated form of analysis to set the structure of the global portfolio. The analysis involves the calculation of an *efficient frontier,* which is designed to determine the precise allocation of assets between U.S. and foreign holdings. The goal is a combination that promises the highest return at the lowest level of risk (i.e., the lowest volatility of return acceptable to the investor). I am skeptical of this approach as well, for the efficient frontier is based almost entirely on *past* returns and *past* risk patterns. That bias may be unavoidable—after all, history is our only source of hard data—but past relative returns of stock portfolios and (to a lesser degree) past relative volatility are hardly reliable harbingers of the future, and may even be counterproductive. (See Figures 4.3 and 4.4.)

Consider how the global efficient frontier has shifted over time. Ten years ago, the highest returns (+23%) had come from a 100% foreign Europe, Australasia, and Far East (EAFE) portfolio, the lowest from 100% in the U.S. (+17%). Yet in the ensuing decade, precisely the reverse was the case—U.S. +18%, EAFE +7%. Slavish reliance on history seems particularly flawed in markets where currency fluctuations create substantial extra risk—a special risk that no investor is obliged to assume. Further, the idea that foreign stock markets do not have high correlations with the U.S. stock market has in itself come

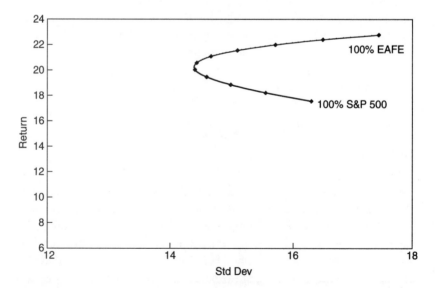

FIGURE 4.3 Efficient Frontier, S&P 500 vs. EAFE (10 years ending 12/31/89).

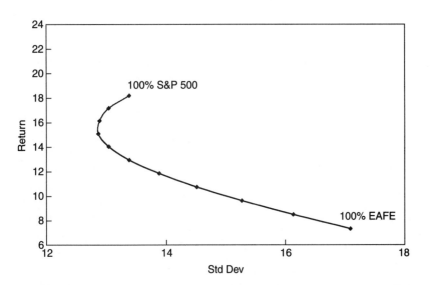

FIGURE 4.4 Efficient Frontier, S&P 500 vs. EAFE (10 years ending 12/31/99).

into doubt. The fact is that, while the correlation was indeed at low levels (about 0.20) during the two decades ending in 1992, the correlation has since leaped up to 0.60. Who is to say that, in an ever more global economy, it won't continue to rise to 0.70 or even to 0.80 or more in the years ahead. So, as in all things, treat history with the respect it deserves . . . *no more, no less.*

Further, extremely small variations in risk often separates the optimal portfolio from those deemed less efficient. For example, in the decade ended in 1989, the lowest standard deviation (60/40 U.S./foreign) was 14.4 percent, compared to 15.0 percent for both a 30/70 mix *and* an 80/20 mix (purportedly the most efficient). Conversely, in the 1999 decade, the 12.8 percent deviation for the lowest risk (70/30 U.S./foreign) portfolio compared with the 13.4 percent figure both for a portfolio holding 100 percent U.S. equities, and one holding 50 percent U.S.—allocations that are, well, worlds apart. These tiny differences in volatility—in both cases, only a half percentage point—are so small as to be almost invisible to any real-world investor, particularly one who is not willing or able to engage in the arcane methodology required for calculating the standard deviation of monthly returns, even assuming that such deviation is a valid proxy for risk. Finally, even when long-term correlations are high, the reduction in standard deviation is often lost in sharp market downturns and in longer bear markets. In the words of Professor Bruno Solnik, "Diversification fails us just when we need it most." With all these weaknesses, such analysis seems a wholly unwarranted triumph of process over judgment.

Did He Say "Gold"? or "Alternative Investments"?

If the idea is truly to reduce risk (or to be clear, standard deviation) by the introduction into the portfolio of asset classes with low correlation to the U.S. market, what about gold? I may be the first serious investor in decades to bring up the subject of gold as a useful portfolio diversifier, but surely it fills the bill! (Others, such as James Grant, discuss gold as an investment opportunity, but I'm just not so sure.) Gold stocks have had a correlation of about 0.05 with the U.S. market, doubtless the smallest figure for any discrete sector of our market. A few decades ago, gold was considered *the* diversifier, just as foreign stocks are in this more recent era. Yet gold proved to be a terrible investment. So I emphasize that while diversifiers may serve a useful purpose, *investors are unwise to diversify their equities ever more broadly merely for diversification's sake.* Rather, we must consider the tangential relationship between standard deviation and risk, the implications for long-term returns when we reduce short-term risks, and the amount of real risk we are assuming.

In this context, I'd like to touch briefly on one more diversifier, made especially popular in recent years by the well-publicized investment strategies of some of the nation's largest college endowment funds. I am referring to *alternative investments,* including hedge funds, venture capital, private equity, and real estate, all of which appear to have low correlations with marketable stocks. These endowment funds (also heavy users of foreign stocks) have undertaken these alternative investments at the expense of their traditional U.S. equity holdings. However, the record is not at all clear that this more diversified bundle of equities has enhanced returns over what a conventional 65/35 stock/bond portfolio, benchmarked to the accepted market indexes, has provided.

What is more, many alternative investments have characteristics that make them considerably *riskier* than U.S. stocks as a group: the business risk of new enterprises, the financial risk of real estate, the leverage risk of hedge funds. And foreign stocks, too, carry larger risks, for the emerging markets, economic risk; for many nations, severe political risk; for *all* such markets, currency risk. I urge you to consider the wisdom of reducing short-term *volatility* risk by assuming the substantially higher *financial* risk in owning alternative investments in the portfolio. Let's never substitute the precise analysis of past data for the wisdom God gave us to make sound judgments.

So far, I've given you two strategies for dealing with risk in today's heady markets: (1) Getting your asset allocation right, maintaining a long-term time horizon, and staying the course; and (2) diversifying some risk away by introducing equities with reliably different correlations with the U.S. market. But what if you can't afford to ignore risk, either because your clients are not prepared to "tough it out" in the difficult markets we may face, or because your client portfolios are not properly structured? And what if you share my misgivings about the real protection available by diversifying into what may be riskier asset classes in the paradoxical quest to reduce the volatility risk of the equity portfolio? One major option remains: Controlling risk by reducing equity exposure.

I conclude that *the single most effective way to control risk is by controlling equity exposure.* For risk, as America's risk guru Peter Bernstein tells us in *Against the Gods,* "is about mystery. It focuses on the unknown, for there would be no such thing as risk if everything were known." Mr. Bernstein quotes Pascal: "Which way should we incline? Reason cannot answer." In short, we simply do not know, and probabilities—that darned "actuarial table" again—do not give us the answer. He then notes, "outcomes are uncertain, but we have some control over the consequences of what does happen. And that is what risk management is all about." Put another way, we must base our asset allocation not on the *probabilities* of choosing the right allocation, but on the *consequences* of choosing the wrong allocation.

Since I agree with that analysis, I am deeply troubled about how the investment profession has come to define risk management today. As Jeremy Grantham recently noted, "when money moves from the hands of amateur investors to the hands of professional investors, the concept of *real* risk is replaced by the concept of *benchmark* risk." And so we have the eleventh commandment of investment management: "Thou shall not permit style drift." The order of the day for investment managers seems to be to limit variations from their benchmark style so that their judgments won't cost them their jobs. As a result, risk control has come to mean, not controlling the client's *principal* risk, but controlling the manager's *career* risk.

"Style drift" means that growth managers can't buy value stocks, nor can small stock managers buy large stocks. If the time horizon is long, the variations moderate, and the principle of mean reversion holds, avoiding style drift may not cause irreparable harm to a portfolio's investment returns. (However, I reiterate my own stock preference for the "style" set by the total U.S. stock market.) But when style drift comes to mean, as Mr. Grantham says, "above all, that equity managers can't buy bonds," there is an obvious flaw in our system of capital formation. For bonds—diversified portfolios of U.S. Treasuries and A or better corporates with little credit risk—are, finally, the investor's only real protection against the most dire consequences of the inevitable uncertainty of equity ownership.

Consideration of bonds as an important asset class implicitly requires us to recognize, as I quoted in *Common Sense on Mutual Funds,* that "risk is *not* short-term volatility, for the long-term investor can afford to ignore that. Rather, because there is not a predestined rate of return, only an expected one that may not be realized, the risk is the possibility that, in the long run, stock returns will be terrible."[3] Put another way, the risk is that the investment portfolio might not provide its owner—individual or institution—with adequate cash to meet future requirements for essential outlays. In short, that the investor will lose a ton of money, just when it is needed the most.

No one knows whether or not bonds will provide higher total returns than stocks over the next decade or quarter century. But we do know this: that bonds will produce far higher *income.* I don't mean to be a Luddite, but income remains important, and a bond portfolio today, without compromising on quality, can produce a yield of 7½%, $75,000 of income per million dollars of capital. An all-market stock portfolio can provide a yield of only about 1%—a bit more than $10,000. Even if its dividends grow at 6% per year, it won't be until 2036 until the stock portfolio pays $75,000, and until 2057 until the *cumulative* dividend payments aggregate to the cumulative bond interest payments. In these days when it is so easy to spend *principal,* it is easy to ignore *income.* But I believe that this situation will prove transitory, not eternal. Nonetheless, fixed-income investments are not only our only real means of controlling risk, they are now our only real means of generating income. In a world of boxcar total returns on

---

3. Lawrence Siegel, the treasurer of the Ford Foundation, writing in the *Journal of Portfolio Management.*

stocks, risk is often ignored, bonds deemed irrelevant, and income old-fashioned. But when the going gets tough, all three—risk, bonds, and income—will come into their own again.

A Final Thought

And so ends this long journey through the thicket of risk and risk control in an era of confidence, and perhaps even greed. I've spent much time telling you why I think stocks are facing outsized risks today, and the recent surge of market volatility may be the harbinger, that after all these years, risk is again coming home to roost. I've also presented three distinct means of dealing with equity risk, from ignoring it, to reducing short-term volatility, to dealing with real protection against losing capital when capital is most needed. While I cannot give any investor a neat formula for risk control, I am comforted to share that inadequacy with the likes of Paul Samuelson, who tells us, "there is no way any professor of economics or any minister of the church can tell you what your risk tolerance must be."

No, nor can any Wall Street seer, nor any money manager, nor any indexing advocate, nor even any grizzled veteran of 50 years in this wonderful business.

5

BUY STOCKS? NO WAY!

OR

IT'S A DANGEROUS GAME. . . . IT'S A VOTE OF
CONFIDENCE THAT THINGS ARE GETTING WORSE. . . .
THE MARKET HAS BECOME A CRAPSHOOT. . . .
THE SMALL INVESTOR HAS BECOME AN ENDANGERED
SPECIES. . . . THE STOCK MARKET IS ONE OF THE
SLEAZIEST ENTERPRISES IN THE WORLD.

The American Association of Individual Investors
Philadelphia Chapter
September 27, 1988

I HAVE GIVEN my remarks this
evening this rather long title to convey to you a clear picture of the low
repute in which common stocks find themselves today. My title is simply the headline from an article that appeared in *Time* magazine dated
September 26, 1988, and a collection of excerpts from the story. And
it suggests that, if there is any substance whatsoever to the theory of
contrary investing, today is far more likely to be a time of investment
opportunity than the harbinger of Armageddon.

Buttressed by a chart (illustrated with an enormous bear) showing
that the percentage of individual investors with immediate plans to
buy more shares has dropped from 35% at the market high in August
1987 to 3.7% in September 1988, the *Time* article is one of a proliferating series of articles in the press purporting to analyze the equity
environment in the year following the great stock market crash of

66

October 19, 1987. It illustrates not only *that* investors have lost their appetites for stocks, but *why* they have.

There are, of course, infinite examples of this change. One of my favorites is the recent disappearance of the NBC "Before Hours" financial news program. A year ago, I (and doubtless many others) turned on our television sets each day at 5:45 A.M. to hear how Tokyo closed, how London opened, and, from seemingly omniscient *Wall Street Journal* reporters, how New York would behave just a few hours hence. Indeed, I was interviewed on "Before Hours" in NBC's New York Studio a few days after the Great Crash (providentially, I advised investors not to panic, and to stay the course), so it was especially poignant for me to witness the program's apparent recent demise. It has been replaced by a show with bouncy music and three rather lithe, leotard-clad young ladies exercising perhaps a million television viewers through their "Morning Stretch." The stock market and *its* bouncy peregrinations seem a long way away!

Investor purchases of mutual fund shares are also a long way away from year-ago levels. During the first seven months of 1987, investors purchased $46 billion of equity mutual funds (often at what proved to be inflated prices). During the first seven months of 1988 (with stocks at more realistic valuations), total purchases had dropped to $16 billion, a 65% decline. *Net* cash flow into equity funds (investor purchases minus redemptions) had dropped even further, from an *inflow* of $25 billion in the first seven months of last year to an *outflow* of $3½ billion this year, a chilling decline of 115%.

These figures are just one more manifestation of one of the great paradoxes of the stock market: When stock prices are high, everyone seems to want to jump on the bandwagon; when stocks are on the bargain counter, it almost seems difficult to give them away. Clearly, the Great Crash has caused a lot of otherwise rational investors to abandon the stock market. While I am the first one to agree with the old adage, "If you can't stand the heat, stay out of the kitchen," it seems to me that sensible, patient long-term investors should continue to stay the course today, just as I urged in my cameo television appearance at the depths of last October's decline.

The Great Crash and Its Aftermath

In this context, it might be useful to consider just why the Great Crash transpired. Writing just two weeks thereafter, in our Windsor Fund

Annual Report for the fiscal year ended October 31, 1987, I said this
to our shareholders:

> **Investors ask, fairly enough, "What caused the market to plum-
> met?" We think that three factors were involved: (1) stock
> prices simply got "too high" relative to their underlying earn-
> ings and dividends, especially in competition with the sharply
> higher yields available on fixed-income securities; (2) there was
> some deterioration in the economic outlook, with no progress
> being made to reduce the Federal budget deficit, no improve-
> ment in our international trade imbalance, and a whiff of infla-
> tion in the air; and (3) the decline that was set in motion by the
> first two factors was greatly accelerated by "program trading"
> in the stock index futures market, where massive computer-
> driven sales took place in an effort to provide "portfolio insur-
> ance," a misnomer if we have ever heard one.**

Now, with the perspective of almost a year, I don't believe that I can
add very much to that thumbnail analysis.

Today, of course, these conditions no longer exist. The common
stocks that comprise the Standard & Poor's Index are selling, not at 23
times earnings (a level that has consistently marked major peaks in
equity prices) as at the August 1987 highs, but at about 11 times, a relative improvement in value of 50%. (The present price-earnings
ration, in fact, is also well below the long-term average of 14 times.)

If our Federal budget deficit is in the same dismal state as a year
ago, an optimist can imagine that once the November elections are
history, it is at least conceivable that our legislators and our new President can begin to take a few steps toward fiscal sanity. Of course, the
trade deficit trends have improved substantially, and the dollar has
strengthened in international markets. And some early signs of a slow-
ing in the economy could mean that inflationary pressures could in
fact be more moderate than anticipated by market participants.

Portfolio insurance, a major factor in making a bad market situation
worse, indeed bringing us to the edge of chaos, failed to live up to the
expectations of those who considered it a panacea. The amount of
assets invested under such schemes has dropped, it is said, from some
$60 billion to $10 billion, reducing its mischief-making potential by
more than 80%. Anyone who thought seriously about portfolio insurance knew as a certainty that it would not work when changes in stock
prices were discontinuous. The issue is hardly either complex or
novel, and was spelled out clearly in James Gleick's book about scien-

tific theory entitled *Chaos,* written long before the crash, explaining what he called "the Noah effect":

The Noah effect means discontinuity: When a quantity changes it can change almost arbitrarily fast. A stock market strategy is doomed to fail if it assumes that a stock has to sell for $50 at some point on its way down from $60 to $10.

In any event, we have witnessed significant turns for the better in each of the three principal areas that troubled us a year ago: (1) market valuations; (2) the economic outlook; and (3) participation in portfolio insurance.

Stock Values vs. Stock Prices

In our 1987 series of Vanguard Fund Annual Reports, we presented a chart showing the relationship of stock prices to book values and dividends since 1960. It made the perhaps obvious point that although prices are exposed to interim, transitory, and even frightening fluctuations, over the long term they are determined by fundamental factors such as book values and dividends, both of which have risen at a remarkably steady rate over the years. In fact, during the 1960–1987 period, dividends on the Standard & Poor's 400 Index rose by +320%, replacement book value rose by +750%, and price rose by 370%. Put another way, the underpinning for the average annual increase in stock prices of 6% during this period of nearly three decades was formed by dividend increases averaging 5½%, and book value growth averaging 8%. So the message is just the opposite of *Time*'s foreboding headline: not "Buy Stocks? No Way!," but rather "Own Stocks, the Course to Stay."

The appropriateness of that advice, I think, is buttressed by the fact that the Great Crash, in truth, was a market spasm that lasted but three business days—or, perhaps more fairly, eight weeks, from August 25 to October 19. Viewed in the light of the gains the stock market enjoyed before then, and the gains that were to follow, it provided a market timing opportunity only to the nimble investor who was either lucky or prescient—twice! (Selling high, then buying low.) The investor who owned stocks when 1987 began, held them through the crash and its aftermath, and stayed the course right up to now, has done just fine. The Standard & Poor's 500 Index, for example, has turned in a total return of +17% during this 19-month period; Vanguard's flagship Windsor Fund has done even better, with a return of +27%. For, as Table 5.1 shows, the unpleasantness of last autumn

TABLE 5.1   S&P 500 Index and Windsor Fund Returns, January 1987 to September 1988

	JANUARY–AUGUST 1987	SEPTEMBER–DECEMBER 1987	JANUARY–SEPTEMBER 1988	JANUARY 1987–SEPTEMBER 1988
S&P 500 Index	+39%	−24%	+12%	+17%
Windsor Fund	+31	−22	+26	+27

came between two delightful winter-spring-summer intervals of salubrious investment results:

I mentioned the role of luck and prescience a moment ago. I know no investors (though there may be a few) who were lucky enough *both* to liquidate their stocks at the highs of August 1987 *and* to buy them back at the turn of the year. Besides, luck is not a very reliable ingredient upon which an investor should stake his financial future. And as to the prescient investor, the market seer, the all-knowing guru, I don't know many of them either. They come and go, and their advice ranges from the erratic to the incomprehensible, as this excerpt from a *Wall Street Journal* interview with Robert Prechter, editor of *The Elliot Wave Theorist,* after "Black Monday," illustrates:

> [Mr. Prechter] said he expected support on the industrial average around 2100. Two hours later, at 12:30 p.m., Mr. Prechter told callers that "he would like to see a close over 2100 today." But at 2:30, Mr. Prechter said he expected to see a support level between 1700 and 1800. In an update after the market closed down 508, at 1738.74—Mr. Prechter predicted that the next support level would be 1500.
>
> Mr. Prechter, who has long predicted that the industrial average would climb to above 3600 by 1988 . . . now says yesterday's action "underscores the magnitude of what lies ahead for the new bear market in stocks." Mr. Prechter could not be reached for comment yesterday.
>
> Less than two weeks ago, Mr. Prechter said that if the industrial average dropped to near 2300, it would represent "an ideal buying spot."

Well, whether the guru is Robert Prechter in 1987, or Joseph Granville five years earlier, or dozens of other lesser-known names at other times, their advice (such as it may be) usually rings hollow in retrospect.

The Hazards of Equity Investing

To be sure, I think that few investors are more aware than I of the hazards that lie ahead. While "peace and prosperity" accurately describe our world today, tomorrow is ever a question mark. "Brush fire wars," now being extinguished in Africa, Afghanistan, and the Middle East, could reignite anywhere, anytime. The U.S. economy will probably face a recession within the next few years. The great industrialized nations of the free world are increasingly dependent upon one another. And the mountains of debt that have been accumulated over the past decade—by our Federal government, by the less developed countries, by U.S. corporations, by leveraged buyouts, and by consumers—is potentially explosive. Nonetheless, it is ever thus: hazards *always* lie ahead, and it is the investors' responsibility to deal with them, by structuring an investment portfolio that rationally looks to protect against each kind of uncertainty.

So, common stocks, which make such good sense for maximum long-term return and optimum protections against inflation, but which carry such frightening short-term and even intermediate-term risks, should comprise only a portion of the intelligent investor's portfolio. Clearly, every investor should also have significant cash reserves, which presently pay generous returns, offer complete stability of principal, and perhaps most importantly, help provide peace of mind for queasy investors on those days when there are drops of 25 points or 50 points or 100 points or more in the Dow Jones Industrial Average. We will continue to experience such declines, I am confident, in the years immediately ahead, just as in the years immediately past, and cash reserves should fortify investors against panic, the better to avoid liquidating equity holdings at prices that reflect fear and pessimism.

Investing in Bonds

I do not want to ignore the third major leg of a three-legged stool of asset classes. You should own *stocks;* you should maintain *cash reserves;* you should also own *bonds.* Of course, I am well aware that in recent years bonds have been subject to periodic short-term—even daily—price fluctuations that are as comparable, and as frightening, as those of the stock market. Nonetheless, if you can ignore the price and enjoy the coupon, four basic reasons commend bonds to investors today:

First, interest rates are generous by historical standards. Best measured on a "real" (i.e., inflation-adjusted) basis, bonds provide a current real return of about 5½% (10¼% coupon on good grade utility bond, less the present inflation rate of 4¾%). The long-term real return on bonds has averaged only about 3½%, so even if inflation heats up somewhat—as well it may—bonds appear relatively attractive.

Second, bond returns are *certain* to be steadier than returns on stocks as the investor's holding period lengthens. This is so because typically 100% of the long-term return on a bond comes from its income stream (interest), while only about 50% of the long-term return on a stock comes from its income stream (dividends). So, in the year that begins today, a bond has a 10¼% coupon "in the bag," while a stock today averages a 3.6% dividend in prospect (based on the current yield of the Standard & Poor's Index). Clearly, the total return on the bond is materially less sensitive to price changes than the total return on the stock.

Third, the rate premium on bonds over cash reserves provides a substantial cushion against even highly adverse changes in long-term interest rates. A compound return on a 10¼% bond over 15 years would provide a terminal value of $44,800 on an initial investment of $10,000; the comparable figure for cash reserves yielding an assumedly flat (which of course it will not be) yield of 7¼% would be $28,500. So, the value of the bond investment could drop by an incredible (and hardly likely) 35% at the end of the period, and still provide an identical return.

Fourth, rising interest rates, however schooled we have been to think of them as baneful, can in fact be a blessing. For most of the long-term compound return on a bond does not come from the regular payment of its interest and the final payment of its principal. Rather, it comes from the reinvestment of the interest coupon (i.e., "interest on interest"). Indeed, taking the 15-year 10¼% bond just described, $15,400 of its total return comes from its coupon; the remaining $19,400 comes from interest on interest. The net result is that if interest rates were to immediately rise to, say 12½%, the terminal value would *rise* from $44,800 to $52,300, or nearly 20%. I should note that this principle holds *only* for the long-term investor. Typically, the "break-even" point for total return comes at about half way through the bond's life (in this case, the eighth year). So, the risk of changes in interest rates should not unduly deter the long-term investor from a substantial position in bonds.

(I have been referring, of course, to *long-term* bonds in these comments. More cautious or more risk-averse investors should also consider short-term bonds, which are substantially less volatile, but yield a nice premium over cash reserves. In many cases, a mixture of long-term and short-term bonds would be appropriate.)

The Appropriate Balance

Now, if I have persuaded you of the importance of maintaining significant positions in stocks *and* in bonds *and* in cash reserves in your investment portfolios, it is fair for you to ask just what "balance" is best. Regrettably, the answer is, "it all depends." It depends most importantly on the amount of your assets (and liabilities!), your financial goals, your tolerance for risk, your need for income, and your age. I can't cover each of these factors for each one of you here tonight, but I can suggest this: a good beginning point might be 50% in stocks, 30% in bonds, and 20% in reserves. For younger investors just beginning to invest—say in an IRA or corporate thrift plan—perhaps 75% to 80% in stocks is the right number, with bonds and cash reserves commensurately reduced. For an investor who has just retired at age 65, stocks might represent 40% of the portfolio, with commensurate increases in the other two asset classes.

I recognize that these examples are grossly oversimplified. For example, there are groups of common stocks with distinct investment characteristics; the younger investor might seek greater returns via stocks with higher growth potential but lower yields and higher risks; the older investor would almost certainly seek stocks with higher yields and a growing income stream, at lower risk. For another example, I have ignored specialty asset classes—such as real estate and gold—which might usefully be considered as ancillary asset classes. For a third example, of course, I have not tried to measure your psyche—your patience, your independence, your determination, in all, the strength of both your heart and your stomach in "pressing on" no matter how compelling the immediate case for abandoning your financial plan. But I hope you will find these brief thoughts on "balance" to be helpful as a starting point.

Return, Risk—and Cost

My emphasis so far in these remarks has been on *return*, and on *risk*, and on how to balance them. They are two of the central elements of *any* investment program. But there is also a third key element, and it is *cost*. Every investment carries a cost, and that cost is a *certain* "drag" on your investment return. It may be a transaction cost (such as brokerage or sales commissions); it may be an advisory fee; it may be the other administrative expenses involved in investing, such as custody and service fees. Usually, it is all of the above. Sometimes they are hidden. But they can be readily quantified in what I believe should be the principal medium of any investment program—mutual fund shares.

It is "hornbook economic" that spreading risk over a variety of investments is essential if the specific risk of any one security is to be substantially eliminated. So, I believe that all investors should be broadly diversified in each of the three major asset classes. And I know of no more intelligent way to achieve this diversification than by investing in mutual funds—surely the most efficient way to own lots of stocks and lots of bonds, and the certificates of deposit of lots of banks. Given that I first studied the mutual fund industry as an economics major at Princeton University some 40 years ago, that I have worked in this industry ever since, and that I have been in charge of a major mutual fund complex for more than two decades, it can hardly astonish you that I come here tonight as an unabashed advocate of the concept of mutual fund investing as the optimum way to capitalize on the rewards and minimize the risks of investing.

And so it is with particular fervor that I discuss the role that *cost* plays in your investment program. In my judgment, this industry has ignored the issue of cost. Indeed, in an ever-more intensive campaign to attract investors' assets, the better to enhance the profits of the typical mutual fund shareholder, mutual fund costs are today escalating beyond belief, and beyond reason. The great mutual fund price war of the 1980s has driven sales costs ever higher (usually through the now nearly omnipresent 12b-1 fees) and advisory fees skyward. It is a paradoxical price war, since economic theory tells us that price wars are supposed to drive prices paid by consumers *down*, not up.

But the competition in this industry is for a sales "push," not a demand "pull." And the best way to attract investor dollars during the halcyon age of the great five-year bull market in stocks and bonds that extended from mid-1982 through mid-1987 (when virtually all diversified investment programs reaped substantial profits) was through massive and costly distribution efforts. This meant paying large (and often hidden) commissions to stock brokers by load funds, and paying for massive (and often misleading) advertising campaigns by no-load funds. In either case, of course, it is the mutual fund shareholder who foots the bill.

The Soaring Costs of Mutual Funds

The shares of the Vanguard Funds are offered on a pure no-load basis without front-end sales charges or deferred sales commissions, or 12b-1 sales fees. So, we are distinctly different from those of our competitors whose shares are often available only on a full-load, low-load or deferred-load basis. I am going to limit my comments on costs, therefore, to fund *operating expense ratios* (the total of advisory fees, 12b-1 charges, administration costs, etc., as a percentage of fund assets). These costs are soaring. According to *Forbes* magazine, the expense ratio of the average stock fund has risen from 1.16% in 1982 to 1.49% in 1987, an increase of nearly 30% in just five years. Even the more easily managed fixed income funds operate at high ratios— 1.04% for the average bond fund and 0.71% for the average money market fund, and new types of funds such as international stock and bond funds operate at still higher ratios, respectively, 1.79% and 1.52%. Further, these increases have in fact been held *down* by the apparent reluctance of fund managers to propose fee increases on existing funds to their shareholders. Rather, they have created new funds (often identical to their predecessors) with expense burdens that once would have been considered "beyond the pale." If we were to examine just those funds newly created during the past few years, a typical expense ratio would likely be in the range of 2% or even higher.

Why would an intelligent investor pay such costs? There are really only three possibilities: one, he expects to achieve returns that vastly exceed the costs involved; two, he doesn't take the trouble to make himself fully informed; and three, he is not presented with cost information in a comprehensible manner. At last, order is coming out of chaos in the cost disclosure area. Previously, important cost information was scattered throughout a fund's prospectus—hidden and often ignored. Now, the Securities and Exchange Commission requires mutual funds to provide integrated cost disclosure in a single, crystal clear tabulation at the front of each fund's prospectus. The table must show the *total* costs that would actually be paid by investors—sales loads (front-end and deferred), advisory fees, 12b-1 fees, shareholder account maintenance charges, and other expenses—assuming his ownership of shares for various time periods. So, the investor can easily make his own cost comparisons, and has only himself to blame if he does not. To give you some idea as to how these costs vary, an investor could incur ten-year costs of $498 for each $10,000 invested in a low-cost fund (I have taken the liberty of using the average Vanguard fund in this example) and as much as $2,564 for each $10,000 invested in a particular high-cost fund. (I won't provide the specific name, but there are plenty of them in that range and even higher.)

The central question, of course, is: "Does cost matter?" I strongly believe that it does. Simply put, if we are measuring long-term returns by historical norms, a conservatively balanced program such as I have described in my earlier baseline example might provide a long-term return in the range of 9%. If the investor's annual cost is ½ of 1%, a $10,000 initial investment would have a terminal value of $39,000 after 15 years. If the cost were 2%, the value of the investment would grow to just $27,600. Just think of that: an increase of $29,000 versus an increase of $17,600. Or to put it another way, an *extra* gain of $11,400—114% of the initial investment, simply by minimizing cost, with risk and return held constant.

Now I fully recognize that it is worth your while to pay a "genius" stock fund manager 2% a year if he can earn, say, 15%, particularly if his "pedestrian" counterpart who is paid ½% a year delivers only 12%. But there are, by my standards, no geniuses in this business. There are, however, lucky managers and managers who take extreme risk, and, after all, those are usually the managers at the very top (and very bottom) of the rankings over most short-term periods. There are also excellent managers with enduring and productive long-term records, but, alas, they are in a distinct minority. What is more, they are not always easily identifiable in advance, and many of yesterday's apparently superior managers will not be among this group tomorrow. Finally, there is not a scintilla—not an iota—of evidence that high-cost funds perform any better than low-cost funds. Indeed, even if the low-cost fund provides marginally *lower* total return performance, it can still win the competition in terms of net return delivered to the investor. One is reminded of the fable of the tortoise and the hare.

If high cost is unlikely to be rewarding to an investor in a stock fund, it is even less likely to be rewarding to an investor in a bond fund, and almost inconceivable to be rewarding to an investor in a money market fund. In this latter case, virtually the *entire* difference in yield among money market funds is accounted for by the difference in expenses—not management expertise—and one can hardly imagine why an investor would give up from 50 to 75 "basis points" (½% to ¾%) in yield, to absolutely no avail. While a handful of high-cost bond funds *may* be able to outperform their low-cost counterparts over time, given the fact that the impact of changing interest rates falls relatively evenly on all classes of bonds, the investor in fixed-income mutual funds who ignores cost is playing very long odds indeed.

Index Funds . . . and Others

On that note, let me now turn to some types of mutual funds that—in part because of their cost efficiency—I believe will become increasingly important in the years ahead—and then some types that I would caution you to avoid. First is the Index Fund—a fund that matches the composition of, usually, the Standard & Poor's 500 Composite Stock Price Index, and hence emulates its investment performance. It is no secret that this Index has been a redoubtable competitor to actively managed equity accounts over a long span of years, and for reasons that are obvious and simple.

Assume the total stock market provides an average annual return of 12%. That is, by definition, the *gross* return that all investors—individual and institutional alike—will share. If we accept the assumption that these investors incur costs—advisory fees, transaction cost, etc.— averaging 1½%, they will share a net return of 10½% per year. But if an Index Fund can operate without advisory fees and with minimal transaction costs, its costs might run to, say, ⅜%, it would turn in a *net* return of 11⅝% per year. Over fifteen years, then, the terminal value of a $10,000 investment at the net market return would be $44,700, while the Index Fund value would be $52,000. Clearly, the typical manager will have his work cut out for him to surpass this unmanaged portfolio.

And that is precisely what the past record shows us. Over the past twenty years, the annual return on the average managed pension equity account has been +8.3%; the annual return on the Standard & Poor's Index has been +9.3%. This actual historical difference of 1% is remarkably close to the simple theoretical difference of 1.1% mentioned a moment ago. (The pension figure is *before* transaction and administration fees. These costs are probably about equal, so the same relationship would prevail on a "net" basis.) During the past five years, the Index superiority is even larger (+16.5% vs. +14.9%), but this high degree of superiority is probably unsustainable in the future.

While indexing has been a major factor in pension management (an estimated $180 billion currently), it has not made much of a dent in the mutual fund field. Indeed, the 500 Portfolio of Vanguard Index Trust, organized in 1976, was, until 1986, the only publicly available index fund, and our assets of about $1 billion hardly mark it as a dominant force among equity mutual funds. And none of our recent index fund competitors seem as determined as Vanguard to minimize costs. (Our Trust's expense ratio will run at about ¼ of 1% this year, the lowest in the entire mutual fund industry, as far as we know.) An investor would have to be very naive to choose a sales-loaded, high-expense ratio index fund when he could select our no-load, low-expense Trust. So, we look for continued growth in this portion of Vanguard's asset base.

Of course, use of an Index Fund precludes the opportunity for extraordinary performance delivered by a truly superior manager, however rare he might be. In return, however, indexing provides an "odds on" bet that an investor can outpace most other equity funds, and a virtual guarantee that his performance will *never* be at the bottom of the deck. For most investors, that trade-off is apt to be worthwhile, and an index account should be considered as at least a core portion of the equity portfolios of most investors.

Indexing, moreover, is moving well beyond a simple "Standard & Poor's 500 Stock Index" approach. This Index comprises about 70% of the value of all stocks, so we have developed our Extended Market Portfolio to index the remaining 30% of the market. By using our 500 Portfolio and our Extended Market Portfolio in these proportions, an investor can in effect "own the entire stock market," a useful hedge against the inevitable periods when small- and medium-sized companies outperform their "blue chip" cousins. (So far, 1988 looks like just such a year.)

Our unique Extended Market Portfolio is but one of three extensions to the basic indexing concept that Vanguard has introduced. A second is Vanguard Bond Market Fund, indexed to the Salomon Brothers Investment Grade Index. A third is Vanguard Quantitative Portfolios, which is "managed" by a computer valuation system with the objective of matching the basic investment characteristics of the S&P Index (industry composition, yield, etc.) but, within that constraint, selecting stocks that appear undervalued. Our goal is to outpace the Index while providing relative performance predictability. In our first year, 1987, we fell short by less than 1%; so far this year, we are about 1% ahead.

I personally believe that more is yet to come in the indexing arena. If mutual funds can be classified as "small company," "capital appreciation," "growth," "growth and income," and "equity income," for example, why can there not be, in effect, index funds emulating each group? We know that their general performance characteristics can be replicated; we also know that if their counterpart index funds are operated at extremely low cost, such index funds will have a strong and favoring wind at their back.

Another new Vanguard fund for which we have high hopes—but realistic expectations—is Vanguard Asset Allocation Fund, which we expect to introduce in November. It will provide a changing mix of stocks (based on the S&P Index), bond (based on the long-term U.S. Treasury bond), and reserves. We have retained Mellon Capital Management as adviser to the Fund. The principals of this firm are pioneers in the field of disciplined strategic asset allocation, and their actual (not, I hasten to add, "back-tested") results over the past decade have been impressive. (We believe that Mellon's highly systematic approach will differentiate the Fund from the "guru approach.") Of course, there are no guarantees of our future success. At worst, the Fund could decline as much as the stock market in downswings and rise much less in upswings. At best, it could do the reverse, matching the upswings and limiting volatility in the downswings. We expect neither extreme. Rather, we hope to garner long-term returns somewhat in excess of those of stocks in general, while moderating risk and minimizing both transaction costs and operating expenses. Only time, of course, will tell.

Beware of Some *Funds*

I hope you will forgive me for emphasizing Vanguard funds in these comments about indexing and asset allocation. But the fact is that few, if any, of our competitors offer mutual funds in these areas, as evidenced by the fact that they have not formed funds designed to implement those concepts for individual investors. Similarly, as I turn to my comments regarding funds to avoid, I am afraid that the reverse will be true—that Vanguard does *not* offer them. Obviously, if we thought these kinds of funds made sense, we would have long since developed them. I do not want to suggest that we are necessarily "right" and our principal competitors "wrong." But we clearly are following distinctly different strategies from most other firms.

Briefly, I would beware of:

1. "Government-plus" bond funds, that seem to generate large yields despite expenses that are often exorbitant. This neat trick is achieved by selling covered call options on the bonds, gaining premium income that enhances their interest income. But such a policy reduces upside participation in the bond markets while maintaining downside participation. In the long-run, in my judgment, that strategy is destined to ratchet down principal, and thus to fail.
2. Actively traded "sector funds," that experience unprecedented transaction activity by their shareholders, and hence huge and expensive portfolio turnover, as well as extremely high cost structures (initial sales charges and annual expense ratios in the 2.5% range). I fear that, if their objective is merely to equal the performance of the industry sectors in which they participate, they too are destined to fail. (Our Vanguard Specialized Portfolios have limited exchange privileges designed to discourage switching, are no-load, and operate at expense ratios of about 0.75%. Most investors, however, seem not to be interested in this combination, and we have achieved very limited success in the marketplace.)
3. "Strategic" funds, with characteristics that permit them to speculate in anything and everything available among today's derivative financial instruments: futures, options, longs, shorts, currencies, and so on. There may well be some managers that can do all of this to the benefit of fund shareholders, but their success will be spasmodic. Interestingly, some of these equity-oriented funds did quite well in 1987, but are doing quite badly in 1988. For better or worse, they seem to totally lack any "baseline" on which to predict relative performance.

Summing Up

Well, in my long talk this evening, I have tried to give you a retrospective on the year since the Great Crash, a syllabus on the need for both balance and diversification, an insight into the counterintuitive idea that unmanaged, index-oriented investing makes good sense, and a few investment concepts that, in my highly subjective opinion, you might be wary of. In all, I continue to believe that common stocks—seasoned with bonds and reserves in amounts appropriate to your own needs—represent a sound centerpiece to the financial programs of most individual investors seeking optimum long-term returns without excessive risk. I hope and expect that *Time* is simply wrong when it suggests that the individual investor is an endangered species. Despite the paroxysms of October 19, 1987, wise and patient investors will be unpersuaded by "Buy Stocks? No Way!" Rather, they will accept the advice that I have presented this evening, which might be rhythmically put as:

> *Own Stocks, the Course to Stay;*
> *Hold Bonds, for They Will Pay;*
> *Keep Cash Reserves for a Rainy Day.*

6

THE DEATH RATTLE OF INDEXING

Keynote Speech
The Superbowl of Indexing III
Palm Springs, California
December 7, 1998

O<small>N</small> FEBRUARY 16, 1993, in the weekly *Investment Perspectives* bulletin published by Morgan Stanley, the author of the Strategy section began his analysis with this headline: "I Hear the Death Rattle of Indexing."

It was based, reasonably enough I suppose, on the fact that after a decade of generally miserable performance relative to the market indexes by money managers during the 1980s, their "stock picking paid off well in 1991–1992," and would continue to pay off during the remainder of the decade. During that two-year period, most managers *were* finally beating "the market." The average mutual fund, for example, had risen at a 22% annual rate, compared to 18% for the S&P 500 Index. The strategist's forecast: "I think many active managers will outperform the popular indexes for most of the 1990s." I salute the courage it takes to issue such a forecast—especially under an unequivocal, contentious headline proclaiming a "death rattle"— for in this business, sticking one's neck out with a forecast of future performance is a very risky endeavor. (Full disclosure requires me to acknowledge that I learned that lesson the hard way!)

Nonetheless, the forecast could scarcely have been worse. For the Standard & Poor's 500 Stock Index, while continuing to lag for the remainder of 1993, quickly moved ahead of the average fund manager, and has not only remained there, but has—almost unbeliev-ably—steadily accelerated its margin of advantage year after year. And this index of large capitalization stocks is putting the icing on the cake this year, with an astonishing advantage of 15 percentage points over the average equity mutual fund manager: +22% vs. +7% for the aver-age fund through December 1. (See Figure 6.1.)

In all, with the bountiful decade of the 1990s nearing its conclusion only a year hence, the S&P 500 Index has produced an average annual return of +17.3%, compared to a gain of +13.9% for the average diver-sified equity mutual fund. That 3.4 percentage point margin, in a sense, conceals more than it reveals. Compounded, the S&P 500 has risen more than 300%, so far during the 1990s, while the average equity fund has gained just over 200%—nearly a 100 percentage point spread. That enormous spread in favor of the Index is so far superior to any decade on record that it brooks no real comparison.

But let's pause just a moment to evaluate what's behind all of these numbers. For the truth (or the closest approximation of truth that we can reach) is that most managers were neither as good as the "death rattle" bulletin reported in 1993, nor as bad as the decade-long results are proving to be. However, the ability of most active managers to out-perform fairly chosen passive benchmarks has been bleak—and so it remains for the future.

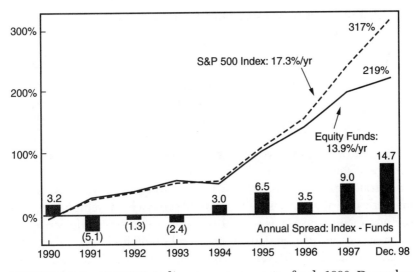

FIGURE 6.1   S&P 500 Index vs. average equity fund, 1990–December 1998.

To explain why this ominous outlook for active managers continues to exist, I want to explore five major myths that, it seems to me, have clouded the vision of investment managers and investors alike, and then to shine the sunlight of evidence on them. Here are the myths:

- One, that the S&P 500 Index is the most appropriate standard by which to measure the returns of active managers.
- Two, that the unusual and allegedly unrepeatable past superiority of passive management over active management implies that the active managers' shortfall will soon be recouped—particularly since we are said to now be entering a "stock picker's market," a related myth.
- Three, that a market index, by being fully invested, will fall more during market declines than funds run by flexible active managers, who can protect their accounts with defensive positions.
- Four, that indexing works only in efficient markets, and that investors in what are alleged to be less efficient markets—say small-cap and international markets—have a superior ability to beat those markets.
- And five, that the anticipated death rattle of indexing, having failed to manifest itself for seven years, will now rattle even louder—a reasonable enough forecast, as far as it goes, if one believes that investment styles inevitably revert to the mean and that the costs of investment advice don't matter.

Myth One: The S&P 500 as the Benchmark

The first myth—curiously perpetuated, despite its counterproductive nature, by the money management profession, and uncritically accepted by regulators and the media alike—is that the S&P 500 Index should be the universal measuring stick for manager performance. However, as anyone who has ever considered the issue for a moment knows, the S&P 500, invested 100% in stocks at all times, is a large-cap index. Currently representing three-fourths of the market value of all U.S. stocks, it would seem a huge sample—and in the aggregate sense it is—but it completely ignores one-fourth of the market, mid-cap and small-cap stocks which periodically prove to have somewhat different performance characteristics than their large-cap cousins. So far during the 1990s, large-cap stocks have carried the day, with an annualized return of +17.3%, compared with 13.3% for the rest of the market (Wilshire 4500 Equity Index).

But the mutual fund industry obviously includes not only large-cap funds, but mid- and small-cap funds as well. While the comparison of the *assets* of equity funds closely resembles the comparison of the total market (about 75% large-cap, 17% mid-cap, 8% small-cap), the *number* of equity funds departs markedly from that pattern: more than 50% of funds are characterized as large-cap, about 25% each as mid- or small-cap. In an area where a perfect benchmark standard seems far too ambitious a goal, the best benchmark for this industry, in my judgment, is the all-market Wilshire 5000 Equity Index. (For the record, despite its fully invested profile, it carries significantly *less* risk than the average equity fund.) Interestingly, over its entire history, dating to 1970, it has earned *precisely* the same annualized return as the S&P 500—13.7% annualized. But within that period there have been many swings to and fro in the relationship between the returns of 500 large stocks in the S&P Index and the thousands of smaller stocks that are not included, and that is surely what we have seen during the 1990s.

Using the Wilshire 5000 as the benchmark, neither the gratifying trends (to active managers) that Morgan Stanley observed in 1991–1992, nor the frightening trends that occurred thereafter, were quite what they seemed to be. In fact, nearly 60% of active managers *underperformed* the Wilshire 5000 during 1991 and 1992, hardly the death rattle of indexing. And for the decade to date, while only 11% of active managers have outpaced the S&P 500, some 20% of managers have succeeded in outpacing the Wilshire 5000. It seems to me that the sooner we use this more realistic standard as the most appropriate—though not a perfect—passive benchmark for active managers, the better it will be for both the industry and the investors we serve. (See Figure 6.2.)

Myth Two: The Past Is Not Prologue

That brings me to the second myth, that the past superiority of passive management is some sort of freak accident, not to be repeated in the future. But I bring bad news to active managers. In this case, the past is all too likely to be prologue. For the past record of equity mutual funds, fairly measured, is largely the direct result of a small series of

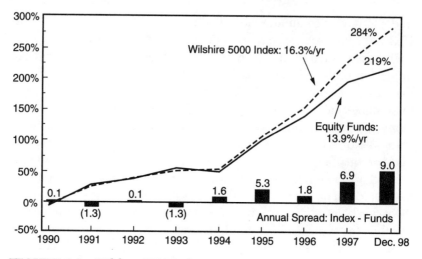

FIGURE 6.2 Wilshire 5000 Index vs. average equity fund, 1990–December 1998.

causative factors that we not only know, but that we know will continue to exist in the foreseeable future.

Let's analyze investment returns during the decade of the 1990s so far. We know that the S&P 500 has provided an annualized return of +17.3%, compared with just 13.9% for the average diversified mutual fund. But this 3.4% spread can be clearly explained. First, since the return on the Wilshire 5000 was 16.3% during the same period, we can count 1.0 percentage points as a "large cap effect," bringing the gap to 2.4%. We know that the expense ratio of the average fund averaged about 1.3% during the period. (It is now 1.5% and rising.) Result: Gap falls to 1.1%. Funds turn their portfolios over at an average rate of 85% per year. (For an industry that is constantly urging its shareholders to invest for the long term, an astonishing result!) So, I'll assume that transaction costs consume at least another 0.7% of annual return, reducing the gap to 0.4%. (See Table 6.1.)

Finally, we know that fund managers held an average of about 8% of their portfolios in cash reserves, an expensive penalty in a great bull market. Taking into account the difference between returns on short-term reserves and fund equities over this period, that cost looks like about 0.7%. Now the gap is a *positive* 0.3% per year. Thus, measured in terms of the ability of managers to pick stocks, they actually seem to

86

TABLE 6.1   Explaining the Mutual Fund Shortfall to "the Market"
Average Nine-Year Return

	GAP	REMAINDER
Total shortfall	3.4%	−3.4%
Large-cap effect	1.0%	−2.4%
Fund expense ratio	1.3	−1.1
Fund turnover cost (est.)	0.7	−0.4
Cash reserve drag	0.7	+0.3
Fund risk premium (est.)	0.6	−0.3

have done a bit *better* than we might have expected. However, given their higher risk profiles, funds should have earned a premium of perhaps 0.6%, meaning their performance was −0.3% less than expected. In fact, however, we're probably talking about a wash: Just as theory would suggest, before their costs are taken into account, fund managers as a group match the market.

But the point is that when we look ahead, future fund returns will carry *at least the same burdens.* The most obvious is fund costs. Expense ratios, perversely, are rising, and will almost certainly be heavier in the coming decade. Transaction costs may decline because of likely enhanced automation in market-making systems and perhaps even lower turnover. But any reduction is not likely to offset the rise in expense ratios. Finally, cash would be less of a relative drag in more subdued markets, although lower equity returns may be too much (or too little!) to count on. In all, I believe that the combination of expense ratios, transaction costs, and cash drag will be at least as high as in the past decade, pulling down the gross returns of actively managed equity mutual funds by something in the range of 2.5% per year. Result: as a group, equity funds supervised by active managers must, and will, again fall short of the passive benchmark represented by the Wilshire 5000 equity index. The past *will* be prologue.

I should note the countervailing thesis that we are now entering what is called a "stock picker's market," in which astute managers will find it easier to pick superior stocks. The logic of this proposition totally escapes me. Aren't we *always* in a "stock picker's market." Didn't smart managers pick Microsoft and Intel and American International Group and Coca-Cola a decade ago? (And wasn't stock picker Warren Buffett rewarded for his skill?) But even if it somehow gets easier to pick stocks (I can't imagine why!), won't 100 *good* stock pickers inevitably make their picks at the expense of 100 *bad* stock pickers? And won't the total stock market provide the same returns as the returns (before costs) of the good stock pickers and the average stock pickers and the bad stock pickers combined? If we apply even the most superficial sort of analysis to the concept of a "stock picker's market" is it evident that it too is just another myth.

Myth Three: Market Timing Will Carry the Day

There is a third myth that, mercifully, may have finally been erased by the 1998 bear market. This is the myth that actively managed funds will outpace passively managed indexes during periods of market decline. The myth was that, since indexes are at all times 100% invested in stocks, the cash reserves held by active managers would lessen the shock of the decline in their portfolios. What is more, so the myth went, smart managers, recognizing that a market decline was in prospect, would raise even more cash in advance, and gain considerable downside protection during the ensuing market storm.

First, the fact is that, at the traditional levels of equity fund cash reserves, cash is the tail and not the dog. Simple logic compels the conclusion that a 5 to 10% tail of cash cannot possibly wag the dog represented by a 90 to 95% equity position. And mutual funds hold equity portfolios that have proven to be somewhat riskier than the portfolios of the major indexes, which are dominated by higher-quality, larger-cap stocks. As a result, the indexes have traditionally provided not less, but more, downside protection than actively managed funds during market declines.

Taking into account both the cash position and the more volatile portfolio of the average mutual fund, the record confirms that index funds based on the Standard and Poor's 500 Index and the Wilshire 5000 Index are somewhat *less* risky. Morningstar Mutual Funds calculates a risk factor for each fund based on returns in the months in which it underperformed the risk-free U.S. Treasury bill. The data show that, over the past decade, the S&P 500 Index was some 15% less risky than the average mutual fund and the Wilshire 5000 Index was 18% less risky. (See Table 6.2.)

Looked at in a different way, over the past decade the standard deviation of return of the S&P 500 has been 3% lower than that of the

TABLE 6.2   Risk Comparisons

	RELATIVE RISK°	DECLINE 7/16/1998 8/31/1998	TOTAL RETURN 12/31/1997 11/30/1998
Average equity fund	1.00	−22.2%	6.9%
Wilshire 5000 Index Fund	0.81	−20.7	15.9
S&P 500 Index Fund	0.85	−19.0	21.6

°Morningstar risk, 6/98.

average equity fund and the Wilshire 5000 has been 5% lower. Given this record, it should not have been surprising that in last summer's bear market, funds again fell more than the averages—8% more than the Wilshire 5000 (off 20.7%) and 15% more than the S&P 500 (off 19%). The average equity fund fell by 22.2%.

What happened to the vaunted ability of fund managers to raise cash before market drops (and to reinvest that cash after the drop is over)? It simply wasn't there. In mid-1998, just before the steepest stock market decline since 1987, reserves represented less than 5% of equity fund assets, close to the all-time lows, compared to 13% at the market low in 1990, close to the all-time highs. This pattern is all too typical. Funds have consistently tended to hold large amounts of cash at market lows and small amounts at market highs. For example, cash equaled only 4% of assets immediately *before* the 1973–74 market crash, but increased to about 12% at the ensuing low; at the beginning of the bull market in 1982, equity funds held cash equal to 12% of assets. Managers in short, have been bearish when they should have been bullish, and bullish when they should have been bearish. It is not a formula for success. (See Figure 6.3.)

Taken together, the recent market decline, the Morningstar risk data, and the relative standard deviations make it clear that, despite the fact that managed equity mutual funds do indeed maintain modest reserve positions—and have the ability to raise even more reserves in anticipation of market dips—their risk exposure has been systematically, and often significantly, greater than that of the fully invested broad market indexes. Yes, index funds decline with the market. So do managed funds . . . only more so. I hope that we have finally heard the end of the silly myth that cash reserves and market timing give active managers an edge in down markets.

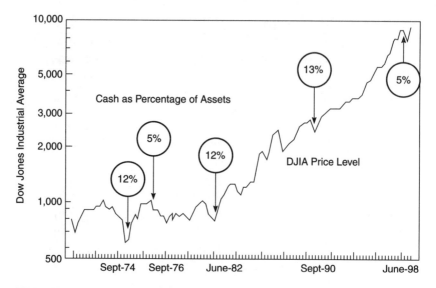

FIGURE 6.3   Unsuccessful "market timing" by fund managers.

Myth Four: That Indexing Works Only in Efficient Markets

As the reality that active managers must fall short of appropriate market indexes by the amount of their costs becomes commonly accepted, the investment community must create another myth to justify its existence. Sadly, much of the academic community seems willing, if not eager, to foster this myth. In any event, myth four has emerged: "Indexing works only in efficient markets," such as those represented by the actively traded, very liquid large-capitalization stocks that overpoweringly dominate the S&P 500 Index and comprise 76% of the U.S. stock market—and not to other presumably less efficient markets.

Plausible as that argument may sound, it is specious. For the success of indexing is based, not on some notion of market efficiency, but simply on the inability of all investors in any discrete market or market segment to outpace the universe of investments in which they operate. Efficiency relates to a market price structure that generally values all securities properly at any one time, which means that good managers and bad alike will have difficulty in differentiating themselves *either* way. In inefficient markets, to be sure, good managers may have greater opportunities to outpace their universe, but the excess returns earned by good managers must inevitably be offset by inferior returns of the exact same dimension by bad managers. (Here again, there are good stock pickers and bad stock pickers.)

However, costs of mutual funds operating in so-called inefficient markets are higher than funds operating in efficient markets. For example, expense ratios and transaction costs of small-cap funds are systematically higher than those of large-cap funds. It also turns out, that, once account is taken for the relatively higher risks that they assume, mid-cap and small-cap mutual funds have actually realized slightly *larger* shortfalls to the indexes in their market sectors than their large-cap cousins have realized. A study of mine that was recently published in the *Journal of Portfolio Management* showed that the advantage in risk-adjusted return—which was 3.5% per year for large-cap funds—was 4.2% for mid-cap funds and 4.4% for small cap funds. Note particularly the almost-rhythmic widening difference in risk as cap-size falls—large-cap funds are 1.6 percentage points riskier than the large-cap index, 2.6 percentage points for mid-cap relative to the mid-cap index, and 3.6 percentage points for small-cap funds versus the small-cap index. (See Table 6.3.)

Costs of international funds are higher still, not only because of higher expense ratios but because of much higher custodial expenses, taxes, commissions, and market impact costs. As a result, not only do the exact same principles of indexing apply in international markets, but an even larger margin of superiority for the passively managed international index should probably be expected. The past results here are erratic, but over the past 20 years, the positive margin for the international index fund over the average international fund was 1.1% annually, while Vanguard's European and Emerging Markets Index Funds have outpaced their actively managed peers by 4.5% and 2.1% annually since their inceptions. Indexing, it turns out, works—as it must—with high effectiveness in all the far-flung corners of the world of equity investing. (See Table 6.4.)

Inefficient markets, to be sure, may provide managers with more opportunities to do well. But the added returns of those who do well must inevitably be offset by the return shortfalls of those who do not. Given the higher costs of owning funds that operate in less efficient markets, it proves to be a bad trade-off. For example, assume that: (a) the top 10% of managers can outpace an efficient market by 3% per year over time, but in an inefficient market by 5%; (b) that the bottom

TABLE 6.3   Fund Categories vs. Comparable Indexes

	RETURN	RISK	RISK-ADJUSTED RETURN
Large Cap			
Funds	13.0%	10.6%	1.04
Index	15.0	9.0	1.28
Index adjusted°	16.5%	10.6%	1.28
Index advantage	3.5%		
Mid Cap			
Funds	13.8%	12.3%	0.95
Index	15.1	9.7	1.22
Index adjusted	18.0%	12.3%	1.22
Index advantage	4.2%		
Small Cap			
Funds	15.1%	14.7%	0.92
Index	15.4	11.1	1.12
Index adjusted	19.5%	14.7%	1.12
Index advantage	4.4%		

°Index return adjusted to equalize index risk and fund risk. Data: 12/31/1991 to 12/31/1996.

10% of managers do the reverse; and (c) that total fund costs are 1½% per year in efficient markets and 2½% in inefficient markets. Result: (1) the top managers provide excess returns of 1½% in efficient markets and 2½% in inefficient markets; but (2) the bottom 10% provide returns of −4½% and −7½% respectively. (See Table 6.5.)

TABLE 6.4   International Indexes vs. International Funds

	1977–87	1987–97	1977–97
MSCI EAFE Index	22.8%	6.6%	14.4%
International funds	17.8	9.0	13.3
	7/90–11/98		
European Index Fund	13.3%		
European managed funds	8.8		
	6/94–11/98		
Emerging Markets Index Fund	−5.9%		
Emerging markets managed funds	−8.0		

TABLE 6.5 Manager Returns Relative to Market Averages (Hypothetical)

	Before Costs		After Costs°	
	TOP 10%	**BOTTOM 10%**	**TOP 10%**	**BOTTOM 10%**
Efficient markets	+3%	−3%	+1.5%	−4.5%
Inefficient markets	+5	−5	+2.5	−7.5

°Assumed fund costs: 1.5 percent in efficient markets, 2.5 percent in inefficient markets.

Clearly, the symmetrical pattern of pre-cost returns quickly becomes asymmetrical after the deduction of costs. Put another way, the onus of costs erodes the superiority of the top equity managers, even as it magnifies the deficiency of the bottom-tier managers. But it does so by larger amounts—in both cases—in inefficient stock markets. Thus, ironically enough, equity indexing may well prove to work more productively in inefficient markets than in efficient markets. "Another myth exploded," as it were.

Myth Five: That Reversion to the Mean Will Finally Triumph

The final myth, in a sense, seems the most reasonable of all. While it is based on a false premise, it deserves to be rebutted because we in the fund industry, and even I personally, have helped to create it. This myth begins with the tacit acceptance that the appropriate benchmark for measuring manager performance is the Standard & Poor's 500 Index. While the analysis I have set forth today has tried to avoid reliance on that Index—and the spectacular returns it has generated, in part by reason of its focus on large-cap stocks—I want to take it on here simply because of its prevalence.

The myth, of course, is that when the seemingly inevitable reversion to the mean of the financial markets takes place and those favorites of yesterday and today—giant-cap stocks such as Microsoft, Coca-Cola, General Electric, and so on—fall back, relinquishing their leadership to small- and mid-cap stocks that have been the serious laggards of the great long bull market, index funds will fall into severe disfavor. I disagree with that thesis.

First, while Vanguard Index 500, with its near-2 million shareholders, soon to become the world's largest mutual fund of *any* type, has become a household name,[1] the fact remains that only half of all managed equity mutual *funds* are large-cap funds and three-fourths of managed fund *assets* are represented by large-cap stocks. Thus a simple comparison of the average fund with our 500 Index Fund is flawed. Yet no matter what I say, the S&P 500 benchmark is going to remain as the prime comparison for some time. And I would be astonished if we were not facing a period in which reversion to the mean—I call it "Sir Isaac Newton's Revenge on Wall Street"—will come into play for that Index. After 15 glorious years in which the *worst* ranking of the S&P 500 Index was just below the 40th percentile of mutual fund managers, and during which it outpaced 96% of all surviving fund managers, it would seem almost obvious that some significant reversion in the Index's relative return lies in prospect.

Nonetheless, I have no ability to predict the *extent* to which this reversion might unfold. So let me turn to index pioneer William L. Fouse. He has both the preeminent credentials in the field and, of all the practitioners, probably commands the most respected intellect. He deserves every bit of that respect. In the July/August edition of *The Financial Analysts Journal,* he considered this issue and concluded: "I expect large stocks to soon cease outperforming the average stock. . . . For the next five years or so, actively-managed portfolios may outperform the S&P 500 by 50 percent or more."

Far be it for someone with my comparatively modest credentials to challenge the experienced wisdom of Mr. Fouse. But permit me to examine what it would take to make his prediction come true in the mutual fund industry, given its configuration and costs. First, assuming a 10% future rate of return for the S&P Index, the *average* fund would have to generate a net return of 15%. As I've noted, 52% of

---

1. In fact, as far back as 1987, I considered *changing* our Index 500 Fund to a Wilshire "Index 5000" fund. I finally decided, however, simply to add an "Index-Extended Market" fund to invest in the remainder of the market outside the 500 S&P stocks, then add a new "Total Stock Market Index Fund" in 1992. I believe that the Total Stock Market Index Fund should be the investment of choice for most investors, covering as it does the entire U.S. stock market, and representing the full practical fruition of the essential theory that the net returns earned by all active investors must, by reason of costs, fall short of the returns of all stocks as a group.

funds are large-cap in focus, 26% mid-cap, and 22% small-cap. If the gross returns of large-cap funds matched the S&P Index return of 10%, the other funds would have to achieve gross returns *averaging* more than 20%. That would be not 50%, but 100%, above the S&P return. (See Table 6.6.)

However, given the possible 3% drag of fund expenses, transaction costs, and cash, the average fund would earn a net return not of 15%, but of 12% for its shareholders, just 2 percentage points ahead of the 500 Index. What is interesting about *that* figure is that it suggests that the Index would nonetheless outperform some 35% of all managers. If this is failure, heaven help the managers when it is followed at some point—as it inevitably will be—by the return of success to the 500 Index. In short, even using the *wrong* benchmark, rumors of the death of S&P 500 Index funds are greatly exaggerated.

What is more—and this is really the central point of these remarks—the S&P 500 is a faulty measuring stick, excluding some 25% of the market's total value. (Better to admit it in these halcyon days than to seem to change the rules after the fact.) If the non-S&P segment of the market's capitalization were to rise by 20%—100% more than the S&P rate—the annual gain in the all-market Wilshire 5000 Index would be but 12.5%. However, when we reduce that figure for our 3% assumed mutual fund lag, the net result could be a gain of 9.5% for the average mutual fund—not only 25% less than the 12.5% return of the 5000 Index itself, but even 5% less than the 10% return of the presumably faltering S&P 500 Index. Further, if the non-S&P segment provided a return 50% higher than the S&P, the fund return could be as little as 8.2%, compared to 11.2% for the Wilshire 5000 and 10% for the S&P 500. Surely no matter which of these relationships hold, they will be bad news for the critics of indexing. (See Table 6.7.)

TABLE 6.6 Implications of Fouse Prediction of a 50% Outperformance by Actively Managed Portfolios

	RETURN	**RELATIVE TO INDEX**
S&P 500 Index	10%	0%
Average fund before costs	15	+50
Large-cap funds	10	0
Small-cap funds	20	+100
Average fund after costs°	12%	+20%

°Expense Ratio + Transaction Costs + Cash Drag = 3%.

TABLE 6.7 Wilshire 5000 vs. S&P 500 (Variation on Fouse Prediction)

	RETURN	RELATIVE TO 500 INDEX
S&P 500 Index	10%	0%
Wilshire 4500 Index	20	+100
75% S&P 500 and		
25% Wilshire 4500	12.5	+25
Mutual funds (after 3% cost)	9.5%	−5%
Funds relative to Wilshire 5000	−3%	−25%

Conclusion

In *Macbeth,* the protagonist says: "The Bell invites me. Hear it not, Duncan, for it is a Knell. That summons thee to heaven or to hell." Similarly, what Morgan Stanley heard in 1993 proved to be a death knell all right, but, as it turns out, it was a knell that was summoning active managers. And since the myths I have described will remain just that—myths—there's every reason to expect that the death knell will again be summoning active managers during the new decade that will begin on January 1, 2000. Now, in a curious turn of fate, the very investment banking firm which predicted the death rattle in the 1990s now seems to agree. For a Morgan Stanley report recently took, perhaps inadvertently, a diametrically opposed position, predicting that in the years ahead the S&P Index will *again* outperform most fund managers.

The basis for its conclusion was reported in its Equity Research Briefing Note of August 7, 1998. After an examination of mutual fund records during the five years 1988–1992, and comparing them with the five years 1993–1997 in terms of return, risk, and risk-adjusted return, the Briefing Note found that, in terms of *return,* 28% of the top quartile funds and 51% of the top half funds repeat their ranking. Par for the course would be 25% and 50%. Randomness writ large! But in terms of risk, the repeat ratios are 63% for the top quartile and 93% for the top half. Impressive! As a result, in terms of *risk-adjusted* return, the predictability figures were 39% and 64%, respectively—both far above the random expectation of 25% and 50%. (See Figure 6.4.) Conclusion: **"Risk-adjusted return has predictive qualities that are lacking in total return."** (Boldface in original.)

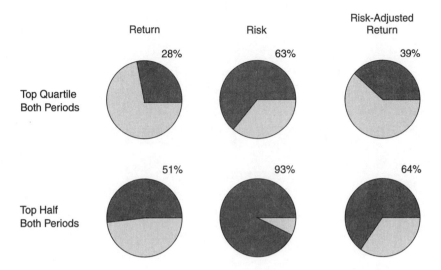

FIGURE 6.4   Persistence in fund return and risk performance in consecutive five-year periods.
SOURCE: Morgan Stanley Dean Witter.

The Note then added: "What about a benchmark? . . . The S&P 500 ranked in the top quartile of risk-adjusted performance throughout the first and second periods. . . . Mutual funds that ranked *below* the first quartile in risk-adjusted return in either period underperformed this benchmark." It therefore follows that since risk-adjusted return is a *highly accurate* predictor of future performance, and that the Index has demonstrated a risk profile that is close to (but in fact below) that of the average fund, the firm's unmistakable conclusion must be this: *The continued top-quartile performance of the S&P 500 Index is highly predictable.*

To be sure, the last sentence in the Briefing Note says: "WARN-ING: This study is backward looking." An appropriate warning indeed, but still a remarkable epiphany for a firm that, only five years earlier, had forecast the death rattle of indexing. But in fact that sound proved to be an early death knell, not for indexing, but for the performance of most active managers—a knell that we now know was not summoning them to heaven. Therefore, according to Macbeth's warning, the knell must have been summoning them to a colder, darker, far less felicitous—but still eternal—dwelling place.

7

25 YEARS OF INDEXING: WHEN ACTIVE MANAGERS WIN, WHO LOSES?

Keynote Speech
The Superbowl of Indexing IV
Phoenix, Arizona
December 5, 1999

JUST A YEAR HENCE, the world's first index mutual fund, proudly named "First Index Investment Trust" at its incorporation on December 31, 1975, will celebrate the 25th anniversary of its birth. What is now Vanguard 500 Index Fund began with assets of just $11 million; on November 16, 1999, assets crossed the $100 billion milestone for the first time, a remarkable compound growth rate of nearly 50% per year. At the outset, the Fund was both excoriated and denigrated—"un-American" was the least of it—so, while I'm rarely one who thinks asset totals are very important as such, perhaps that date may serve as a useful landmark of the moment that heresy finally turned to dogma.

Index funds, of course, have spread far beyond Vanguard, and now constitute an important subset of the financial services industry. Assets of equity index funds total $300 billion, nearly 10% of the equity mutual fund total. There are 334 index mutual funds, 139 modeled on the Standard & Poor's 500 Index, and 195 in other categories, some of which make considerable sense, and some of which do not. Among those that *do not* are 69 funds which carry sales loads; the reason for their existence totally escapes me. Among those that *do* are international index funds and fixed-income index funds. Because of the extra costs of *managed* international funds—higher fees and expense ratios, higher portfolio turnover, and higher transaction costs—the advantages of low-cost index funds are proportionately even larger than in the domestic arena. Although so far only a single mutual fund firm has made a serious commitment to bond indexing, that arena too makes consummate good sense. Given the smaller margins of potential performance superiority that are possible among fixed-income funds, together with the truly outrageous fees charged by most bond funds, this area holds great potential.

But the new index industry includes far more than scores of index managers (some managing their funds at low costs—at least for a while—and some at costs that are confiscatory). It also includes large numbers of creative marketers engaged in proving that the number of indexes that can be used to create new "products" is virtually limitless; and numerous purveyors of methods to beat the indexes, or reshape them, by one obscure statistical technique or another—from computer-assisted mathematical models to portfolios composed solely of mortgage-backed bonds and S&P 500 futures—and hundreds of providers of legal, financial, technological, and communications services to all of those countless souls who are engaged in the creation, management, and marketing of index funds. Indexing has also spawned a new magazine—a Dow Jones publication called *Indexes,* of all things—and, to state the obvious, the annual Superbowl of Indexing itself, now meeting for the fourth year, with 97 speakers and 300 participants.

Our initial 500 Fund, a quiet first-born, was an only child for nearly a full decade. It was not until 1984 that the second index fund was born, and it proved to be a pale imitation of its older sibling. Its high costs, predictably, have utterly destroyed the fund's ability to do what its sponsors implicitly promised: To match the return of the S&P 500 Index. While this fund, which is managed by one of the largest and most respected banks in America, has persevered to this day, its shareholders have been ill-served. A $10,000 investment when the fund began, hit at the outset by a 4½% sales charge, and then by operating costs of some 1% each year, would have been worth just $116,000 as 1999 drew to a close. The same investment at the same time in the first index fund, the fund that the copier was emulating, was worth $143,000—a gap of a mere $27,000. (When asked by the press how the fund could justify its lofty costs, a spokesman answered: "It's our cash cow." And of course it *is.*)

A Better Standard?

With the passage of time, I have become convinced that the most intelligent index fund strategy is modeled not on the Standard & Poor's 500 Stock Index, but on the Wilshire 5000 Equity Index. (It recently became the "Wilshire 5000 Total Stock Market Index," from my perspective a change long overdue.) Later on, I'll discuss the merits of the total stock market index as a performance standard against which active managers of funds should be measured, but for now let me say that owning an index fund based on the total U.S. stock market virtually *guarantees* that investors will capture 98% to 99% of the stock market's annual return. By way of contrast, active investors as a group are virtually guaranteed to capture but 75% to 85%, simply because of the costs of investing. The search to identify, *in advance*, the few winning funds is like looking for a needle in the total market haystack. *Why bother looking for the needle when you can own the haystack?*

Owning an all-market index fund, simply put, means *buying businesses*—in essence, every publicly held business in America—and holding them for Warren Buffett's favorite holding period: Forever. Owning the average actively managed mutual fund, on the other hand, means *trading pieces of paper*, holding each sheet for this industry's favorite holding period: 406 days. (Fund turnover now averages 90% per year.) Believe me, there is a difference between these two strategies—in the complex and speculative task of mutual fund selection, in the certainty of future relative returns, in management fees and expense ratios, in portfolio turnover costs, and in sales loads too. And, lest we forget, in tax efficiency. (The grotesque tax *inefficiency* of most active mutual funds, while assuring irreparable harm to *taxable* fund investors, has provided no demonstrable advantage to *tax-deferred* fund investors in IRAs and retirement plans.)

Too Many Index Funds?

The selection of the large-cap S&P 500 as the appropriate benchmark at the outset of indexing has earned a lot of money for index fund shareholders. But I don't believe that it should remain the standard in the years ahead. (Though I wouldn't dream of encouraging satisfied investors in the S&P 500 Index funds to make the switch. After all, those 500 stocks represent 75% of the weight of the all-market index.) The consummate simplicity and comprehensiveness of the all-market index fund has me questioning, more than ever before, the wisdom of other, narrower index strategies.[1] Here, to be forthright, I am questioning no judgment other than my own, for we started the first small-cap index fund just over a decade ago, and the first growth index and value index funds in 1992—just as soon as the corresponding Standard & Poor's/BARRA growth and value indexes made their debut. The problem with small-cap index funds—and, lest I paint with too narrow a brush, small-cap funds in general—is that by maintaining what is called "style purity" (i.e., never having the temerity to jump out of the small-cap style box), such a fund *must* sell its winners and begin all over again. Such a move not only defeats the long-term nature of investment strategy, but has powerfully negative tax consequences. We all ought to be reconsidering this strategy to make it work more effectively.

The growth and value index strategies, too, ought to be reexamined. By definition, each accounts for 50% of the capitalization of the Standard & Poor's 500 Stock Index. But with the soaring market value of the technology stocks, the number of growth stocks comprising that 50% has dropped from 232 companies a decade ago to 128 today. The 1060% appreciation in Microsoft stock alone since 1994—increasing its weight from less than 1% of the Index to nearly 4%—has taken as many as 25 former *growth* stocks and transmogrified them into 25 new *value* stocks, making the value index "growthier" than ever before. Furthermore, as companies are elbowed out of the Growth Index into the Value Index, there are potential adverse tax consequences to taxable investors in a growth index fund. Again, as "style" index strategies are tested by time, we owe them some reconsideration. In any event, it is high time for better disclosure of the implications and consequences of "style purity," in index funds and active funds alike. Today is no time for dogmatism.

The Newest Fad

But if these modest—and well-intentioned—departures from the majesty of broad stock market indexing should be carefully reconsidered, what can one say about the latest fad in indexing? Exchange-traded funds, already acronymically known as ETFs (which, I confess, I still confuse with the completely unrelated "electronic funds trans-

---

1. Index funds following narrower styles, however, remain an intelligent medium for investors who own particular actively managed funds and wish to gain total market exposure.

fer") are the hot item of the day. They've taken indexing far beyond what any of us present at the creation a quarter-century ago could have imagined. Fair enough. But what is *wrong* is that this new breed of index funds, by accident or design, seems to be frustrating the original purpose of the index strategy—efficient *long-term investing* in a diversified portfolio of businesses—giving us instead a vehicle for *short-term speculation* in the stock market.

This is not to knock, in any way, the Spiders (SPDRs, modeled on the Standard & Poor's 500 Index). I've acknowledged for years my respect for the creativity that went into their design, their low operating costs and fine tracking of the index, and their tax efficiency, in which the investor, in substance, is solely responsible for his own taxes. I happen to believe, however, that the services, conveniences, and low costs offered by the best Standard & Poor 500 index funds, along with the absence of brokerage commissions, make them the superior vehicle for long-term investors. Of course, the tax issue (for taxable investors) remains, and it may well be that some long-term investors may prefer to own conventional index funds through a newly created Spider-like series by today's conventional index funds. Such an eventuality should neither surprise nor concern investors. In any event, I expect no interruption in the robust growth of index mutual funds, which now account for nearly 40% of equity fund cash flow.

The real-time pricing of Spiders, on the other hand, makes them by far the superior vehicle for short-term speculators, doubtless well worth the brokerage commissions involved. The marketplace supports that judgment: While our index fund investors turn their holdings over at a rate of just 10%, the annual turnover of Spider shares is running at an annual rate of 1800% in 1999, about 22 *times* the 80% turnover rate of the average share of stock on the New York Stock Exchange. In the stock market today, the average share is held for about 456 days (itself a period that is hardly a monument to long-term investing), while the average Spider is held for just 20 days. *Not even three weeks!* And relative to the burgeoning ETF universe, Spiders investors are models of decorum. Their counterparts who trade the even-gamier Nasdaq 100, are turning over their "QQQ's" at an annual rate of 7800%, an average holding period of just over four *days!* Long-term investors might consider extreme caution before investing in a program—however inexpensive, whatever its tracking success, and irrespective of its potential long-term tax efficiency—in which most investors are, well, four-day wonders.

Of course, ETFs have been carried far beyond Spiders and QQQ's. There are now 17 WEBS (with much higher expense ratios—in the plus 1% range) based on global indexes, soon to be joined by 51 new ETFs called iShares (cost not yet disclosed), presenting an even wider selection of domestic and foreign markets. But these new ETFs have been designed with a purpose diametrically opposed to the purpose of that pioneering index mutual fund of 1975. Our purpose was to create an investment that would serve long-term shareholders, to be bought and held, to be the hedgehog who knows one great thing, rather than the fox who knows so many things, bringing simplicity rather than complexity to the world of investing. The purpose of the ETFs seems to be to create a product that will sell, a product that, if all goes well, will serve speculators efficiently, but will serve its sponsors whether things go well or not. Indeed, an executive of a major ETF sponsor recently said, "Brands have always existed in consumer products. We see investors buying (our) brand just like they buy a brand of toothpaste." That's one point of view. But it's not mine. For believe me: *There is a critical difference between designing a product that sells, and creating an investment that serves.*

Active Managers and Indexes

Last January, when I offered up "When Active Managers Win, Who Loses" as the title I would use for these remarks, I assumed that this would be a year in which the average mutual fund, after five consecutive years in the doghouse, would finally beat the S&P 500 Index. During the 1994–1998 period, the average fund lagged the 500 by an astonishing 75 percentage points (+119% vs. +194%). What is more, as a dyed-in-the-wool believer in reversion to the mean in the financial markets, I suspected that the time for the smaller stocks to rise again was at hand. I was well aware that while the 500 Index is invested 100% in large-cap stocks, about one-half of the industry's general purpose stock funds are large-cap funds (and with a slightly smaller average cap size at that) and one-half are mid- and small-cap funds. This distribution almost assures superiority for the average fund when non-S&P stocks outperform.

As the year draws to a close, my guess is looking pretty good. The non-S&P stocks are up 22.0%, while the S&P 500 is up 16.0%. And the average fund has produced a gain of +18.0%—two percentage points better. The 500 triumphed in the first quarter, but the average fund led the second quarter lap, as *Indexes* magazine headlined, "Man Bites Dog! Pros Beat Indexes." And the average fund led again in the third quarter lap, which *The New York Times* (somewhat more temperately) headlined, "A Small Victory for Stock Picking." If the year ends with the S&P Index still lagging, we can expect to see more dramatic headlines as year 2000 begins.

So, at least for the moment the tables have turned ever so slightly toward the active fund managers, and we indexers must be ready with a rational response. So let's begin with the basics: *The fact is that indexers always win.* That is, in any financial market—and any segment of any financial market—indexers owning all of the securities in that market at low cost *must* provide better returns than the other investors in the market in the aggregate, simply because the costs incurred by active investors—commissions, fees, taxes—are substantially higher. Costs matter. Costs *always* matter. And that is why active managers as a group can *never* win.

So the answer to the question: "When active managers win, who loses?" is: *other* active managers. Perhaps hyperactive managers, or inactive managers, or managers not included in the database. Nonetheless, simple data being simple data, there will be years when it *looks* as if active managers win. Mutual fund history, indeed, shows that the average fund beat the S&P 500 in 1991–1993, in 1977–1982 (right after our index fund began), and in 1965–1968 (the Go-Go era). But there is much more to the data than meets the eye—especially over the long run. Let me give you just a few examples:

- First, the S&P 500 is the wrong index to compare with the diverse and ever-changing mutual fund industry. Why would one compare a 100% large-cap index with the average fund in an industry in which large-cap funds as a percentage of all funds have shrunk from 75% 15 years ago to 44% today?
- Second, "selection bias" distorts fund industry returns. Many mutual funds have records that are more than suspect; invalid records that count in the industry data side by side with the valid records. The worst offenders are incubator funds, which, *if* they fly, fly high, and if they flop, flop right out of the database. But those that fly remain in the record book, which includes many mainstream funds of today that began with tiny assets, providing remarkable returns until size and reversion to the mean took

over, and then fading to average and below. But their long-term records are accepted uncritically. *Caveat Emptor!*

- Third, "survivor bias" plays a *major* role in industry records. The meek, in short, do not inherit the mutual fund earth, and the dimension of fund failure is astonishing. For example, of 355 equity funds that existed 30 years ago, 186—more than one-half!—have vanished into thin air. Even in the mutual fund boom of the past 15 years, 70 of the original 454 funds have vanished. Analysts from academe, such as Princeton's Burton Malkiel and University of Southern California's Mark Carhart, have estimated survivor bias ranging from as little as 1.4 percentage points annually in 1982–1991 to as much as 4.2 points in 1976–1991. It is now clear that the evanescence of so many funds—surely the weakest performers—sharply overstate long-term industry-wide averages.

- Fourth, front-end sales charges are almost universally ignored in the publicized performance data. As a result, the returns of the average mutual fund *investor* inevitably lag the reported returns of the average *mutual fund.* The resulting diminution of returns, amortized over the typical holding period, may cut the reported returns by as much as a full percentage point.

- Fifth, amazingly, fund comparisons—again, almost universally— ignore taxes. Managed mutual funds are shockingly tax *inefficient,* while market index funds are highly tax *efficient,* largely subject only to taxes on dividend income. In the ebullient market of the past 15 years, the *relative* reduction in active fund returns as a result of taxes has been about 1.8 percentage points per year.

So what's to be done in assessing comparisons of industry returns with the stock market? There are lots of complex statistics we can develop (I've surely developed my share!), but there are also some simple and obvious steps we can take. Here are three:

- When comparing the results of the average mutual fund with the market, abandon the use of the S&P 500 Index and use the Wilshire 5000 Total Stock Market Index. By bringing small- and mid-cap stocks into the equation we get a reasonably fair long-term comparison. In fact, the correlation (R^2) of the returns of the average value and growth equity fund with this index has been .998 over the past 15 years. During that period, the annual return of the average surviving fund has been 14.4%, compared to 16.9% for the 5000 Index. Adjusting that 2.5% spread to take into account the impact of both sales charges (.5%) and survivor bias (at least 1%), and throwing in another 2.7 percentage points for tax impact gives rise to an average annual fund return of 11.1% for a taxable investor; all-market index fund return (also after costs and taxes), 15.8%. Cumulative fund return: +384%. Cumulative index fund return: +804%.[2] No further comment is required.

- When using the S&P 500 Index as the comparator, limit the comparison to funds following the large-cap style (or, even better, Morningstar's 933 "Large-Cap Blend" funds, owning both large growth and large value equities). Yes, you'll still find short-term differences that may favor or disfavor active managers. For example, active funds presently hold positions in Microsoft, General Electric, and Coca-Cola that are well below their market weights. But in the long run, the comparison ought to be fair, though it ought to be adjusted for sales charges and taxes; survivor bias is least significant among large-cap funds.

- When using the Russell 2000 or 2500 Indexes as the comparator for small and mid-cap funds, be absolutely certain to estimate the impact of survivor bias, for here it is highly significant. Morningstar recently placed survivor bias in small-cap funds, over the five years 1992–1996 *alone,* at 1.1% per year. Result: While small-cap blend funds—with an annual return of 10.3% over the past ten years compared to 10.9% for the Russell 2000—seemed competitive, if we assess a 1.5-point survivor bias, that 0.6-point loss zooms to 2.1 points, not far from what we'd expect based on fund costs. When we adjust for another one point for sales charges and perhaps two points of tax differential, that deficit burgeons.

And when the day comes that active managers *seem* to win, remember that it is only because the data—proliferating far beyond what even the most farsighted of the index pioneers might have dreamed

---

2. For the tax-deferred investor, the relative returns are: Active fund, +12.9% annually and +517% cumulative; Index fund, +16.7% annually and +914% cumulative.

25 years ago—fails to capture the results of *all* active managers is burdened by statistical errors such as disregarding survivor bias, sales charges, or taxes, or ignores data anomalies, of which the most notable is calculating fund returns based on *number* of funds rather than *assets* of funds.

A Retrospective

So, fellow indexers, be of stout heart: *Active managers as a group never win.* As we begin to commemorate the 25th anniversary year of the birth of the index mutual fund, amid the surfeit of data available today, let's never lose sight of that immutable fact—time-honored to a fault. As Peter Bernstein tells us in his remarkable book *Capital Ideas*, it was way back in 1908 that the French economist Louis Bachelier spelled out the unequivocal brute fact in his thesis: *"The mathematical expectation of the speculator is zero."* However, Bachelier ignored the costs of investing, the proceeds raked off by the numerous croupiers at work in the marketplace. After these costs, as I expressed it most recently in a *New York Times* Op-Ed piece last summer: *"In the stock market casino, it is the croupiers who win."* Paraphrasing the title of a book of the 1940s, I asked "Where are the customers' private jets?" Where, indeed.

Nobel Laureate Paul Samuelson has said that his view of indexing theory, "oscillated from regarding it as trivially obvious (and almost trivially vacuous) and regarding it as remarkably sweeping." Of course, it is both, giving further testimony to the ancient wisdom of William of Occam. In 1330, he formulated a rule that came to be known as Occam's Razor, essentially that, "when confronted with multiple solutions to a complex problem, choose the simplest one." Yes, the secret of success in investing is the obvious one: The haystack trumps the needle, *almost* every time. No matter what the data that compare active managers with market indexes *appear* to show, we'd best never ignore that immutable fact. As Oliver Wendell Holmes reminded us, "we need education in the obvious more than investigation of the obscure." I hope my message tonight has reinforced that wisdom.

8

SELECTING EQUITY
MUTUAL FUNDS

WHY IS IT VIRTUALLY IMPOSSIBLE TO PICK *THE* WINNER,
YET SO EASY TO PICK *A* WINNER?
AND WHAT SHOULD YOU DO ABOUT IT IN THE 1990S?

Journal of Portfolio Management
Winter 1992

*I*NVESTMENT MANAGEMENT is a field fraught with fragility and fallibility, a field in which today's careful, rational fund selections are too often tomorrow's embarrassments. There is little doubt in my mind that few portfolio managers actually believe that there are easy means to *providing* performance superiority, and that few financial advisers or intelligent investors believe that such superiority can be consistently recognized *in advance*.

This article considers what I believe to be a peculiar paradox of investing: how difficult it is to pick "the winner." I would like to present the logic of my observations in the following manner:

1. A study of the randomness of equity fund performance that shows, using past performance as the criterion, how difficult it is to pick *the* winner in advance.
2. A real-world long-term study of the actual results achieved by an intelligent and careful system of fund selection.
3. Given the results of that study, an obvious means of owning a winner, and being guaranteed never to own a loser.

4. Assessment of techniques for evaluating past performance that are emerging in the "information explosion" regarding mutual funds today.
5. A look at a theory of "rational expectations" for stock market returns during the decade of the 1990s, and its implications for equity fund selection.

Why Is It So Difficult to Pick "the" Winners?

Let me begin with a hypothesis: The relative return achieved by an equity mutual fund yesterday has virtually no material predictive value for tomorrow. While investors are likely to think that this is the case, the premise is subject to careful testing in the laboratory of fund performance. The basis (not necessarily the fairest) format for analysis is simply this: Calculate the actual past records of all general equity funds, select the top twenty in each period, and then record the future returns actually achieved. Our data include both short-term and long-term analyses.

First, we examine how the one-year "champions" perform during the following year. To minimize the possibility of randomness in any single year, we have made comparisons of fund rankings in *each year* during the past decade (i.e., how the top-twenty mutual fund performers of 1980 ranked in 1981, and so on through to how the top twenty of 1989 ranked in 1990). For simplicity's sake, we then average the results for each individual period, as shown in Table 8.1. Here are the conclusions:

1. A top fund's performance in one year has borne no systematic relationship to its ranking in the subsequent year.
2. A typical top-twenty fund in the first year provides a phenomenal return of +45.5%—nearly three times the average for all equity funds of +15.5%. In the second year, the return falls to +14.6%, still above the average of +11.5%, but only by a modest 3.1 percentage points.
3. Funds that rank in the top twenty in a given year have, on average, ranked 249 (of 554 funds) in the subsequent year. (*That* can fairly be described as "regressing to the mean.")

Over the long term, these three general conclusions are reaffirmed, as is also shown in Table 8.1. In a ten-year study (1971–1980 versus

TABLE 8.1 Rank and Order of Top-Twenty Equity Funds*

Rank in First Year	One Year											Ten-Year Rankings	
	1981	1982	1983	1984	1985	1986	1987	1988	1989	1990	Avg.	1970–1980	1980–1990
1	302	1	125	405	179	7	2	23	13	15	107	1	176
2	314	145	263	NA	316	391	43	757	443	814	387	2	126
3	58	31	317	416	306	1	5	132	136	124	153	3	186
4	318	55	228	183	230	33	297	647	811	494	330	4	309
5	223	264	269	19	235	34	84	316	364	723	253	5	136
6	299	330	46	39	96	28	272	609	37	783	254	6	20
7	319	85	72	124	99	14	24	749	64	109	166	7	298
8	78	308	148	298	NA	406	256	726	291	747	362	8	35
9	329	89	203	34	305	23	113	199	721	802	282	9	119
10	242	175	277	233	229	27	3	335	824	516	286	10	1
11	15	204	14	113	415	500	134	411	352	612	277	11	242
12	296	11	101	164	239	48	60	341	537	829	263	12	239
13	282	100	169	145	278	17	52	532	436	427	244	13	161
14	203	9	40	348	257	24	384	127	54	165	161	14	78
15	117	83	223	127	138	400	377	224	159	699	255	15	21
16	322	124	210	398	390	19	159	701	366	14	270	16	36
17	287	225	230	107	399	40	94	187	401	330	230	17	259
18	327	284	67	252	134	268	120	577	722	162	291	18	60
19	230	302	59	235	109	75	345	176	198	579	231	19	172
20	57	134	172	14	410	47	15	33	470	421	177	20	57
Avg. return top-20 funds (%)	45.5	-8.2	28.9	22.6	-1.8	25.5	37.3	13.8	13.5	24.7	-10.2	14.6	19.0	11.1
All funds (%)	15.5	-1.3	25.0	20.2	-2.1	27.2	13.4	0.5	14.4	24.0	-6.3	11.5	10.4	11.7
Number of funds	500	330	340	372	420	466	552	639	763	825	829	554	177	309

*Sector and option income funds excluded.

1981–1990), the rankings are even less meaningful, with the average member of the top twenty providing a premium average annual return of 8.6 percentage points (+19.0% versus +10.4%) in the first decade, then lagging the average return by 0.6 percentage point in the second (+11.1% versus +11.7%). Some of the specific results are dramatic:

1. The average rank of the top-twenty funds in the first decade falls to 137 (of 309 funds) in the second.
2. Only two of the top twenty funds in the first period remain there in the second.
3. The fourth-ranked fund in the first decade ranks dead last of all funds in the second.

In short, even when we examine the question from the vantage of a full decade, it appears that investing in the winners of the past, sheerly in terms of highest relative return, adds no significant value to the selection of the winners of the future.

A More Sophisticated Real-World Test of Fund Selection

There are quite a few criticisms that could be leveled at these simple tests. So, we shall present a more sophisticated test. Rather than simply picking the *top* performers, we carefully select the *better* performers, taking into account their total return over a period of at least ten years, their relative performance in both rising and falling markets, and the continuity of their portfolio management over at least seven years.

What I have described is the Forbes "Honor Roll." It is an eminently sensible and fair system of equity fund selection, and it has been consistently prepared by the magazine each year since 1973—nearly two decades.

The Honor Roll has encompassed large funds and small, well-known and obscure alike. At one time or another such respected funds as Fidelity Magellan, Investment Company of America, Templeton Growth, Twentieth Century Growth, and Vanguard's Windsor have graced the list (although none of them does so at the moment). Nonetheless, little-known funds—by way of example, Axe Houghton "B," Central Securities, Castle Convertible, Philadelphia, and Union Income—have scarcely been ignored. So, we have a diverse group of funds, a sensible system for selection, and an extended time period for evaluation.

We propose to test the Honor Roll in retrospect by creating a hypothetical mutual fund investor who studies the Forbes Honor Roll when it is published each year. This investor purchases (or holds) an equal amount in each fund on the list, eliminating funds as they drop from the list. Such an approach avoids the inevitable bias of back-testing (i.e., massaging past numbers until they produce the desired result, or, as it is said, "applying different tortures to the data until they finally confess"). We examine first, whether the Honor Roll is able to select a group of funds that provides better returns than other comparable funds; and second, whether the choices provide better returns than the stock market as a whole.

As to the first issue—selected funds versus all funds—the Honor Roll list provides a total return of +605% compared with +566% for the average general equity fund. (See Table 8.2.) The annual rate of return on the Honor Roll is +12.2% versus +11.8% for the equity average. I should note that this small advantage is more than accounted for by an excellent relative return (+40% versus +29%) in 1979. Excluding that single year, the score would have been: Honor Roll return +10.6%, average equity fund +10.8%. So, I think that it is fair to call the comparison essentially a draw.

This test, however, overstates the results of both the Honor Roll funds and the equity fund average, because in neither case is an adjustment made for sales charges. In the latter case, the data are simply not readily available. In the former case, however, it is relatively simple to account for the front-end sales commission on each of the non-no-load funds when they are added to the list. We do precisely that in the next example, and then compare our results with the U.S. stock market as a whole (as measured by the Wilshire 5000 Index). Now, the relationships shift. As you can see in Table 8.2, the Honor Roll return drops to +440% (+10.4% annually) as we introduce the real-world reality of sales commissions. The return of the market as a whole—as measured by the Wilshire 5000 Index—totals +633%, an average of +12.4% annually. This difference of 2.0 percentage points per year represents a statistically significant extra return. (I believe the Wilshire Index is a better comparative standard for the diverse mutual fund industry than the more conventional Standard & Poor's 500 Composite Stock Price Index; just for the record, however, the average annual return on the S&P 500 was +12.2% for the period under review.)

TABLE 8.2 Equity Honor Roll

	1974	1975	1976	1977	1978	1979	1980	1981	1982	1983	1984	1985	1986	1987	1988	1989	1990	CUMULATIVE
Before sales charges																		
Forbes Honor Roll*	-25.2	23.6	24.7	5.9	6.9	40.4	34.7	-4.7	23.5	23.8	-4.7	27.5	12.1	2.0	14.9	28.4	-4.5	604.8
Lipper general equity fund	-25.3	32.3	24.5	1.3	11.1	28.7	33.5	-1.3	25.0	20.2	-2.1	27.2	13.4	0.5	14.4	24.0	-6.3	565.6
After sales charges																		
Forbes Honor Roll*	-28.9	23.6	23.6	5.3	4.9	38.8	30.4	-5.8	21.6	20.5	-6.9	27.4	10.6	1.4	14.9	26.2	-6.7	439.7
Wilshire 5000 Index	-28.4	38.5	26.6	-2.6	9.3	25.6	33.7	-3.7	18.7	23.5	3.1	32.6	16.1	2.3	17.9	29.2	-6.2	633.4

*Performance figures exclude international and balanced funds.

Assume now that such a total market fund—following a "passive" investment strategy—had been available in 1973. (The fact is that a Standard & Poor's 500 mutual fund has been available since 1976, and a "completion fund" to facilitate matching the Wilshire 5000 since 1987.) These funds are available on a no-load basis, so there is no adjustment for sales commission, although we reduce the market return by estimated annual expenses of 0.2% (today's going rate for such funds) to account for operating costs. Now, we can calculate that the naive (if intelligent) investor would have garnered an annual net return of +12.2%, compared with +10.4% for the Honor Roll (+11.6% and +8.9% if we adjust for that devilish 1979, but perhaps it is now I who am torturing the data to excess).

During the 1973–1990 period, this difference in annual return would have provided a phenomenal increase in terminal investment value, as indicated by the growth of $10,000 invested in each program on December 31, 1973:

	TOTAL VALUE DECEMBER 31, 1990
Honor Roll funds	$53,800
Total stock market	70,700

I am sure that you can now see the basis for the title of this article: seeking to select "the winners" has, at least in this instance, proven far less rewarding than selecting "a winner." This conclusion is generated almost entirely from the fact that the sales charges, advisory fees, and portfolio turnover costs involved in mutual fund investing must *inevitably* cause actively managed investments in the aggregate to fall short of the market as a whole.

A Simple Strategy for Picking "a" Winner

I choose the word "inevitably" because it is indeed inevitable that a passive market strategy will, under *all* circumstances, past and future alike, outperform the combined result of all active strategies in the aggregate. Let me take you through this simple syllogism of proof:

1. If passive equity managers can match the aggregate market return (and it has been proven over and over again that they can do precisely that), then it logically follows that active managers—

that is, all other institutional and individual investors—must also match the market. For example, in a +10% total return market, the passive managers will produce a *gross* return of +10%; it logically follows that active managers—the remainder of the market—must divide up the +10% gross return that remains.

2. If passive managers operate at lower cost than active managers, it therefore logically follows that passive managers must provide excess *net* returns. It is an undisputed fact that passive managers operate at far lower fees than active managers, and—because of substantially lower portfolio turnover rates—incur lower transaction costs. The conclusion, then, is self-evident.

As the mathematicians would say: QED.

What can go wrong with this thesis? The answer is "nothing." Unless one is to put forth the far-fetched arguments that passive managers somehow lose track of their target index, or that their computers take on a sudden "virus." Despite all the other uncertainties of investing, it is *certain* that passive equity strategies have, and will, and must, outperform active equity strategies in the aggregate.

If nothing *can* go wrong, I hasten to add, at least three things can *appear* to go wrong:

1. When subsets of the equity market provide different results from the market as a whole. The most notable case is the use of the Standard & Poor's 500 Index as the market standard, when it in fact includes only large-capitalization stocks. The S&P 500 aggregates about 75% of the market's weight, leaving 25% remaining to be accounted for. It will outperform the total market in some periods (as in 1982–1990) and underperform in others (as in 1975–1981 and during the first three quarters of 1991). So, the all-encompassing Wilshire 5000 Index should, I believe, be the relevant standard.

2. When a subset of active managers provides better equity results than another subset. For example, it is quite possible that mutual funds will outpace the market from time to time, given differences in portfolio structure. Under this circumstance, one or more of the other subsets—say, bank trust accounts, pension funds, or individual investors—*must* underperform by a commensurate amount. (There is no empirical evidence that this phenomenon systematically occurs.)

3. When exact measures of the returns of active managers are un-
   reliable. There is, in fact, no way to measure precisely the returns of individual investors; pension fund data are notoriously
   crude; and what we refer to as the "average general equity mutual fund" is unweighted by fund size. An asset-weighted return—adjusted to take into account the cash reserve position of
   the average equity fund—would be a more exact standard.

Despite these caveats, the past record has validated the passive/
active syllogism presented above. The thesis is, implicitly at least,
accepted by scores of large pension funds that have committed
something like $300 billion to this concept. Why has it not found
similar acceptance in the mutual fund field? Again, I would cite
three reasons:

1. Indexing is decidedly counter-intuitive. ("You mean that *no*
   management is better than professional management?") Presumably few mutual fund investors have the patience to labor
   through the proof presented in my syllogism.
2. Indexed accounts are far less profitable to investment advisers
   than actively managed accounts. It simply flies in the face of reality to expect an active manager with an advisory fee of 50 to
   100 basis points to offer—at least with much enthusiasm—an
   index fund at 1 to 5 basis points.
3. "Hope springs eternal." Some investors will choose funds carefully and outpace the market; some will make lucky choices and
   do the same. In total, however, it is inevitable that these investors in the aggregate will be a minority.

Applying Analysis and Judgment to Identify Future Winners

I want to underscore that the "active/passive" issue is not intended to
demean the skills of the very best money managers. Despite the drag
of expenses and transaction costs, they have succeeded in assembling
portfolios that, over an extended period of time, have provided measurably higher net returns than the market as a whole. The issue is
whether *these* winners can be systematically identified in advance in
such a way as to provide excess returns over passive investing—always
a winner.

If (and I underscore the "if") there is a systematic way to identify equity fund winners that can win bigger than the sure winner that is readily available through the techniques of passive investing, it would surely be in this new era of the microcomputer, with the fantastic explosion of information that is now available to mutual fund investors. Indeed, investors have at their disposal the means to effect intelligent investment analysis, most notably through the use of various financial publications that compile statistical data on mutual funds.

Perhaps none of these publications is more promising than "Morningstar Mutual Funds," a remarkable conception of Morningstar, Inc. It goes to the heart of the information that intelligent investors can and must grasp, to which they must apply their own judgment, and finally make their selections. The question, of course is "will the system work?" Will it in fact enable mutual fund investors to earn enhanced risk-adjusted returns? It is to this issue that I now turn.

I propose to gauge the effectiveness of Morningstar's statistical compilations by investigating the results of its star rating system. In this rating system, each equity mutual fund is awarded an overall rating of from one to five stars, depending on the fund's total risk-adjusted return over a variety of periods. (Risk is defined as the cumulative total of all the months in which a fund *underperforms* the results of U.S. Treasury bills, divided by the *total* number of months in the period.) The top 10% of all equity funds receive five stars (highest), and the bottom 10% receive one star (lowest). The remaining 80% of funds are assigned ratings as follows: 22.5%, four stars (above average); 35%, three stars (neutral); and 22.5%, two stars (below average).

Because the Morningstar system was first published only five years ago, no definitive conclusions can be drawn regarding the predictive value of the star ratings. Nonetheless, as a preliminary test, we compared equity fund ratings over the past three years (July 31, 1988 to July 31, 1991) for the five-star and one-star funds at the start of the period. Here are the results:

CATEGORY	AVERAGE INITIAL RATING	AVERAGE SUBSEQUENT RATING
Five-star funds	5.0	2.8
One-star funds	1.0	1.9

In short, in this simple test there is a remarkable (if hardly surprising) regression to the mean, with five-star funds on average falling just below the three-star (middle 35%) group, and one-star funds moving almost to the two-star category. This combination would suggest a moderately helpful predictive value for the system, primarily because the initial poor performers remain well below average in the subsequent period. (An interesting sidelight: of the initial 46 one-star funds, fully 9 liquidated or merged during the subsequent three years.)

Upon further analysis, we have concluded that the Morningstar system is somewhat better than the evaluation above suggests. A review of the data shows that 22 of the initial 57 five-star selections were mutual funds with international portfolios. Such funds, of course, were favored with an excellent investment environment through 1988, and a poor one thereafter. When compared against a list dominated by U.S. portfolios, then, their fall from grace in 1989–1991 is hardly unsurprising.

If we consider only the U.S. fund portfolios, however, the average rating for the three years ended July 31, 1991, was 3.3 stars, substantially above the 2.8 star average shown in the table above. (I believe that if the star system rated funds in terms of their returns relative to funds with comparable objectives—i.e., international, growth and income, small company—the system would be significantly more useful to investors.) The preliminary indication, then, is that the Morningstar system provides some basis for selecting the better-performing funds and for avoiding the worse-performing. Even if substantial predictive value-added does not materialize over time, however, there can be no doubt that Morningstar is an outstanding source of copious relevant information about each fund under consideration.

It includes, by way of example, a description of the fund's objectives and policies; past performance, including its consistency over a variety of periods; careful measurement of the degree of risk assumed by the fund in the past; divided history; components of its current portfolio (by asset class, by sector, and by major stock positions); portfolio statistics (price/earnings ratios, earnings growth rate, leverage, market capitalization, etc.); name and tenure of portfolio manager; and last— but far from least—the costs incurred in acquiring and holding the fund's shares (sales charges, if any, as well as expense ratios). In short, this new service enables serious investors to *understand* the investment characteristics of the funds that they select, and that may prove to be the greatest gift of all.

Implications for the Decade of the 1990s

During the 1980s, virtually all equity mutual funds were winners, in the sense of remarkably high absolute rates of return. (The Standard & Poor's 500 Index provided a compound annual return of +17.5%.) In this salubrious environment, fund shareholders may well have been forgiving of relative shortfalls that were not substantial. How will these same shareholders evaluate their results during what may well be a less productive future equity environment?

In particular, how will investors justify paying high expense ratios (the average equity fund carries an expense ratio of 1.40%) or the substantial transaction costs entailed by portfolio turnover (88% for the average equity fund)? If we take into account sales charges (where applicable), expenses, and transaction costs, the cost of an average fund may approximate 2.5% annually. Such a cost would have consumed one-seventh of the +17.5% annual market return we enjoyed in the 1980s, but it would consume fully one-quarter of the +10% return that stocks have returned during their modern (1926–1990) history.

So, the fifth and final issue of this article: What return can we expect of the stock market during the decade of the 1990s? A narrow range of forecasts can be established for an investor willing to make intelligent and reasonable appraisals of just three basic factors:[1]

- The dividend yield when the initial investment is made.
- The earnings growth rate over the ensuing period.
- The *change* in the price/earnings multiple during the period.

We can all quickly agree on the first of these three factors: the yield on common stocks as we entered the 1990s was 3.1%. So now we are down to but two, and I have presented some expected ranges in the matrix labeled Table 8.3. Looking first at earnings growth, a disgruntled bear might look for 4.0% a year in the 1990s, a roaring bull, let us say, 10.0%. Combining these earnings growth rates with the entry yield of 3.1% would provide an annual return of +7.1% to +13.1%, other things held equal.

As for the third factor, the price/earnings ratio of the market at the beginning of the 1990s was 15.5 times. If it remains the same at the

---

1. Initial price/earnings = 15.5x; terminal Price/Earnings of 18x, 12x, and 14x, respectively.

TABLE 8.3 Stock Return Matrix (Initial Yield: 3.1%), Projected 10-Year Total Return

TERMINAL PRICE/EARNINGS RATIO	Earnings Growth Rate			
	4.0%	6.0%	8.0%	10.0%
6.0x	−1.7	0.0	+1.8	+3.6
10.0x	+3.1	+4.9	+6.8	+8.7
14.0x	+6.4	+8.3	+10.3	+12.2
18.0x	+8.6	+10.6	+12.6	+14.6

end of this decade, stock returns will perforce fall within our range of +7% to +13% annually. Each one-point change in this price/earnings ratio will add or subtract about 0.6% to the annual return over a decade, however. To be more precise, if you believe that price/earnings ratios will be at 18 times earnings in 1999, add 1.5% to the base rate of return; if you believe that they will be at 12 times, subtract 2.5%, and so on. Thus, as shown in Table 8.4, a theoretical range on annual stock returns in the 1990s would be from +14.6% (high earnings growth, higher price/earnings ratio) to +4.6% (low earnings growth, lower price/earnings ratio).

Investors are free to make their own assumptions. But they all *must* deal with this matrix of rational expectations when they do so. We need not waste time debating stock returns in the abstract. Rather, we should accept the current yield as a starting point, and then debate the dimension of the two remaining factors: the "fundamental" factor of earnings growth and what the resultant earnings will be in 1999, and the "technical" factor of what multiple the marketplace will then apply

TABLE 8.4 Components of Stock Return

	1990s (Projected*)			
	1980S	BEST CASE	WORST CASE	MOST LIKELY
Entry yield	+5.2	+3.1	+3.1	+3.1
Earnings growth	+4.5	+10.0	+4.0	+8.0
Price/earnings impact	+7.8	+1.5	−2.5	−1.0
Total return	+17.5	+14.6	+4.6	+10.1

*Initial Price/Earnings = 15.5x; terminal price/earnings of 18x, 12x, and 14x, respectively.

to those earnings. (There is a large emotional component—to say nothing of a large interest rate component—in this factor!)

Let's close by evaluating possible returns in the 1990s relative to the "Golden Decade" of the 1980s. Table 8.4 also presents these data.[2] It shows that the market's extraordinary return during the 1980s was based not on particularly good earnings growth but on a high yield (5.2%) at the start of the period, and a doubling of the price/earnings ratio from 7.3 to 15.5 times, which added 7.8% annually to return—nearly one-half of the +17.5% total rate.

Simply put, the entry yield of 3.1% at the close of 1989 compares with 5.2% at the close of 1979, and thus will reduce annual return by 2% in the 1990s. To repeat the 1980s return of 8% from price/earnings impact would require *another* more than doubling of the ratio, to an almost unprecedented 33 times. Perhaps the most rational scenario would be a 2-point drop in the multiple to a more normal level of 14, and an earnings growth rate of 8%. (The compound earnings growth rate over the past 30 years was 6.5%, so this assumption is an ambitious one.) Under these circumstances, the annual return on stocks would average about +10% for the decade, a close counterpart to the long-term historical norm.

Conclusion

I would like to conclude by answering the questions posed at the beginning of this article:

1. Picking *the* winning fund is virtually impossible, because reliance on past performance is of no apparent help.
2. Picking *a* winning fund is made easy by selecting a passive all-market index fund, or perhaps by engaging in thorough research and careful analysis.
3. If the stock market in the 1990s offers annual returns well below those of the 1980s, intelligent investors simply cannot disregard the heavy burden of costs endemic to most actively managed funds, and clearly should consider index funds for at least a core portion of their equity holdings.

---

2. Despite its limitations, the Standard & Poor's 500 Index is issued as the proxy for the stock market in this analysis, because it is the only reliable source of long-term historical data.

9

THE THIRD MUTUAL FUND INDUSTRY

WHY INVESTORS SHOULD OWN BOND FUNDS

FIVE RULES FOR BOND FUND SELECTION

FIVE WARNINGS TO BOND FUND INVESTORS

Keynote Address
American Association of Individual Investors
Chicago, Illinois
June 12, 1992

*R*ARELY A WEEK goes by without a major story about equity mutual funds and their portfolio managers surfacing in the news. We could hardly avoid knowing, for example, when Peter Lynch and, more recently, Morris Smith retired, both having done a superb job in managing Magellan Fund. Newspapers and magazines print extensive stories about equity managers who often praise their own prescience, comment on their favorite stocks, and come close to forecasting the stock market (no mean task!).

At least each quarter, *Business Week, The Wall Street Journal,* and *Barron's* lionize the managers of the "top performing" equity funds (at least for the previous quarter, but sometimes, in fairness, for a full year or longer). *Money,* a monthly publication, does so every month. And nearly every financial publication provides an annual performance overview. (Interesting enough, the focus is almost always on the winners, almost never on the losers.)

Since equity funds began it all back in 1924, I suppose that we can call this asset class the *first* mutual fund industry. Money market funds as the industry's largest component with $575 billion of assets, are doubtless perceived as the *second* mutual fund industry. These funds, which arrived on the scene in the mid-1970s, expanded mutual fund horizons to include, not only investors, but savers.

And now, I would argue, there is a *third* mutual fund industry. It is the bond mutual fund industry. While this industry subset commands relatively little public attention, and its portfolio managers are almost never lionized, and rarely even featured, in the press, the growth of bond funds is one of the most remarkable aspects of the soaring popularity of mutual funds. In fact, today bond fund assets of $440 billion remain in excess of the stock fund total of $430 billion—as they have since 1984—despite the boom in equity prices.

- Bond fund assets, $3 billion 25 years ago, represented just 7% of the assets of long-term mutual funds. Today they represent 51%.
- During the 1967–1992 period, bond fund assets have grown at a compound growth rate of 22% annually. Equity fund assets have grown at 10%, less than one-half of the bond fund rate, and indeed, less than what the total return of the stock market would suggest.

So, to borrow a line from *Death of a Salesman*, "attention must be paid." And I shall pay that attention to bond funds today. I recognize the risk that I am taking by *not* discussing equity funds, their performance, and their portfolio managers, but I think the risk is worth taking as I try to provide some stimulating ideas about that third mutual fund industry, composed of bond funds.

It is perhaps paradoxical that the diversity of types of stock funds pales by comparison with that of bond funds. Stock funds largely comprise some combination of three investment sectors (growth, value, and mixed), focusing on one of three general market capitalization levels (large, medium, and small).[1] These nine "boxes" compare with 21 for the bond fund arena, with three major maturity levels (short-term, intermediate-term, and long-term) and seven distinctly different investment sectors (U.S. Government, Investment-Grade Corporate,

---

1. These are the basis differentiations utilized in the new Morningstar equity mutual fund system. International and industry specialized would be important subcategories.

Medium-Grade Corporate, "Junk" Corporate, Investment-Grade Municipal, High-Yield Municipal, and Global). (Table 9.1) While not all of these 21 neat "pigeon holes" are filled, we have "forced" some other types of funds (such as GNMA and Adjustable Rate Mortgage funds) to conform to the table in the exhibit. In any event, 21 is not a bad estimate for the variety of bond funds available.

In my remarks, I shall discuss three aspects of this subject: first, why own bond funds at all; second, five general rules for investors to follow in their decision as to what types of bond funds they should consider; and third, five strong warnings about funds with specific characteristics that should be avoided or, at the very least, viewed with great skepticism. Let's turn first to the question of the value of bonds as an investment opportunity.

Why Own Bond Funds?

First, why indeed should investors own bonds at all? Is not the historical record clear that the long-term (since 1926) *nominal* return on corporate bonds is but **+5.4%** per year, compared with an average return of **+10.4%** for stocks? (The *real* returns of each, adjusted for inflation, are of course some 3% lower.) I believe that we should *disregard* this historical evidence—I call it "hysterical" evidence—since the current level of long-term interest rates suggests, indeed it virtually guarantees, that future bond returns will be far higher than in the past. In fact, the average initial interest rate on such bonds in the 1926–1981 period is estimated at **4.9%,** compared to a rate of **8.8%**— nearly twice that level—today. So, I believe that the odds suggest that, during the coming decade, bonds will give a much more favorable account of themselves relative to stocks. Assuming today's price-earnings ratio of about 19 times remains at that level during the coming decade, stocks may provide returns in the **+9.2%** range—2.9% current dividend yield plus 6.3% estimated earnings growth.

Even if the returns on *long-term* bonds fall somewhat short of stock returns (a situation that is by no means guaranteed), they provide investors with a useful asset class—fixed-income securities—with which to diversify their investment portfolios. At the minimum, bonds will moderate the price volatility of an investment portfolio; at the maximum, they should provide a haven against a severe deterioration in the ever-volatile stock market—*always* a hazard to the investor's capital.

TABLE 9.1 The Fixed Income Fund Industry, April 1992 ($ Billions)

	U.S. GOV'T	INVEST.-GRADE CORP.	MEDIUM-GRADE CORP.	"JUNK" CORP.	INVEST.-GRADE MUNI	HIGH-YIELD MUNI	GLOBAL	TOTAL
Short-term	25.5[a]	10.2	—	5.1[c]	4.5	—	23.8	69.1
Inter.-term	68.5[b]	9.1	—	31.5	8.9	—	—	118.8
Long-term	51.3	16.2	16.0	—	141.4[d]	19.9	8.1	252.9
Total	$145.3	$35.5	$16.0	$36.6	$154.8	$19.9	$31.9	$440.0

[a] Includes Adjustable Rate Mortgage Funds: $15.5.
[b] Includes GNMA Funds: $64.6.
[c] "Prime Rate" Funds.
[d] Includes insured ($12.6) and state ($74.7).
SOURCE: Strategic Insight.

At the same time, *short-term* bonds presently offer a high yield premium relative to cash reserves, in exchange for only a modest increase in principal risk. With today's steep yield curve, a three-year Treasury bond offers a yield of 5.9%, fully 2.1% (210 "basis points") above the 3.8% yield on Treasury bills. (Figure 9.1) Put another way, even if interest rates rise sharply, a bond with a constant three-year maturity could lose 2% of its principal value every year for three years, and still earn the same *net* total return. (The chance of a symmetrical *decline* in rates is probably 50–50; under that circumstance, the notes would deliver an annual return of +8.0%.)

It is but one small step from bonds to bond funds. Their portfolio management and remarkable range of shareholder conveniences are of the same high intrinsic value as with stock funds. They maintain a "constant maturity," rather than one which gradually shortens as the day of maturity approaches. And, very importantly, their broad diversification can—without *extra* cost to the investor—mitigate the substantial principal risk that can easily "come home to roost" to haunt an investor who owns only one or a handful of bonds that are downgraded or default. Bond funds—at least when "the price is right"—are

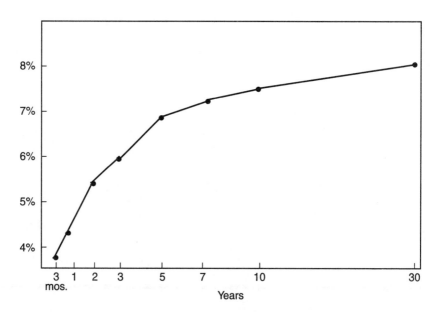

FIGURE 9.1 Treasury Yield Curve, June 1992.

essential components of the investment program of the prudent investor.

So, the case for bond funds is strong, both for equity investors seeking to reduce overall portfolio risk and for money market investors seeking to enhance income. Let's now discuss five general rules for the selection of bond funds.

Five General Rules for Bond Fund Selection

GENERAL RULE 1   Recognize that bonds carry "interest rate risk." But consider not only risk to principal but also risk to income. *Principal risk increases with length of maturity.* That is, rising rates means lower prices, and *vice versa. Income risk,* however, *decreases with length of maturity.* Simply put, a 90-day Treasury bill has no principal risk, but an *enormous* income risk. (In fact, its annualized yield has fallen from 9.3% to 3.8% during the past three years!). An 8% 30-year Treasury bond, on the other hand, will crank out $8 per year for each $100 initially invested for three *decades,* but interim fluctuations in principal value of plus or minus 20% should be expected. So, the investor's task is to consider short-term bonds and long-term bonds and to balance out principal risk against income risk.

GENERAL RULE 2   Consider the impact of income yield and principal change on total return, in the light of *the length of time* that you expect to own the investment. For the very short-term investor, the principal risk embodied in rising interest rates will overwhelm the lower income return; for the long-term investor, potential principal losses will be reduced by the higher interest rates usually available on longer-term maturities. (Currently, the "spread" between the yield of 8.0% on long-term Treasury bonds and the yield of 3.8% on Treasury bills is 4.2%—420 basis points—dwarfing the average spread of 120 basis points during the past 25 years.)

For example, a 25-year Treasury bond would provide a one-year total return of −10% if interest rates rose by 200 basis points and a return of +31% on a commensurate rate *decline;* however, after five years the range of respective rates of return narrows to +6% and +11%. After eleven years the gap is in fact eliminated, and the interest rate rise then turns to the bondholder's advantage. At maturity, the average rate of return would be +9.2% in a *rising* rate environment and +7.0% in a *declining* rate environment.

The perhaps obvious long-term value to investors of higher rates versus lower rates is dramatic. A $10,000 investment in a 25-year Treasury bond would have a terminal value (including interest) of just $9,000 one year after the 2% rate increase, and a value of $13,000 following the 2% rate decline. Then, the values begin to converge, crossing in the eleventh year. After 25 years, when the bond ultimately matures, the $10,000 investment is worth nearly $94,000 in the *rising* rate environment and just $55,000 in the *declining* rate environment—a 60% difference in value! This reversal is, in a sense, a reaffirmation of the centuries-old aphorism that "it's an ill wind (indeed) that blows no good." The reason is that higher yields, while they have a negative *short-term* impact on prices, have a positive *long-term* impact on returns since interest payments are reinvested at higher (i.e., more attractive) rates.

GENERAL RULE 3 Consider—very carefully—investment quality. Interest rate risk (remember, the longer the maturity, the greater the portfolio's near-term sensitivity to interest rate changes) is but one of two major risks assumed by the bond fund investor. The other is quality risk—the risk that a bond will be unable to meet its specified interest coupon and, at maturity, to repay its principal. In terms of quality, U.S. Treasuries are the safest of bonds, junk bonds the riskiest. The recent "quality curve" showed the yield for a 30-year U.S. Treasury bond at 8.0%, an Aa bond at 8.7%, a Baa bond at 9.4%, a Ba at 9.9%, and a B (junk) bond at 11.9%. (Table 9.2) Thus, the market is saying, for example, that Baa bonds (the lowest "investment quality" grade by the definition of Moody's Investor Services) must provide the investor with a 140-basis-point premium over U.S. Treasuries in order to compensate for the extra risk.

TABLE 9.2 Yield by Quality Rating

	3-YEAR BOND	10-YEAR BOND	30-YEAR BOND
U.S. Treasury	5.9%	7.6%	8.0%
Aa industrial	6.3	8.1	8.7
Baa industrial	6.7	8.6	9.4
Ba industrial	10.0	9.8	9.9
B industrial	11.5	10.5	11.9

SOURCE: Salomon Brothers.

GENERAL RULE 4   Consider at least two *other* kinds of risk. (Yes, there are still other risks in fixed-income investing.) One is *prepayment risk*—most typically the risk that mortgages held by GNMA "pass through" certificates will be prepaid. This process, which *invariably* accelerates when rates decline, can appreciably shorten what would otherwise appear to be a steady long-term string of payments. (What is more, when rates rise, prepayments slow, also an unfavorable outcome.) The second is *currency* risk, which exists in foreign bonds. Specifically, the value of foreign bonds fluctuates inversely with the value of the dollar in international currency markets—a strong dollar means lower prices for foreign bonds, and *vice versa*.

GENERAL RULE 5   Consider the taxability of interest payments. Interest payments on municipal bonds are generally free from Federal income tax, and (importantly in states with high income tax rates) bonds of that state are usually free of state taxes too. As a result—since financial markets are highly efficient—municipal bonds provide lower yields than taxable bonds. Investors, then, must calculate which alternative produces the most after-tax income. For example, a 10-year Aa corporate bond presently yields 8.1%, compared with 6.0% for a comparably rated municipal bond. Since the latter rate is 26% below the former, the municipal bond represents approximately "fair value" only to investors paying marginal combined state and Federal tax rates in excess of 26%.

With these five general rules in mind, let's now turn to my five warnings regarding the selection of specific types of bond funds.

Five Warnings about Bond Fund Selection

WARNING 1   Never, never, never invest in a bond fund without knowing its expense ratio. While some stock funds, some of the time, may provide premium performance despite prodigious costs, most bond funds, most of the time, will fail to do so. Specific types of bond funds—for example, those investing in long-term U.S. Treasury bonds—tend to be homogeneous in nature, and differ most importantly only in their expense ratios (operating expenses as a percentage of net assets). Such expenses represent the amount taken by the fund's management from the *gross* interest income earned by the fund before the distribution of *net* income to the fund's shareholders.

In fact, the cost differences are staggering. (Table 9.3) General government bond funds have annual expense ratios ranging from 2.40% for the highest five funds to 0.36% for the lowest five. Their average expense ratio is 1.14%. For investment-grade corporate bond funds, expense ratios are 1.69% for the highest, 0.30% for the lowest, and 0.89% for the average. For municipal bond funds, the expense ratio range is 2.31%(!), 0.25%, and 0.87%, respectively. It is virtually inevitable that, when maturity and quality are held constant, higher costs will result in lower returns and *vice versa.*

Within the major bond fund categories, most, if not all, funds exhibit relatively comparable quality standards and little significant difference in maturity. U.S. Treasury bonds, for example, all have identical credit ratings, and are segmented into fund portfolios that are fairly clearly identified as long term, intermediate term, and short term. Insured municipal bonds are all rated Aaa. And so on.

So, powerful odds suggest that a lower cost bond fund will provide a higher return than its higher-cost cousin. With the wide variety of funds available in each category, it does not make much sense to own one with annual expenses of 1% or 2% or more, which, simply put, would reduce an 8% yield to 7% or 6%. And, even expenses much over 50 basis points seem a bit rich. In any event, the investor should, *without fail,* be aware of what portion of his income is consumed by fund expenses.

(I should add that it has become increasingly difficult to get meaningful fund expenses information. Many new funds begin with "teaser" yields that are substantially enhanced by waiving expenses. They then "guarantee" midrange expenses for several years, before the expense ratio moves to a permanently higher level. Be sure to get all three expense ratios, and a copy of the "guarantee." Lots of luck!)

WARNING 2   Do not take quality for granted. I have never seen a corporate bond fund advertisement that addressed the quality issue, and, so far as I can tell, most bond funds do not report quality standards in their prospectuses, nor do they provide the quality ratings of their current portfolios in their reports to shareholders. Yet many so called investment-grade funds are reaching out for yield, in part doubtless to offset their higher expenses. The differences in quality are often dramatic. Consider the selected examples in Table 9.4.

TABLE 9.3 Bond Fund Cost Factors (Expense Ratios)

	Total Funds	Top Five	Bottom Five	Average	Front Load	Deferred Load	No Load
Gov't—Treasury	29	1.07%	0.37%	0.75%	7	0	22
Gov't—General	134	2.40	0.36	1.14	71	19	44
Gov't—Mortgage	54	1.85	0.36	0.95	36	4	14
Corp—Inv. Grade	68	1.69	0.30	0.89	25	5	38
Corp—General	104	2.29	0.34	1.03	51	6	47
Muni—National	182	2.31	0.25	0.87	101	22	59
World—Short Term	27	2.51	1.00	1.62	10	12	5
Totals	598				301	68	229

SOURCE: Morningstar Mutual Funds.

TABLE 9.4 How Bond Funds Differ—Some Extreme Examples

	1991			Portfolio Maturity (Years)	Portfolio Quality		Average Coupon	Sales Charge
	Net Yield	Expense Ratio	Gross Yield		A and Above	BBB and Below		
U.S. Treasury								
Fund A	7.9%	0.8%	8.7%	6.0	100%	—	8.4%	0
Fund Z	6.5	1.9	8.4	8.8	100	—	7.6	6.0%°
GNMA								
Fund A	8.8	0.5	9.3	7.4	100	—	8.3	0
Fund Z	7.7	1.9	9.6	6.0	100	—	9.6	5.0°
Short-term corporate								
Fund A	7.9	0.3	8.2	2.5	87	13%	8.2	0
Fund Z	8.2	0.9	9.1	2.9	38	62	9.7	0
Inter.-term corporate								
Fund A	7.9	0.2	8.1	8.3	92	8	8.9	0
Fund Z	8.1	1.5	9.6	8.0	28	72	10.2	0
Long-term corporate								
Fund A	8.9	0.3	9.2	20.2	82	18	9.1	0
Fund Z	9.1	0.9	10.0	14.9	40	60	11.1	4.75
Long-term municipal								
Fund A	7.1	0.3	7.4	18.1	98	2	6.6	0
Fund Z	5.8	2.0	7.8	24.0	50	50	7.9	6.0°
Insured municipal								
Fund A	6.2	0.6	6.8	21.6	90	10	6.8	0
Fund Z	5.6	1.7	7.3	23.9	100	—	6.7	5.0°
State muni (CA)								
Fund A	6.2	0.3	6.5	15.1	100	0	6.7	0
Fund Z	5.4	1.9	7.3	23.9	60	40	7.2	6.0°

°Contingent deferred sales load.

- Two short-term corporate bond funds in Table 9.4 have portfolios including, respectively, 13% and 62% of bonds rated Baa or below. Yet the lower quality portfolio—given its high expenses—provides only a marginally higher yield (8.2% vs. 7.9%).
- Two long-term municipal bond funds in Table 9.4 hold portfolios rated, respectively, 98% and 50% A or above. Given its astronomical expense ratio (even while ignoring its sales charge), the lower-quality fund provided a net yield of 5.8% vs. 7.1% for the high-quality fund.
- The portfolio of one California state municipal bond fund Table 9.4 is rated 40% Baa and below; another comprises 100% Aaa *insured* municipal bonds (which may be especially important in an earthquake-prone state!). But the insured fund provides a net yield of 6.2%, compared with 5.4% (ignoring the hefty sales charge) for the uninsured fund. (Just imagine an investor being *paid* 0.8% for buying an insurance policy!)

I believe that a lower quality bond portfolio with a commensurately higher expense ratio than other funds with comparable maturities should *never* be purchased by an investor. That is to say, if one hypothetical portfolio has a gross yield 1% or higher than another, and an expense ratio 1% higher, both funds will deliver the same net yield. A gross yield premium of 1% happens to be the spread between a 10-year Treasury bond (7.6%) and a Baa industrial bond (8.6%), as shown previously in Table 9.2. Thus, the higher expense ratio means that you are, in substance, paying the *price* for a Treasury bond, but receiving in return the *value* of a medium-grade industrial bond for your money. It is not a sensible trade-off.

WARNING 3   Beware of the impact of sales charges. Such loads are incurred by investors in 369 of the 598 bond funds listed in Table 9.3. Front-end loads immediately reduce the principal value of your investment, resulting in a significant reduction in yield. For example, a net yield of 6% in a no-load fund would be reduced—all else held equal—to 5.7% in a fund with a 5% sales commission. And, even this reduced yield implies that the fund's shares are held to infinity. Spreading the load over five years reduces the 5.7% yield to 5%; and, obviously, if the shares are held but one year, the yield drops to a mere 1%. The sales charge, then, is a factor that is particularly important in choosing between fixed-income funds with comparable quality, maturity, and expense ratios. (Some bond funds—unbelievably!—also assess a sales charge when a shareholder reinvests his dividends. This practice reduces yield by *another* 0.3%. Avoid it like the plague!)

Front-end sales charges are often hidden by the use of "contingent deferred sales charges." If you exit from the fund in the first year, there is typically a 5% load penalty, which usually drops to 0% in the sixth year. In such funds, you normally pay another 1% each year in expenses, often during your entire holding period. However hidden the charge, it has the same impact as a front-end sales load during the first five years, and an impact that is truly baneful in each subsequent year, during which the 1% charge is paid over and over again.

WARNING 4 Do not take yield calculations at face value. There are simply too many ways to calculate yields, to say nothing of enhancing them, to facilitate comparative analysis. For example, bond fund yields may be calculated on a "current yield" basis (income as a percentage of market value) or on a "yield to maturity" basis (amortizing premiums and discounts over the life of the bonds). You have a right to know both of these yields; if you can't get them, take your money elsewhere.

To clarify this point, if, for example, a bond fund owns a portfolio of "premium" bonds selling, on average, at a price of $105 and with a five-year maturity, the current yield (assuming a 6% coupon) is 5.7%; the yield to maturity, however, is 4.9%, since principal will decline by 1% annually. It is generally municipal bond funds that have invested heavily in "high coupon" bonds, issued for the most part during the high interest rate environment of the early to mid-1980s and now losing their (initial 10 years of) call protection. With coupons well in excess of the current market level, such bonds are highly likely to be "called back" by their issuers during the next few years. They will be replaced *inevitably* with bonds providing much lower yields. As a result, dividends on municipal bond funds that follow a "high coupon" strategy are riding for a fall.

Perhaps nowhere is the complexity of yield calculations more evident than in mortgage obligations. Calculating a yield to maturity for GNMA securities, for example, requires some assumptions about mortgage prepayments under existing market conditions. But both current yield and yield to maturity calculations ignore possible prepayments. It is clear that GNMA funds which own obligations with high coupons run a far greater risk of acceleration in prepayments than those funds emphasizing low coupon obligations (which reduce such prepayment risk). Complex as it may sound, the wise GNMA investor should know this data. (Average coupon data for GNMA funds is provided in Morningstar; any prepayment assumptions are available only from the fund sponsor.) The issues are even more complex when collateralized mortgage obligations (CMOs) are held in a bond fund's portfolio, but the information should nonetheless be obtained from the fund sponsor.

Under circumstances such as these, there is a clear tendency for fixed-income funds of all types to maximize apparent yields by owning premium bonds with high coupons and by making heavy commitments to mortgage obligations. These practices cry out for full disclosure.

WARNING 5   Avoid fixed-income "gimmick" funds. A few years ago, an apparent investment miracle took place with the creation of "Government Plus" bond funds, which were to provide, miraculously enough, higher yields than government bonds, even after hefty fund expenses. The trick was to add to the interest income substantial premium income by selling options on the bonds. This would be a marvelous strategy indeed if the managers could accurately forecast the rises and falls of interest rates. Apparently, however, none did. So the Government-Plus fund held on to the bonds when they *dropped* in price and had them called away when they *rose*. This highly predictable *ratchet effect* had the obvious result: Principal was gradually eroded, and income gradually deteriorated. The theory—predictably—failed in practice. It was a "black eye" for the mutual fund industry—even though it seemed to escape much public notice.

Are other gimmicks likely to lead to other black eyes? I believe that the answer is "yes." The most likely present candidate, in my view, is the "Prime Rate" fund—investing in bank loan participants of dubious quality and liquidity. These funds were to have periodic "tender offers," allowing investors to redeem. At least one such fund, however, has suspended its tender offer, but, to provide shareholder liquidity, listed its stock on the New York Stock Exchange. The shares, ostensibly still valued at the initial $10.00 per share, recently traded at $8⅞. For shareholders in these funds, presented as money market fund substitutes, it is a sorry situation.

It is too soon to say whether or not other "hot new products" from this most creative of all industries will prove to be gimmicks. Presently, there is a boom afoot in global short-term bond funds and adjustable-rate mortgage funds, both of which have very limited histories over which to make a fair evaluation. Moreover, both own highly complex investments and engage in equally complex strategies. Certainly they carry *at least* the principal and income risks of short-term corporate bond funds. So, the yields of all three types—two novel, one fully tested—should be compared with one another, and *not* with the yields of money market funds, which carry far less principal risk.

Conclusion

Let me summarize and conclude. First, bond funds today, it seems to me, represent an attractive investment opportunity: long-term bond funds by providing potentially competitive returns and substantially lower risks relative to stock funds; and short-term bond funds by providing higher and more durable income while assuming measurably higher risks than money market funds, but not *much* higher.

Second, the choice of bond fund sectors will vary substantially from one investor to another, depending on that person's income requirements, tolerance for interest rate risk, willingness to assume quality risk, and expected holding period.

Third, once investors decide on the types of bond funds that fit their needs, they should be careful and thorough in their individual fund selections. They should ignore advertisements that point to high yields ("the highest-yielding short-term bond fund!) if they do not disclose, *in the same size type,* the quality, maturity, coupon structure, and other relevant portfolio characteristics of the fund. And, investors are also entitled to the same forthright and prominent disclosure of the fund's expense ratio.

Finally, I believe that most investors will conclude that bond fund returns can be predictably enhanced by only two factors—one, higher risk, generally measured by longer maturities and/or lower investment quality; and two, lower operating expenses. To state what I believe is obvious, the latter is the more sensible and more productive strategy for enhancing yield. So, as improved disclosure is demanded by investors and regulators, as perceptions about yield are replaced by the hard realities I have discussed today, and as expenses are driven to more realistic levels that are fairer to the investor, bond mutual funds should continue to provide excellent opportunities, and "the third mutual fund industry" should continue to grow apace.

Part II

Taking On the Mutual Fund Industry

OVER THE YEARS, I've become less and less constrained in speaking out with candor on what I perceive as serious shortcomings in the principles and practices followed by the mutual fund industry. While not all fund organizations are equally tarred by the broad brush with which I paint, a sufficiently large majority of firms is subject to these failings—high costs, excessive portfolio turnover, focus on marketing over management, delivery of inadequate long-term returns to shareholders, failure to hold stewardship as their defining characteristic—for me to comfortably take on "the industry."

In this context, I'm reminded of what President Harry S. Truman said during his whistle-stop campaign aboard a train, a campaign that proved to be the key to his election in 1948. At each train stop, someone in the crowd would interrupt his scathing denunciation of "that do-nothing 80th Congress" and yell, "Give 'em hell, Harry." He would respond, "I'm not giving them hell. I'm just telling the truth and they *think* it's hell." Whether the industry thinks I'm giving it hell or not, I've yet to hear a single serious rebuttal to my criticisms of the fund industry. So I conclude that, because their veracity is self-evident, my words are accepted as truths.

The first speech ("Mutual Funds: The Paradox of Light and Darkness," Chapter 10) describes the bright stars of the fund industry's growth, including the Great Bull Market, an increasingly favorable tax environment, the blessings of technology, and our industry's remarkable capacity for innovation. But I quickly note the paradox: Each of these stars has a dark side that may come back to bedevil us. I suggest that mutual funds must take off their blinders and see the industry as it really is, and then promptly get to work on improving today's imperfect model of mutual fund principles and practices. Plato's *The Allegory of the Cave* provides an apt metaphor from the classics: "The prisoner emerges from the dark cave and comes into the sunlight, dazzled by a new vision." One day, so it will be for the mutual fund industry.

The next two chapters deal with the economics of the mutual fund industry, "Economics 101: For Mutual Fund Investors . . . For

Mutual Fund Managers," as Chapter 11 is entitled. There I contrast the extraordinary profitability of fund management companies with the lagging returns of fund shareholders relative to those provided in the financial markets. Because fund costs account for most of that shortfall, the contrast represents a definitional *quid pro quo*. I challenge the accuracy of the allegation by the industry's Investment Company Institute that fund industry costs are declining and present evidence that they are actually soaring. As a result, I urge the Securities and Exchange Commission to begin the process of bringing fund costs under control by undertaking an economic study of the mutual fund industry. (So far, alas, to no avail.) In the next chapter, I discuss the reasons that Vanguard's rivals have no interest in challenging our low-cost business model.

The final three chapters relate to fund governance issues. Both "Creating Shareholder Value" and "The Silence of the Funds" note that by abdicating their corporate governance responsibilities, mutual funds have failed to focus on creating shareholder value in the stocks they own. Funds have also failed to create shareholder value for their own investors, earning returns that fall well short of their cost of capital, the standard popularized by the phrase "economic value added" (EVA). The final chapter takes on the very independence of mutual fund "independent directors," asking first, "Where are they?" and closing with, "I hope they'll be back soon." I delivered that speech in 1991, almost a decade ago, but they haven't come back *yet*. But my hope—that directors will better honor their stewardship obligations to fund shareholders—springs eternal.

10

MUTUAL FUNDS: THE PARADOX OF LIGHT AND DARKNESS

Distinguished Speaker Series
The Houston Club
Houston, Texas
January 14, 1998

*M*Y 1993 BOOK on mutual funds concludes with what I describe as "Twelve Pillars of Wisdom" for investors. The final chapter begins with this lofty quote from Ecclesiastes: "Wisdom excelleth ignorance as far as light excelleth darkness." That book is described as a "how-to-invest guide," but as I considered my mandate to speak in this respected forum for airing the ideas of so many distinguished speakers over the years, it occurred to me that the theme of light and darkness might also profitably be used to accommodate a rather different approach.

My remarks today, while I hope they will stimulate your investment thinking, will focus, not on the use of mutual funds in your own investment and savings programs, but on the diverse factors—some widely known, some less so—that have fostered the growth of the mutual fund industry, as funds have replaced, first savings deposits, then life insurance, and then pension plans to become the investment of choice for America's families. If we have ever had a clear case of "creative destruction"—the phrase the economist Joseph Schumpeter chose to describe the process by which one industry strikes at the heart of another by providing a novel solution to society's needs—surely this industry's rise to preeminence is its apotheosis.

But, as the laws of physics tell us, a strong action engenders an equal and opposite strong reaction, and I shall also discuss some of the problems created by our industry's growth. These issues are rarely discussed, even (and perhaps especially) within industry circles. But I do not hesitate to do so before this distinguished forum. I have come here neither to promote our industry's interests nor to heap additional encomia on its good works. Rather, I want to offer a broad perspective from the viewpoint of one who thinks we can do a much better—and surely a much more responsible—job of serving investors than we have in the past.

By way of full disclosure, I freely acknowledge that I speak from the perspective of a unique mutual fund enterprise that was created to lead the way, to be "in the vanguard" of a new and better industry. Our very structure—based upon having mutual funds owned and controlled by their own shareholders and not upon existing as mere *products* (an unfortunate term used in our industry to denote mutual funds) of an investment adviser—shapes our focus on the primacy of the interest of the shareholder, not the interest of the adviser.

Since our inception 23 years ago, we have become the second largest firm in this burgeoning industry. Yet, ironically enough, not a single follower has appeared on the horizon. Our innovative structure has yet to be copied. Nonetheless, if this industry hardly needed (or wanted) *Vanguard* as such, I believe that it did need *a* Vanguard, a firm to offer a second and perhaps *better* way to serve investors—an alternative to the traditional structure. It's only fair, I think to warn you in advance that you'll see some of this contrarian spirit—missionary zeal, if you will—in my comments today.

The Biggest Star: The Bull Market

In this industry's rapid ascent to public acceptance and even acclaim, many stars have shone their light on us. The greatest star of them all is the most remarkable bull market in U.S. history. The longest advance in the prices of common stocks, now more than 15 years of age; the steadiest, with just a handful of brief and quickly recouped declines; and by all odds the strongest, with the Dow Jones Industrial Average rising tenfold, from less than 800 to more than 8000 (when I prepared this speech!), an astonishing rate of total return (including dividends) of 19% *per year.* I assure you that there has never been another bull market—in *anything,* as far as I know—that has approached the sheer power of this one.

Since August 1982, when the bull market began, fund industry assets have risen 17 times over, from $260 billion to $4.3 trillion, a compound annual growth rate of more than 20%. Assets of equity mutual funds alone have risen from less than $40 billion to $2.5 trillion, a starkly faster 32% growth rate—an incredible rate that doubles assets every two-and-one-half years. This growth has taken mutual funds from cottage industry to financial behemoth in just 15 years—perhaps the most powerful force in U.S. financial markets today.

Fifteen years ago, funds owned but 3% of the value of all stocks; today, funds own 22%, and, adding in other accounts supervised by fund managers, fully 33% of all stocks. Our investment accounts likely are responsible for 60% or more of all equity market transactions. Our latent ownership power has helped to encourage U.S. corporations to focus on operating efficiency, restructuring, and the creation of economic value, which in turn have contributed to unprecedented corporate earnings growth. At the same time, of course, the massive capital flows into funds has created new demand for stocks which has helped to drive stock prices to today's lofty levels, simultaneously making funds a prime beneficiary of the market boom. The great bull market, then, has been the first and brightest of the stars that have shone on this most-favored industry, as we have ridden the crest of the market wave.

Three More Stars: Taxes, Technology, and Innovation

But the bull market has by no means been our only shining star. There are at least three others. A second star, surprising as it may seem, is the Federal tax code. In 1976, it was amended to enable municipal bond funds to exist; in 1980, it was amended to enable individual investors to open tax-deferred IRAs; and in 1984, it was interpreted as enabling the establishment of tax-deferred 401(k) thrift plans. These three salutary tax changes helped cause wide shifts in individual savings preferences and brought new focus on personal saving for retirement. Mutual funds had at the ready the investment programs to meet the needs of this diverse and ever-more-knowledgeable public. Together, municipal bond funds and investor-directed savings programs account for a truly remarkable $2 trillion of fund assets today—nearly one-half of the industry total.

And we can't ignore a third star that has shone on us. The technology revolution. The computer has provided us with communications technology, transaction technology, and record-keeping technology without which today's mutual fund simply could not exist. Imagine a mutual fund without an 800 number. Without daily asset valuations for retirement plan investments. Without the ability to handle huge daily cash flows. Without seemingly instantaneous liquidity (for our investors, as well as our portfolios). Without exchanges among funds. In a real sense, technology has shaped the character and development of what we know as the modern mutual fund industry.

Finally, there is a fourth star. While we can hardly take credit for the benefits bestowed on us by the other stars, we can claim this star as our own creation. I shall call it creative innovation. This industry has not only quickly capitalized on an environment of radical change—in the stock market, in the tax code, in the technology transfiguration—but has fostered a transformation of its own. During the past 15 years, the number of mutual funds has increased from 700 to 7,000. The industry has greatly broadened its historical dependence on equities to include bonds (which have enjoyed a bull market of their own, as inflation rates have tumbled and interest rates have followed suit) and short-term investments (causing the very cream of the savings market to desert banks in favor of money market mutual funds).

At the same time, we've vastly expanded our equity fund offerings, and we now include not only funds with the industry's traditional focus on U.S. blue chip stocks, but also funds emphasizing small-cap stocks, international stocks, and stocks in particular industries. It is probably safe to say that whenever the investor marketplace has demanded a "product" (again using the industry lingo)—or whenever we have sensed a demand for one—we have promptly created it, offered it, and marketed it. "A fund for every investor, a fund for every purpose under Heaven" could serve as an accurate slogan for the modern mutual fund industry.

And we've created the "fund family" to replace "the fund" as the preferred mode of doing business. Compared to supervising perhaps a dozen funds in 1982, a major fund family now manages an astonishing array of 150 individual funds, sometimes even more. There are a score of fund families with assets at the level of $50 billion or above. These 20 industry powerhouses account for about $2.5 trillion of the industry's $4.2 trillion of assets. And, in another amazing change, the two largest firms, and eight of the top 20—together holding $1.2 trillion of assets—have taken "the road less traveled by" 15 years ago: we offer principally no-load funds—purchased directly, without sales commissions, by investors. It could well be said "that has made all the difference" in bringing Main Street to Wall Street.

The Dark Side of the Bull Market

But, even as "all that glitters is not gold," each of the four stars that have shone so brightly on mutual funds has a dark side. If a "black hole" scenario might be too strong a phrase to describe the reaction to the powerful forward action we've enjoyed in this industry, it would nonetheless be unwise to ignore the reaction potential created by the dark side of the stars that I've just described.

Let's begin with our first star, the stock market. First, with a simple question: Have fund investors shared adequately in the rewards of the great bull market? Alas, while our asset upsurge places us at the very crest of the market wave, the investment returns we have delivered to our shareholders leave us trailing in the market's wake. Compared to the annual return of 17.5% for the Standard & Poor's 500 Stock Index during the past 15 years, the average equity fund has returned far less: 14.1%. Result: $10,000 invested at year-end 1982 in an unmanaged market index would have been worth $112,000 as 1998 began; if invested in the average fund (ignoring initial sales commissions, if any) it would be worth $72,000—less than two-thirds of the unmanaged index. The typical fund investor has $40,000 less than he might have expected, a tangible manifestation of the reality that fund managers as a group have not measured up to the task at hand: they have failed to provide an excess return sufficient to overcome their heavy cost handicap of some 2% per year. It has been an expensive failure for fund shareholders.

The record is clear, then, that in the past these investment professionals have fallen well short of earning their keep. But what of the future? With fund costs now running at the highest levels in history, it would be unrealistic to expect future *relative* returns to improve very much. Nor would it seem realistic to expect that in a highly efficient market with prices set largely by fund transactions, funds owning one-third of all stocks could somehow outpace the returns of investors owning the other two-thirds.

To make matters even more difficult for the funds, long-run *absolute* returns are, at least in my view, likely to regress to the long-term mean of about 11%—and probably even below it. Why? It is much more than the simple rationale of believing that "trees don't grow to the sky." (After the incredible performance of the stock market during the past three years, I may be alone in continuing to believe that ancient aphorism!) Rather, it is that in today's stock market, corporate stocks are valued far more highly than when the great bull run began 15 years ago. Then, stocks were valued at seven times actual earnings; today valuations are at 23 times earnings. Then, stocks sold at book value; today, at four times book. Then, stocks yielded 5.5%; today, just 1.6%. Of course, Wall Street says that dividend yields don't matter any more, but I remind you that, over the past century, the dividend yield has accounted for 40% of the total return on stocks. If— *if*—that relationship were to prevail in the coming decade, stocks would return but 4% annually, a far cry indeed from the 19% annual return that this flourishing bull market has lavished on them.

The Dark Side of Taxes, Technology, and Innovation

If our stock market star may dim, what of the tax star that has shone so brightly? Ever the pragmatist, I don't expect to see further major changes in the tax code that will favor us. But I fear that the industry faces a major challenge to its far-less-than-benign neglect of the tax issue in the past. *Simply put, the fact of the matter is that fund managers in general run their portfolios without regard to tax considerations.* It is not without evidence that I suggest that, in their drive to attract tax-deferred assets—now more than one-half of industry cash inflow—funds have flatly ignored the interests of the taxable investors that constituted the traditional backbone of this industry. Fund portfolio turnover now averages some 90% per year, meaning essentially that only 10% of the stocks in a given portfolio at the start of the year remain there at the end of the year. Imagine! The performance record of mutual funds that I cited earlier offers no suggestion that such turnover enhances industry-wide returns. Indeed, with funds largely buying and selling stocks among one another, turnover cannot reasonably be expected to do so.

And while high turnover fails to enhance the normally stated *pre-tax* fund returns, it has a powerful negative impact on *after-tax* returns. Indeed, the lag of three percentage points per year in pre-tax fund returns that I have already demonstrated would have increased to more than four percentage points on an after-tax basis. As a result, more than 20% of the market's total annual return would have been sliced away, largely by fund expenses and taxes. I estimate that funds realized and distributed $150 *billion* of capital gains during 1997, which will cost taxable shareholders some $22 billion when the tax bill comes due on April 15, 1998.

In the coming year, *no matter what the stock market does,* still more realized gains are certain to come pouring out. Given the industry's casual approach to taxes, some capital gains will be short-term, taxed up to the 40% maximum on ordinary income, some at 28%, with only some—perhaps even the smallest portion—taxed at the newly lowered 20% long term rate. Yet, with this newer rate, capital gains have become more attractive relative to dividend income than at any time since World War II. Perversely, this industry seems intent "on making the least of it" by virtually ignoring the colossal benefit of deferring the realization of gains to the maximum extent possible.

And what's the problem with the computer revolution star? "The law of unintended consequences" strikes again. For all the remarkable business assets technology has given us, it has given us some considerable business liabilities. First, all of that information has seemed to bring with it powerful little wisdom. But, even as seemingly infinite information about fund records permeates the marketplace, the simple truth—that the past records of top-performing funds are rarely, if ever, repeated in the future—seems to be lost. Yet the financial section of the newspaper reports fund performance each day, and the mere punch of a computer button can bring us a Morningstar analysis of the returns, risks, portfolio characteristics of any fund we select—with statistics of unimaginable detail—all on a single page. But when investors select a fund, it is predominantly on the basis of its past performance.

And there is an even more serious problem: instant communications and fast-as-lightning transaction facilities have enabled us to effectively turn mutual funds into proxies for individual common stocks. Since the early 1980s, the average holding period for a mutual fund share has dropped from more than ten years to less than three years. Whether or not this increase in investor share turnover is engendered by the same forces that have energized the soaring turnover in mutual fund portfolios I described a moment ago, it is simply another form of what I call *casino capitalism.* And it flies in the face of intelligent investing.

I ask simply: to what avail? To what avail have we converted the finest medium for long-term investing ever devised into a device for trading on market swings, for buying and selling funds on the basis of recent performance, for giving "hot" funds an apparently cost-free entry (although it is anything but that) into the investor marketplace, often based on little more than an idea and a short-term record of uncertain provenance. Yet as an industry we too often fail to adequately inform the investing public of the risks and costs involved in our funds, and indeed actively promote, not our typical offerings—and most assuredly not our offerings with inferior performance (and *no* firm is bereft of them!)—but the hottest-performing funds we have.

And that brings us to the star of creativity, our fourth star. Its dark side is that we have turned our remarkable record of innovation away from seeking creative ways to enhance the investment results that we provide to our shareholders, and toward the rather less lofty task of bringing more assets into our fund families. The marketing of mutual funds has become highly aggressive, far too much so for an industry which I conceive of, not as a modern-day collection of Procter & Gambles, Budweisers, and Coca-Colas, hawking "consumer products" for their "franchise brands," but primarily as a trustee for other people's money. In this business, investing is becoming the poor relation of marketing. We appeal far too much (for me at least) to the desire to accumulate substantial wealth with ease, the apparent certainty of doing so through equity funds, and the ease of picking super-funds based on their past performance. *The message is becoming the medium.*

Marketing and distribution, of course, are highly expensive. So, "money is no object" seems to have become our industry's tacit watchword in the search for the holy grail of market share. Yet it is the fund *shareholder* whose money is no object, but the fund *manager* who reaps the benefits of the money spent on marketing, earning rising fees as the assets roll in. At the outset of the growth curve, some beneficial economies of scale may accrue to a fund's shareholders. Then shareholders neither gain nor lose, and the benefits of growth accrue to the manager, who enjoys rising fees without commensurately rising costs. Finally, as the fund grows to an extremely large size, fees continue to soar but asset growth may lead to excessive portfolio diversification, limited liquidity, and rising transaction costs, all negatively impacting returns to shareholders. Shareholders have paid to foster the fund's growth, yet they have suffered in return.

In part because of soaring marketing expenses, fund expense ratios have risen sharply. Fifteen years ago, the expense ratio of the average equity mutual fund was 1% of assets. Despite the enormous 65-fold (!)

growth in assets since then, today's equity fund expense ratio has increased by half again to 1.55%—although only about one-tenth of the revenues generated by funds are expended on investment advisory services. Obviously, huge economies of scale now exist in this business, but it is the fund *manager*, not the fund *shareholder*, who has been the beneficiary.

Where Do We Go from Here?

If you believe in capitalism and free markets—and I can assure you that I hold their value to be self-evident—what must happen to resolve the deeply troubling issues that I've laid before you today? The fundamental, but I think only preliminary, response must be to let the problems work themselves out in the marketplace. For most competitive industries, that is clearly the sole recourse.

If this industry is to be reshaped by its investors, by supply and demand if you will, present and potential mutual fund investors will have to become much better informed. "Trial and error" is one answer, and investors who get badly burned by a long period of underperformance, or even (and much more memorably) a short-term bear market in stocks, will not soon return to our fold. Investors buying hot funds, experimenting with market timing, and shopping and swapping funds with untoward frequency in the supermarket casinos will one day learn by painful experience that these short-term approaches have been not only unproductive, but counterproductive.

More optimistically, the promulgation of better investor information may gradually turn the tide. Investors have clearly learned that *costs matter.* In the money market fund arena, they entrust far more of their savings to the lowest cost, and therefore highest yielding, funds at the expense of the highest cost, and therefore lowest-yielding, funds. A similar trend, if one of lesser degree, is evident in the bond fund arena. And there are at least hints of a similar pattern in the stock fund arena, most notably in the increasing attention being given to market index funds, which are making their mark solely through capitalizing on the simple values of extremely low cost and broad diversification. Fostered by corporate benefits executives who are responsible for selecting funds for tax-deferred employee stock plans with assets now approaching $1 trillion, by self-motivated investors with substantial assets, by the SEC tentatively mounting "the bully pulpit" to take up the cost versus performance issue, and by the increasingly sophisticated financial media, the mantra of *costs matter* will finally take hold. But all of that will take time, and—as long as present excessive costs persist—time is not running in favor of the fund shareholder.

As investors come to "vote with their feet"—learning to favor long-term investing over short-term and low cost over high cost—fund managers will finally get the picture. A focus on long-term portfolio strategy will supplant the frenetic—and costly—trading of portfolio securities today. Funds will more clearly define their investment objectives, describe their performance standards, report far more candidly on how their results compare with their expectations. The implicit promise of equity fund managers is "we can do better" than the market—or, in this tough world in which beating a broad market index sometimes seems beyond hope—at least bettering the results of their peers with similar objectives and strategies. So managers would seem to have an obligation to describe how they'll meet that goal, and then to disclose regularly the extent to which they are meeting it.

Corporate managers have become well aware that the creation of economic value—to earn a return on invested assets in excess of the cost of capital—is a "do or die" responsibility, with the price of failure the loss of their jobs, or even their corporations. Why shouldn't mutual fund managers who fail to provide shareholder returns in excess of those provided by the stock market be subject to the same discipline? Surely it is a fair question.

And investors should demand that industry creativity turn away from costly marketing efforts and expensive media advertising. What is really the point of selling past performance that is almost surely unrepeatable? Or the value, as one senior industry marketer stated approvingly, citing perfume as analogy, of selling hope? Rather, we should be focused on better solutions to investor needs. It shouldn't take too much curiosity for an investor to learn that the shortest, simplest route to top-quartile performance is bottom-quartile expenses. And it shouldn't take much more to figure out that the taxable investors in this industry—more than half of our shareholders—are being ill-served by the baneful tax and trading cost impact of high portfolio turnover.

This all may sound both dubious to achieve and too idealistic to prevail. But, without apology for my idealism (or, given the Vanguard shareholder-owned structure I described briefly at the outset, for my vested interest), I offer a simple solution. It comes from my conviction that *strategy follows structure.* And a structure in which fund shareholders are in working control of a fund—as distinct from one in which fund advisers are in control—will lead perforce to meeting nearly every important requirement in the litany that I have just recited. Once the industry's sole focus turns to serving investors as productively as possible, some critical things happen. Funds—at least large fund families—will run themselves. They will be "mutualized," having their own officers and staff, and the huge profits earned by their external managers will be diverted to their shareholders. They won't waste money on costly marketing campaigns designed to bring in new investors at the expense of existing investors. With lower costs, they will produce higher returns and/or assume lower risks. They will improve their disclosure, and report to their shareholder-owners with greater candor. They might even see the merit of market index funds. It's quite an imposing bundle of improvements.

In preparing these remarks, I found it easy to identify with the prisoner in *The Republic.* In his "Allegory of the Cave," Plato describes men living in a cave, shackled to the same spot, eyes covered with blinders so that they can see not the fire burning behind them at a higher elevation, but only the shadows cast in front of them by the fire:

> **Then . . . one prisoner is freed from his shackles; he walks, looks toward the light, and is pained by the glare and unable to see the objects whose shadows he used to see. He comes into the sunlight, dazzled by a new vision and unable to see what he called realities only moments earlier. He returns to the dark cave, and is laughed at for his vision. But he has seen the reality of beauty and justice, and knows the idols and shadows for what they are.**

Clearly, leaving the darkness of the cave—the safety and comfort of the place one has known—is difficult, unpleasant, and challenging. But Plato's allegory is a powerful symbol of the need for change. And as mutual fund shareholders come to see the light—and realize that "light excelleth darkness," as in my citation from Ecclesiastes at the outset—and recognize the realities I have described today, they will demand a change in industry focus, a change that, in my view, can be best accomplished by a change in industry structure.

A truly *mutual* mutual fund industry would be structured precisely like every other corporate enterprise in America—management that serves solely the shareholders, and creates economic value, *or else*. I wish that I could be sure that this brave new world of mutual funds will begin to emerge during my remaining span of years. Alas, I fear not. But someday, somehow, just as 1997 inevitably rolled into 1998 two weeks ago, we will ring out the old structure for operating mutual funds, and ring in the new.

11

ECONOMICS 101: FOR MUTUAL FUND INVESTORS . . . FOR MUTUAL FUND MANAGERS

The Economic Club of Arizona
Phoenix, Arizona
April 20, 1999

*I*T'S A SPECIAL PRIVILEGE to be asked to speak to the Economic Club of Phoenix. For while this lovely city is a long way from the boundless seas that HMS *Vanguard* sailed centuries ago, it is the place we chose four years ago to develop Vanguard's first office space away from our home in Valley Forge, where I founded the firm. Given your Club's mission, I'm going to present some strong and perhaps controversial opinions about the nature of the economics of mutual funds—as they affect fund investors, and as they affect fund managers as well. As you will see, there *is* a difference. That difference has created serious flaws in the record of the mutual fund industry, flaws ignored during our era of incredible economic growth.

I've called the talk "Economics 101," for what I intend to do is give a sort of basic college survey course explaining the nature of this industry, and its remarkable acceptance. For in the wink of an eye, mutual funds have at once become:

- The investment of choice among America's families, not only the dominant way in which we invest in stocks and bonds, but the dominant way we save our cash reserves.

- The largest institutional investor in common stocks, holding (when private accounts managed by fund advisers are included) fully one-third of all U.S. equities.
- The major force in the largest stock market in the world, accounting for almost two-thirds of all trading in U.S. stocks.
- Perhaps the most cost-efficient medium through which individuals can accumulate assets, even though the general level of costs charged by mutual funds are, in my view, grossly excessive.

In all, it is quite an imposing record. And it comes in an industry that, a mere 20 years ago, looked to be in the throes of a slow and painful death.

When we think of our enormous $5½ trillion industry today, it is hard to imagine that two short decades ago, assets were less than $50 billion, less than ¹⁄₁₀₀ of today's size. In 1978, the industry was composed almost entirely of common stock funds, and in the aftermath of the 50% stock market crash in 1973–74, cash was flowing out of these stock mutual funds at a heavy rate. Steady outflows during 1974–1982 reached a cumulative total of $14 billion—a withdrawal of fully one-third of the industry's assets in mid-1974.

During those dog days, fund firms had begun, reflexively, to diversify their so-called product lines with bond funds, but there was not nearly sufficient investor interest to produce capital flows that would offset the equity fund bloodletting. Even so, hope sprang eternal in the industry's breast. I should know, for at the very bottom of the bear market, an odd series of events conspired to make September 24, 1974, the time for me to start The Vanguard Group, a new mutual fund organization with a unique mission. Our economics, as I'll explain later, were different from the economics of our peers.

Some 265 years ago, Alexander Pope warned mankind that, "hope springs eternal in the human breast. Man never *is*, but always *to be* blessed." Our industry, however, defied his warning, and was indeed blessed by opportunity to create a new kind of fund, designed to capitalize on a peculiar inefficiency of the U.S. savings market. In an era of high (10% to 15%) short-term interest rates, the nation's savings institutions were limited by Federal Reserve regulations to paying but 5¼%.

The Leopard Changes Its Spots

The new mutual fund—the money market fund—owned short-term U.S. Treasury bills, certificates of deposit, and commercial paper, money market investments paying, of all things, money market rates, rates that were far higher than the regulated institutions could pay. Almost overnight, our industry, soon dominated by cash management funds, had changed its spots.

Assets still trickling out of stock funds were dwarfed by staggering inflows into money market funds. By the end of 1982, the mutual fund industry leopard, only shortly before spotted almost entirely with stock funds, was now spotted largely with money market funds. Measured by total dollars invested, in 1982 fully 76% of our leopard's spots represented the assets of money market funds, 8% bond funds, and barely 16% the stock fund segment that had comprised 90% of the spots only five years earlier. An amazing transformation! In less than a decade, industry assets had soared to $265 billion—a near eightfold increase from their 1974 low of $36 billion. We were blessed manyfold by the money market fund, for our industry's asset base—now with stock funds, bond funds, *and* money funds, essentially every form of liquid investment—became a virtual Rock of Gibraltar.

Perversely enough, then, just as equity funds touched their *smallest-* ever all-time share of the fund industry, the *biggest* bull market in history began. In August 1982, interest rates began to tumble from their all-time highs of 12% to 15% reached shortly before, falling from 12% to 9% in August alone. Bond prices soared, with stock prices not far behind. Over the following 16 years, to this very day, both bull markets have remained substantially intact, providing the best returns in the recorded history. Since 1982, stock fund assets have grown 50-fold, bond fund assets 40-fold, and even money market fund assets have grown sixfold from this huge base at the outset. Today, industry assets approach $6 trillion, and our leopard is covered 55% with stock spots, 18% bond spots, and 27% cash management spots. "Something for everyone" is a fair characterization of what the mutual fund industry is now offering investors.

The fund industry's share of savings flows has grown from nominal levels to levels that are now truly staggering. Last year, net additions to the savings of American families totaled $406 billion. Some $401 billion—nearly 99% of this huge amount—was represented by cash flows into stock, bond, and cash funds. Imagine that! A quarter century ago, the fund share was only slightly above 0.5%—$1 billion of $180 billion. Truly, we are seeing a stampede into mutual funds.

And total industry flows seem immune to fluctuations in the markets. Stock prices soar (and sometimes even drop), interest rates move bond prices up and down and alter yields on savings, but the industry's cash flows remain a pattern of steady growth: $10 billion a month in 1994, $20 billion in 1995, $30 billion in 1996–97, $40 billion in 1998. But yes, fund investors are market-sensitive to a fault; the stock fund portion can change radically. Stock fund flow, $20 billion a month before last summer's brief bear market, has tumbled $2 billion monthly since then—but money market and bond funds have consistently made up the shortfall.

It is fair to say that, for the moment at least, the mutual fund industry, with its diverse "product line" of stock, bond, and money funds, is meeting the perceived needs of America's investors and savers alike. Surely, our industry's position must be the envy of our rivals in the fields of insurance, savings, and even stock brokerage, to say nothing of the often-troubled financial institutions around the globe. Industry leaders, so often given—unwisely—to bragging, can fairly raise their arms and give the "V" symbol, and announce, as James Cameron, producer and director of *Titanic* did at Hollywood's Academy Award ceremony a year ago, "I'm the king of the world."

I do not wish to be included among the braggarts. Yes, it would be easy to say that our extraordinary history over the past two decades has brought mutual funds to the point at which we are, as it were, *bulletproof*. But I hardly need tell the audience of economic club enthusiasts that nothing is quite so simple. In this rapidly changing world, it is fair to say that *nothing* is bulletproof. Indeed, with our industry's huge size have come potential flaws—and they are major flaws—concealed by the great dual bull markets in stocks and bonds, their impact almost unnoticed so far. But they do not, I assure you, escape the notice of this grizzled veteran of the mutual fund wars, who last December entered his 50th year of involvement with mutual funds. I'm now going to discuss those flaws and the major challenges they have created for our industry.

The Flaw of Past Performance

First, the bull markets have served to conceal our performance inadequacies. If I may be permitted to mix a metaphor, while we have ridden the crest of the two bull market waves in one respect, we have trailed—badly—in their wake in another, and far more vital, respect. And it is a major shortcoming. In a stock market with record annual returns averaging 18.6% annually, since the bull market began in

1982, our industry's stock funds have earned an annual return averaging just 15.8% for their investors, an *annual* shortfall of 15%! Final result of $10,000 invested at the outset: stock market, $167,000; average stock fund: $113,000. With 85% of the *annual* return of the market, the *total capital* accumulated by the fund investor amounted to but 65% of the capital that would have been accumulated had he simply *owned the market.*

The bond fund story is little different: annual return of bond funds 9.1%, annual return of bond market 10.9%. Result: bond funds provided 83% of the market *annual* return, but only 76% of the market's accumulation during the full period. In both cases, the aggregate of annual shortfalls grows geometrically over time, a sort of "tyranny of compounding." Over the long term, seemingly small annual lags in annual return grow to become yawning gaps in capital accumulation. "Little things mean a lot." This failure to provide our shareholders with returns that can keep pace with the financial markets in which we invest is our first major flaw.

The Flaw of High Fund Costs

Our second flaw, rarely recognized, is that the high cost of investing in funds is principally—indeed overwhelmingly—the cause of this performance lag. The stock fund annual shortfall of 2.8% closely parallels the all-in costs of 2%-plus for equity funds—expense ratios that averaged some 1.3% and portfolio transaction costs of perhaps 1% annually during the period. (These cost and performance figures, moreover, ignore fund sales charges, costs which are paid by about two-thirds of fund investors.) In bond funds, the performance lag of 1.8% closely parallels all-in bond fund costs of 1.2%—about 1.0% expenses and 0.2% trading costs. (Again, sales charges would increase the fund shortfall.)

To make matters worse, fund expense ratios have steadily risen during the period. For stock funds, from about 1.1% to 1.6% or nearly 50%. For bond funds, from 0.9% to 1.1%, more than 20%. (Money fund ratios, however, declined from 0.7% to 0.6%.) These expense ratio increases, coming in the face of the quantum increase in fund assets from $265 billion in 1982 to $5½ trillion today, have raised industry revenues from about $2 billion annually to $60 billion annually (taking into account that fee rates tend to decline slightly for funds that attain large asset size). Clearly, this is a great business for *the fund managers.* The costs of fund managers have not risen nearly so fast as their revenues. Yet they have failed to adequately share the enormous economies of scale in fund management with their fund shareholders. They have effectively turned economies of operation into outright diseconomies in the costs that investors pay. High costs, then, represent our industry's second major flaw.

"Follow the Money"

I freely acknowledge that it costs money to operate a mutual fund. Let's examine how much. This year, on the operating side, the aggregate expenses paid by fund investors to fund managers this year will total about $50 billion—50 *billion* dollars. Where does this money go? We don't know exactly, but it looks to me that about one-tenth of that amount—up to $5 billion—is spent on portfolio management and investment research. (However vain the search for market-beating returns, that's presumably what investors *expect* their money to be used for.) About $8 billion of that total is spent on marketing fund shares; that is, on the effort to bring more money into the funds. (Of course, this expenditure adds *nothing whatsoever* to the funds' returns; it *reduces* them by the amount of the expenditure . . . perhaps by even more, but that's another story.) About $17 billion, I think, is spent on services to fund shareholders, which is fine as far as it goes, although some of these "services" are thinly disguised marketing efforts; others are actually counterproductive for investors. That comes to a total of $30 billion.

But the total management fees and operating expenses paid by fund shareholders are actually $50 billion. Where, you may ask, is the other $20 billion? According to my rough estimates, $20 billion represents the aggregate pre-tax profit earned by the fund management companies—a rather handsome reward, considering the failure of fund managers to provide investors with the full returns earned by the market. By now the fundamental economics of the fund business itself are apparent. If we assume that the $5 billion spent on portfolio research and management is reasonable; that $2 billion could be spent, however counterproductively, on marketing; and that shareholder service expenses could be stripped down to say, $13 billion; then a total of $20 billion should be sufficient to operate this industry. Even if we conceded that managers are entitled to, say, $5 billion a year in profits, hardly an insubstantial sum, that would represent an annual savings to investors of $25 billion.

And now, a caution: I want to be clear that these figures should be considered only as informed estimates. The industry does not disclose such data, nor do I expect it to be voluntarily disclosed in the foreseeable future. But, in an environment of enlightened full disclosure, it *ought* to be disclosed. Indeed, I have recommended to the U.S. Securities and Exchange Commission that it undertake an economic study of the industry so that, one day, soon I hope, we shall all have a public awareness of, not good estimates of, the profitability of industry managers, but hard facts. The sunlight of full cost disclosure is the best remedy for awakening the awareness of where the shareholders' $50 billion is being spent. It's high time, as was said in the Watergate scandal years ago, to "follow the money."

The Flaw of Future Returns

Our third flaw comes in the fact that our two great bull markets seem unlikely to clone themselves in the next 16 years. The U.S. stock market began this bull run with a dividend yield of 6.2% and a price-earnings ratio of 7.7 times. Today, the yield is 1.3%, the price earnings-ratio 30 times. It is this increase in the price-earnings multiple—not in the fundamental factors of dividend yields and earnings growth—that has largely driven the bull market. For example, the Standard and Poor's 500 Index of stock prices was at 120 when the bull market began. It now reposes at 1300. But had the P/E ratio *remained* at 7.7 times, the Index would now repose, not at 1300, but at 320, almost 1000 points lower. *But in the long run, it is dividend yields and earnings growth that are the fundamental driver of stock returns.*

Now let's apply some elementary economics to the stock market. If we assume that today's 1.3% dividend yield is accompanied by future earnings growth of 8% (the long-term earnings growth rate is 6%), future stock returns based solely on our dividend yields and earnings growth would be 9.3%. Now let's make three different assumptions: (1) If today's price-earnings ratio valuation remains at 30 times a decade hence, this 9.3% would be the exact stock market return for the next decade. (2) If the price-earnings ratio fell to 18 times, the annual return on stocks would be but 4.3%. (3) If a future return of

16% were to be achieved, a price-earnings ratio of 57 times in 2009 would be required. I'd simply rule out #3. It seems inconceivable to me that a further substantial upward revaluation in multiples lies before us. So, I'd guess the best case for the future would rest between #1 and #2. Perhaps future stock market returns might lie in a 5% to 10% range. Because of their heavy operating and trading costs, then, equity *funds* would return as little as 2½% to 7½% over the next decade.

In the bond market, the case for lower future returns seems even clearer. The bond market began this great run in August 1982 with an 11% yield on long-term Treasury bonds, and subsequently delivered an average return of 10.9% annually. With a yield below 6% today, their most likely future return over the next decade would be, well, 6%. It would be unlikely, I think, for returns over the next decade to stray far outside a range of 4½% to 7½%. Future returns on bonds, really, cannot match those of the past 16 years—or come even close.

The high portion of fund returns confiscated by fund managers in our bull market era would rise even higher in markets in which returns were lower. For unit costs (the expenses paid on each dollar invested by shareholders)—are collected by managers as a percentage of *assets,* so, as market returns recede, the same asset charges consume a higher percentage of *return.* So, if we anticipate future returns in the 7½% range for common stocks and all-in stock fund costs of 2½% (due to ever-rising fund expenses), stock fund costs would consume, not 15% of the market's annual return as in the past, but fully 33%. Applied to a future bond market return of 6%, costs of 1.1% would result in bond funds providing, not 85% of the market's return, as in the past, but 81%. Under these conditions, fund investors would at last begin to recognize the extraordinarily baneful role that excessive fund costs play in the economics of mutual fund investing. Hidden in the current bull market, fund costs would truly be devastating in a less salubrious environment. When future market returns are lower, fund costs will have a far higher negative impact on investor returns, and that is the industry's third flaw.

The Flaw of Great Success

And now this fourth flaw: Fund industry growth. There is no longer any hope whatsoever that mutual funds can overcome the odds and beat the market in such a manner as to overcome their high cost handicap by a meaningful margin. That is because the funds are simply too large. Our industry's thesis of success has created its own antithesis. *The lore is wrong:* The truth is that "nothing *fails* like success." As Warren Buffett puts it, "a fat wallet is the enemy of performance superiority." Mutual fund managers, including the private accounts they oversee, now control one-third of America's $13 trillion of equities.

Even if it were arguable that the managers holding $4 trillion plus of stocks in our highly efficient markets could somehow, by dint of some superior skill, outpace the other professional and public investors holding the remaining $9 trillion by an amount sufficient to overcome the awesome burden of their heavy expenses, that hope would be quickly dashed by the fact that, with their stupefyingly high portfolio turnover rates—85% in 1997 alone, nearly twice the market's turnover—funds now account for almost two-thirds of all trading. The managers are clearly trading largely with one another, inevitably leaving fund investors as a group in a neutral position *before costs.* Relative to the stock market (and the bond and money markets, too) funds are playing a zero-sum game *before* management and trading costs, but a loser's game *after* the croupiers rake off their generous share of the wagers.

Even before funds grew to their current gargantuan presence in the market, funds had been unable to "beat the house"—the market. Indeed, way back in 1975, when I recommended to our directors that Vanguard form the first stock market index mutual fund, I presented data showing that over the previous 25 years, managed funds had experienced an annual shortfall of about 1½% to the S&P 500 Index. (The shortfall was smaller because fund costs were lower then.) Now, with a half-century of evidence of index superiority, it is high time for investment managers, brokers and financial planners, industry analysts, and the financial media to disavow, once and for all, the notion that "beating the market" is a realistic objective for the mutual fund industry.

The Industry Responds . . . Sort of . . . on Fund Performance

So far, the mutual fund industry has found little, if any, need to respond to the issues manifested in these four crucial flaws. The industry itself takes no position on the appropriate financial market indexes for comparing the performance of funds. When the SEC in

1993 required fund annual reports to include comparison with appropriate annualized market indexes—the Standard & Poor's 500 Stock Index, the Wilshire 5000 Equity Index of the *total* stock market, or the Lehman Aggregate Bond Index (covering the total investment-grade bond market), for example—the industry complained, but grudgingly complied, although most funds find few reasons to highlight the comparison and lots of reasons to bury it deep in the annual report. And, despite the SEC requirement to do so, substantive comments on the reasons a fund's return falls short (mostly) or exceeds (rarely) the return of the index are conspicuous by their absence.

But the fact is that even the most casual economic analysis suggests that if market indexes are almost impossible for managers to beat, the industry response should be to offer index funds. Why accept 85% or less of the market's annual return when an index fund can virtually guarantee 98%–99%? Indeed, long before he became a television celebrity, Fidelity's Peter Lynch was willing to concede, that "most investors would be better off in an index fund." And a former fund chairman has publicly said that investors ought to realize that "mutual funds can *never* beat the market" (italics added). Other fund executives, however, have a different view. One recently brushed aside the index comparison by scoffing, as quoted in *Money* magazine, "it's [the S&P 500 Index] a large-cap growth fund," and defending his firm's managed funds by saying that they are "like everybody else. Our managed funds have done well over the long term but less well in recent years."

Well, there are brute facts that can be brought to bear when statements like these are made. Fact 1: The S&P 500 Index is *not* a large-cap growth fund. A large-cap fund, yes, but, by common consensus, structured to include 50% growth stocks and 50% *value* stocks. Fact 2: As to "recent years," the return of that executive's flagship growth fund trailed the S&P 500 by a cumulative total of 84 percentage points (+159% vs. +243% for the Index) during 1994–98. I guess "less well" is an acceptable, if rather generous, description of that shortfall. Fact 3. "Over the long term," the annual return of this same flagship growth fund trailed the S&P 500 by 3 percentage points (+12% vs. +15%), meaning that $10,000 invested in the growth fund 25 years ago would presently be worth $160,000 vs. $324,000 for the same investment in the Index. That result surely pushes the definition of "done well" to some sort of world-class limit. People who live in glass houses, I think, shouldn't throw stones.

The Industry Response on Costs

There is no question that since 1980 the annual expense ratio of the average equity fund has risen by 40%—from 1.10% to 1.57% of fund assets. It has been documented, well, everywhere. But, the industry takes the position that the cost of fund *ownership* is declining. Or that's what the industry's Investment Company Institute *says*. What it *means* is that, according to its rather tortured and convoluted methodology, the cost of *purchasing* funds has, in fact, declined, from 2.25% annually in 1980 to 1.49% in 1997. The industry reaches this conclusion by including sales charges *plus* expense ratios, and then *weights the results by the sales volume of each fund each year.* High-cost funds that don't sell, in short, don't count. Virtually ignored in the ICI methodology, the managers of high-cost funds prosper and their shareholders suffer accordingly.

Given the dynamic combination of (a) the increasing importance of no-load funds (sold without commissions); (b) the rapid growth of low-cost market index funds; and (c) the remarkable rise in market share of the industry's sole *mutual* mutual fund complex—the unique structure adopted by a firm that operates its funds on an "at cost" basis (you'll recognize that firm as Vanguard)—the industry's claim, while rather pushy, may well even be valid, as far as it goes. However, it doesn't go nearly far enough. It ignores the fact that the heavy cost of portfolio transactions is a *major* "cost of fund ownership" which probably adds—the industry is tight-lipped on this subject—up to a full percentage point to fund costs, raising the total annual cost to as much as 2½%.

Even to the extent that the industry's overly generous appraisal of the data, along with its somewhat specious series of definitions, can be regarded as valid, however, what the data really show is that, quoting from the independent Morningstar Mutual Funds analysis, "the drop has been driven by investors, not by shareholder-friendly mutual fund companies," and that a few fund families "deserve credit for keeping their expenses down, but one shouldn't credit the entire industry for the virtues of a few—and for the diligence of investors in seeking them out." In any event, there's not a lot of point in arguing over the difference. The industry's 1.49% figure is hardly different from the 1.57% average expense ratio that is, I believe, a realistic figure.

The Industry Response on Price Competition

Finally, the issue comes down to the sharing of the economies of scale between fund managers and fund owners. The managers have grabbed the lion's share—that is, to be clear, *almost all*—of these economies. For this industry prices its wares at what the traffic will bear, not at what is fair to investors. Price competition—at least, competition to *reduce* prices (there is plenty of competition to *increase* prices)—is conspicuous by its absence in this mutual fund industry. To say the very least, the industry disagrees with that conclusion. The official position of the ICI: "Let there be no doubt in anyone's mind—mutual funds compete vigorously, based on price."

Why, then do fund expense ratios remain so stubbornly high? Because they are virtually invisible, lost in the shuffle of fund performance during the greatest bull markets in all history. How many investors are aware that the gap between stock market returns and average equity fund returns have cost investors 35% of their capital potential during the bull market? How many are aware that the huge gap is explained largely by fund costs? How many investors realize that it is their market intermediaries—fund managers, promoters, and brokers—who rake in those revenues? While the fund shareholders put up 100% of the initial capital when they invest, and then assume 100% of the market risk, they receive only 65% of the stock market's long-run return. It is our capital market croupiers who, without providing *any* of the capital or assuming *any* of the risk, rake in the remaining 35% of the return. These economics hardly represent capitalism's finest hour.

Is There "Vigorous Price Competition"?

If there is vigorous price competition, how can the industry explain the fact—buried deep (and without comment) in the Investment Company Institute analysis of the costs of fund "ownership"—that the *lowest cost* 10% of funds have raised their expenses from 0.71% to 0.90% per year? A 27% cost increase.[1] (In fairness, the ICI report also calculated that the high-cost 10% of funds did experience a modest

---

1. Given that Vanguard dominates the low-cost universe—and that our expense ratios have *declined* by 53% since 1980—I would estimate that the other "low cost" funds in the ICI survey raised expenses by as much as 40%.

9% decline in cost, from a confiscatory 3.45% to a marginally less confiscatory 3.15%. One wonders what the justification for those funds
may be!) Again, if there is price competition, how can the industry
possibly explain how the industry's *sole* VLCP ("very low cost
provider," if you will) has, in the past year, accounted for an eye-
popping 90% of the cash flow into direct-marketed (no-load) stock
and bond funds . . . without significant competitive response. (That's
right: Vanguard cash flow, $49 billion; other direct marketers $5 billion.) In what other industry could a relative upstart capture a 90%
market share and not have a single competitor imitate its strategy?
How one can equate this picture with the allegation that mutual funds
compete vigorously based on price is beyond my comprehension.

What would real price competition look like? The answer is as simple as it is obvious. Vanguard's philosophy is based on long-term
investing at low cost. Competitors would have to plunge enthusiastically into the index fund fray. (A "kicking and screaming" entry won't
do the job.) They would have to cut their management fees and the
portfolio turnover of their managed stock funds. They would have to
slash fees and raise the portfolio quality of their bond funds. These
changes would make money for their *investors*. But it would slash
profits for their *managers* and *their* shareholders. The simple economic truth is this: There is simply *no* increase in market share that
would be adequate to maintain the managers' present awesome levels
of profitability. As long as today's awesome level of profitability is priority number one for the managers, fund shareholders will pay the
price, and industry expense ratios will edge ever upward.

The fact is that price competition can *not* be proven by the admitted fact that one VLCP—Vanguard—exists in this industry. (Does
the existence of Savings Bank Life Insurance prove that the life
insurance industry is price competitive?) Since the low prices established by that single competitor are substantially ignored by other
fund firms, there can hardly be said to be "vigorous competition."
Indeed such an allegation flies in the face of hornbook economics:
*Price competition is defined, not by the behavior of consumers, but by
the behavior of producers.*

Solutions: Unclear

If the aggressive entrepreneurship of fund managers, rather than
fiduciary trusteeship, is the force that controls competition in the

mutual fund industry—*and believe me, it is*—and if these managers, with their own management company shareholders to please before they please their fund shareholders, make more profits by relinquishing market share in favor of maintaining and increasing prices—*as they do*—how will the mutual fund industry *ever* give its shareholders the fair shake that they deserve?

So far, classical economics—the relationship between supply, demand, and price—shows but faint signs of being the agent of change. Not *no* sign, for the marketplace is demanding index funds; a few other firms are adopting index-like strategies (albeit at index-plus prices); at least *one* other bond fund manager with relatively low fees is building large assets; and, *mirabile dictu,* the hugely respected TIAA-CREF organization is adding low-cost mutual funds to its fixed—and equity—annuity base. May they flourish! Vanguard needs some high-quality, low-price competitors to hone our own competitive edge.

But if competition in the marketplace shows little sign of supplanting the serious, performance-penalizing economics of the financial markets for fund investors, there is another factor. The law of the land—The Investment Company Act of 1940—clearly intended to protect fund shareholders from the failure of competition to give them a fair shake. The Act doesn't even *hint* at allowing managers to charge what traffic will bear. Rather, it imposes on *mutual fund directors* the duty to place the interests of shareholders ahead of the interests of advisers. The SEC is evaluating whether independent directors are doing their job. Section 4 of my new book, *Common Sense on Mutual Funds* will, I hope, provide the Commission with important information. (No less an investment icon that Warren Buffett has recommended, in writing, that section of the book to the SEC.) The House of Representatives has held hearings on "improving price competition," and while the industry designees espoused the party line, at least one university professor and "The Motley Fool" were allowed to speak. And speak they did, bless them, endorsing my own iconoclastic views.

There is life, then, and there is hope, for fund shareholders. By building public awareness with groups like this one, and by writing another book—that, while primarily designed to help fund owners become more successful investors, also takes aim at improving industry values and structure—I'm trying my best to do my part.

"*Show Me the Money*"

This economic analysis of the fund industry I've presented today has, I fear, been a bit didactic and tedious, to say nothing of disillusioning, given the industry's remarkable growth over the past two decades. But I hope that my analysis has clearly revealed some of the important economic realities of investing, reflected both in the chinks in the armor of a potent industry and in the unlikelihood that this bull market is destined to last forever. I've been transfixed by the economics of this industry for nearly 50 years now—I began to write my senior thesis, entitled "The Economic Role of the Investment Company," at Princeton University in December 1949—but I find these economics more interesting today than ever before, and certainly more challenging.

But never forget that the most important economic role of the mutual fund industry is to make it possible for investors—large and small, knowledgeable and naïve alike—to reach their financial goals in the most advantageous way possible, under the best terms, provisions, and, above all, costs. Yes, costs matter. And they'll matter even more when the financial markets at last revert to more normal returns, as seems to me inevitable. Two years ago, in a major mutual fund article, *Newsweek* magazine laid down a good rule for investors to consider in their mutual funds investments: "Your mantra as a low-cost investor: *Show me the money.*" *Your* money is at stake and it is high time you demanded it. Show me the money? Yes! And, since time is money, and compounding entails both magic and tyranny, the sooner investors recognize this simple fact, the better.

12

HONING THE COMPETITIVE EDGE IN MUTUAL FUNDS

The Smithsonian Forum
Washington, D.C.
March 23, 1999

*I*N A RECENT ARTICLE, *Forbes* magazine raised the question of the competitive edge in the mutual fund industry, beginning with these words: "How common is it for a relatively unadvertised brand without any mass sales force to be a top name in a mass marketed industry?" *Forbes'* answer: "Freakish . . . unusual . . . very unusual . . . maybe even unique." So why has that very situation happened in the mutual fund industry? Again, *Forbes'* answer: "Maybe that strange business called Vanguard isn't a business at all. It's a religion."

Well, as you can imagine, these words—though far more objective observers than I will have to judge their accuracy—provide considerable reaffirmation to the faith that Vanguard's founder has had in our mission since I started the firm on September 24, 1974, just short of a quarter century ago. But the objective facts surely support Vanguard's rise to industry leadership. Beginning as an also-ran with $1 billion-plus in assets, our firm has grown to become the second largest mutual fund firm in the world. We now manage $460 billion of assets, now growing by about $6 billion *per month* of net cash inflow.

The 30% annual growth rate that we have enjoyed during our history is the highest of any firm in our industry, and our competitive edge has enabled us to move from a rank of #12 in our industry to #2 today. Our market share of assets among directly marketed U.S. funds (those sold without sales charges) has grown from 8% to 28%, and our market share of *net cash flow* has grown from zero (!) to 60%. In other words, six out of every ten dollars now flowing into no-load mutual funds are invested in Vanguard funds. It may surprise you—it surely surprises even me!—that this substantial market share is being earned by a firm whose marketing philosophy is based on these two basic rules I set out early in our history: (1) Market share is a measure, not an objective; (2) market share must be earned, not bought.

We honor these two rules. Yet Vanguard's market share is rising. Why? I can only presume it is rising because we are earning the confidence of mutual fund investors by providing them with superior returns. Indeed, the very same issue of *Forbes* that described Vanguard in such generous terms suggests that is the case. In the magazine's regular listing of "Best Buys in Mutual Funds," fully 30 of 86 funds—more than one-third—were Vanguard Funds. The next six fund firms *together* had but 29 "Best Buys," one less than the Vanguard total. The magazine's selections tell us something important about Vanguard's investment philosophy: Our stock market index funds constitute one-half of the "best buy" index funds (2 of 4), our bond funds almost one-half of the "best buy" bond funds (18 of 41), and our actively managed stock funds about one-fourth of the "best buy" stock funds (10 of 42). Clearly, *Forbes* sees Vanguard's index and bond funds as our principal strengths. And so our market share suggests. We enjoy more than 70% of industry cash flows in each of these sectors.

Index Funds and Managed Funds

It is in the index and bond fund arenas that cost plays the principal role in determining investment success. Index funds invest in a list of stocks determined by a stock market index; for example, all 500 stocks in the Standard & Poor's 500 Composite Stock Price Index, weighted according to their market capitalizations. So, the difference between the market index return and the index fund return is determined largely by the expense ratio of the index fund. Result: a low-cost index fund produces 98% to 99% of the return earned by the market index. For example, in a market with a 12% annual return, an index fund with a cost of 0.2% per year should provide a return of 11.8%, or 98.4% of the market return.

As it happens, few—*very* few—actively managed stock funds perform with such effectiveness. In fact, over the past 15 years, only 12 of the 289 stock mutual funds in business throughout the period— one in 24—outpaced the return of the Standard & Poor's 500 Index.

And only two did so by a statistically significant margin (that is, their annual margins of advantage were reasonably stable). As a result, despite the fact that relatively few fund organizations offer index funds, such funds now claim more than 60% of all of the cash flowing into equity mutual funds during recent months. It is not that index funds are so *good*—they have not beaten, and never will beat, the market—but that most mutual funds are *not* very good. I recently read an apt phrase about the Pulitzer Prize for fiction: "It takes dead aim on mediocrity, and almost never misses." So too the same thing might be said about mutual funds. Except, of course, that "mediocrity" means, roughly stated, "neither good nor bad," and this industry's record relative to the market has to be characterized as . . . well, I really don't need to characterize the record. Let the figures speak for themselves.

What the figures tell us is that, during the past 15 years, the S&P 500 Index has earned an annual rate of return of 17.9% per year. The average equity fund (including only those that survived the period, and eliminating those poorer performers that did not) provided a return of 13.7%. This represents a shortfall of 4.2 percentage points per year. In fairness, however, the S&P 500 Index is dominated by giant corporations with huge market capitalizations, which fared considerably better than mid-size and small stocks during the period. The mutual fund industry has an investment profile more akin to the profile of the Wilshire 5000 Equity Index, which represents substantially the *entire* U.S. stock market. The return of the Wilshire 5000 averaged 16.7% annually during the past 15 years, so the industry shortfall was a smaller, but a still impressive (in its own perverse way) 3.0 percentage points per year. Net result: funds delivered just 82% of the return earned by the total U.S. stock market—when 98%-plus was there for the taking for investors, by the simple expedient of owning a low cost, all-market index, mutual fund.

The Powerful Relationship between Costs and Returns

But the decision as to whether to characterize the industry's record as mediocre—"neither good nor bad"—shouldn't end there. For when these returns are totaled up for an investor who put $10,000 to work at the beginning of the 15-year period, the fund investment (even ignoring sales charges that must be paid at the outset to purchase shares of most managed funds) would have grown to $68,600, while a similar investment in the market would have grown to $101,400. The capital appreciation earned on the $10,000 invested by the fund buyer, through the magic of compounding—or was it the tyranny of compounding?—represented only 64% (not 82%) of the accumulated appreciation of the investment in the stock market. The industry, as far as I know, has not attempted to characterize the outcome of its labors. But I believe that nearly all investors would characterize it, not as "mediocre," but as "bad."

The severe shortfall of equity mutual funds to the stock market is easily explained. It arises largely from the (I would argue, excessively high) costs incurred by fund managers. As a group, these managers, it turns out, have stock-picking skills that are about average, not in any demonstrable way superior to the man on the street, nor, for that matter, to throwing darts randomly at a wall of stock listings. With average skills, fund managers generate average returns before costs, and then lose to the market by the amount of their costs. (Obviously, all investors as a group *must* do precisely the same thing.) During the past 15 years, the average fund has had an annual operating expense ratio of about 1.3% (it's even higher now), and incurred portfolio transaction costs that can be fairly estimated at perhaps another 1.0%, bringing the total cost of doing business to 2.3%, or nearly 80% of the 3.0 percentage point shortfall. (The remainder is attributable largely to fund holdings of cash reserves, with a consequent loss of market appreciation on that portion of equity fund assets.)

The issue of mutual fund cost applies, too, in bond funds. Last year, for example, the average general bond mutual fund provided a return of 7.5%, compared to 8.7% for the Lehman Aggregate Bond Index, which is of roughly comparable quality and maturity. That difference of 1.2 percentage points was largely caused by the all-in (expense ratio and turnover) costs of 1.1% annually for the average bond fund. Result: the 1998 *annual* return of the typical bond fund investor was 86% of the return of the bond market. What if we assume that these returns were to prevail over the next 15 years? (Given the 6% +/– level of interest rates today, that assumption would be optimistic.) The *cumulative* appreciation earned by the investor who put $10,000 to work at the start of the 15-year period would be just 79% of the appreciation (including reinvested interest income) earned by the same investment in the bond market.

For money market funds, the same fundamental things in life apply as time goes by. It is in money market funds of course, that the causal nexus between cost and return should be most obvious and most immediate. It is. After all, how could one expect *any* manager—limited as he must be to investing 100% of assets at all times in U.S. Treasury bills and top-quality bank CDs and commercial paper, all with average maturities of less than 60 or 70 days—to find substantial extra value hidden deeply within these highly efficient markets that are dominated by professional investors? Or to out-guess Federal Reserve Chairman Greenspan as to whether short-term rates will rise or fall?

Well, even if it *could* conceivably happen, it *hasn't* happened. Over the past 15 years, each one of the 73 money market funds in business throughout the period has earned a return of about 6.7% per year before costs. After costs, which averaged 0.7%, the average net return was 6.0%. But the *net* returns of the individual funds ranged from 5.3% (gross return of 6.7% less expenses of 1.4%) to 6.4% (gross return of 6.7%, less expenses of 0.3%). *Cost* was all that truly mattered. Compounded over 15 years, $10,000 grew to $23,900 in the average fund, compared to $26,400 in the money market itself. Net result: Money funds earned 89% of the money market's annual return, and 85% of the cumulative appreciation.

Vanguard vs. the Competition

So, whether we evaluate stock funds, bond funds, or money market funds, the record is clear: Cost is the culprit. And here is where a powerful part of Vanguard's competitive edge comes into play. From the figures that I have presented, it is easy to see how important it is to maintain the *lowest possible level* of operating expenses so that the fund investor receives the *highest possible proportion* of market returns. And Vanguard's unique structure—without parallel in the industry—gives it not only the *willingness*, but the *desire*, to maintain the lowest possible level of expenses, and the *ability* to attain that goal.

Other mutual fund organizations lack the willingness and desire, and the ability as well. Why? Because they are operated by external organizations, privately held management companies which seek to earn high returns for fund investors, to be sure, but seek at the same time to earn the highest possible returns for themselves. Some of these companies are publicly held, in which case their shares are held by investors who own their shares for the same reason that investors own Microsoft or General Motors: To make money for themselves.

These public investors, as compared to the fund managers, have little reason to be much concerned about the earnings of the investors in the *funds* the company manages. This conflict of interest between fund shareholders and fund advisers lies in the very *structure* of the mutual fund industry. And with the managers controlling *both* fund affairs *and* management company affairs, there is a powerful tendency, borne out by the figures you have seen today, for managers to resolve this conflict in their own favor.

Now let's sum up where we are. *It is clear that, in the long run, investment success has been based on the apportionment of market returns between fund investors on the one hand and investment managers on the other hand.* What would happen in a mutual fund structure in which that conflict was resolved entirely in favor of the fund shareholders? This was the nature of what I called *the Vanguard experiment* when it began a quarter century ago. Rather than being structured like other fund organizations—operated by an externally owned manager—the Vanguard Funds literally *own* The Vanguard Group, our management company, and operate it under a joint cost-sharing agreement with the Funds. We operate at cost, and the Funds control how much we spend on administration, on marketing, and on investment management. Net result: our operating costs average about 0.25% of assets annually vs. about 1.25% for the average mutual fund (including stock, bond, and money market funds). Savings: 1.0% per year. That may not sound like much, but 1% of $460 billion dollars is $4.6 billion—and *per year,* at that—representing a tangible and material enhancement of the investment returns our shareholders receive. Less of the market return to managers, more to investors.

It's More Than the Expense Ratio

I don't want to leave you with the thought that the expense ratio advantage of an internally owned fund management organization is the only advantage of a structure that, in effect, creates *mutual* mutual funds. From this structural difference, a whole new system of corporate values can flourish. Of course, the key advantage is that the truly mutual firm, without an incentive to earn highly superior returns on the capital of external entrepreneurs or profit-seeking public investors, is in business solely to create superior returns for its fund shareholders. The entire corporate strategy of such a firm is shaped by its structure. "Strategy follows structure," as it were. For example:

- **Lower prices.** There is a big difference between cost-based pricing and charging investors the highest prices that traffic will bear.
- **Extra emphasis on high-quality investor services.** A truly mutual enterprise treats its fund clients as its owners, because they *are* its owners.
- **Reduced tolerance for risk.** If a mutually oriented fund can hold risk constant with its peers, and provide extra return simply by virtue of its lower cost, why would it seek extra return by assuming extra risk? It need not. It does not. (This advantage is especially critical in bond and money market funds.)
- **Minimal marketing expenditures.** The enormous marketing budgets that permeate this industry cost fund *investors* hundreds of millions of dollars each year, but benefit only the fund *managers*. Why would a truly mutual firm spend, well, *anything* on marketing? It wouldn't. Or at least it wouldn't spend much.
- **Developing mutual funds.** The structure of the conventional fund firm calls for offering whatever funds—however speculative or opportunistic—the marketplace demands. (That's how advisers earn fees.) The structure of the shareholder-owned firm calls for offering funds that offer the highest value—and, by definition, the lowest cost—to investors. Index funds, for example, do not fit the first example; they fit the second. That, in fact, is why we started the first index fund 24 years ago. (It took nearly a decade before our first index competitor joined the fray.)

At this point, I want to add a further thought about managers and index funds. In the conventional firm, managers and index funds clearly threaten one another's existence. *Allocating substantially all of the market's return to fund investors doesn't help managers to earn high profits for themselves.* In the mutual firm, however, index funds do *not* threaten the firm's existence. *Every* fund is operated at cost. Think about that. And index funds represent the closest approximation we can find for emulating the success of America's most successful investor, Warren E. Buffett. Mr. Buffett rails against "short-term *trading* of pieces of paper." Instead, he prefers "long-term *ownership* in businesses." He's right. Mr. Buffet doesn't succumb to the wiles of "Mr. Market," who bids for his properties each day. But few mutual funds maintain such discipline. With a staggering average portfolio turnover rate of 85% per year, generating billions of dollars of extra transaction costs, this industry has aligned itself with the short-term traders. We can call that *speculation*. But an index fund is clearly a long-term owner of businesses. We can call that *investment*. Investment is better.

Mr. Buffett says his favorite holding period for a stock is "forever." I say that owning an all-market index fund is owning *every publicly held business in America . . . forever.* No wonder Mr. Buffett repeatedly endorses the index fund: "By investing in an index fund, the know-nothing investor can actually outperform the professionals." There is a sharp difference—both in cost and in investment philosophy—between a conventionally managed mutual fund and an index fund, and therein lies a difference, not merely in *degree,* but in *kind.* In my bolder moments, I believe that the index fund will, by its crystal-clear example of the causal link between cost and return, finally prove to be the vehicle that will not only change the focus of the mutual fund industry, but its very structure.

Revolutionary Words

A change in the structure—indeed the entire *modus operandi*—of this industry is imperative. Yet change seems nowhere in sight. Costs must be cut, simply because all those expenditures incurred by mutual funds—on management fees and operating expenses, on marketing fees and sales charges, and on the execution of portfolio transactions—have consumed at least a quarter of the stock market's annual return, more than 4 percentage points per year, not even counting taxes, during the long bull market. When market returns fall back to more normal levels—*as they will*—the diminution will be cataclysmic.

Question: So what's to be done?

Answer: Gentlemen[1], you must recognize (1) that companies having the smallest expense will have the ultimate advantage; (2) that companies having this advantage are the most desirous of correcting present abuses, and (3) that companies which cannot long survive the present condition of affairs are determined to nullify every effort for reform. To save our business from ruin we must at once undertake a vigorous reform. To do this, the first step must be to *reduce expenses.*

---

1. Today, the quotation would properly read, "Ladies and gentlemen."

Those words may sound rather idealistic and fiery—even revolution-ary—so I quickly confess that they are neither new, nor mine. They are the words—right down to the italics—of my great-grandfather Philan-der B. Armstrong, who conceived the idea of mutual insurance in the property field, and formed the Phoenix Mutual Fire Insurance Com-pany in 1875. A decade later, he spoke those words to his fellow lead-ers of the insurance industry in St. Louis, Missouri. The fact that my own career in the mutual fund industry, and my own convictions as well, so closely resemble his must stand as a monument to the fact that even the apple's apple's apple's apple doesn't fall very far from the tree.

The fact is that costs still matter, today as in 1875. They matter in insurance and in mutual funds, and in *all* financial service industries. And they matter most where they are at once very large, compounded over time, and easily measurable relative to the value of the services provided. The confluence of those three factors is vividly etched in the investment record of the mutual fund industry. And it is high time that fund costs, after rising for decades, begin a long cycle of decline.

Four Generations—Two Authors—One Idea

Bringing fund costs down to proper levels will take a long time. I know that, if only because of the experience of Great Grandpa Armstrong, an insider taking on the property insurance industry in the 1880s and 1890s. According to his biography, "His methods were original and dia-metrically opposed to almost every recognized underwriter in the country." Perhaps frustrated by the failure of his ideas to catch hold in the fire insurance industry, by the turn of the century he had turned his critical gaze to the life insurance industry. He wrote a classic, if rather intemperate, book entitled, "A License to Steal," subtitled, "Life Insur-ance, The Swindle of Swindles. How Our Laws Rob Our Own People of Billions," published in 1917. His concluding words were these:

> **Why talk about correcting the present evil? The patient has a cancer. The virus is in the blood. He is not only sick unto death, but he is dangerous to the community. Call in the undertaker.**

When Great Grandpa Armstrong wrote those words, he was the same age as the apple of his apple's apple when my own new book, *Common Sense on Mutual Funds: New Imperatives for the Intelligent Investor,* was published two months ago. While my book about mutual funds is rather more temperate than his about life insurance, it makes the same point: ". . . the industry has embraced practices that seriously diminish its shareholders' chances of successful long-term investing. . . . Mutual funds should provide the greatest sum of investor returns with the least management expense, (but) the natural order has been turned on its head. The result not only defies nature, it offends common sense. . . . Common sense demands that funds be governed in the interests of those who own them."

Common Sense on Mutual Funds

On that note, let me add just a few comments on my new book. It aims, not only to help its readers become more successful mutual fund investors, but to chart a course for change in the mutual fund industry. While it is designed to be read sequentially, just as a typical book, it is in fact a series of 22 essays, each of which can be read independently. The first three parts of the book are purely about investment issues, encompassing (1) investment strategy, including the nature of financial market returns and asset allocation; (2) investment choices, including index funds, investment styles, and stock, bond, and global funds; and (3) investment performance, including the powerful role reversion to the mean plays in the financial markets, tax-efficiency (and tax-*in*efficiency), and the effect of *time* on return, risk, and cost.

The next two parts of the book turn to critical industry issues that have played a key role in the disappointing past records of mutual funds of all types. Part four, "On Fund Management" describes the industry's deviation from its original principles, discusses the ascendancy of marketing over management as our talisman, rails at the failure of fund directors to uphold shareholder interests, and suggests the positive implications of the change in industry structure that I discussed a few moments ago. This subject matter, of course, is unusual stuff for a book on fund investing, but the subject of part five, "On Spirit," is even more unusual. Here, I conclude that a mutual *structure*, as helpful to shareholders as it may be, is not enough. Irrespective of their structure, the firms in this industry need a mutual *attitude* toward serving investors, an attitude conspicuous only by its virtual absence today. So in part five, I take the liberty of describing the mutual values and spirit that, as Vanguard's founder and leader, I have endeavored to inculcate in our enterprise.

"Common Sense" is the theme that suffuses each of the book's subjects. Not only common sense as you and I understand it today, but

"Common Sense" as Thomas Paine used it in his pamphlets some 225 years ago, presenting sentiments to the citizens of the Colonies "not yet sufficiently fashionable to procure their general favor . . . offering nothing more than simple facts and plain arguments," and asking the reader to "generously enlarge his views beyond the present day." I present similar sentiments to fund investors in my book.

Except for the final section, the book is *not* about Vanguard. It *is* largely about my deeply held convictions on how to invest successfully. Vanguard's growth, which I described at the outset, seems to reflect an improving, indeed burgeoning, acceptance of the investment ideas, policies, and principles that I urge fund investors to adopt. And it is primarily by these means that we have established whatever competitive edge it is that we have, an edge that has enabled us to establish the structure and spirit that *Forbes* found to so clearly differentiate us from our rivals.

The Competitive Edge

Given what we observe in most competitive industries—and the mutual fund industry is ferociously competitive in all respects save one, the setting of prices—we might expect our competitive edge to be challenged. In an industry with perhaps 30 *major* competitors, how many firms would you expect to challenge a leader who captures a 60% share of cash flow? Five firms? Ten? All 30 firms? The answer, however, is: *None.* No fund leader, as far as I can tell, has called a meeting of his senior officers and said: "These guys are eating our lunch! Let's take them on, toe to toe! Now!" That hasn't happened. Why? Because taking on Vanguard would require aggressively challenging us with low-cost index funds, low-cost bond and money market funds, and low-cost conservative stock funds focused on long-term investing. The fact is that the returns of the clients of our rivals—their fund shareholders—would be markedly enhanced, but the returns of their own management firms would be slashed—*no matter how much their market share improved.* In the face of the competitive edge we have created, the industry's silence has been, well, deafening. There's no money for fund managers, or so it seems, in giving their clients— the *owners* of their funds—a fair shake.

Despite our competitive edge, honestly, I worry about the bright outlook for Vanguard's future growth. Huge size, at our awesome levels even today, is a mixed blessing. And we won't be any smaller tomorrow, or a year hence, or a decade from now. *Investing money* doesn't get easier as you get bigger, though the minimal turnover strategies of our index and bond funds greatly vitiate the challenge. But neither does *managing an enterprise* get any easier. Our crew (we don't have "employees") has burgeoned from the 28 human beings on board when we began to 9,000 human beings today. Bureaucracy looms. Technology supplants more and more human interaction. Judgment battles to hold its own against process. Our managers and crewmembers today are mounting a superb offense, but merely holding the line to maintain our spirit and values remains a challenge. With an admittedly far more unremitting opponent than asset size, King Canute failed, as was inevitable, to hold back the onrushing tide.

But maintaining the competitive edge we now hold at Vanguard will remain a challenge. Curiously perhaps, it is a challenge I recall first facing up to when our assets were but $8 billion, only about *one-sixtieth* of our size today. As far back as 1984, I spoke to our entire crew (then, there were just 350 crewmembers) on the subject of "Two Axioms." One was "nothing succeeds like success." The other was "nothing *fails* like success." I warned our crewmembers that our success—even in those ancient days—could easily lead to failure, pointing out that "countless business enterprises, at the very moment of their greatest triumph, were planting the seeds of their own destruction."

Turning to the incipient competitive edge that we were even then establishing in 1984, I warned the crew that when a company is doing as well as we were, "the danger is to think it can do no wrong." I also pointed out that "when an institution goes down, one condition may always be found: it forgot where it came from." *It forgot where it came from.* Today, I think it is fair to say that our competitive edge has been established. But now, even as in 1984, *"whether we can keep it is up to us."* If we continue to give each of our shareholders a fair shake, hold to our long established values, continue to do the right things in just the right way, remember where we came from, and hone our competitive edge to an ever-finer point, we will meet the challenge. Of that I have no doubt. But it would be a lot easier to keep our competitive edge sharply honed if at least a few mutual fund firms would seriously compete with Vanguard on our terms. With that expectant hope, I welcome all comers.

13

CREATING SHAREHOLDER VALUE: BY MUTUAL FUNDS ... OR FOR MUTUAL FUND SHAREHOLDERS?

Keynote Address
Annual Conference of the Investor
Responsibility Research Center
Washington, D.C.
October 26, 1998

IT IS AN EXTRAORDINARY honor to be invited to give this keynote address as the IRRC begins its second quarter-century of service to the shareholders of America's publicly held corporations. In fact, as I understand it, I am the first senior executive of a mutual fund firm to be so honored. Clearly our industry—now representing the largest single pool of institutionally owned equities in the nation—has been conspicuous by its absence from participation in your annual conference.

While there are some valid reasons for why you might not have sought our participation in the past, there are—paradoxically enough— also some disturbing reasons why we might not have been particularly enthusiastic about participating in discussions regarding the creation of shareholder value in Corporate America. For reasons that I look forward to discussing with you today, our self-interested modesty—if that is not an oxymoron—is now at the inflection point of change.

The creation of "shareholder value" as the explicit focus of corporate strategy is largely a phenomenon of the 1990s. It has been driven, in part, by the leadership of large institutional investors, notably the states of Wisconsin and Florida, CALPERS, and the New York City funds, supported by the vigorous advocacy of the Council of Institutional Investors. The important research provided the IRRC and others has also been invaluable. This handful of heroes fully deserves the accolades of America's shareholders who are—lest we forget—the *owners* of our publicly held corporations.

Enhancing Corporate Value

As the responsibility to enhance economic value has become the prime article of faith in corporate America, it has often been codified in Mission Statements of Boards of Directors. For example, the mission statement of the Mead Corporation, the Fortune 500 papermaker, on whose board I've served as an independent director for 20 years, states:

> **The mission of the Board is to achieve long-term economic value for the shareholders. The Board believes that the Corporation should rank in the top third of peer companies in the creation of economic value ... which is created by earning returns over full cycles which are higher than the cost of capital, usually reflected in total return to shareholders.**

In Mead's case, total return is measured by Return on Total Capital, with our ROTC then compared with the average ROTC of both our peers and Corporate America in the aggregate. In addition to serving as the benchmark for the evaluation of corporate success by the Board, this joint measurement serves as the basis for Mead's incentive compensation system.

The focus of the Board—and Mead's Board is hardly unusual in this respect—is on the creation of additional economic value, measured by achieving an ROTC that exceeds the cost of capital. If we cannot earn the cost of capital for our shareholders, so the essential logic goes, why should they entrust us with it? As *Fortune* magazine put it: "The true cost of equity is what your shareholders could be getting in price appreciation and dividends if they invested instead in a portfolio about as risky as yours."

The idea that companies must recover their cost of capital is not new. According to a recent article in *The Financial Times*, the eminent British economist Alfred Marshall stated it clearly a century ago. "But," the article added, "it was not systematically applied to management until the 1980s." One current fashion is to cast the issue in the form of "economic value added," or EVA®.[1]

EVA can be simply described as the amount by which the corporation's return on total capital exceeds the weighted market value of the corporation's cost of capital, measured by the capitalization-weighted average of the interest rate on its debt and the market return on common stocks as a group (adjusted to reflect the riskiness of its stock, using Beta, the conventional measure of the volatility of a company's stock price relative to that of the Standard & Poor's 500 Composite Stock Price Index). In a simple example, if the return of the S&P 500 Index were 15%, a corporation with 100% of its capitalization represented by equity (i.e., without debt) and a Beta of 0.90 would have a cost of capital of 14%.[2] EVA, therefore, would depend on investing capital only in new projects earning, say, significantly more than 14%. While the *precision* of this statistical measure is subject to well-deserved skepticism, the *concept* represents rather elementary common sense.

Time Horizons and the Sources of Investment Return

But if we all can agree that the creation of shareholder value is the critical responsibility of the business corporation, a second important issue remains: how to measure value, and over what period? In the *long run* the returns on a corporation's shares in the stock market are determined by its investment fundamentals—earnings growth and dividend yields. For example, the real earnings and dividends (after inflation) of U.S. corporations have aggregated just short of 7% over the past two centuries, almost precisely equal to the real return of 7% in stock prices. Over the long pull, investment fundamentals, not market valuations, are the piper that calls the tune.

Over the *short run*, however, the fundamentals are often overwhelmed by the deafening noise of speculation—the price at which the stock market values each dollar of earnings. This noise can be surprisingly durable. On a one-year basis, as shown in Table 13.1, the gap between annual fundamental rates of return on stocks and their mar-

---

1. While it may seem anomalous that such common words can, in effect, be patented, EVA® is a registered service mark of Stern Stewart & Co. The logic of U.S. patent law never ceases to amaze me.
2. Risk-fee rate + Beta (stock market return − risk-free rate) = Cost of capital. Therefore: 5% + 0.9 (15% − 5%) = 14%.

ket return can be staggering, exceeding 10 percentage points (!) in more than two-thirds of the 125 rolling 10-year periods since 1872, and exceeding 5 percentage points in more than 8 out of 10 periods. On a 10-year basis, the gap shrinks considerably, almost never exceeding 10%, but exceeding 5% in one-fourth of all periods, and 2% in two-thirds. Over 25 years, however, the gap shrinks radically, exceeding 2% in fewer than one-quarter of all periods and never exceeding 5%.

One need look no further than the 1970s and 1980s to see that wide variations can take place during decade-long periods. As shown in the Table 13.2, during the 1970s the *fundamentals* of investment, measured by earnings growth and dividend yields on the S&P 500 Index, provided a return of 13.3% per year, but the total stock market return was but 5.9% annually. The *reduction* in valuation of –7.6% per year reflected a drop in the price-earnings ratio from 15.9 to 7.3 times. During the 1980s, by contrast, the fundamental return of 9.6% came hand in hand with a valuation increase of 7.8%, as P/E ratios more than doubled, from 7.3 to 15.5 times, bringing total annual return to 17.6%. While, measured in nominal terms, corporate America's performance was *worse* in the 1980s than in the 1970s in terms of fundamentals (+9.6% vs. +13.3%), it was far *better* in stock market terms (+17.6% vs. +5.9%). Turnabout, apparently, is fair play. For during the two decades combined, the fundamental return of 11.5% was virtually identical to the market return. The cacophony of speculation was, on balance, conspicuous by its absence.

We *know* that in the long-run, market returns represent the triumph of investment fundamentals—earnings and dividends—over speculation in the market's valuation of these returns. Yet I have no doubt that during recent years it is speculation that has been in the driver's seat. This trend would not have surprised the worldly-wise

TABLE 13.1   Examining 125 Years of Market History

HOLDING PERIOD	Difference between Fundamental and Market Returns		
	+2%	+5%	+10%
1 year	94%	84%	68%
10 years	62	27	3
25 years	23	0	0

Note: A 5% gap, for example, would mean that if the fundamental return were 10%, the market return might be more than 15% or less than 5%.

TABLE 13.2   The Golden Decade Follows the Tin Decade

	1970s	1980s	1970s AND 1980s
Fundamental return[a]	13.3%	9.6%	11.6%
Speculative return[b]	−7.6	+7.8	−0.1
Market return	5.9%	17.6%	11.5%
P/E ratio—Start	15.9x	7.3x	15.9x
P/E Ratio—End	7.3x	15.5x	15.5x

[a]Earnings growth + Dividend yield.
[b]Annualized impact of change in P/E ratio.

Lord Keynes, who warned of the powerful role of speculation in the markets, concluding (in the early 1930s) that ". . . the conventional valuation of stocks [is] based on the mass psychology of a large number of ignorant individuals." Unable to offset the mass opinion, he predicted, professional investors would focus their investment strategies on endeavoring to "foresee changes in the public valuation."

His conclusion has been reaffirmed—and then some! In the past three decades, expert professional investors have come to dominate the financial markets. Managers of pension funds and mutual funds have largely replaced ignorant individuals in the investment marketplace. Rather than endeavoring to place appropriate values on business enterprises, these pros are, in a real sense, focusing their professional careers on attempting to foresee changes in the public valuation of stocks. In the long run, of course, precious few will succeed in doing so.

The Consequences of Using Market Returns as the Standard

What is more, there are some deeply troubling aspects in the acceptance of the returns generated in the stock market as the sole ingredient of the cost of equity-capital. The stock market—as recent wild fluctuations have demonstrated yet once again—is a fickle, flighty investment in the short run—"a tale told by an idiot, full of sound and fury, signifying nothing," to borrow a phase from the Bard. In the long run—as every intelligent investor, from Alan Greenspan to Peter Bernstein to Peter Lynch knows—it is the sum total of earnings and dividends that controls market returns. Nonetheless, in the short run it is the valuations that speculators place on these investment fundamentals that drive market returns—from day to day, and even from decade to decade, before the fundamentals finally reassert themselves and the market reverts to its long-term norm. But only until the next cycle begins.

Because of these periodic swings between optimism and pessimism, between greed and fear, the considerable success of corporate managers in building earnings and dividends at a 13% annual rate during the 1970s was translated into a shabby total market return of less than 6%. While corporate managers were *less* successful in the 1980s, providing a return from earnings and dividends of less than 10%, investor emotions took a 180° turn and valuations more than doubled, carrying the market to an outstanding 17% return.

The reliance on market returns as the ultimate standard gives rise to an important issue in corporate governance: the emergence of stock options as the driving force in executive compensation. During the second half of the 1990s, this system has provided huge rewards to managers of corporations whose stocks have soared to new heights in the great bull market. Leaving aside the issues of paying executives on the basis of what often prove to be market whims, and accounting for option costs without diluting reported earnings, there is the critical question of what to do when the law of gravity in the financial markets—reversion to the mean—strikes, and stock prices tumble, even in the face of uninterrupted earnings growth.

When this happens, it must not be unheard of for management to tell the directors: "our options are so far underwater that we have no incentive to improve. We need motivation; we need our team to stay; we need to enhance shareholder value. So please reprice the options." And the directors are apt to do just that. It is a perverse sort of argument, but the practice is taking hold. Nearly 10% of the 1500 large companies tracked by IRRC have repriced options in the past two years. And given the precipitous drop in the prices of so many stocks in recent months, repricing seems certain to expand in the months ahead.

Repricing is clearly an emerging corporate governance issue. Necessary as it may—or may not—be, this creation of wealth without risk (a nice way to live!) clearly dilutes shareholder value. I believe that institutional shareholders should take a firm stand with the companies who shares they own, demanding that such repricings be submitted to shareholders for approval. At the same time, the terms and conditions of repricing should be monitored, for repricing schemes range from "grossly unfair" to "reasonable under the circumstances." We should oppose the former and accept, however reluctantly, the latter. The time is now—well before the 1999 proxy season—for institutional investors to communicate their position to the directors and managers of their portfolio companies.

The whole stock option process, moreover, based as it largely is on simple price appreciation, needs serious reconsideration. Why shouldn't options be related to the extent to which the corporation earns returns in excess of its cost of capital, or to its performance relative to its peers, or even to the performance of its shares relative to the stock market as a whole? Targets that are too easy to hit result in the disproportionate sharing of corporate value between the corporation's management and its shareholders, and distort our financial system.

I hope that institutional investors and individual investors alike will recognize the folly of applauding corporate managers solely on the basis of evanescent market returns, without due regard for the hard work involved in generating the underlying investment fundamentals that are required to deliver returns that exceed their cost of capital over the long run.

The Rise of the Institutional Investor

The fact that *market* return seems to have taken the place of fundamental *investment* return in measuring shareholder value has had important implications for corporate governance. Surely the fact that shareholders must be served is as it should be, but the responsibility of focusing on the nature of returns, and the time frame over which they should be measured, will devolve largely on the institutional investor.

Today, institutional investors have the power to make a difference in corporate governance. When the 1950s began, institutions controlled less than 5% of all U.S. equities. Pension funds were just coming into being, and mutual funds, then the largest institutional investor, accounted for just 2% of the stock market's value. By the time that 1970 rolled around, the institutional share had risen to 27%, growing to 43% in 1990. Today, institutional investors own more than 70% of all U.S. stocks. In fact, the 100 largest financial institutions alone now own more than half of all U.S. corporate equities, valued at about $5 trillion. It is this handful of firms that can be the force that controls Corporate America.

The latent power represented by these institutions has the potential to reverse the trend toward the separation of corporate ownership and control that so concerned Adolf Belre and Gardiner Means in the early 1930s.[3] As then-Comptroller Ned Regan of New York told this convocation a year ago, financial institutions have "sent a wake-up call to American business." He described this wake-up call as the third such call to rouse corporate CEOs, following the force of global competition, and then the explosion in corporate takeovers. The call from institutional investors, eager to enhance returns and bound by their fiduciary duty to prudently maximize returns for their beneficiaries and shareholders, may well be the final wake-up call that American business needs to receive. Final call or not, it surely has a ring whose intensity has risen measurably over the years, and it is now a call that can not be ignored by Corporate America.

Institutions have the power to make their will be done. The three principal classes of investors alone—mutual funds, state retirement plans, and corporate pension funds—hold fully 40% of the market value of the nation's publicly held corporations today, eight *times* their 5% share in 1980. But the relationship of the holdings of these three groups of institutions has changed substantially during this period. As shown in Table 13.3, 15 years ago, long after mutual funds had relinquished their leadership, corporate pension funds held sway, holding 68% of these institutional assets. But that share has since been cut by one-half, to 34%. State and local retirement plans have increased their share from 17% to 25%. Fastest growing of all has been the group's previously deposed leader, for mutual funds have leaped from 15% to 41% of the group's aggregate, and now represent its largest single unit.

The response to corporate governance issues by the trustees and managers of these three institutional asset pools has traditionally been so different in degree that it can easily be mistaken as a difference in kind. The *public* funds have been, dare I say, in the vanguard of corporate activism, while the private funds—corporate pension plans and mutual funds—have been conspicuous by their absence from the fray.

The Changing Focus of Institutional Voting Activism

It is relatively easy to understand why the private investment sector stood back when significant institutional activism emerged in the early 1970s. Most of the early issues related to proxy proposals by small

---

3. *The Modern Corporation and Private Property*

TABLE 13.3   Assets Held by the Three Major Institutional Investors

	Corporate Retirement Plans		State and Local Retirement Plans		Mutual Funds		Total	
	$ BILLION	PERCENT	$ BILLION	PERCENT	$ BILLION	PERCENT	$ BILLION	PERCENT
1983	350	68	90	17	79	15	519	100
1990	562	51	293	27	249	23	1,104	100
1993	938	45	531	25	634	30	2,103	100
1996	1,422	37	956	25	1,514	39	3,892	100
1998°	2,005	34	1,482	25	2,396	41	5,882	100

°First quarter.

shareholders on social and ethical issues—minority hiring, pollution, recycling, and the like. Many institutional managers had either a sort of ho-hum reaction to these proposals, or a view that it was up to the corporation's managers to resolve them. So far as I know, none of these proposals ever received a significant portion of shareholder votes.

In the late 1970s, however, the first issue to receive compelling public attention arose: South Africa. The rigorous separation of races under the doctrine of apartheid caught the investment world's attention, and shareholder proposals that corporations divest themselves of business interests in the Union of South Africa were rife. Without, I think, adequate consideration of whether U.S. corporations were part of the problem—or, instead, could be part of the solution—this pressure, especially from public funds and college endowment funds, caused many corporations to withdraw from South Africa, even as it brought others to adopt the Sullivan Principles for acceptable practices in doing business there. Ever quick to spot an investment opportunity, many institutional managers ducked the issue by offering "South-Africa-Free" portfolios. (Even index fund managers offered "S&P 500 Lite" portfolios.) Changes in South Africa, however, have now made this issue substantially moot.

But as we moved into the 1980s, issues of corporate performance, corporate governance, executive compensation, and mergers and takeovers rose to the fore. These issues get to the heart of the question of the corporation's determination to enhance shareholder value, and the extent to which shareholders can influence corporate policy, strategy, and management. These issues are not going to vanish any time soon.

The institutional community has had a split response to these new, bottom-line-related, issues. On the one hand, the members of all three pools—private plans, public funds, mutual funds—have generally proved ready to respond at a moment's notice to a merger proposal, or a takeover bid offering a steep premium over the current market value. "Analysis of long-term prospects be damned, let's tender first and ask questions afterward," was the implicit response.

On the other hand, the large public funds, almost alone, became corporate activists, seeking greater management focus on the creation of shareholder value, and in some cases placing proposals in the proxies of corporations whose managements appeared not to get the message. The large public funds—with long-term investment horizons, low portfolio turnover, and a market indexing orientation—also took initiatives with managements of corporations deemed to be underperforming in the stock market, even demanding changes in boards of directors. The record would seem to confirm, in particular, that the handful of large state retirement plans that I applauded at the outset have enjoyed some success when they have undertaken initiatives to influence the policies of major corporations.

The Silence of the Mutual Funds

During those corporate battles, mutual fund managers in general (Michael Price being a rare exception) were well behind the lines. Few, if any, made proxy proposals. Many, if not most, performed their proxy voting on a rote basis, failing to carefully attend to the issues raised and automatically voting in favor of management recommendations.[4] Why is it that mutual funds, now with the most potential power of the three groups, have been the quietest, almost absent from the policy debate?

There are lots of reasons. First, improving shareholder value is a long-term proposition, and most mutual funds are short-term

---

4. Note: Vanguard, I acknowledge, has rarely played an activist role, although John B. Neff, longtime portfolio manager of Vanguard Windsor Fund, was a vocal critic of a number of corporate proposals, and unstinting in writing to the boards of directors involved, alas, without notable success. Our own procedures entail a thorough examination by our staff of all issues raised in the proxies we receive (our funds own shares in some 5,000 U.S. companies), and we vote them in accordance with principles approved by the Directors of the Vanguard Funds. These principles include generally leaving social responsibility issues to the corporation's board, opposing barriers to mergers or takeovers, and supporting competitive compensation packages unless excessive dilution is involved. We rely heavily on the work of the IRRC. My impression is that only a minority of mutual funds follow such thorough procedures. TIAA-CREF also has excellent voting procedures, and is a more active participant in governance issues than is Vanguard.

investors. The industry's annual rate of portfolio turnover is 85%, suggesting an average holding period of about 1.2 years for a given security. (The average turnover rate for the highest quartile of funds is 196%—barely a six-month holding period—while the large state retirement funds are estimated to have turnover in the 10% to 20% range.) As Columbia Law School Professor Louis Lowenstein expressed it in a recent article, mutual fund managers "exhibit a persistent emphasis on momentary stock prices. The subtleties and nuances of a particular business utterly escape them."

Happily, there is every reason for this situation to improve. For there is, by definition, one type of equity strategy that is ironbound to invest for the long term. This strategy precludes both the short-term "I don't care" approach, and the longer-term but threadbare "If I don't like the management, I sell the stock" approach. It is called market indexing, and mutual fund investors are increasingly embracing this approach. A decade ago, index funds, then as now largely targeted to the S&P 500 Index, represented barely 1% of equity fund assets. Today, thanks to a combination of excellent Index performance and strong cash flow, index funds now represent nearly 8% of equity fund assets. Given that this year index funds are accounting for fully 25% of equity fund cash flow, it would not be unreasonable to expect index funds assets to reach a 15% share of mutual fund assets well within the next decade.

With that penetration, index mutual funds would be on their way to approaching the present 22% share that indexed equities represent in public and private pension plans. This number, however, has grown at a snail's pace; in 1990, the index share was 20%. Thus it may be that, through index mutual funds, the fruition of the long-delayed participation of the public in the indexing strategy will add considerable weight to the dominant role that indexing now plays in the retirement plan world. Since the growth in indexing by retirement plans since 1990 has been glacial (up only from 20% to 22%), it is not a moment too soon for the average investor to adopt this remarkably successful investment strategy, and at the same time add momentum to its growth.

Indexing strategies now represent 17% of the total assets of the combined institutions, up from 12% in 1985 and 16% in 1990, yet even now only about 8% of the market value of *all* equities (including individuals, endowments, and bank trust accounts owning stocks directly) is committed to this approach. Surely much more growth lies ahead. Table 13.4 highlights this growth:

TABLE 13.4 Indexing as a Percentage of Equity Assets ($ Billions)

	Private and Public Pensions		Mutual Funds		Total Pensions and Funds		U.S. Stock Market	
	INDEXED DOLLARS	**% OF ASSETS**	**INDEXED DOLLARS**	**% OF ASSETS**	**INDEXED DOLLARS**	**% OF ASSETS**	**INDEXED DOLLARS**	**% OF ASSETS**
1985	$ 90.6	14.7	$ 0.6	0.5	$ 91.2	12.4	$ 2,195.0	4.2
1990	172.7	20.2	4.9	2.0	177.6	16.2	2,957.6	6.0
1993	293.0	19.9	23.3	3.4	316.3	15.1	4,791.0	6.6
1997	672.0	21.9	141.7	7.2	813.7	17.0	10,271.0	7.9

Once investors adopt the market-indexing strategy, they hold stocks in the same companies, in effect, forever. So the only way to add economic value becomes the exercise of the same governance responsibility as would characterize the sole owner of a private business: the shareholder comes first. It is hard to imagine that the trend toward indexing will not mean that all institutions—including mutual funds—will become far more assiduous, not only in their voting policies and in making proxy proposals where necessary, but in expressing their informed opinions to corporate directors and managers.

But the mutual fund industry is still largely driven by a marketing system that places a premium on short-term performance, which leads to an incentive system in which rewards go to fund managers who have achieved outstanding past returns (High fund returns yield more fund assets, and more assets generate higher fees to advisers.) Inertia ("we've never *done* it that way") is inevitably part of the for-bearance problem, too. While the costs of greater attention and thoroughness would be trivial to any but the smallest fund groups, the benefits of activism are apparently deemed too uncertain for most funds to undertake the effort.

Another issue our industry faces—and it is an important one—is that of potential conflicts of interest. When a fund group is selected to run a corporation's $1 billion-plus retirement or thrift plan and issues regarding shareholder value, or even a hostile takeover attempt, arise, the fund manager may well be tempted to consider the interests of the corporation's management (i.e., its client) rather than the fund's shareholders. As one example, in the early 1990s, one large fund organization (not, I hasten to add, Vanguard) that was among the most vocal critics of a tough Pennsylvania anti-takeover bill, switched sides and became a supporter. The target corporation, a strong advocate of the bill, promptly retained the fund firm to manage its 401(k) thrift plan. Whether it was a mere coincidence or an isolated example, it surely sends up a warning flag.

Mutual Funds: The Artillery or the Target?

In addition to the reluctance of the fund industry to actively participate in corporate management generated by our short-term focus, our inertia in governance issues, and the conflicts of interest we face, there is all too likely a final factor that may dissuade mutual funds from an activist-investor stance. This issue gives me a neat transition to the final section of my speech: corporate governance and shareholder value issues in the fund industry itself. Taking a "people who live in glass houses shouldn't throw stones" stance, we would prefer not to advise the companies in our portfolios about governance when our own houses are so fragile. We may not mind being the artillery of shareholder activism, but we don't want to be its target.

In short, a challenge *by* mutual funds to Corporate America to create economic value is problematic unless we can create greater economic value *for* our own mutual fund shareholders. Our responsibility to do so is particularly large since the traditional mutual fund governance system is, as far as I can determine, a unique exception to the rules under which ordinary business and financial corporations are governed. In our business, the fund corporation is merely a corporate shell, a holding company for marketable stocks and bonds, which delegates virtually all of its activities—from the choice of its very name, its investment strategy and policies, and its administration, distribution, and portfolio management—to an external corporation.

The process begins when the fund's manager sets its own fee for managing the fund. It is duly approved by the fund's independent directors, unaffiliated with, but appointed by, the manager. The result as you might expect, lives up to Warren Buffett's aphorism, "negotiating with one's self seldom produces a barroom brawl." To those who are unfamiliar with our industry, this structure must seem bizarre and rife with potential conflicts of interest. And so it is, especially since the ownership of mutual funds is so diffused among investors of relatively modest means. As a result, the kind of institutional intercession we see in Corporate America is conspicuous only by its absence.

The industry, however, advances powerful arguments that the system effectively serves mutual fund shareholders. It is the shareholders, after all, who *elect* the directors, who in turn assume a fiduciary duty to protect them. Excessive or not, the costs, like the past returns and potential risks, are fully disclosed. Shareholders can vote against a fee increase, and, if they aren't satisfied with the fund, they can redeem their shares without cost (leaving aside capital gains taxes and sales loads). All of this is quite true in principle. But in practice, does the mutual fund governance system work effectively to serve shareholders?

The Inevitable Failure to Earn the Cost of Capital

The best way to answer that question is to return to the issue of the creation of economic value with which I began these remarks. Whether or not the fund governance system works effectively depends upon the extent to which mutual funds earn the cost of capital for their shareholders. Doing so, of course, would require that funds earn for their shareholders at least what they could otherwise "be getting in price appreciation and dividends if they had invested instead in a portfolio about as risky," using the words from *Fortune* that I cited at the outset.

A business corporation, as I have noted, calculates its cost of capital based on its debt-equity ratio, but since 100% of a given mutual fund corporation's capital is equity, its cost of capital is the return of the stock market (adjusted for the fund's relative risk). *Given that standard, mutual funds as a group must fail to earn their cost of capital.* The record is clear on that point. Measured over the past 50 years, the average equity mutual fund has carried a volatility risk quite similar to that of the market, but has *lagged* the market return by about 1½% annually over the long term, and about 2¼% over the past 15 years.

The reason that mutual funds as a group have earned only about 85% of their cost of capital is the heavy costs that they incur—not only operating expenses and advisory fees, but portfolio transaction costs. As a group, their professional managers, despite their expertise, have failed to outperform the market *before* the deduction of costs. So their costs doom them to below-market returns. And their costs have been rising, as advisory fees move ever upward, as new fees (such as 12b-1 marketing fees) are added, and as portfolio turnover escalates. The expense ratio for the average equity fund has risen from about 1.0% in the early 1960s to 1.6% now. During the same period, industry-wide portfolio turnover has risen from less than 20% to nearly 90%. The "double whammy" represented by this rise in total costs appears primarily responsible for the rise to more than 2% in the shortfall of annual fund returns relative to their cost of capital.

How Effective Are Fund Directors?

The mutual fund governance system, it seems to me, bears considerable responsibility for these problems. If directors of funds that fail to earn their cost of capital by a wide margin believed, as corporate directors do, that earning the cost of capital for shareholders is valid policy goal, they might at least consider terminating their manager and getting a new one. While they are legally free to do so, such an action has virtually *never* transpired. Or they could get to the root of the problem by reducing advisory fees. But in fact they persist in increasing them, and in adding yet new types of fees, even as the evidence of this proposition is crystal-clear: *The shortest route to top-quartile investment performance is bottom-quartile expenses.*

What is more, even in the face of compelling evidence that portfolio turnover has a neutral impact at best on pre-tax fund returns to shareholders and a devastating impact on their after-tax returns, directors apparently accept without challenge today's high turnover mania. Why do they not press managers to reduce turnover if there is no evidence that demonstrates that all of our industry's feverish and costly transaction activity benefits shareholders? Why don't they demand that the adviser make available low-cost, passively managed index funds, which have, for obvious reasons, outpaced high-cost, actively managed funds? Yet few of the major fund groups have been willing to do so. Low-cost index funds, in fact, have earned net returns equal to about 99% of the cost of capital, a remarkable margin over the 85% ratio for the average managed fund.

Faced with the cost of capital as a standard—measured with such surpassing ease in the mutual fund field—and the clear reasons for the persistent shortfall of most mutual funds, where *are* the independent directors? While this industry describes them as watchdogs for the fund shareholders, Warren Buffett calls them "cocker spaniels" and *The New York Times* depicts them as "empty suits." Suffice it to say that the record is bereft of evidence that directors of any mutual fund have taken affirmative action when the fund has persistently failed to earn its cost of capital, even when the margin is wide. It's not a record of which this industry should be proud.

Paradoxically, however, even as we display no interest whatsoever in using tough standards of corporate governance for our own shareholders, we increasingly apply them to the corporations in our portfolios. A few years ago, the chairman of one giant fund complex lectured the directors of corporations whose shares were held in his fund's portfolios. He said that his funds wanted "directors who will mind the store for us, making sure management's doing a good job. . . . If not, the board has to fire, rehire, and pay new managers. . . . [We need] boardrooms that are responsible to shareholders' interests and not passive rubber stamps for the Chairman's agenda."

What can one say other than, "physician, heal thyself." I simply can't imagine that even the most vigorous defender of the peculiar governance structure of the mutual fund industry would dare to say that our own governance standards meet the stern and valid test laid down by this fund leader, even as we begin to apply these standards to Corporate America with increasing vigor. Yet state corporate law makes no distinction between the duties of corporate directors and fund directors. Federal law, in fact, imposes an added responsibility on the shoulders of fund directors, an explicit directive that funds must be organized, operated, and managed in the interest of their shareholders, rather than in the interests of directors, officers, or investment advisers.[5]

Creating shareholder value as the pre-eminent priority of corporate management is a sound concept, an article of faith in the financial system of the United States, now spreading all over the globe. Only the mutual fund industry seems to be immune from the process. It is high time for this issue to be raised, and high time that we focus on the principle of earning the maximum possible portion of our cost of capital for our shareholders. They deserve no less. For they are our *owners*.

---

5. Investment Company Act of 1940, Section 1(b)(2).

14

THE SILENCE OF THE FUNDS: MUTUAL FUND INVESTMENT POLICIES AND CORPORATE GOVERNANCE

The Corporate Governance and Shareholders Rights Committee
The New York Society of Securities Analysts
October 20, 1999

WHEN I WROTE my Princeton thesis on the mutual fund industry nearly 50 years ago (!), I explored the funds' role in corporate governance. While funds were quite hesitant to make their votes count in those ancient days ("If you don't like the management, sell the stock"), I was able to find a number of examples of fund activism. The most notable was the Montgomery Ward case of 1949, in which mutual funds joined in the effort to remove Chairman Sewell Avery from his job. (The effort followed by just a few years the famous removal of Mr. Avery from his office in his desk chair by a pair of soldiers.)

My thesis reflected my then-as-now idealism, and I predicted that it was only a matter of time until mutual funds exercised their duties as corporate citizens, "basing their investments on enterprise rather than speculation . . . and exerting influence on corporate policy, often in a decisive manner, and in the best interest of investment company shareholders." In 1951, when I wrote those words, mutual funds owned less than 3% of the stock of U.S. corporations, and I expected their voice would strengthen in tandem with their muscle.

Alas, I could hardly have been more mistaken. Now, a half-century later, even though mutual funds own about 23% of all stocks, and mutual fund *managers* (who also typically provide investment management services to pension plans and other institutions) control some 35% of all stocks—making them by far the controlling force in corporate America—the strong voice I expected is barely a whisper. Switching metaphors and putting a reverse twist on the saying that "the spirit is willing but the flesh is weak," the mutual fund flesh is strong but the spirit is unwilling.

As far as I can tell, while the managers of most large fund groups carefully review corporate proxies, they endorse the proposals of corporate management almost without exception. But simply voting— usually doing just as they are asked—in accordance with management's recommendations, too often without adequate review, is a far cry from not only activism and advocacy, but from the very process of corporate governance. *Mutual funds have failed to live up to their responsibility of corporate citizenship.*

Why Are Mutual Funds Passive Participants in Corporate Governance?

The reasons for this passivity are not hard to fathom. First, funds are essentially short-term investors. In the two decades after I wrote my Princeton thesis, annualized portfolio turnover of the average equity mutual fund averaged less than 20%. This year turnover is at an all-time high of 112%. For the highest decile of funds, the average turnover is 166%; for the lowest decile (excluding index funds), 64%. That shocking 112% turnover means that a fund with $1 billion of assets buys $1.12 billion of portfolio securities *and sells* $1.12 billion— $2.24 billion of transactions *in a single year.* Put another way, the typical holding of an average mutual fund lasts for but 326 *days.* Such turnover has *nothing whatsoever* to do with long-term investing. But it has *everything* to do with short-term speculation. And when speculation is the name of the game, it is the *price* of a stock that matters, not its *value.* As Columbia Law School Professor Louis Lowenstein has said, fund managers "exhibit a persistent emphasis on momentary stock prices. The subtleties and nuances of a particular business utterly escape them." Pure and simple, most mutual fund managers don't care about corporate governance.

One might ask: To what avail is this hyperventilating level of portfolio turnover? It is costly, for the croupiers of the financial market-place have wide rakes. And it is even more tax inefficient than it appears. While realizing capital gains *at all* is expensive for fund shareholders, funds realize something like one-third of their gains on a *short-term* basis, taxable as ordinary income at rates up to 40%. And while the capital gain tax on a stock held for one year or more consumes 20% of the gains, that 20-cent drag on each dollar would drop to just eight cents of present value were the gain deferred for 15 years. But few funds hold *any* shares for a period of that length.

Further, with fund managers owning some 35% of all shares outstanding, much of their trading—likely more than half—is done with *other* fund managers. Such transactions clearly cannot advance the interests of fund investors *as a group*. Indeed, the presence of the croupiers in the stock market casino *inevitably* reduces the returns that fund shareholders receive. But the fundamental point is that funds following *short-term* investment policies based on anticipated changes in stock prices are hardly good candidates to become *responsible* participants in a corporate governance process in which shareholder value is the watchword. (I'm speaking of *fundamental* investment value here, and not the kind of *speculative* shareholder value that has become a euphemism for raising, by fair means or foul, the price of stock.)

A second obstacle to mutual fund activism is the commercial nature of the mutual fund business. We've become a marketing business. Investment managers seek corporate clients, for that is where the big money is . . . and where the big profits lie for the managers. Corporate 401(k) thrift plans have been among the driving forces in generating new fund assets since the mid-1990s, and corporate pension funds— absent the need for all of that complex and costly subaccounting—are also considered plums by fund managers. Given the drive for corporate customers, the reluctance of fund managers to risk the opprobrium of potential clients by leaping enthusiastically into the controversial areas of corporate governance is hardly astonishing, though it is discouraging.

A third obstacle, or so it has been alleged by the fund industry, is that corporate activism would be an expensive process for the funds to undertake. And in a sense, it would be. TIAA-CREF, whose stock and bond portfolio totals some $300 billion, is unique in this industry in taking on the responsibilities of corporate activism, spending an amount approaching $1 million per year on the implementation of its splendid—and productive—corporate governance program. This expenditure, however, amounts to but 0.003% (3/1000ths of a basis point) of its invested assets. The benefits generated to TIAA-CREF's participants have been measured in hundreds of millions of dollars.

While small-fund managers could hardly spend the resources necessary for a broad-gauge program, they could at least engage their security analysts in some kind of serious review of the governance of their major corporate holdings. Given the fund industry's $6 trillion of assets, an industry-wide governance effort that entailed just 1/1000th of a basis point would produce an annual commitment of $60 million for an active corporate governance program—far in excess of what such a program would require. Even those dollars, however, would be but a drop in the bucket relative to today's near-$60 *billion* annual fund expenditures on management fees, marketing fees, and operating costs. Even if the governance costs were paid by the funds themselves rather than by their managers (a peculiar notion in and of itself), the change in fund expense ratios would be invisible. So, to paraphrase the adage: "Money is not the object."

A fourth and final obstacle might be described as a "people-who-live-in-glass-houses syndrome." The mutual fund governance system has itself come under severe and well-deserved criticism. Where else in corporate America is there a parallel for the control of a giant publicly held financial corporation by a small outside firm—with its own shareholders—whose principal business is providing the giant corporation with all of the services required to conduct its affairs? Nowhere else, as far as I can tell. And it is that structure that has led to the steady rise in mutual fund expense ratios, generating huge rewards to the shareholders of fund managers at the expense of fund shareholders. It is easier to understand than to accept the reluctance of fund managers to throw stones from their own glass houses at the management of the corporations whose shares they own by becoming corporate activists.

The Effects of Passivity

What are the consequences of a corporate governance system where the owners fail to exercise control? Where mutual funds are silent. Where corporate pension plans are muted. Where individual investors are powerless. Where only a few state and local government pension funds have the voting power *and* the willpower to make a difference. This is the very problem that Adolph Berle and Gardiner Means confronted in 1933 when they wrote *The Modern Corporation and Private Property*. Their concern was essentially that corporate governance problems would develop as ownership and management were separated. While it took a long time for their prophecy to be realized, it is starkly before us today. But the institutional forces that might resolve the problems surrounding today's separation of corporate ownership and corporate control has yet to emerge.

What Berle and Means could not have imagined, however, is that a new arbiter of this separation would emerge: The financial markets. Specifically, the stock market itself has become the arbiter of conflicts of interests between management—who seek, I suppose, high compensation, perquisites, job security, and control over the corporation's affairs—and owners—who want, and arguably deserve, the maximization of true shareholder value. Even as President Clinton's campaign manager James Carville wanted to manage our nation's economy by being reincarnated, "not as the President or the Pope, but as the Bond Market," so a seemingly benevolent despot named "the Stock Market" is the driving force that now bridges the gap between ownership and control in corporate America. And the stock market not only demands efficiency, presses for lower costs, and insists on rationalizing business strategy, but also places a high premium on managed earnings. Given these mixed motivations, however, the stock market is proving to be an imperfect mechanism for this task.

Managed Earnings

Today, we live in a world of managed earnings. While it is corporate executives who do the managing, they do so with at least the tacit approval of corporate directors and auditors, and with the enthusiastic endorsement of institutional investors with short-term time horizons, even speculators and arbitrageurs, rather than in response to the demands of long-term investors. Like it or not, corporate strategy and financial accounting alike focus on meeting the earnings expectations of "the Street" quarter after quarter. The desideratum is steady earnings growth—manage it to at least the 12% level if you can—and at all costs avoid falling short of the earnings expectations at which the corporation has hinted, or whispered, or "ballparked" before the year began. If all else fails, obscure the real results by merging, taking a big one-time write-off, and relying on pooling-of-interest accounting (although that procedure will soon become unavailable). All of this creative financial engineering apparently serves to inflate stock prices, enrich managers, and to deliver to institutional investors what they want.

But if the stock market is to be the arbiter of value, it will do its job best, in my judgment, if it sets its valuations based on punctiliously accurate corporate financial reporting and a focus on the long-term prospects of the corporations it values. However, the market's direction seems quite the opposite, and there is much room for improvement. For while the accounting practices of America's corporations may well be the envy of the world, our nation's financial environment has become permeated with the concept of managed earnings. The accepted idea is to smooth reported earnings, often by aiding security analysts to establish earnings expectations for the year, and then, each quarter, reporting earnings that "meet expectations," or, better yet, "exceed expectations." Failure to meet expectations may be preceded by lower "whisper earnings," which must, in turn, be met. It is an illusory world that ignores the normal ups and downs of business revenues and expenses, a world in which "negative earnings surprises" are to be avoided at all costs.

Managed earnings are reflected in the values of America's most respected companies. Microsoft, for all its rapid growth and essentially conservative practices that tend to *understate* reported earnings, focuses on producing steady quarter-after-quarter gains, even as it prominently discloses "below the line" the huge dilution of earnings resulting from its usage of stock options to reward officers and employees. The odd failure of accounting principles to include stock option costs as compensation, of course, can result in a large overstatement of bottom-line income (prompting Warren Buffett's questions: "If options aren't a form of compensation, what are they? If compensation isn't an expense, what is it? And, if expenses shouldn't go in the calculation of earnings, where in the world should they go?"). But forget that nuance. "The bottom line"—ignoring option dilution—is the number that Wall Street accepts as reality.

General Electric, with or without accounting gimmickry surely one of America's most successful companies, also produces regular double-digit quarterly earnings growth. While many of its businesses are cyclical, analysts have somehow been able to forecast its earnings within 2% of actual for the past ten quarters in a row, an accuracy said to be a 1-in-50 billion chance. It is creative financial engineering that fosters this remarkable precision.

American Express, another blue-chip stock, also regularly meets the market's growth expectations. In this year's second quarter, the firm securitized a pool of credit card receivables in order to produce the expected earnings. When at a meeting with management one analyst raised doubts about the practice, the company's chairman defended the smoothing of earnings, and then took a poll of the security analysts in attendance. The vote: Ten to one in favor of avoiding the decline in reported earnings. A landslide! Wall Street clearly endorses the managed earnings that corporate America targets.

I share SEC Chairman Arthur Levitt's concern that earnings management has gone too far. He cites abuses in huge restructuring changes, creative acquisition accounting, "cookie jar" reserves, excessive "immaterial" items, and premature recognition of revenue. And I surely agree with the Chairman that "almost everyone in the financial community shares responsibility [with corporate management] for fostering this climate." It is, in a perverse sense, a happy conspiracy. But I believe that no corporation can manage its earnings forever, and that managed earnings misrepresent the inherently cyclical nature of business. Even as we begin to take for granted that fluctuating earnings are steady and ever-growing, we ought to recognize that, somewhere down the road, there lies a day of reckoning that will not be pleasant.

Short-Term or Long-Term?

Closely tied to all of this creative financial accounting is the stock market's focus on short-term events—aberrations rather than long-term valuations. The most fundamental tenet of investing, in my view, is *owning businesses and holding them,* for the long term, even "forever," which is said to be Warren Buffett's favorite holding period. But today most investors seem to be doing the opposite, *buying pieces of paper and trading them back and forth,* with one another and with alacrity. It almost goes without saying that playing such games in the stock market casino increases the proportion of the market's returns that is arrogated by the croupiers, and reduces the residual proportion of the market's returns that remains for the gamblers. Where, indeed, are the customers' yachts, or, in today's coin of the realm, the customers' jets? In such an environment, it would seem obvious that the successful strategy is to buy stocks and hold them, never again entering the casino.

And yet short-term *speculation*, not long-term *investing*, is the order of the day. Turnover in the stock market now approaches 100% per year, five times the 20% level of the 1960s and 1970s, and closing in on the 1929 high of 112%. Make no mistake about it, however: The speculators of 1929 were largely individuals; in 1999 the speculators are largely institutions. Alas, Lord Keynes was right: "Professional investors, unable to offset the mass psychology of a large number of ignorant individuals, will strive to foresee changes in the public valuation of stocks."

Reversing Course I. Index Funds

What finally will make institutional managers reverse this counterproductive flight from long-term investing and toward short-term speculation? What will make these managers head in the more sensible direction of focusing on fundamental corporate values? First, I think, will be the growth of indexing investment strategies at the expense of active management strategies. The ultimate index strategy is owning the stock market and holding it forever—by definition a more rewarding strategy than rapidly trading stocks in the marketplace. Put another way, the investor who stays out of the casino earns the market's return, while the investor who enters the casino shares the market's return with the croupiers, earning less in proportion to his level of trading activity. While the rapid growth in the use of index strategies by pension funds during the 1980s has virtually dried up during the 1990s, still, some 20% of pension assets are now indexed. But during the 1990s, index mutual funds have enjoyed strong growth, coming from virtually nowhere to account for nearly 10% of equity fund assets today.

Since the mid-1980s, the indexed portion of pension and mutual fund assets combined has grown from 12% to nearly 20%. So, the management of one-fifth of all institutional assets has nothing to do with trading and speculation, and everything to do with long-term investment fundamentals. Since these institutions act as *owners* of businesses, not *traders* of pieces of paper, their sole recourse to improving shareholder value is to be active participants in the corporate governance process.

With time, I expect that the success of indexing strategies will cause active managers to lengthen their own time horizons. In an increasingly institutionalized financial system, the stock market is populated with skilled, highly trained, and increasingly experienced professionals who are, finally, competing with one another on an ever-more-level playing field. As they face the increasing costs and challenges of outsmarting an ever-more-efficient market, they will surely come to question their ability to add value by their feverish trading, and recognize that a strong focus on governance will be one of the few remaining ways to further enhance fundamental shareholder value.

Reversing Course II. The Ticking Time Bomb of Executive Compensation

The second reason that institutional managers will at last look to fundamentals is that, for all of this short-term focus and approval of managed earnings, they can no longer afford to ignore what I believe is a ticking time bomb on corporate America's balance sheet: The soaring use of executive stock options. Part of the problem is the nature of the options themselves. Options provide corporate managers with incentive-related increases in *stock market* prices rather than increases in the fundamental value of the enterprise. And in this great bull market, the rewards are staggering. Compensation of chief executives, largely through stock options, has risen to 419 times the compensation for the average worker, compared with 85 times in 1990 and just 40 times in 1980. At some point, this extreme distortion of traditional norms alters the nation's social equilibrium.

Yes, stock options align the interests of management and shareholders. But consider these negatives: First, the very relationship between stock *price* and stock *value* may be distorted, as I believe it is today. Second, despite the fact that *any* business which merely reinvests all or part of its earnings should grow in value during any given period, options offer a free ride to managers who put up no capital and take no risk. Third, a rising stock market, unlike the proverbial rising tide, may not lift all boats equally, but it provides enormous rewards even to those who manage companies whose stocks lag the market. Fourth, even if the stock market were deemed the ultimate arbiter of success, it rewards *any* success, irrespective of performance relative to a company's peer group. In short, the fact that there is no "hurdle rate" for the prices at which options are exercisable fails to provide valid incentives and creates rewards where there are no risks.

The amount of potential earnings dilution is huge. One analyst estimates that reported earnings on the S&P 500 Index would be reduced by 50% when diluted by the exercise of existing options, raising today's *adjusted* price-earnings ratio to more than 60 times. Corporate shareholders are giving too much, and getting too little in return.

The most ominous aspect of the flawed option process is only now rearing its ugly head. Time and again, when a corporation's stock price tumbles, management reprices the options, all in the name of continuing to assure that its executives have incentives that are attainable. Understandable as it may be for corporate executives to see things in this way, the question is: What would an *owner* do? Is it fair to the stockholders—any more than to a sole owner of a corporation—to engage in wholesale repricing at a new low price, perhaps in a stock whose shares are temporarily depressed, or even the stock of a company whose prospects have remained stable over a decade but whose stock price has merely soared with a soaring market or plunged with a plunging market? When, as, and if, the stock market takes a big tumble—and all of that earnings management suggests that such a tumble lies ahead when the bubble breaks—the trickling stream of option repricing in recent years will become a torrent. If unopposed by stockholders, it will result in material earnings dilution, likely exacerbating the market decline. Institutional investors, beware. Indeed, be aware enough to tackle the issue head on.

Reversing Course III. Taking Action

My expectation—I hope not vain—is that fund managers will, well, come to their senses. Sooner or later—I pray sooner—they will gradually see the light and adopt long-term investment strategies. Then the industry's nearly single-minded focus on marketing, marketing, marketing will shift to a focus on the stewardship of the assets investors have entrusted to the funds. The issues I've discussed today regarding short-term speculation in the stock market, managed earnings, and executive stock options must be addressed. Mutual funds have the voting power to implement constructive change. It is high time for funds to make their ownership muscle felt by joining the pension funds of state and local governments and TIAA-CREF in actively participating in the process of corporate governance, with a view to enhancing shareholder value.

How to bring this force to bear? One means of doing so would be to have our Investment Company Institute take the lead in organizing an industry-wide corporate governance effort, and today I urge that such an effort begin. So far, however, the industry's efforts have focused not on the interests of investment companies and their shareholders (as the ICI name might seem to suggest), but on the interests of investment managers and *their* owners. However useful and productive the ICI's lobbying, regulatory, and marketing efforts may be to the managers, it is hard to discern that the interests of fund shareholders are at the top of its priority list. I'm not sure whether the ICI has *ever* held a roundtable or forum on the role of funds in corporate governance or on the responsibilities that funds may have as corporate owners. Yet today, with the huge voting power of mutual funds and their managers, the subject can no longer be ignored. It is high time for an industry-wide, ICI-sponsored effort.

Failing action there, however, there is no valid reason that the large fund groups could not meet on a regular basis to discuss corporate governance issues and the activities of particular corporations. Perhaps the Council of Institutional Investors—in which most large state and local government pension funds, but no mutual funds, actively participate—could serve as a role model. The voting power wielded by even a small group of large managers would surely catch the attention of corporate managers. For example, the funds and accounts managed by Fidelity, Vanguard, and Capital Group alone own 100 million to 200 million shares of most large companies, often representing 5% to 10% of each firm's voting control. While these managers have thus far seldom taken up corporate governance issues, were they to form a nucleus of activist firms, other like-minded funds would surely climb aboard the bandwagon. As I understand it, since 1992 SEC policy has been to permit greater communication among shareholders, so if the industry does not act, I urge all major firms that have a long-term investment philosophy and a sense of responsible corporate governance to band together and begin the task.

Way back in 1940, as I reported in my Princeton thesis, the SEC called on mutual funds to serve "the useful role of representatives of the greater number of inarticulate and ineffective individual investors in corporations in which investment companies are also interested." Even though 60 years have elapsed since then, it is not too late to begin. The point is that mutual funds today are owners of huge blocks of stocks. Together, they can wield their power through the controlling influence they hold over corporate affairs. With this ownership comes not only rights, but responsibilities. If the role of this industry is to add value for its own shareholders, the sooner the effort toward enlightened corporate governance—toward working intelligently with corporate managers with no bias other than the interests of the shareholders—begins, the better it will be for investors, and for the financial markets.

15

LOSING OUR WAY: WHERE ARE THE INDEPENDENT DIRECTORS?

*The North American Securities Administrators
Association, Inc.
San Diego, California
October 21, 1991*

*I*T SEEMS ALMOST endemic that, from time to time, every industry loses its way. In a burst of opportunism—or in ignorance of a changed world—firms and even entire industries have lost sight of the principles that made them successful. Scandalous conduct by major Wall Street firms is but a recent example. The automobile industry's failure to treat foreign competition seriously and to "drag its feet" on quality and safety is another. The savings and loan industry's massive move from home mortgages to real estate investments is yet another.

And, it seems to me, the mutual fund industry is in this same position today. In too many areas, we have lost our traditional bearings. Too many management companies—large and small alike—are engaged in a chase for more assets, and for more profits (with correlatively less profits to the shareholders we serve), no matter what the cost, and no matter whether or not the investor is fully and fairly informed.

Let me present, in the brief time allowed this morning, some of the concerns I have: (1) diseconomies of scale that should have been economies of scale; (2) fee increases and fee structures that are appalling; (3) the baneful effect of the notorious 12b-1 plans that encumber existing fund shareholders with the cost of attracting—for whatever reason—new fund shareholders; (4) disclosure in fund reports that, in some instances, verges on the outrageous; and, last but not least, (5) advertising that hawks "reward" and ignores the two other determinants of investment return—*risk* and *cost*. Then I'll conclude with some thoughts as to what, in my opinion, might be done about these problems.

1. DISECONOMIES OF SCALE   When I came into this industry 40 years ago, it was an equity-based industry (i.e., no money market funds and few bond funds) with assets aggregating $2.5 billion, and an average fund expense ratio of 0.72%. Thirty years later, in 1981, assets of equity funds totaled $40 billion, and the average expense ration was 1.04%—an average increase of one basis point (1/100 of 1%) per year.

Now, in 1991, with equity fund assets totaling $250 billion, the average expense ratio has risen to 1.45%—an average increase of *four* basis points per year, or four *times* as much. As a result, since 1981, industry expenses are up nearly eightfold from $470 million to $3.5 billion, with industry assets up only fivefold. The real issue is *not* why expense ratios are up by so much, or even at all. The issue is why they have not declined. For believe me, there are substantial economies of scale in this business—and my next two points—on management fees and 12b-1 plans—will examine why expenses have increased so far in excess of our industry's staggering rate of asset growth.

2. FEE INCREASES AND FEE STRUCTURES   Despite the industry's awesome profitability, many mutual fund managers have in recent years extracted substantial fee increases from the funds they manage. How can these fee increases be justified? Well, each organization will have to answer that for itself, but I will give you just one extreme example.

The annual cost of managing one of the investment companies in a $5 billion complex was stated to be $820,000 for 1990. The previous annual fee was $5,370,000, which provided the adviser with a seemingly adequate operating profit of $4,550,000 per year. However, apparently it was not adequate enough; the fee was raised to $7,050,000, increasing the manager's annual profit to $6,230,000—or 88% of revenues. [These are not my calculations. They come directly from the Fund's proxy.]

Fee increases on existing funds, however, are only part of the problem. Failure to scale down fees in a material way to reflect clear economies of scale is another. But perhaps most significant is the high—one might even say unconscionable—costs sometimes imposed on new funds as they are formed. Here are two examples.

A *money market* fund was offered in 1987 with an expense ratio of 2.1% (last year it was 2.2%). Today, with yields on money market instruments at about 5.8%, the leading money market funds—with expense ratios in the 0.5% range—provide a net yield of roughly 5.3%. This fund's yield is 3.6%. (You must be wondering why anyone would own it.)

A $3 billion *Government-Plus* fund (perhaps more aptly named Government-*Minus*—its net asset value has dropped from $9.47 per share to $7.17 since it was first offered in 1987) has an expense ratio of 1.97%. The manager graciously has agreed to reduce its advisory fee, so the reported ratio is 1.92%. The advisory fee totalled $25,565,000 in 1990 (before that reduction of $1,675,000). What does the shareholder get for that awesome fee? A portfolio consisting of three repurchase agreements, one FNMA issue, two GNMA issues, and seven U.S. Treasury bonds. It simply doesn't seem like the fund should need $25 million worth of advice, particularly since, as I understand it, you don't need to do much, if any, credit analysis on a government bond portfolio. To add insult to injury, the first sentence in the President's letter in the 1990 Annual Report says: "As part of our continuing efforts *to reduce expenses,* we have combined in this report the annual report of the six (same organization's) fixed income funds." Why don't shareholders redeem their shares? Probably because (a) they don't want to realize their losses; and (b) they would have to pay a commission—as high as 6%—to get out. (This so-called contingent deferred sales charge is one of the better kept secrets from mutual fund investors.)

3. *12B-1 DISTRIBUTION PLANS*   Such plans, stripped of all of the verbiage, amount to charging existing fund shareholders for the cost of bringing in new shareholders. Since their introduction in 1980, they have become the rule rather than the exception. Today, 1,861 funds—58% of the 3,226 funds in existence—have such plans. In total, 12b-1 plans cost mutual fund shareholders a cool $1.23 billion last year, representing, in and of itself, an addition of 0.26% to the expense ratios of the funds that incur them.

These distribution plans are often said to enable funds to build their assets, thereby engendering economies of scale. However, the fact is that—except for the very smallest funds—the economies of scale are a fraction of the amount spent to garner them. That is to say, even a fund with a base advisory fee of 0.75% that is scaled to 0.50% as assets rise—a reduction that goes far beyond anything I have seen—would literally *never* recover its sunk costs from a 0.50% distribution fee. I would add, perhaps a bit cynically, that spreading such items as auditors fees and shareholder report costs over a larger asset base are highly unlikely to provide measurable benefits.

These plans are also said to enable funds to improve their returns by better assuring cash inflow, thus minimizing the likelihood that share redemptions will require funds to liquidate portfolio holdings when stock prices are declining. That I have seen no evidence whatsoever that this objective will be accomplished is not the point. The fact is that, even if distribution plans do build cash flow, there is no evidence whatsoever that funds with positive cash flow have better returns; nor that cash outflow creates portfolio management problems (the need to sell securities) that are any different from those created by cash inflow (the need to buy securities).

It should be apparent to a novice, furthermore, that funds cannot spend themselves into success. A poor-performing fund, for example, could spend (and many do) millions of dollars in vain to overcome the shortcomings of its investment adviser. Funds—like all other corporations—should have no guaranteed right-to-life.

But I am not saying that 12b-1 plans are totally wrong. Rather, I am saying that they can be justified, only when, first, the capital investment represented by distribution expenditures can be recaptured to benefit the fund shareholders who are paying the bills; and second, when full and clear disclosure is provided. The truth, as a shareholder proxy statement should say, but does not, is this: "This plan will increase your expenses and commensurately reduce your returns. There is no realistic expectation either that cash inflow will enhance, or outflow diminish, the fund's performance. While an increase in fund assets may be beneficial or harmful to shareholders, it will have the certain effect of increasing advisory fees, providing additional revenues which the adviser may expend to benefit the fund, or to sell more shares, or to receive additional profits, or all three."

4. *FUND REPORT DISCLOSURE*   The quality of disclosure to fund shareholders in shareholder reports is too often superficial, and the quantity minuscule. Many reports are bereft of the most basic information on the fund's returns during the year and over the long term.

Often there are no standards for evaluation of performance (i.e., market indexes or peer groups with comparable objectives), and there is almost never a word from the fund's chief executive—normally the chief executive or an officer of the adviser, but nonetheless responsible to the fund's directors—about whether the fund's results were regarded as satisfactory or unsatisfactory. Too many fund reports make up in glossiness what they lack in substance.

The annual report of the money market fund with the 3.6% yield (described above) does not even state the fund's yield at year-end. (Nor is it published in the weekly press reports showing current money market fund yields.)

In the annual reports of two equity funds in the same mutual fund complex, one states that it outpaced the return of the Standard & Poor's 500 Stock Index for the year, provides the data, and brags about it. The other, having fallen short, does not provide the data, and is silent about it.

A high-yield bond fund, after a disastrous fiscal 1990, provides an annual report, in living color, printed on heavy coated paper, with lots of lovely photographs, and a statement that "negative newspaper headlines raised concern among investors in high yield bonds." Buried deep in the financial statements at the end of the report, is the first and only reference to the fact that during the year the net asset value dropped from $7.48 to $6.30 per share.

5. *FUND ADVERTISING*   I believe it has gotten completely out of hand. It hawks "return" and virtually ignores—except in tiny footnotes—risk and cost. This has become an industry of which it can be truly said: *Don't forget to read the fine print.* And that is hardly a compliment.

"We're number one" advertising is, in my view, philosophically outrageous. While all ads note that "past results cannot be predicted in the future," it seems to me that there is an implicit suggestion that if an investor wants to be number one in the future, that is the fund he should buy. Of course, the linkage between past and future is in fact close to zero—and those who publish the ads know it. Such advertising is also mathematically ridiculous. There are so many time periods, and so many funds, with so many objectives, and with such a variety of asset sizes, it should almost be an embarrassment *not* to be number one in *something*. Here's just one example: "Number one in performance"—but only among 12 growth funds with assets between $250 million and $500 million, for the period March 31, 1971, to March 31, 1991. (For the prior 12 months, the fund ranked 18 of 24 funds.)

In the past few years, much fund advertising has resembled white-sale ads that would do Bloomingdale's credit. Much of this advertising is based on being the "highest yielding" money market and bond funds, in that position only because their advisers have *temporarily* waived their fees, hoping to attract investors who won't notice it when the fees go up. (I hope it is not inappropriate to note that this practice would seem to fly in the face of Section 15(a)(i) of the Investment Company Act, which says that advisory contracts must "*precisely* describe all compensation.") Speaking of these off-again fees, one industry observer said: The mutual fund industry has its own law of gravity: *What goes down, must come up.* Again, it was not intended as a compliment.

So much for my litany of charges: They all spring from essentially the same source: an increasingly pervasive philosophy that this is just another consumer products *business,* rather than a *trust service* offered for the prudent management of other people's money. The mutual fund industry has, I acknowledge, elements of both, but I believe that during the era of the 1980s—and continuing today—the business aspect (a drive for market share, no matter what the cost) has sharply increased, and the fiduciary aspect (sound investment programs, fairly priced and fully explained) reduced commensurately.

Assume, for the purpose of argument, that my concerns are valid. What can be done to protect the investors in your own states?

STATE SECURITIES REGULATIONS   I believe that the gradual elimination of state expense ratio limitations since 1978 (and, where they still exist, almost total waiving of the requirements "on demand") has played a major role in the rise of fund expense ratios. Under these limitations, essentially, large funds were limited to 1% expense ratios, small to 1½% (You should recall that the industry *average* itself is now nearly 1½%.) However, I also believe it is unrealistic to expect their return, nor do I believe that state oversight of fund literature and advertising would prove effective, even if it were feasible.

THE MEDIA   The press has virtually ignored fund proxies that propose advisory fee increases and 12b-1 plans. With 37,000,000 mutual fund shareholders out there, it is hard to believe that these specific fee changes, and these trends as well, are not news. But when there is no glare of sunlight when added costs are imposed on shareholders, a major governor for over-reaching is abandoned. It is probably too late to worry about this, for the continuing escalation of fees cannot go on *forever.* (I don't think.) But the interest of the investing public would be served by more publicity about fund costs. It would also do no harm if there were less press focus on the "best" funds for the prior quarter or year, because it generally results from mere chance. That some fund will be number one is just as certain as that, in 1,024 flips of a coin, someone will flip heads ten times in a row. The difference is that the successful coin flipper goes ignored, while the successful portfolio manager is lionized and credited with extraordinary skill—at least for the moment.

THE SECURITIES AND EXCHANGE COMMISSION   I believe that the Securities and Exchange Commission should *promptly* move forward with its proposed rule that would require each fund to provide in its annual report a Management Discussion and Analysis (MD&A) of its results. This discussion would include complete data on fund performance, comparative data for various standards (appropriate market indexes and peer groups), and a narrative providing commentary on the year's results and how they are evaluated. Of even greater importance, I also urge the Commission, in its forthcoming Investment Company Amendments Act, to require an express statutory fiduciary duty standard for mutual fund directors. With such a federal fiduciary standard, I believe the problems that I have addressed will be largely solved.

THE INDEPENDENT DIRECTORS OF THE FUNDS   The independent directors have a solemn responsibility to place their sole focus on the best interest of mutual fund shareholders. But, for mutual funds, this principle has never been, as far as I know, formally articulated and codified. A federal fiduciary standard would, I believe, be a forceful reminder to directors that fee increases must be fully justified, that expenditures on distribution must carry at least the possibility of being recouped, that annual reports must portray specific fund returns (and how the directors have evaluated them), and that new shareholders who join the fund do so only through advertising that includes full and open disclosure about risk and cost—and not in tiny footnotes—as well as return.

What I am recommending scarcely goes beyond the philosophy expressed in the original Investment Company Act of 1940, which was passed 51 long years ago: "The national public interest and the interest of investors are adversely affected ... when investors do not receive adequate, accurate, and explicit information, fairly presented ... or when investment companies are organized, operated and managed in the interest of investment advisers, rather than in the interest of shareholders ... or when investment companies are not subjected to adequate independent scrutiny." Clearly, that language has been honored more in the breach than in the observance, so my proposal would simply codify those worthy objectives.

Let me conclude by emphasizing that this is a great industry, providing financial services that are useful, if not essential, for investors. But, investors would benefit from some hearty price competition (to reduce prices, *not* to increase them), and far more complete and candid disclosure. For we have, perhaps understandably after a golden decade of growth that has taken fund assets from $100 billion to $1.2 trillion, lost our way, as we have departed to too great a degree from the principles that got us here in the first place. While not all firms in this business have participated in the problems I have described, I think it is fair to say that all of us—Heaven knows, including Vanguard!—have room for improvement. And in the long run, any improvement that helps to make mutual funds a better investment is in the best interest of our shareholders, to say nothing of ourselves as fund managers.

In short, I am confident that this industry will return to its original bearings, if we will but respond positively to these three questions:

- "Whose money is it that we manage?" Our fund shareholders' money.
- "Who represents these shareholders?" The independent directors.
- "Where *are* the independent directors?" I hope they will be back soon.

Part III

Economics and Idealism: The Vanguard Experiment

*T*HESE NEXT FIVE chapters describe how Vanguard has developed over the years. Together, they describe not only why and how the firm came to be formed, but the philosophical ideals inspiring our novel "mutualized" corporate structure, as well as the investment ideas and human values that have remained, to this day, at the very heart of our enterprise.

In Chapter 16, I present a short chronology of our history, focusing on the seemingly endless series of random accidents that made it possible to test my idealism, financial ideas, and organizational values on the hard anvil of the business world. These fortuitous events begin with the genesis of my Princeton senior thesis in 1949, followed by my first job, offered to me by my great mentor Walter L. Morgan; a failed merger, the happy event (as it turned out) of my being fired; the founding—and even the *naming*—of Vanguard in 1974. Each of these events offered the opportunity to take "the road less traveled by." Without them, Vanguard would never have come into existence.

From the outset, given the unprecedented nature of our structure and strategy, I frankly referred to our mission as "The Vanguard Experiment," part of the title of a speech I gave to the Federal Bar Association in March 1975, six months after our founding (Chapter 17). In it, I urged, perhaps too boldly, that our industry rivals, in their enlightened self-interest, "might want to consider" a similar approach. (So far, none has done so.) Initially, our structure—described in detail in the talk—called for the mutualization only of our fund governance and administration. But within two years we had undertaken our first step toward mutualization of investment management and completed our mutualization of distribution. While we were barred from both activities at the outset, I argued (perhaps a bit disingenuously) that we could undertake them by *not* engaging in them at all. Our management of the index fund entailed no *active* management, and our going no-load—after a half-century of distributing funds which carried sales charges—entailed no *active* distribution. So Vanguard's present business model—internalization of *all* aspects of fund management—became fully functional early in 1977 and has remained essentially unchanged to this day.

The concept of an ideal industry structure, however, had occurred to me much earlier. First aired in my 1951 thesis, I spelled it out with surprising candor to my associates at Wellington Management Company in 1971 in my fifth annual "State of the Firm" address as Wellington's chief executive. In the speech entitled "Deliverance," (Chapter 18) I made so bold as to suggest a coming need for investment managers to measure up to higher standards of professional responsibility and fiduciary duty, perhaps through some form of mutualization. I described the concept as "a great objective to be accomplished by 1976." And accomplished it was, but only through the harrowing sequence of fortuitous events that led to Vanguard's foundation.

In recent years, I've thought a great deal about the strong link between Vanguard's economics and its idealism, from the principles I advocated in my thesis to the Vanguard structure itself, to our low costs, and to our index and index-oriented funds. When I studied the enlightened economic philosophy manifested by that great Princetonian Woodrow Wilson as the 23rd President of the United States and his own extraordinary idealism, I sensed a similar connection between the two. In Chapter 19, I explore that parallel, concluding with a citation of Wilson's inspiring 1901 message of hope for the 20th century as the harbinger of my own hope for the 21st century that now lies before us.

The final chapter of Part III may be the most idealistic of all. "On the Right Side of History" was the keynote speech at the 1998 Conference of the Greenleaf Center for Servant-Leadership. In it I discuss the idea of building a model institution, how the superior company can arise from a liberating vision, and what can happen when a company grows from small to large. My words may seem poignant—and in a sense they *are* poignant—but I have no difficulty in reaffirming my confidence in our extraordinary crew, "who know what *ought* to be done, and have done the *right* things at the right time." Our structure and strategy, and the ethical foundation that is our rock, place us, I suggest, "on the right side of history." And so to this day I continue my mission, facing the marvelous challenges that life has always afforded me with an enthusiasm and idealism that remain undimmed by time and tide.

16

VANGUARD—CHILD OF FORTUNE

The Pennsylvania Partnership for Economic Education
Harrisburg, Pennsylvania
January 31, 2000

*I*T'S A THRILL both to be in the capital of this great Commonwealth and to address this distinguished group of business and government leaders. I'll focus this evening on Vanguard's role in the mutual fund world, especially our focus on the elemental principles of investing and economics.

In the 1999 annual reports of the Vanguard mutual funds, I began my message with one of my favorite passages, a quotation from the evocative poetry of Robert Frost:

> *Two roads diverged in a wood, and I—I took the one less traveled by, and that has made all the difference.*

Those few words tell, far better than I could, the story of Vanguard's founding more than 25 years ago. Indeed, we took, not merely a road less traveled by, but a road that no firm in this industry had ever taken before. The well-traveled road—then as now—was one on which mutual funds were managed by an *external* management company, in the business to make a profit for itself by charging a fee for its services. But the Vanguard funds—there were only 11 of them then—would be controlled by *their own* shareholders and operate solely in *their* financial interests. The outcome of our unprecedented decision was by no means certain. We described it then as "The Vanguard Experiment."

Well, I guess it's fair to say it's an experiment no more. During the past 25 years, the assets we hold in stewardship for investors have grown from $1 billion to more than $500 billion, and I believe that our reputation for integrity, fair-dealing, and sound investment principles is second to none in this industry. Our staggering growth—which I never sought—has come in important part as a result of the simple investment ideas and basic human values that are the foundation of my personal philosophy. And I have every confidence that they will long endure at Vanguard, for they are the right ideas and right values, unshakable and eternal.

Fortune and Princeton

The Vanguard you know today—the largest pool of assets in the Commonwealth of Pennsylvania—exists only by remarkable chance. Hard as it is for me to imagine an investment world without Vanguard, we are here by the grace of the Lord. The first piece of good luck came 50 years ago, when I was determined to write my senior thesis at Princeton University on a subject which no previous thesis had ever tackled. (There went Adam Smith, Karl Marx, and John Maynard Keynes!) In December 1949, during my junior year, I stumbled across an article in *Fortune* magazine that described the mutual fund industry as "tiny but contentious." I had never before even heard the term "mutual fund," and I decided on the spot that this industry should be the topic of my thesis, which I entitled, "The Economic Role of the Investment Company." And so my long journey in this industry began.

It seems problematical at best that my thesis, as some have generously alleged, laid out the design for what Vanguard would become. But whether that is true or not, many of the practices I specified then would, 50 years later, prove to lie at the very core of our success. "The principal function of mutual funds is the management of their investment portfolios. Everything else is incidental. . . . Future industry growth can be maximized by a reduction of sales loads and management fees. . . . Mutual funds can make no claim to superiority over the market averages." And, with a final rhetorical flourish, funds should operate "in the most efficient, honest, and economical way possible." Were these words an early design for a sound enterprise? Or merely callow, even sophomoric, idealism? I'll leave it to you to decide. But whatever was truly in my mind all those years ago, the thesis clearly put forth the proposition that mutual fund shareholders must be given a fair shake. Since our outset in 1974, that is what Vanguard has been all about. And, I can assure you, it works!

The next wonderful piece of good fortune came my way when fellow Princetonian Walter L. Morgan, who founded Wellington Management Company and Wellington Fund in Philadelphia in 1928, read my thesis. He was impressed enough to offer me a job after my graduation from Princeton in 1951. While I should have leapt at the chance offered to me by this great man, and my good friend until his death at age 100 in 1998, I agonized about the risks of going into what was then a tiny business. But, my courage strengthened by the conclusion in my thesis that the industry's future would be bright, I finally accepted the offer. And a good thing, too!

By 1965, Mr. Morgan had made it clear that I would be his successor. At that time, the company was lagging its peers, and he told me to do whatever it took to solve our problems. Young and headstrong (I was then but 36 years of age), I put together a merger with a high-flying group of four "whiz kids" who had achieved an extraordinary record of investment performance over the preceding six years. (Such an approach—believing that *past* performance has the power to predict *future* performance—is, of course, antithetical to everything I believe today.) Together, we five whiz kids whizzed high for a few years, and then whizzed low. The speculative fever in the stock market during the "Go-Go Era" of the mid-1960s died, and was followed by a 50% market decline in the early 1970s. The once-happy partners had a falling out, and in January 1974 I was fired from what I had considered "my" company.

In the Business and Out

But without both the 1951 hiring, which providentially brought me *into* this industry, and the 1974 firing, which abruptly took me *out* of it, there would be no Vanguard today. Nonetheless, removed from my position as head of Wellington Management Company, I decided to pursue an unprecedented course of action. The Wellington Management Company directors who fired me comprised a minority of the Board of Wellington Fund itself, and I went to the *Fund* Board with a novel proposal: Have the Fund, and its then-ten associated funds, declare their independence from their manager. It wasn't *exactly* the Colonies telling King George III to get lost, as it were, in 1776. But *fund independence*—the right to operate in the interest of their own shareholders free of conflict and outside domination—was the heart of my proposal.

Thanks largely to the determination of a key Wellington Fund director named Charles D. Root, Jr., the Fund Board, after seven months of heated debate, accepted my proposal by the narrowest of margins. Perhaps because there are so few true leaders in our corporate society, such leadership by an independent director is rare in America today. I can assure you that it was even rarer all those years ago. But happen it did, yet another happy accident, and the new firm—a firm that would be owned, not by outsiders, but by the funds themselves—was incorporated on September 24, 1974.

Whether these events were fortuitous, or accidental, or Heaven-sent—I'll leave that for you to decide—another was about to happen. The new firm needed a *name*. In September, not a moment too soon, a dealer in antique prints came by my office with some small engravings from the Napoleonic War era, illustrating the military battles of the Duke of Wellington, for whom Mr. Morgan had named his first mutual fund all those years before. When I bought them, he offered me some companion prints of the British naval battles of the same era. Ever enticed by the sea and its timeless mystery, I bought them, too. Delighted, the dealer gave me the book from which they had been removed. After he left I browsed through it, even as I had browsed through *Fortune* 25 years earlier. I came to the saga of the historic Battle of the Nile (recently designated by *The New York Times* as the greatest naval battle of the millennium), where in 1798, Lord Nelson sank Napoleon's fleet. There, I paused, and noticed Nelson's triumphant dispatch "from the deck of HMS *Vanguard*," his victorious flagship. The naval tradition of the name "Vanguard," together with the leading-edge implication of the noun *vanguard* were more than I could resist. And two weeks later, on September 24, 1974, "The Vanguard Group, Inc." was born—in a profound sense, the child of fortune.

The Character of Vanguard

But, truth told, there is more to Vanguard than this incredible series of happy accidents. So let me take you now to the character and nature of the company that had just come into existence. By having the mutual funds themselves responsible for their own governance and administration—after all, that's what independence was all about for the funds in 1974 even as it was for the colonies in 1776—we had broken new ground in the fund industry. Not only would we operate the funds at cost, but we would operate them at the lowest *possible* cost, disciplined and sparing in every expenditure, always asking ourselves: "Is this expenditure necessary?" Or, to put it another way: "If this were my own money rather than the shareholders' money, would I spend it?" (Happily for our investors, I really hate to spend even my own money!)

In many businesses, all of this cost discipline could be merely an interesting observation, a harmless diversion. But in investing, *cost matters*. It doesn't stretch reality to point out that in most respects the stock market is a casino. A casino in which the investor-gamblers swap stocks with one another, a casino in which, inevitably, all investors as a group share the stock market's returns, no more, no less. *But only until the rake of the croupiers descends*. Then, what was a fruitless search by investors to beat the market *before* costs—a zero-sum game—becomes a negative-sum game *after* the costs of investing are deducted—a loser's game.

And the way the mutual fund game is played carries heavy costs and entails lots of croupiers, each wielding a wide rake. The cost of sales commissions when (most) funds are purchased. The opportunity cost when stock funds hold cash reserves in rising markets. The cost of fund management fees, marketing—all those television advertisements you see—and operations. The transaction costs expropriated by brokers and investment bankers when fund managers buy and sell the stocks in fund portfolios. The cost—and it is *huge*—of the excessive taxes to which fund shareholders are subjected unnecessarily, the result of the incessant, often mindless, turnover of fund portfolios—now nearly 100% per year. One can only be reminded of Pascal's words: "All human evil comes from this, man's inability to sit quietly in a room."

How *much* do costs matter? Hugely! Taking into account sales charges, management fees, operating expenses, and portfolio turnover, the average mutual fund deducts about 2½% per year from investor returns. Assuming—an arbitrary assumption indeed—that the manager is able to match an annual stock market return of, say, 12½% *before costs*, the shareholder would receive a net return of 10% *after* costs. Result: 20% of the investor's return is consumed by costs in one year, 29% in a decade, and fully 45% of the return is consumed in a quarter century.

Nearly one-half of the cumulative return generated by the stock market has been confiscated by the costs incurred by the typical mutual fund. And that's *before taxes*. In a market returning 12½%

annually, excess taxes could easily reach 2% per year, further slashing that 10% after-cost return to an 8% after-tax return. Now, the croupiers have consumed 36% of the investor's return in a year, with compounding it leaps to 48% in a decade and—I'm glad you're sitting down!—fully 68% in a quarter century. That leaves 32% of the market's return remaining for the investor, who put up 100% of the capital and took 100% of the risk. Yes, *costs matter.*

The First Index Fund

It was my conviction that costs are crucial that inevitably brought Vanguard to the two major mutual fund innovations with which I've been most closely identified—one very well known, the other barely known at all. Well known—indeed it seems almost folklore now—is our pioneering formation of the first index mutual fund. It was the very first step in the development of our corporate strategy. In mid-1975, only months after we began operations, I began to develop the rationale for the index fund. A quarter century earlier, the concept of an index fund had received at least tangential focus in my Princeton senior thesis. (Remember, "mutual funds can make no claim to superiority over the market averages.") And by the mid-1970s, the academic financial journals had published several articles suggesting the development of index funds. In order to prove that the gambling casino theory I mentioned earlier worked in practice, I calculated by hand the annual returns generated by the average mutual fund during the previous 30 years, and then compared them with the returns of the Standard & Poor's 500 Index. The Index won by a 1½% annual pre-tax margin—virtually identical to the actual costs assessed by the mutual fund croupiers during that earlier era. Voilà! *Practice confirmed theory.* By December 30, 1975, we had incorporated the industry's first index fund.

Why was it Vanguard, rather than some other fund firm, that was the pioneer? Many financial firms must have recognized, just as easily as I did, the mathematics of the marketplace that define investment success by the apportionment of returns between investors and managers, even as between gamblers and croupiers. But external fund managers had a powerful vested interest in maintaining their own extraordinarily high profitability. We alone had an internally managed structure and a mission to be the lowest-cost provider of financial services in the world. So even if, at the same instant we did, 100 mutual fund firms had grasped the opportunity of a lifetime that indexing presented, 99 would have prayed that the cup of indexing pass quickly from their hands.

But, as fate would have it, as the evidence in favor of indexing mounted, one firm had just been formed that—like the suspect in a good murder mystery—had *both* the opportunity and the motive to seize the day, and take the first step that would one day re-landscape the financial firmament. After recognizing our opportunity, only force of will—persistence, patience, and determination, along with a healthy dollop of missionary zeal—were required. Implementation, after all, has always been far tougher than ideation! But we implemented with zeal, watching acceptance follow, and have seen indexing move from heresy to dogma.

The First Multi-Series Bond Fund

No comparable sea change was required in our second major innovation in mutual fund investment strategy—a new strategy for managing bond funds. It came less than a year after we formed our index fund, and had precisely the same basis—the knowledge that, in any given sector of the financial market, managers as a group must lose by the amount of the aggregate costs of the croupiers, along with the fact that we had both the mission to provide our services to investors at the lowest possible cost, and the structure to do exactly that. Again, opportunity *and* motive!

In June 1976, Congress had passed a law making it possible to offer municipal bond mutual funds. The first such funds were traditional actively managed bond funds, charging high costs. Ever the contrarian, I was deeply skeptical that *any* manager could consistently forecast interest rates with accuracy, and thus significantly outpace the famously efficient bond market over the long run. This situation presented Vanguard with the opportunity to change, not merely the structure of fixed-income management in mutual funds, but its very nature. Given our low operating expenses, we were in a position to offer a municipal bond fund that could deliver to our investors the highest *net* yields in the field, winning the performance derby not by genius, but by combining minimal cost with a less active approach to bond management.

But how would we deal with the question of managing bond maturities? The proverbial lightbulb went on: An idea so simple and so obvious as to defy description. We created, not a single "managed" municipal bond fund—as was the accepted custom of the day—but three separate series: A long-term fund; a short-term fund (essentially the first tax-exempt money market fund); and—you guessed it!—an intermediate-term fund. Each would own high-grade tax-exempt bonds, rigorously maintain a defined maturity range, employ professional managers, and minimize portfolio turnover. And the shareholders would be rewarded with top performance.

It is difficult to be very proud of such an elemental conception. Yet the simple notion of the three-tier bond fund is now firmly established as the industry norm, for tax-exempt and taxable bond funds alike. In its obviousness, its elemental simplicity, and its reliance on rock-bottom costs, the three-tier, fixed-income strategy we pioneered in 1976 had the same genesis as our 1975 pioneering of the index stock fund: The banal insight that it is the *costs* of investing that determine the gap between the returns the stock and bond markets *provide* and the returns investors as a group *receive*. Conclusion: To the victors—the shareholders of the lowest cost funds—belong the spoils.

It is Vanguard's stock indexing and bond management investment strategies—and the reputation we have earned for their efficient implementation—that have accounted for the lion's share of our growth. Of the $540 billion of assets we manage today, fully $370 billion—two-thirds of that total—is accounted for by funds following those two elemental strategies. Of course, success hardly came overnight. After a decade, for example, the assets of our first index fund (we now have 28 index funds, keyed to various stock and bond market indexes), totalled less than $500 million. But with our missionary zeal and our focus on simple investment strategies and investor education, we have, I think, begun to change the mutual fund industry, to make it a better place for investors to entrust their hard-earned dollars.

Education and Economics

Much of my career, in fact, has focused on educating investors about the elemental economics that drive this business and the simple economics of investing. Indeed, though it happened a half-century ago, it seems like only yesterday that I was writing my thesis on "The Economic Role of the Investment Company." Amazing as it may seem, in recent years, I've used passages from that ancient document as the platform for talks about corporate governance, the sources of investment returns, fund performance, and the challenges confronting this industry. (Indeed, it may be some form of vindication that the thesis and a series of my speeches will be published by McGraw-Hill this autumn, the first volume of their planned series, *Great Ideas in Finance*.)

On this grand occasion, right here in the capital of our great home state—this remarkable American commonwealth that has been the source of fine governance, such fair taxation, such hospitality to business, and the home of such a splendid, motivated, and well-qualified labor force—it seems only fair to attribute considerable credit for our growth to being here in Pennsylvania, as well as to the kind of simplicity Pennsylvania's founder, William Penn, cherished when he came to his newly chartered lands in 1621. For Penn's own words come preciously close to describing the conduct of Vanguard's affairs:

Method goes far to prevent trouble in business: for it makes the task easy, hinders confusion, saves abundance of time; and instructs those that have business depending, both what to do and what to hope.

And so, even as William Penn looked at Pennsylvania as his "Holy Experiment" for human rights and perfect freedom, I began Vanguard as an experiment—though hardly a holy one—to test whether a mutual fund enterprise of, by, and for the shareholders could succeed in a competitive, dog-eat-dog industry. With Quaker-like simplicity in our investment philosophy and with Penn's stubbornness, candor, and thrift in our business strategy, we've surely met the test so far.

My own role from the outset—and particularly in recent years—has been one of spreading the word. Speaking out all over America, not so much on Vanguard itself, but on the elementary principles that are embodied in the investment philosophy, strategies, and human values that I've inculcated into Vanguard, principles that are hardly proprietary, principles that any firm in this industry could adopt if only it has the wit and wisdom to do so.

In that context, I take this moment to applaud the Pennsylvania Partnership for Economic Education for the splendid work it is doing to raise the level of economic, financial, and investment understanding of our citizenry, and especially our youth. I know my trust is not misplaced that this mission will not lose sight of the fact that economics does not stand apart from idealism, that, quoting Woodrow Wilson, "There are other things besides material success with which one must supply our generation . . . we need men who care more for principles than for money, for the right adjustments of life than the gross accumulations of profit . . . for sober thoughtfulness and mere devotion as well as practical efficiency."

My belief that the economic functioning of a business enterprise cannot be separated from the values it holds high has worked splendidly in practice. And at this stage of my life, I recognize more than ever the special meaning of William Penn's credo:

> *I expect to pass through this world but once. Any good therefore that I can do, or any kindness I can show to any fellow creature, let me do it now. Let me not defer or neglect it, for I shall not pass this way again.*

And so I will press on in my mission, comforted with some closing words of Robert Frost that parallel those describing the journey that I cited at the outset, a journey taken down a long road in a woods less traveled by:

> *The woods are lovely, dark, and deep, but I have promises to keep, and miles to go before I sleep. And miles to go before I sleep.*

17

THE WINDS OF CHANGE:
THE VANGUARD EXPERIMENT
IN INTERNALIZED
MANAGEMENT

*FBA-CCH Conference
on Mutual Funds and Investment Management
San Diego, California
March 12, 1975*

I AM MOST PLEASED to have this
opportunity to appear before this meeting of the Federal Bar Association, and to talk about something that is truly unique in the mutual
fund industry: the restructuring of one of the pioneer mutual fund
groups in a manner designed to give the Funds corporate independence and self-sufficiency, and the ability to obtain investment advisory and distribution services under terms which are negotiated at
arm's length. From a business standpoint, we have done something
useful, novel, and exciting; from an independent standpoint, we have
something that is clearly designed to serve our shareholder; and from
a legal standpoint, we have, in a real sense, converted the theoretical
letter of the Investment Company Act of 1940 into the real spirit of
this statute.

Wellington Fund, the original member of our Fund Group, was
founded in 1928—just short of a half century ago. With the other ten
Funds that were added during the ensuing years, our Group's assets
presently aggregate $1.7 billion. For a large and established complex,
we have taken a giant step. And you might ask "why?"

I will try to answer that key question definitively today, for there
are, we believe, many good solid business and philosophical reasons

behind our actions. But at the outset, I must frankly acknowledge that our new structure was born of corporate conflict. In January, 1974, our Fund directors were faced with this situation: The Funds' Management Company had replaced its chief executive, who also served as the Funds' chief executive. This situation compelled the directors to examine all of the courses of action that were open to them. I propose to say no more about this corporate background, except to emphasize that it provided only the precipitating issue. The underlying issue—involving the fundamental relationship between the Funds and those who serve them—is much more important, and it is this issue that I will deal with in depth today. Specifically, I want to cover six areas involved in our restructuring:

1. The *mandate* from the Fund Directors;
2. The *concept* of internal management;
3. The *timetable* for implementation;
4. The *challenges* we faced;
5. The *opportunities* our new structure holds;
6. The *implications* for the industry.

1. The Mandate

Faced with the *fait accompli* I have noted, the Fund independent directors (8 of the 11 Board members, and essentially the same for each Fund) made some prompt decisions. They made them solely with a view to serving the interests of the Fund shareholders, and I think it is fair to say that they were assiduous in their efforts, incredibly diligent, and, as a result, are probably among the best-informed and most knowledgeable group of directors in the entire mutual fund industry today. The independent directors decided, first, to constitute themselves as a working group, assuming primary responsibility for resolving the issues facing the Funds; second, to hire independent legal counsel to advise them; third, to continue their own chief executive in office, at least for an interim period; and fourth, to give him a mandate.

The mandate I received, as the Funds' chief executive, was to undertake a definitive study of how our Fund Group could best be organized to obtain the highest quality administrative, investment advisory, and distribution services at the lowest reasonable cost. This was a substantial project: a review of the past, an analysis of the present, and an appraisal of the future. It required an exhaustive study—

ultimately encompassing five volumes (perhaps 300 pages in all)—of financial data, performance and distribution results, organizational and personnel specifications, legal and regulatory aspects, and plans and projections. (The Management Company, of course, also prepared a substantial amount of material of its own for the Fund directors.) If it would be premature at best to characterize our study as an industry landmark, it in fact proved to be just that for our organization. Our "Future Structure Study," as it came to be called, may be seen as the outgrowth of one of the basic issues facing the mutual fund industry: What structure would provide the optimum means for a major fund group to meet the challenges of today and capitalize on the opportunities of tomorrow?

The Directors requested that our Future Structure Study cover *all* the options available to them. It occurred to us, of course, that was a lot of options, and the number was quickly reduced to seven. They ranged from Option 1—the status quo (meaning the standard structure in the fund industry, with a management company totally responsible for all fund activities)—all the way over to Option 7, starting anew by terminating the existing advisory and distribution contracts, and having the Funds form their own organization exclusively to serve all of their needs.

However, the most serious consideration was given to what we defined as Options 2, 3, and 4:

Option 2—Internal Management, whereby the Funds would assume full control of their administrative and financial activities, contracting out investment advice and distribution.

Option 3—Internal Management and Distribution, whereby the Funds would assume direct internal responsibility for all distribution activities as well. (This course raised some interesting regulatory issues, since the Funds would directly pay part of their distribution costs. I will return to this point later on.)

Option 4—What we defined as "Mutualization," whereby the Funds would *purchase* the mutual fund business assets and certain other assets of their management company, thus controlling all of the administrative, distribution, and investment advisory services provided to them. Such a step was without precedent (as were Options 2 and 3) but would have undergone close regulatory scrutiny, and might not, of course, have received the requisite regulatory blessing.

Option 2, of course, was the option ultimately adopted. In July, the Fund Directors formally decided to internalize Fund corporate management and administrative activities, and to retain Wellington Management Company as investment adviser and distributor for the Funds. Their decision to take this unprecedented step was not an easy one. If some see it as a conservative step, in view of the other options available, I can only say that the decision reflected an honest judgment that the Fund shareholders would be best served not only by the intrinsic merit of the arrangement itself, but by the relative simplicity of the step, the likelihood of quick regulatory approval, and the maintenance of the existing Fund officers and staff, and the existing organization of the adviser and distributor. Further, it is often good judgment to take small steps, when the issues are novel and complex.

2. The Concept

The adoption of Option 2—the Funds assuming control of all their administrative activities—was based on one crystal clear concept: *Independence.* The Fund Directors wanted to be independent of those who provided them with the services they required—not just independence for its own sake, but for the sake of the shareholders they serve. This concept rests on the conviction that the quality and efficiency of these services can best be maintained if the Funds are *clients,* rather than *creatures* or *captives,* of the adviser and distributor. Here is how we defined "independence," quoting excerpts from our application to the SEC that I will later discuss:

> **the real and practical ability of the Funds (1) to make day-to-day policy and operating decisions with the interests of the Funds as the sole consideration; (2) to evaluate effectively and thoroughly the quality and costs of all services provided to them; (3) to price appropriately such services and make changes, if appropriate, in the persons or companies providing them.**

If *independence* was relatively easy to define, defining *administration* was more of a challenge. That is to say, exactly what functions would the Funds assume for themselves? The Directors ultimately decided the Funds would have their own executive officers, who would assume full responsibility for these functions:

1. Financial, including accounting, budget, and control
2. Legal and compliance
3. Operational, including shareholder account maintenance and custodianship
4. Shareholder reporting and communications
5. Monitoring and planning, including the evaluation of all services externally provided to the Funds
6. Any additional services the Funds may request

These responsibilities will be assumed by a Fund staff of approximately 60 persons—now fully in place—who will be compensated exclusively by the Funds, who will have no economic interest in the adviser, and who, in the last analysis, will have their professional careers tied to the Funds.

Perhaps a reasonable way of viewing the scope of the Fund staff's responsibilities is to look at the financial dimensions, based on 1975 pro forma estimates:

Staff personnel and operating expenses	$1,500,000
Shareholder account maintenance	2,500,000
Custodian fees	300,000
Shareholder reports and proxies	500,000
Taxes	600,000
Legal, auditing, insurance, directors' fees, etc.	800,000
Total	$6,200,000

This total compares with about $6,500,000 of investment advisory fees estimated to be paid by the Funds in 1975 under the revised advisory contracts that were agreed to. The basis of the agreement was that the Funds' achievement of the real—but highly intangible—benefits of independence should be accompanied by tangible savings to shareholders. The net result was to reduce Fund management fees by about $1,045,000 (based on net assets on July 31, 1974), representing $621,000 of costs to be assumed from the management company (the Funds were, of course, already bearing most of the costs outlined above), plus $424,000 of savings to Fund shareholders. These savings were an implicit recognition that, as the management company's responsibilities to the Funds were reduced, it was both fair and appropriate to provide for a commensurate reduction in its profits.

Having determined the conceptual, operational, and financial steps required to bring the Funds to an independent and self-sufficient posture, we then had to decide on the optimum *structure* for our complex. To optimize operational efficiency and economy in dealing with the 11 separate Funds that comprise our Group, we decided to create a new corporation—we call it a service company—to carry out the Funds' affairs. It will be owned entirely by the Funds. It will have essentially the same officers and directors as the Funds themselves, will directly employ all members of the staff, and will provide to the Funds the services earlier outlined. A service contract defines the Funds' relationship with the service company; provides for its initial capitalization of $300,000 and subsequent changes; spells out the services to be provided to the Funds and the basis for cost allocation; and specifies the basis on which Funds may join the Group. Most importantly, the service company provides its services to the Funds at cost, on a non-profit basis. The service company is, in sum, simply the vehicle through which the Funds carry out their individual and collective activities.

The concept of a service company also enabled us to deal with another difficult business and conceptual issue: how to collectively identify our Fund Group. Our problem here was rather unique, since our Funds do not have a common name (e.g., Dreyfus, Fidelity, Eaton & Howard, etc.), a situation that developed from a court decision (*Taussig v. Wellington*) that, in essence, gave Wellington Fund exclusive rights to the name "Wellington" in the investment company, as distinct from investment advisory, field. Even putting aside this question, it seemed somehow inappropriate under our newly achieved independence to continue referring to "The Wellington Group of Investment Companies," when it was hardly clear whether "Wellington" referred to Wellington Fund or Wellington Management Company. So we decided to develop a new name for the service company, and also to use that name as the means of collectively identifying the Funds. The name we chose was *Vanguard—The Vanguard Group* for the service company, *The Vanguard Group of Investment Companies* as the identifier for the funds collectively. Perhaps it goes without saying that the principal reason for our name selection is that we believe our new structure indeed places us "in the forefront" of this changing industry.

A final word on our concept of internal management. It contemplates that the Funds (through Vanguard) are (1) *directly* responsible for the performance, at cost, of all administrative services required by the Funds in carrying out their corporate business and financial affairs, and (2) *ultimately* responsible, through a continuous process of monitoring and evaluation, for the performance of all investment advisory, distribution and other services provided to the Funds by external organizations, and for assuring that these services are provided at reasonable cost. As I have noted, the Funds decided to retain Wellington Management Company as adviser and distributor, under contracts with revised terms and conditions. Interestingly, the revisions required were small in number, with the major one (other than the fee reduction) being the simple deletion of the adviser's responsibility under the previous management contract "to administer the affairs of the Fund," limiting the new responsibility solely "to managing the investment of the assets of the Fund."

3. The Timetable

Let us now turn briefly to the timetable involved in this restructuring. Following the decision by the Board in late July to adopt an internal management structure, it took most of August and September to turn our concept into a tangible plan (functions, staff, structure, fees, name, etc.). In particular, the renegotiations of the financial terms of the Fund advisory agreements was no small task, for two reasons: (1) to assure the independence of each individual Fund, we decided to abandon the "complex-wide" element of our existing fee structure (under which approximately one-half of each Fund's fee was based on the aggregate assets of all of the Funds in our Group) and have each Fund's fee stand on its own; (2) to assure that our restructuring provided financial benefits (in the form of demonstrable cost savings) to each Fund, we had to examine literally dozens of fee schedules, expense allocation formulas, and asset projections. We ultimately agreed upon a sliding scale of advisory fees beginning at .445% on the first $250 million of assets and declining to .10% on assets in excess of $700 million.

On October 4, we filed our application with the SEC, essentially to obtain several required exemptions from Section 17(b) of the Investment Company Act of 1940. These exemptions were required to allow the Funds to engage in a "joint transaction"—the formation, capitalization, and ownership of the service company—and to permit the Funds to purchase the certain furniture and fixtures from the

Management Company, for approximately $60,000. The creation of the service company enabled us to face the joint transaction issue squarely. However, it is interesting to speculate as to whether an SEC application would have been necessary if no assets were purchased from the Management Company, and if, rather than determining to carry out the Funds' activities through a service company, we had simply determined to have each Fund staffed by its own employees, who would also serve all of the other Funds.

Proceeding the way we did, however, enabled us to make a definitive articulation of our position as being "consistent with the provisions, policies and purposes of the Act"—particularly with respect to fostering the operation and management of investment companies in the interests of their shareholders rather than other (Section 1(b)(2)), the duty to evaluate investment advisory and principal underwriting contracts (Section 15), and the fiduciary duty sections (36(a) and (b)).

On January 17, 1975, the SEC acted on our application, releasing without comment our documents for public notice. They asked no change or amendment whatever, a remarkable tribute to our lawyers, who had no boilerplate to copy from in this unprecedented arrangement. During the ensuing notice period, there was no request for a public hearing, and the SEC determined not to order one. Hence, on February 18, our application was approved, with the SEC finding "on the basis of the information stated," that our proposed transaction is "reasonable and fair and does not involve overreaching on the part of any person concerned, and consistent with the policies of the Funds and the general purposes of the Act."

Our Fund proxies, providing for the formation and operation of Vanguard, and submitting revised advisory agreements to shareholders, were cleared by the SEC last week. Proxy solicitation will ensue immediately, with our annual meetings scheduled during the last three weeks of April. If all works according to plan, and we have every reason to assume it will, the new contracts will be approved, the new corporation will get under way, and Vanguard group will be handling the Funds' affairs on May 1, 1975.

4. The Challenges

If I have oversimplified the development of the Vanguard concept, or if I have understated the complexity of its implementation and the length of time it took, one thing is clear: internalizing a fund group's management is a substantial undertaking with a set of risks, costs, and challenges that should not be underestimated. Lest you consider taking this step unaware of the consequences, let me summarize them briefly:

- Perhaps the events which precipitated our restructuring made us particularly susceptible to the challenge of public relations. The press loves controversy and will inevitably personalize conflict to the extent possible. Our restructuring was, to a degree, therefore conducted in a "goldfish bowl." With the financial press covering rather fully the executive changes, the deliberations of the directors, the restructuring announcement, the SEC filing and approval, the Vanguard name, and so on. It would have been better to deal with these matters with a lower profile, but one's span of control only goes so far.

- As a result of this publicity, we attempted to track the impact of the restructuring on our Fund sales and liquidations. It is my conviction that the impact on liquidations was no more than normal (e.g., our liquidations remained at approximately industry-wide levels), and the impact on new share sales was moderately negative (e.g., a decline in market share slightly greater than that might have been anticipated, based on other known factors.

- Organizational change is another important factor. Internal management means that, in general, the Fund staff members assume new full-time responsibilities and with them new attitudes. Some of their relationships with previous associates may take on an adversary (hopefully not an antagonistic) character; and the executives and staff of the adviser will inevitably reflect some uncertainty about the change. Positive and open communications can allay these transitional problems. But I would not underestimate the advantages to the Funds in having experienced people in place to do the job; intimate knowledge of how all of the Fund management, advisory, and distribution affairs are conducted is most valuable.

- This experience and knowledge play a key role not only in establishing the new structure and in forming the new organization, but in the real arm's length negotiation that is involved both in defining operational responsibilities and in establishing new financial terms. I can only say that until one gets into such a negotiation—with respect to fee rates, allocation of expenses, etc.—one cannot be fully aware of the multiplicity of issues that exist.

- Another challenge is preparing the compilation of data for Fund directors to review and evaluate the proposed new advisory and distribution agreements. In our *Directors' Annual Review—1975,* we had to make not only definitive and complex studies of investment and distribution performance, and of comparative *management* fees and expense ratios, but also of comparative *investment advisory* fees, recognizing that the new contracts are of the *advisory,* not the *management,* variety. Suffice it to say that such studies must be scrupulously fair and objective.

- Finally, a word about State expense ratio guarantees. An external advisory firm, newly independent, will doubtless raise the question as to why it, any more than, for example, the Fund's transfer agent or custodian, should guarantee the Fund's expense ratio. If that question is far less complex than its answer, it must nevertheless be answered. This is one loose end we have not yet dealt with definitively.

In sum, the challenges—and I have only had time to highlight them here—are numerous, complex, and worthy of your consideration.

5. The Opportunities

If I had to identify the single key opportunity in our new structure, it would be that the Vanguard Group concept should be good for shareholders. Our Fund Group will now have its own staff, with an eye sole to the interests of the shareholders, without conflict of interest, divided loyalties, or the lure of other business activities. Our duty is to make sure that the Funds' interests come first and that they are well served. Now I recognize that is a generality, and a pretty glittering one at that. But it can be translated into some rather clear specific advantages:

1. *The Incentive for Performance.* The Fund shareholders can be confident that, if the adviser fails to provide satisfactory performance, he faces the same risk faced by any adviser to any large institutional client. In this sense, all of the advisory fees paid by

the Funds are, in the finest sense, incentive fees. And we hope this incentive in itself will help to enhance the investment results realized by our shareholders.

2. *Sophisticated Quantitative Evaluation of Performance.* The Fund staff will apply the same rigorous, sophisticated—and sometimes technical—standards of performance evaluation, fairly and objectively, that any major institution uses in evaluating its advisers. The ability to monitor results soundly is, as you know, beyond the capability of all but the most sophisticated investors.

3. *Quality of Advisory Service.* The shareholder can also be sure the Fund staff is carefully monitoring and evaluating the adequacy, competence, and quality of the people who comprise the staff of the adviser and distributor, to ensure that the Funds are receiving the services for which they have contracted.

4. *Fund Policies Consistent with Fund Objectives.* The Fund staff will also be in a position to see that each Fund's investment program is consistent with the Fund's policies and objectives, as spelled out in the prospectus.

5. *Fair and Competitive Expense Ratios.* Our Fund contracts have been negotiated at arm's length; not only as to the amount of advisory fee, but also as to the allocation of expenses as between Fund and adviser—clearly, a very important area. This negotiation, as I mentioned, has already laid the groundwork for a significant reduction in Fund expenses.

6. *Shareholder Reports: Objectivity and Perspective.* The shareholder will receive Fund reports that will "tell it as it is," with candor and fairness. If results are good, we will say so; and if they are not, we will be equally candid. In short, our reports will be written from the perspective of the shareholder.

7. *Encouragement of Distribution Activities.* The Fund Group will be in a position to encourage distribution activities. A good cash inflow should be in the interest of Fund shareholders, for our Fund Group expenses are relatively fixed, and thus become lower in ratio as assets increase; our investment advisory fees do the same, by reason of the scaling down under our new fee schedule.

8. *New Funds and the Negotiation Process.* The formation of new funds—their objectives, markets, cost structure—has a particular advantage under the Vanguard concept. These funds must be valid in purpose, sound in their objectives, and with reasonable

expenses. An analysis of the prospectus of our new money market fund, for example, shows particularly attractive advisory fee and expense provisions.

In total, then, our structure is designed to provide clear and specific advantages to the Funds and to their shareholders, present and future. At the same time, most of the advantages are presently only theoretical. They must be turned into practical advantages if we are to successfully capitalize on the opportunities our new structure provides.

6. Implications for the Industry

It is difficult to be certain what implications, if any, the new Vanguard concept has for the mutual fund industry. If the background for our change was unique, it is nonetheless easy to identify a number of perfectly valid reasons why other Fund complexes might want to consider some form of internal management:

- Organizational pressures, arising from legitimate but major differences of opinion between a fund group and its management company about executive leadership, business issues, or performance evaluation
- Financial pressures, ranging from a management company's lack of earnings viability to capital inadequacy for the company or its parent
- Legal pressures, including private litigation, conformance with federal law and SEC regulation, etc.
- Or, most hopefully of all, an enlightened sense of self-interest about the optimal structure for the conduct of the Fund Group's activities

In an industry as traditionally imaginative as this one, perhaps the Vanguard concept will spark other—and perhaps even better—structural innovations to deal with the issues I have discussed today. After all, our concept is similar to that of Union Service Corporation, which is owned by the Broad Street Fund Group, and has carried out *all* of those Funds' activities throughout its history. If we elected not to go as far as Union Service, we have gone a good bit beyond the steps earlier taken by the Investors Mutual Group (which has its own President, independent of, although paid by, its management company) and by the Putnam Group (which recently named a Vice Chairman with a small staff to assume responsibility for representing the Funds' interests).

The principal impact of our Group's declaration of independence is, as I have noted, to make the Funds clients of the adviser rather than its creatures, a clear parallel to the investment counsel field. This would seem to be the direction in which the Putnam and Investors Groups are also heading. On the other hand—like many a large pension plan (U.S. Steel, for example), university endowment fund (Harvard), and private foundation (Ford)—the Broad Street Group has placed its emphasis on in-house investment advice. It is difficult to find fault with their investment results, and almost impossible to argue with their low expense ratios. In any event, there are numerous precedents and parallels in the field of institutional money management for what we at Vanguard have done, and for what others may do.

The direction in which our industry will move, further, may depend importantly on the outcome of a number of concerns that we intend to come to grips with sooner rather than later. Three of these, in particular, may have industry implications, and I will conclude by reviewing them.

One is the objective of giving the Fund Group a clear identity in the shareholders' minds. In our case, we want to make it clear that Vanguard is a cooperative undertaking of a family of funds with common management; that its function is to provide investors with a broad range of financial management services at the minimum reasonable cost; that its staff is concerned solely with the interests of the shareholders. This "identify" problem is a real one for any group which restructures. In our case, it is exacerbated to a degree by our need to create a new name.

The second item is the question of financing fund distribution activities. It is no secret that, at present, mutual fund distribution activities rarely produce self-sustaining sales revenues. If sales activities are to be maintained, then, the only resource remaining to support them is management fees. In our case, the issue becomes especially clear, for there are no administrative fees or functions encompassed in our purely investment advisory contracts. I believe that it is better in the long run to face this issue squarely than to avoid it, and we will soon be working toward separate pricing of investment advisory and distribution services. To clarify this issue, we need look only to the Broad Street Funds, which already have an asset charge for distribution services, and to some of the joint bank-mutual fund products, in which an investment adviser may receive one-fourth of the total management fee, with an administrator/distributor receiving the remaining three-fourths to pay administrative sand sales costs. These practices, of course, seem to conflict with SEC policy as expressed in the 1972 *Statement of the Future Structure of the Securities Markets* and reaffirmed in a 1974 letter to the Axe-Houghton Funds:

> **The cost of selling and purchasing mutual fund shares should be borne by the investors who purchase them and not, even in part, by the existing shareholders of the fund, who often derive little or no benefit from the sale of new shares. To impose a portion of the selling cost upon the existing shareholders of the Fund may violate principles of fairness which are at least implicit in the Investment Company Act.**

Nonetheless, I believe separate pricing will prove to be both good law and good economics, and will ultimately enable our Fund directors to judge the investment adviser's and distributor's services separately, rather than jointly.

The third concern that has industry-wide implications is the development of a structure that provides the best possible investment advisory services to shareholders. The internally managed fund group, calling on the services of an established professional investment counsel organization, is a new approach to this question. We believe it will enhance the probabilities of attaining performance excellence for each of our funds, measured against other institutional accounts with similar investment objectives. We intend to give our adviser the maximum of cooperation and support in our attempt to meet this goal. But there are a variety of other organizational forms in existence also seeking the same goal, so we will be continuously evaluating the accuracy of our basic judgment, as well as continuously monitoring how other institutional accounts are providing for the delivery of investment advisory services, and the results that they obtain.

The Winds of Change

Let me close by emphasizing this: The winds of change are blowing in the mutual fund industry. The business, economic, legal, structural, philosophical, and ethical challenges are great. Perhaps, in the last analysis, the principal implication of the Vanguard concept is not that it is the only, or even the best, way to deal with these challenges, but that it is an early signal that major structural change is in the air. Bob Dylan tells us, "You don't need a weatherman to know which way the wind blows." That is true. But while they will be strong and gusty, we believe that the winds of change are blowing in our direction.

18

DELIVERANCE

Wellington Management Company Partners
Boston, Massachusetts
September 9, 1971

D*ELIVERANCE* is an extraordinary novel by James Dickey. On the surface, it is an adventure story—telling of four men on a canoe trip in an isolated area, running rapids that are soon to be flooded and forgotten. It tells us something of what it is like not to know what natural dangers or man-made perils, not to know what excitement, may lie at the next turn, not to know how a risky and adventurous trip will end—for four individuals, not all of whom, as it turns out, are equipped to be adventurers. But, much more than this, its theme is the role of danger and stress on the individual, and how deliverance from peril can help us find self-realization and liberation.

The relevance of *deliverance* to our meeting today goes far beyond the fact that one of the four principals who undertake this canoe trip is a mutual fund salesman. It goes to the fact (I hope I am not overdramatizing this) that in the money management profession all of us—surely I am much as you—are at this very moment rushing down a river whose course is exciting, if not wholly known; navigating a canoe that is solidly seaworthy, if not entirely stable; operating in an environment that has precious little predictability, a certain sense of mystery, and an aura of danger ahead. Our ability to deal with the money management world we live in today will depend, I think, on the skills and abilities and energies each of us bring to this task.

There is so much that has happened, that is happening, and that will happen to our company and our industry that it is hard to know how to cover very much of it, even superficially, in less than an hour. What I propose to do this morning is spend just a brief moment on the past five years and the colossal change wrought in the Wellington Management Company organization, and then look ahead to the future (my charter is to look out to 1976), with special emphasis on the two challenges that I see as having particular importance to our company:

First, *Professional Responsibility:* What performance standards will we have to meet in the next five years?

Second, *Fiduciary Duty:* What demands will the shifting legal environment make upon us in this period?

Our ability to deal with these critical questions, of course, will depend importantly on our flexibility—by which I mean a combination of our ability to make decent guesses about the future environment, and our willingness to respond with changes in our organizational structure and strategy. I believe we have demonstrated these qualities in the past. Interestingly, when I looked back five years, I discovered the notes for my remarks to our District Sales Representatives meeting at the announcement of the Wellington/Ivest combination. These comments were made on September 9, 1966, five years ago today. In describing the reasons for this combination (which, as you know, profoundly altered the shape and future of both organizations), I talked about change, using this quotation from a *Fortune* magazine article entitled: "Tomorrow's Management: A More Adventurous Life in a Free-Form Corporation":

> **The essential task of modern management is to deal with change. In this situation, a company cannot be rigidly designed, like a machine, around a fixed goal. A smaller proportion of decisions can be routinized or precoded for future use. The highest activity of management becomes a continuous process of decision about the nature of the business. Management's degree of excellence is still judged in part by its efficiency of operation, but much more by its ability to make decisions changing its product mix, its markets, its techniques of financing and selling. *Initiative, flexibility, creativity, adaptability* are the qualities now required.**

Looking Back and Then Ahead

In 1966, this was our challenge, which I went on to quantify by speci-
fying a set of five-year financial objectives for our combined organizations. Now that the moment of truth is here, I would like to review
four objectives briefly:

- We were to maintain Wellington Fund assets at $2 billion. We
  failed in this objective. Wellington Fund is now $1.33 billion.
- We were to build our other mutual funds from $150 million to $1
  billion. We *succeeded* in this objective and then some—other
  fund assets are now $1,190,000,000—a sevenfold increase.
- We were to develop our investment counsel assets from $190
  million to $1 billion. We *more than met* this goal. These assets
  are now $1,140,000,000—a fivefold increase.
- We were to triple our market share of mutual fund sales from 2%
  to 6%—and we *will meet* that objective.

If the score of three to one in favor of good guesses—and that is all
they were—is not too bad, I hasten to claim no personal credit. Others too numerous to mention, many of whom I see before me this
morning, deserve whatever credit is due. But, change we did. And—
miracle of miracles—our change paid off. The five-year period that is
ending at this moment is now past, however. It is over. It is done. It is
probably of little interest even to the narrowest historian. Its only
importance to our organization is in what we have learned—individually and collectively—from the many trials and tribulations, from the
hard experience of this five-year period. I will remember, and I
soberly urge each one of you to remember, too!

I want to emphasize this morning how important it is to focus on
this extraordinary change in our company in the past five years. We
have changed Wellington *Fund* Management Company (while it was
not called that, 96% of our revenues were derived from Wellington
Fund) to Wellington *Management* Company—a diversified money
management firm which at this point in time, derives 24% of revenues
from Wellington Fund, 24% from investment counseling, and 52%
from other mutual funds.

Now we must look forward to the next five years, not backward
over the past five. I am not going to concern myself with *how* our

assets will be distributed. But, I would guess that if we are to gain the revenue growth we must, we ought to be managing $5 billion in 1976—which I suggest as our goal, even though it is a modest goal, representing only about a 7% growth rate. And, if we are a new company and we are a different company, we are a company with greater *resources* and, hopefully—if we have learned as we should have from the past five years—greater *resourcefulness*. We will surely need both greater resources—whether $5 billion is enough or not I am not sure—and greater resourcefulness to deal with the two challenges I spoke of earlier—professional responsibility and fiduciary duty.

The Challenge of Professional Responsibility

Let's turn then to the challenge of professional responsibility. In the years ahead, we will have to meet far more exacting performance standards for our fund and counsel clients. I cannot describe to you the precise nature of these standards. But I can do a little brainstorming, and lay out some broad areas of change based on my conviction that the actual performance of an investment account will be analyzed with increasing intensity. These new standards will incorporate most, if not all, of the following four elements:

1. The total return of an account will be subject to *exact* measurement. This concept, so familiar to those in the mutual fund industry, will be extended with comparable precision—and by that I assume asset valuation will be generally made on a unit basis no less frequently than monthly—to counsel accounts. Performance measurement will be all-pervasive, and will include the banks, pension funds, individual clients, all types of investment counsel accounts.
2. The concept of *risk* will come into its own. "Risk-adjustment" to returns will be made with mathematical, though surely not conceptual, precision. In mutual funds, investors will be *told* about the volatility (is this really risk?) they can expect from a given fund. In the counseling field, investors will be *asked* about the amount of volatility they can tolerate in keeping with their objectives.
3. The ultimate measurement of performance—in both fields—will be on a units-of-reward-per-unit-of-risk basis. I am not sure which standards will prevail, only that there will be some.

4. With performance standards established, there will also be an increasing scrutiny of the entire investment management process by investors—

- in the mutual fund field, by statistical services (Lipper *Insight*, etc.)
- in the investment counsel field, by large corporate investors.

In 1976, the world—or at least the investors involved—will want to know whether and what the account was buying when the market was down—and we will have to say what, and why. It will want to know what industry groups were favored, and we will have to answer. Our selection of companies will have to be defended and articulated. Under these circumstances, it is entirely possible that our clients and financial publications may well have more information about what we are doing than we do. (With their computers abuzz, they may detect portfolio trends we are not even aware of, or patterns that emerge without our knowledge.)

The impact of the trends will be profound: To remove much of the *mystique* from the money management profession—especially the mysterious counseling profession as compared to the mutual fund industry—for two perfectly good reasons: First, the trend toward quantification and rationality I have here reviewed; and second, because the stage for this development has been set in part by the tragic failure of many money managers to provide satisfactory investment accomplishment in the 1969–71 period.

When you consider the impact—magnified by all the accompanying public relations—of Fred Mates, of Fred Carr, of Jerry Tsai, on the investment world, there are few who are not aware of these past shortcomings. As it has been said, we came to realize "that Mates are only mates, a Carr is just a car, a Tsai is but a Tsai"—when we should have realized all along that, as the old song goes, "the fundamental things apply as time goes by." And if we can't make a song out of John Hartwell or Fred Alger, or Bill O'Neil, or David Meid, we *can* say each made his own contribution toward taking the mystique out of money management. (While the managers I have mentioned found their inadequacies most evident in the mutual fund field, it is clear that their counseling accounts experienced equally tragic failures.)

I am not *blaming* these people, none of whom planned to fail. I am merely saying that they helped to set the stage for the 1971–76 era, during which only those firms that can demonstrate consistent standards of excellence in money management will be able to grow and prosper. Only those firms that do an excellent performance job and meet acute investment standards will gain the cash inflow so necessary, not only to provide future growth and resources, but to avoid the drain of steady cash outflow. And within those firms, only those individuals who meet the same tests will enjoy the substantial rewards that accomplishment will bring.

On the evidence—and we should not expect it to be otherwise—few firms have met this standard of excellence in the past. And it is disappointing but true that our own firm, in the last decade, must be counted among those that have not provided consistent excellence. If we are to succeed in the next five years, we *must* demonstrate consistent excellence in money management. Given our record so far in 1971, we are not starting from a particularly secure base.

In any event, our focus for the next five years must be on meeting standards of excellence, of measuring up to our performance responsibilities. We will have to do so if we are to build our assets. The amount of information on the subject of performance will explode, I am confident, and you can expect and assume that we will have new measurement devices, new evaluation processes, and ever more numbers with even greater complexity. Our 1976 world, then, will be one of greater professionalism, measured in a more rational climate, for all money managers, whatever types of accounts they manage.

I would not predict what adjustments we will have to make to deal with these developments. However, I would assume that new standards will ultimately call for possibly profound changes in our money management procedures, our organizational structure, our compensation programs, and our research activities. *Initiative, flexibility, creativity,* and *adaptability,* repeating the *Fortune* quote, will be critical to our success.

To sum up: Because of the sins and excesses of the past, as well as the communications revolution of the present and future—the quantification and information explosion—the profession of money management will lose much of its mystique. Among the changes that I suspect will emerge would be these:

- First: The big competition for major corporation pension plans *may* not be other established investment counsel firms, and *will* not be trust companies. It will be (1) new small investment counsel firms that limit the number of accounts they manage (and thus the regulation they are exposed to), and (2) possibly— even more importantly—the corporations themselves—a trend toward "internalization" of money management. In this context, I would also guess that the trend toward "multiple management" is not too far away from its peak.

- Second: The big competition in the mutual fund field will continue to be within the conventional system of dealer distribution. The dealer, after all, can help the average investor cope with the complex new measurement standards. But major inroads will be made by no-load funds at the expense of captive distribution. The astonishing trend in this direction is little noticed thus far, but is one of the most significant in the mutual fund industry— the no-load funds are now out-selling the captive distribution funds.

- Third: The big competition for equity money management for the average investor may not revolve around one mutual fund marketing system vs. another, but one type of *product* vs. another. We cannot be sure, for example—despite the Supreme Court decision in the *First National City Bank* case—that banks are barred from the mutual fund industry; that decision merely bars them from acting as underwriters of, not as investment advisers to, mutual funds. Further, we have no protection, nor are we likely to get any, against other means of marketing equity management in packages that may well prove to have more efficient service, or different cost structures, or more generous sales commissions, or more favorable tax characteristics or regulatory status, than mutual funds. (Here, I refer to the competitive threat of the variable annuity and variable insurance.)

In any event, the competition is not going to get any easier, and performance excellence must be our goal.

The Challenge of Fiduciary Duty

Let me now turn to an equally compelling and critical challenge for money managers in the future—*fiduciary duty*. We live in a world that is increasingly intolerant, not only of conflicts of interest, but even the appearance of conflicts. It is hard to argue either that this trend is baneful or that it is likely to abate. For this is but one aspect of the "consumerism" whose impact pervades almost every aspect of our society, and certainly is not limited to the world of money management. It seems beyond question that consumerism, along with the entire thrust of the legislative, regulatory, and judicial overview of our profession, will play a critical role in how we conduct our affairs in the years ahead.

What are some of these conflicts in money management that have existed in the past, and how are they likely to be resolved in the future?

- *The question of brokerage utilization for various forms of sales and research reciprocity.* While I totally disagree with the Appellate Court's reversal of the *Fidelity* decision in the lower court, and the judgment that the Fund has a right to recapture "give-up" commissions for 1967–68, I have little doubt that the future environment will make any available recapture mandatory. We are in a new world, and even the Supreme Court's unlikely reversal of *Fidelity* would effect only past practices, not the future. At the same time, the available pool of reciprocal will continue to represent a smaller portion of the money managers' resources.

- *The question of exchange membership.* Certainly, the potential for considerable abuse exists in this area, for there is a fundamental conflict between a *pure* investment judgment where the commission is paid to a disinterested broker and an investment judgment where the manager himself earns the commission. There are, in fact, many managers who depend on generating commissions for their profitability, and (in certain cases) for their survival. It occurs to me that these kinds of pressures are patently wrong. They will ultimately be resolved, not by structural separation, but by the *de facto* separation that would occur if the negotiated rate level comes down once again.

- *The question of asset size and the investment process.* Clients—fund directors and investment counseling accounts alike—will not accept massive size *unless* we can show them that its benefits—and I tried to make the point earlier that substantial resources are important in doing a responsible performance job—outweigh its detriments. I don't think I have to spell out to anyone here what these detriments are.

- *Other questions* are also in the process of resolution—resolution that must consistently be made in the interest of the client. I would include here the valuation of restricted stock, combined order (bunching) procedures, allocation of orders among different accounts, the apportionment of expenses between fund and adviser, and ultimately the setting of the level of fund advisory fees.

Fund Industry Structure

This last issue—the arm's length setting of advisory fees—is truly a jugular issue. For, if mutual fund independent directors ultimately assume the position of the trustees of an eight- or nine-figure counsel account, one has to raise a question of the very role of a management company—as a separate and distinct entity—in the future. This is a question that has been surprisingly ignored. Listen to Howard Stein of Dreyfus *Fund,* for example:

> **Should an investing institution have any responsibility other than to those who entrust their money to it? I do not believe so.**
> **Should those who manage other people's money do anything else—have corporate or other financial relationships that give the appearance of conflict? I do not believe so.**

Or, is this Howard Stein of Dreyfus *Corporation* speaking? Or, has he ever considered the applicability of his comments to our own industry situation. (He does not always display consistency in these areas; i.e., opposing institutional access while doing business on the Philadelphia-Baltimore-Washington Exchange and applying for membership on the New York Stock Exchange.)

Indeed, one of the most significant legal decisions affecting our business in over a decade effactually raises this same question. The *Lazard* case rules in effect—and on a specific set of circumstances—that profits from the sale of a mutual fund management contract belong to the shareholders of a fund, *not* the sellers of the contract. In the Court's words, "A trustee may not sell or transfer such office for personal gain. . . . No matter how high-minded a particular fiduciary may be, his duty is to eliminate any possibility of personal gain." The panel of three eminent jurists appeared to realize that this decision could fly in the face of the court decision in the 1958 *ISI* case, which enabled management company shareholders to capitalize on the value of the management contract. Some have said the *Lazard* decision "opened Pandora's box"; my own view is that it is more likely to have *closed* it. Nevertheless, the *Lazard* decision raises a profound question: What happens when the common law prohibition against a trustee's profiting from the sale of his office conflicts with the implied right of a businessman to capitalize on the entrepreneurial value of the enterprise he has created? As SEC Chairman Casey recently noted, the *Lazard* decision is right on fiduciary law, but harsh on businessmen, and may require legislative remedy.

The ultimate answer, I suspect, will be to allow some entrepreneurial profit, but only on terms negotiated at arm's length by a truly independent fund board of directors. It is not inconceivable for such a board to consider steps like these, if they appear important to protect the rights of the fund shareholders:

- In instances of failure to meet adequate performance standards, forced transfer of contract, or contract termination.
- In instances of the proposed merger of a management company, evidence of positive benefits to fund investors, including lower fees, strengthened management, marketing, or administration, etc.
- In any event, more frequent and flexible fee negotiation.

This would seem to say that the ultimate outcome will be neither the "black" of *Lazard*, nor the "white" of *ISI*, but rather a true negotiation at which both sides are represented. Certainly, this was one of the original intentions of the Investment Company Act of 1940 (which was aimed, in part, toward prevention of "trafficking" in investment advisory contacts), and more recently, in the Investment Company Act of 1970, which specifically laid down a fiduciary duty with respect to the amount and determination of the advisory fee. If this is correct, it seems clear that excessive management profitability is likely to be under some restraint. There are those who say this is bad, and there are those who say *Lazard* would eliminate the entrepreneur from the mutual fund business. But, I, for one, am not entirely clear that the entrepreneurs who came into our business in 1967–1969 have served either fund investors, or our industry.

"A Man Cannot Serve Two Masters"

These problems, to be sure, are not new. They merely recur as history is forgotten. Listen, for example, to Justice Harlan Fiske Stone speaking in 1934:

I venture to assert that when the history of the financial era which has just drawn to a close comes to be written, most of the mistakes and its major faults will be ascribed to the failure to observe the fiduciary principle, the precept as old as holy writ, that "a man cannot serve two masters" . . . the development of the corporate structure so as to vest in small groups control over the resources of great numbers of small and uninformed investors, make imperative a fresh and active devotion to that principle if the modern world of business is to perform its proper function. Yet, those who serve nominally as trustees, but relieved, by clever legal devices, from the obligation to protect those who interests they purport to represent . . . consider only last the interests of those whose funds they command, suggest how far we have ignored the necessary implications of that principle.

I endorse that view, and at the same time reveal an ancient prejudice of mine: All things considered, absent a demonstration that the enterprise has substantial capital requirements that cannot be otherwise fulfilled, it is undesirable for professional enterprises to have public stockholders. This constraint is as applicable to money managers as it is to doctors, or lawyers, or accountants, or architects. In their cases, as in ours, it is hard to see what unique contribution public investors bring to the enterprise. They do not, as a rule, add capital; they do not add expertise; they do not contribute to the well-being of our clients. Indeed, it is possible to envision circumstances in which the pressure for earnings and earnings growth engendered by public ownership is antithetical to the responsible operation of a professional organization. Although the field of money management has elements of both, differences between a business and a profession must, finally, be reconciled in favor of the client.

Nevertheless, Wellington Management Company is publicly owned—unlike many of our finest competitors. We have a responsibility to those public investors, who are, in effect, the financial heirs of the entrepreneurs who created this company. They are entitled to a return on their investment, and I would suggest that our management has bent over backward to recognize this responsibility. However, *if* it is a burden to our fund and counsel clients to be served by a public enterprise, should this burden exist in perpetuity? And if we believe that it is in the interest of our fund and counsel clients that our firm should be owned by its active executives and not by the public, shouldn't we work to solve this problem in a way that is equitable to all? What a great objective to be accomplished by 1976!

Mutualization?

I wish there were a simple way to accomplish what I am talking about, let alone to describe it. But, let me say that a variety of options may open up as the legal atmosphere clears. For example, there may be "mutualization" whereby the funds acquire the management company. (Students of the development of the life insurance business will know how this can come about.) There may be "internalization" whereby the active executives own the management company, with contracts that are negotiated on some type of "cost-plus" basis, providing incentives for both performance and efficiency, but without the ability to capitalize earnings through public sale. (This would be consistent with the changing tax treatment favoring earned income at the expense of capital gains.) And, there may be other variations on these ideas. At the same time, for that matter, we must face the fact that there may be *no way* to accomplish this goal.

This brainstorming is an important part of what we have to do, for I think a restructured Wellington Management Company may—I repeat the phrase, *miracle of miracles*—enable us both better to fulfill our performance obligations and more effectively to honor our fiduciary responsibilities. Above all, however, any restructuring must *not* be at the expense of the organization we have developed. I believe, and I hope you agree, we have created an organization that is worth holding together. Our fund and counseling areas are increasingly interdependent, and not only within the investment management group, but also within the administrative group, which, in turn, interacts with the mutual fund and investment counsel marketing groups.

In candor, I do not know whether maintaining our organizational unity means there will be *no* change in these various relationships. Legally, for example, cannot funds "mutualize" in a sense that is difficult to conceive of for investment counsel firms? From a regulatory standpoint, is not the fund industry—at least to date—vastly different from investment counsel? Does not fiduciary duty mean one thing when a client can negotiate for himself, and another when he must rely on an independent board of directors? Operationally, is it not conceivable that the funds could be internalized and made self-sustaining with respect to administration and distribution, but continue as at present in their relationship with respect to investment management?

The Challenges Ahead

Questions like these suggest the complexity of the issues that face us as we deal with the next five years and beyond. I hope I have not gone too far in suggesting that the seeds of their resolution may be surprising. But let me emphasize that we will bring to this future the same qualities, toughened by hard experience, that we have tried to bring to past problems. As Howard Johnson, President of MIT—the University, not the restaurateur, and not the mutual fund—warned us at the April Investment Company Institute Membership Meeting, we have to "take a longer view. If we wait until all can see," he said, "there is no room to act. So many bad decisions are made when there are no longer good choices."

Speaking personally, the events of the past five years have been an incredibly satisfying experience for me. I hope I am different and better for the challenges we have faced, and for the people with whom I have worked, for both what we have succeeded in doing and where we have failed, for all of the trials and tribulations we have endured. It has been fun, and I only hope that each of you has experienced at least some of this range of sensations—for that, not to be too melodramatic, is what life is all about.

In Wellington Management Company, we—with the emphasis on *we,* for *I* is neither critical nor important—have built something that is quite precious. A young organization. An open environment. A professional orientation. A responsive and alert group of people who have great ability, people who (to quote Schow's Law, which is said to govern hiring at Capital Research and Management Company) "it is at least *possible* to like." Our future is no more uncertain than the future of anything else, and I see no reason you cannot earn a generous enrichment here—personal, professional, and financial—in an organization that *must* remain both independent and unified, irrespective of whatever structural change may evolve.

Lest there be any possibility of misunderstanding, let me put my conclusions in a more simplified form:

What we have built as an independent professional organization, we must maintain as an independent professional organization, so long as it is financially possible to do so.

What we have built as a unified, cooperative organization, we must maintain as a unified, cooperative organization, whether we do so through one corporate entity or half a dozen.

In 1976, then we may well be a *different* company than we are now, but one that is better rather than worse. I repeat what I said earlier: *initiative, flexibility, creativity* and *adaptability* are the attributes that are required, as we go about the task of providing consistent excellence in investment management, under increasingly stringent standards of fiduciary duty. If we do so, our ride down the river I described to you at the outset today will be exciting. We will enjoy the sense of adventure in a financial world where it is all too often lacking. And, we can achieve, hopefully, a "deliverance," not in the narrow sense of a safe arrival at a final destination—surely we wouldn't want that even if we could have it—but in the broader sense of liberation, an enhancement of our very selves.

Or maybe *Deliverance* is just another adventure story.

19

THE LENGTHENED SHADOW, ECONOMICS, AND IDEALISM

Annual "Wilson and Princeton" Dinner
Woodrow Wilson House, Washington, D.C.
September 30, 1999

GOOD EVENING, LADIES and gentlemen. Thank you, Ambassador Lukens and distinguished members of the dinner committee for honoring me with the invitation to address you. In the spirit of this grand occasion, I'd like to begin with some comments about what I find especially remarkable about President Wilson; in particular, how his lengthened shadow lies over America today, and how his economic policies were shaped by his idealism. I'll then turn to Vanguard, the now-giant mutual fund enterprise that I founded just 25 years ago. Only time will tell whether the lengthened shadow of my economic vision of fund management and my own idealism will lie over my firm a century hence. But I hope so.

As I understand it, it is Vanguard's distinctive approach to the stewardship of investors' assets that led to Princeton University's decision earlier this year to honor me with the Woodrow Wilson Medal—presented annually to an undergraduate alumnus for "distinguished achievement in the Nation's service." My humble delight in receiving this award almost (but not quite!) equals my utter astonishment at having been chosen, the first businessman in a long and distinguished line of public servants, artists, scientists, and authors who preceded me.

Wilson and Economics

In the course of preparing my Wilson Lecture, given in conjunction with the presentation of the medal, I studied again the stunning legacy of Woodrow Wilson as President, first of the University, and then of the United States of America. As a member of the financial community at the 20th century's end, I was profoundly impressed by one of his little-recognized but most far-sighted contributions: Setting a new direction for American economic and financial policy.

You would not have to walk very many blocks from here to read these words in the lobby of a handsome Greek Revival building: "We shall restore, not destroy. We shall deal with our economic system as it is and as it may be modified, not as it might be if we had a clear sheet of paper to write upon; and step by step we shall make it what it should be . . ." This quotation, from Wilson's brief (for him) First Inaugural Address on March 4, 1913, appears, as some of you doubtless know, at the main entrance of the Federal Reserve Bank in Washington, D.C.

Wilson proposed the Federal Reserve Act in order to bring monetary and banking reform to the nation. He worked gradually with the Congress, making numerous concessions to the existing financial system. And before the year had ended, the United States had a central bank, absent since Andrew Jackson abolished the Second Bank of the United States in 1836. Wilson's goals were to prevent the recurrence of banking panics, and to break the private monopoly of credit, so that banks would serve, in his words, as "the instruments, not the masters, of business and of individual enterprise and initiative." The Federal Reserve Bank evolved gradually over the years, finally to become the most powerful financial institution in the world. While no one—Wilson included—could have foreseen that development, surely his shadow lies over the Fed today.

Wilson's desire to fundamentally change the American economic order hardly stopped there. In that same Inaugural, Wilson proposed to cut tariffs and open America to global commerce (the Underwood Tariff Act of 1913) and to improve the administration of the Sherman Anti-Trust Act and enhance its fairness (the Clayton and Federal Trade Commission Acts of 1914). His overriding goal, articulated time and again, was to create an environment in which free enterprise and unfettered competition could prevail. His passion for this goal was hardly hidden: to restore "that ancient time when America lay in every hamlet, when America was seen in every fair valley, when America displayed her great forces on the wide prairies, ran her fine fires of enterprise up over the mountainside and down into the bowels of the earth, and eager men everywhere captains of industry, not employees . . . America stands for opportunity. America stands for a free field and no favor. America stands for a government responsive to the interests of all." Could it be better said today?

Liberal or Conservative?

In his first Inaugural, Wilson also addressed safeguarding the health of the nation, protecting the environment for future generations, equality of opportunity, pure food, and labor conditions. Quite an agenda! But if these goals would today be characterized as liberal, surely his bedrock philosophy was conservative: "The fundamental safeguarding of property and individual right; to lift everything that concerns our life as a Nation to the light that shines from the hearthfire of every man's vision of the right." No radical he, Wilson expressed the consummate gradualist perspective: "Step by step we shall make (our economic system) what it should be. . . . Justice, and only justice shall be our motto."

As I read his first Inaugural, I wondered what might have been the source of his economic insights. In Princeton's Seeley G. Mudd Manuscript Library, I uncovered his essay on Adam Smith, written at Bryn Mawr College in 1887 for use in his course on Political Economy. But, alas, it focused on Adam Smith's mastery of the art of academic lecturing. Wilson's essay ("An Old Master") emphasized that the miscellany of economic thought contained in the *Wealth of Nations* was but a supplement to Smith's *Theory of Moral Sentiments*.

In that earlier book, Adam Smith had reckoned with such unselfish motives as "love, benevolence, sympathy, and charity in filling life with kindly influences." So, Wilson's essay excused the exclusive concentration of self-interest and expediency in the *Wealth of Nations*. But it is in *Moral Sentiments* (though Wilson did not cite this passage in his essay) that we find an overriding ethical principle that might surprise today's conservatives who trumpet Adam Smith's philosophy of free competition:

> **It is reason, principle, consensus, the inhabitant of the breast, the reason within, the great judge and arbitrator of our conduct . . . who shows us the propriety of generosity, of reining in**

the greatest interests of our own for yet the greater interests of others, the love of what is honorable and noble, the dignity of our own characters.

It is my view that the idealistic spirit of those lines—and I don't think I am mistaken in hearing in them the cadences of Woodrow Wilson's later addresses—had more to do with his shaping of the program of economic and monetary reform enunciated in his first Inaugural address than a detailed understanding of the workings of the economic system of the early 1900s. I believe, in short, that Wilson's idealism was the inspiration for his economics.

Whether the issue was control of our nation's monetary policy or the reduction of tariffs, Wilson fashioned economic policy to restore the democratic ideals of the nation's founders. In his first Inaugural, Wilson lamented that "we reared giant machinery which made it impossible that any but those who stood at the levers of control should have a chance to look out for themselves." Wilson's administration would seek to redress the imbalance between the broad citizenry and the powerful financiers and industrialists of the Gilded Age. Wilson would undertake a moral crusade to "square every process of our national life again with the standards we so proudly set up at the beginning and have always carried at our hearts."

Even 90 years later, in this age of global economics, Wilson's shadow lies on the institutions and policies through which the American business and financial community conducts its affairs around the world. His shadow also, of course, lies on Princeton University. On becoming President of the University in 1902, he implemented the preceptorial system and revolutionized teaching, added greatly to the University's physical plant, established a new curriculum, added an honors program, and inspired today's system of residential colleges. (His "favorite dream of a collegiate Quad Plan" was rejected in 1908, a setback that contributed to his decision to leave Princeton and run for Governor of New Jersey. But by 1966 "Woodrow Wilson College" became the first of Princeton's five residential colleges.[1])

---

1. Writing about Wilson in 1945, Professor George McLean Harper, who knew Wilson at Princeton, opined, "some day perhaps a residential college such as he envisioned will be incorporated into the University and named for him." A fine prediction!

So too his lengthened shadow lies on the United Nations, the realization of his failed dream of a League of Nations, a crushing defeat for this idealist that doubtless contributed to the stroke he suffered in 1918, ending his political life. Nonetheless, we cannot miss the echo of Emerson's epigram (and we know that Wilson was an avid reader of Emerson's essays): "An institution is the lengthened shadow of one man." Whatever the case, surely the shadow of Wilson lies unmistakable, unwavering and dominant today, over Princeton, our economy, and the United Nations.

Turning now from Wilson's formidable shadow, I now turn inward to discuss, with some trepidation, the career of the Woodrow Wilson Medalist for 1999. As I reflect on the matter, it occurs to me that Wilson would have delighted in the precedent-breaking award of the Medal to a businessman. In evidence, I offer his Princeton Inaugural Address: The University must "serve a free nation whose progress, whose power, whose prosperity, whose happiness, whose integrity depend on individual initiative and sound sense." He expected "the merchant and the financier (to) have traveled minds . . . for every considerable undertaking has come to be based on knowledge, on thoughtfulness, on the masterful handling of men and facts." It is, he said, "the free capital of the mind the world most stands in need of, spiritual as well as material, which advance the race and help all men[2] to a better life. . . . No task rightly done is truly private. It is part of the world's work."

The Economics and Idealism Behind Vanguard's Founding

I've tried to dedicate my career to, using Wilson's words, "a task rightly done." It was almost 25 years ago to the day when our firm was incorporated. I chose the name "Vanguard" for the new enterprise, hoping to capture the tradition of HMS *Vanguard,* Lord Nelson's flagship, which led his victory over Napoleon's fleet at the Nile 200 years ago. (Nelson's triumph was recently crowned by *The New York Times* as the greatest naval battle of the millennium.) If Vanguard has distin-

---

2. In Wilson's day, of course, "men" was synonymous with "humankind." We must not forget, however, that it was in his administration that the 19th amendment (women's suffrage) was added to the Constitution.

guished itself, it is through our mission of stewardship, our single-minded devotion to giving the mutual fund investor a fair shake.

It is hardly an exaggeration to say that, without Princeton, there would be no Vanguard. For my interest in this industry sprang to life in the University's spanking-new Firestone Library, quite by accident, in 1949. There, I stumbled across an article in *Fortune* magazine that described the mutual fund industry as "tiny but contentious." I decided on the spot that it should be the topic for my senior thesis, which I entitled, "The Economic Role of the Investment Company." So, thank you President Wilson, for making the departmental thesis a requirement for the bachelor's degree!

It seems problematical that my thesis, as some have generously alleged, laid out the design for what Vanguard would become. But, true or not, many of the practices I specified then would, nearly 50 years later, prove to lie at the very core of the success reflected in the growth of our fund assets from $1 billion in 1974 to $500 billion in 1999. "The principal function of mutual funds is the management of their investment portfolios. Everything else is incidental. . . . Future industry growth can be maximized by a reduction of sales loads and management fees. . . . Mutual funds can make no claim to superiority over the market averages." And, with a final rhetorical flourish, funds should operate "in the most efficient, honest, and economical way possible." Were these words an early design for a sound enterprise? Or merely callow, even sophomoric, idealism? I'll leave it to you to decide. But whatever the case, it works!

The fact is that Vanguard's economics, like Wilson's, were in important measure shaped by idealism. For what distinguishes Vanguard from the typical business enterprise is our mission: To place the interest of our investors before our own commercial interests. Our truly *mutual* mutual fund structure is unique in the fund industry: The funds' management is controlled by the fund shareholders, not by an outside management company, and is operated on an "at-cost" basis, not for a hefty management fee. With the substantial profits normally earned by the management company eliminated, this mutual structure has been the major contributor in generating aggregate savings to our investors—and hence added returns—that now approach $20 *billion*. The other contributor has been our deep, assiduous, slavish, passionate dedication to providing our stewardship to the shareholders who have entrusted their resources to our care at *rock-bottom* operating costs; that is, "in the most economical way possible."

Down with Costs, and Carthage Too

All of this is important only if costs matter. They do. *Costs matter.* I repeat this phrase so often that one journalist compared me with Cato, the Roman orator whose speeches in the Forum always ended with a call for the defeat of Carthage: *"Carthago delenda est."* In my shameless repetition of this theme in speech after speech, I'm reminded of Wilson, who, when asked how often he used the same idea in his addresses, replied: "You will have to wait a long time for me to be able to answer that question." (That is, he expected to continue to use the same ideas over and over again.)

How *much* do costs matter? Hugely! Taking into account sales charges, management fees, operating expenses, and portfolio turnover, the average mutual fund deducts about 2½% per year from investor returns. Assuming—an arbitrary assumption indeed—that the manager is able to match an annual stock market return of, say, 10% *before* costs, 20% of the investor's return is consumed by costs in a year, 29% in a decade, and—I'm glad you're sitting down!—fully 45% of his return is consumed in a quarter century. Nearly one-half of the cumulative return generated by the stock market has been confiscated by the costs incurred by the typical mutual fund.

It was largely in the context of minimizing costs that I entitled my Woodrow Wilson lecture "The Hedgehog and the Fox." The title comes from Archilochus' ancient dictum, "The fox knows many things. But the hedgehog knows one *great* thing." In my remarks, I contrasted the many financial foxes in the money management field—often brilliant, clever, and wily, vulpine to a fault—who trade stocks constantly in a futile effort to beat the stock market, only to be destined finally to failure, dragged down by the heavy costs of their active investment approach. The one great idea of the hedgehog, on the other hand, is simply to buy a diversified list of stocks and hold them, well, forever. This is, of course, a fair depiction of the strategy of Warren Buffett. But it is also the driving force in Vanguard's success: The passively managed market index fund. In its most pristine form, the index fund—operated at a cost best described as trivial—owns a share in every business in America, and never sells it.

Who wins, the fox or hedgehog? Well, let's look at the record. If you had invested $10,000 with the typical mutual fund fox at the outset of this 17-year bull market—the greatest in all history—it would today be valued at $136,000. The same investment with the all-market fund hedgehog would be valued at $182,000. Just owning American business—at low cost—and doing *nothing* else, resulted in an extra $46,000 in return. The difference lies *solely* in relative cost. No wonder investors are starting to appreciate indexing. And no wonder the financial foxes hate it. For, as the record shows, foxy active management, with its heavy fees and costs, simply results in a diversion of the market's returns *from* the shareholders *to* the managers.

More than any other firm, Vanguard has been the fund industry's hedgehog, applying its one great thing to pioneer in many of the fund industry's most productive and investor-friendly innovations: the mutual (investor-owned) structure; the index fund; the tax-managed fund; the money market fund; the management of bond funds in defined asset classes; the direct marketing of shares to investors through no-load funds, without salesmen or commissions; and many others. While we were not always first to adopt these strategies, we have been widely credited as being the driving force in their acceptance, for our single-minded focus on low costs has made them work for investors in an extraordinarily effective way. It was said of Wilson, "He may not have *coined* all of his vital ideas, but he *mined* them as no others did." So too it might be said of Vanguard.

A Lengthened Shadow?

Is Vanguard, too, "the lengthened shadow of one man?" I'm not so sure. But I hope and pray that the shadow of the investment philosophy and the human values—the economics and the idealism—I have championed will lie forever on our firm. For they are the right philosophy and the right values, sound, enduring, even eternal. As for the man himself, I assure you that Vanguard today is far more durable than its now-aging founder, and indeed far greater than *any* one man. Our superb crew, now numbering more than 10,000, is committed and deeply dedicated to our core values. And our investors, from whom I hear with extraordinary frequency, demonstrate a remarkably sophisticated understanding of what Vanguard is all about. Even as Wilson placed his hopes in the people and believed that the real wisdom of human life is compounded out of the experiences of the common man, so I freely place *my* trust in the wisdom and common sense of our shareholder-owners, and in their continued recognition of the soundness of Vanguard's approach to investing.

Of all that I admire about Wilson—his powerful intellect; his commanding presence; his graceful, flowing use of the English language; the length of his foresight and the breadth of his vision—I admire most his stubborn, uncompromising idealism, reflected, in a colleague's view, in "his recklessly, passionately-outspoken, crusading spirit." He was not above responding to a statement that there are two sides to every question with a curt, "Yes there are. A right side and a wrong side." Nor was he beyond telling a colleague, "Do as you think best," while always leaving underneath the veiled injunction, "but do it this way." And as he freely admitted, he hardly became easier and more placable with age. "The older I get, the hotter I get," Wilson said—and he was only 52 then! I confess that my colleagues at Vanguard might see these same traits in me.

It was Wilson's stubborn idealism that stood in the way of accomplishing his final goals while at Princeton—a collegiate campus—and while at the White House—a League of Nations. I can only recall F. Scott Fitzgerald's statement: "Show me a hero, and I'll write you a tragedy." But is tragedy truly the right word? Both developments have now come to pass. And for me, whether one finally succeeds or fails, steadfast commitment to one's own principles and values is what a man's life is all about. In the words of Theodore Roosevelt, Wilson's predecessor in the White House, "The credit belongs to the man in the arena, . . . who knows the great enthusiasms; . . . who strives valiantly in a worthy cause; . . . who, at best, knows in the end the triumph of high achievement; and who at worst, if he fails, at least fails by daring greatly, so that his place shall never be with those cold and timid souls who know neither victory nor defeat." The qualities that result in compromise, while valuable, even priceless in some circumstances, are rarely responsible for the building of a great institution.

Finally, my idealistic view—for which I offer no apologies—is that the mutual fund firm should be of the clients, by the clients, and for the clients, holding their interests above the financial interests of the manager-entrepreneur; providing a service of stewardship to the human beings who place with the firm their assets and their trust alike. And low cost is so central to that view that, even as in Wilson's case, the idealism that I've invested in Vanguard leads to its economics. "And there are other things," he wrote in his Princeton Inaugural, "besides material success with which we must supply our generation. It must be supplied with men who care more for principles than for money, for the right adjustments of life than for the gross accumulations of profit. The problems that call for sober thoughtfulness and mere devotion are as pressing as those which call for practical efficiency."

President Wilson closed that address with this ringing peroration, with which I close my own remarks this evening: "I have studied the history of America. I have seen her grow great in the paths of liberty and of progress by following after great ideals. Every concrete thing she has done has seemed to arise out of some abstract principle, some vision of the mind. Her greatest victories have been the victories of peace and of humanity. And in days quiet and troubled alike, Princeton has stood for the nation's service." Continuing his vision—and remember, this address was given in 1902, nearly a century ago—he added this profound prophecy: "A new age is before us, in which we must lead the world . . . the spirit of the age will lift us to every great enterprise, but the ancient spirit of sound learning will also rule us . . . and the men who spring from our loins shall take their lineage from the founders of the republic." And so in the United States of America the spirit of the age remains, this very evening.

20

ON THE RIGHT SIDE OF
HISTORY

*The 1998 International Conference
on Servant-Leadership
Indianapolis, Indiana
August 7, 1998*

*T*ODAY, I WANT TO mix some corpo-
rate history and some personal philosophy, and try to impart some
sense of how the idealistic vision of the servant as leader, and of the
leader as servant, can have—and has had—an impact on the pragmatic, dog-eat-dog competitive world of American business. I'm
going to use as my example the burgeoning mutual fund industry, next
to the Internet, I suppose, the fastest-growing industry in the United
States, and the Vanguard Group, its fastest-growing major firm.

What is of interest, I think, is not our mere success—a word so elusive in its connotations that I use it here with considerable reluctance—but the fact that, whatever we have achieved, it has been by
marching to a different drummer. Our unique corporate structure has
fostered our single focus on being the servant of our fund shareholders, our disciplined attitude toward the costs that they bear, and our
conservative investment strategies and concepts (many of which we
created *de novo*). In remarks that I hope will be especially relevant to
all of you who are interested in servant-leadership, I plan to demonstrate how so many of those concepts have served us well—implicitly
to be sure, but served us well nonetheless—in bringing us to where
we stand today.

The Fund Industry and Vanguard

Hesitant as I may be to do so, I must establish my *bona fides*, as it were, by drawing a brief sketch of the mutual fund landscape today and identifying Vanguard's position in the scene. The mutual fund industry is booming:

- Its asset base has swelled to $4.7 *trillion,* compared to just $50 billion a quarter century ago—a 90-fold increase, equivalent to a compound growth rate of 20% annually.
- Cash inflow from investors is running in the range of $500 billion per year, compared to an *outflow* of $290 million in 1974. Mutual funds have become the investment of choice for American families at the moment, accounting for 100% of net additions to the financial assets of our households.
- Twenty-five years ago, the market was tumbling, with the Dow Jones Industrial Average on its way to a 12-year low of 578. Today, the Dow is at the 9000 level. While the *relative* returns of the average managed equity mutual fund have fallen far short of those achieved by the unmanaged market averages, the *absolute* returns of even the most mundane funds have been little short of spectacular.
- As a result of the great bull market, common stock funds are again the driving force of the industry with 53% of its assets, although money market funds have had their turn as the industry's largest component (75% of industry assets in 1981), followed by bond funds (37% of assets in 1986). This is a market-sensitive industry!
- The character of the industry has changed rather radically. As investors have become better educated, more aware, and more self-reliant, the no-load (no sales commission) segment of the mutual fund industry has become its largest component—surging from just 15% of industry assets in 1979 to 35% currently. In fact, the industry's two largest firms, and five of its ten largest, offer primarily—often solely—no load funds.

Using the conventional measuring sticks, Vanguard, a firm that did not even exist 25 years ago, is emerging as the industry leader. We have by far the fastest growth rate of any major firm, and as a result have become one of the two largest fund organizations in the world. A scattering of measures makes the point:

- Assets recently topped $400 billion, up from $1.4 billion in the mutual funds for which we assumed responsibility at our inception in 1974—a near 300-fold increase, equivalent to a compound growth rate of 27%.
- Cash inflow is running at a $50 billion annual rate, compared to an outflow of $52 million in 1975, an even more extreme turnabout than the industry has enjoyed.
- Typical of the industry, Vanguard funds carried sales loads at the outset. However, we abruptly made an unprecedented switch to no-load distribution in 1977, less than two years after the firm began operations. We led the industry shift to no-load dominance, and are today that segment's largest unit.
- Our market share has risen from 2% of industry assets in 1980 to 8% today, and from 9% of no-load assets to 24%—one dollar of every four invested in no-load funds.
- And, driven by our preeminence in money market funds, bond funds, conservative stock funds, and index (market-matching) funds, we currently account for fully 50% of the net cash flowing into no-load funds. Our three nearest rivals account for 15%, 7%, and 6%, respectively.

My point in presenting you this context is not merely to illustrate, with what I hope is not false pride, our position in the industry, but to set the stage for how and why this situation has developed, and what it says about the important principles of business ethics—so closely aligned with the principle of servant-leadership—we have established for ourselves. Most important of all, I want to strike an important and optimistic keynote at this meeting: that it is possible to do well by doing good, to succeed by serving others, to lead by having principles hold sway over opportunism. Indeed it is my deeply held conviction that, by doing the right things in the right way, we are on the right side of history.

Turning Back the Clock

Let me now turn back the clock. In 1925—nearly three-quarters of a century ago—an aging professor said to his university class, "There is a new problem in our country. We are becoming a nation that is dominated by large institutions—businesses, governments, universities—and these businesses are not serving us well. I hope that all of you will be concerned about this. But nothing of substance will happen unless people inside these institutions lead them to better performance for the public good. Some of you ought to make careers inside these big institutions and become a force for good—from the inside."

Those words could have as easily been said today. But, as some of you here today will surely recognize, they were in fact the words that inspired a college senior named Robert K. Greenleaf to cast his lot with business as a career. On graduation, he joined American Telephone and Telegraph Company, in important measure because it was then the largest employer in our nation. He described himself as one who knew how to get things done and as a pursuer of wisdom, and his objective was to work on organizational development for the company. He worked there for nearly 40 years, until he retired in 1964.

I have no way of knowing about the influence that Robert Greenleaf exerted on the AT&T organization. But the work he did after his retirement, beginning with his brilliant 1969 essay, "The Servant as Leader," has surely brought much-needed wisdom and insight to the subject of corporate and institutional leadership in the United States. And I salute with admiration the leadership of the Greenleaf Center for its extraordinary accomplishments in carrying on his crusade.

Remarkable Relevance

I must acknowledge that I did not read "The Servant as Leader" until the early 1980s, well after it had become one of a series of a dozen related essays, published in book form under the title *Servant-Leadership*. But as I read his words then, and as I re-read them again in preparing my remarks for today, I was thunderstruck by the power and relevance of his philosophy. Not merely to the great world out there, beyond my ken, but to me. To me, directly and personally, as if this man of my own parents' generation had placed me in the crosshairs of his telescopic sight, and would not rest until he captured the mind of his quarry.

Now, I hope—and indeed I suspect—that many others who have shared in his concepts feel the same way. And that acceptance, that feeling of revelation, more than anything else suggests the force of his mind and the power of his ideas. In this sense, then, the fact that he speaks to me with such relevance may be far more important than if he had in fact been directly responsible for inculcating in me the values and principles of the enterprise I founded in 1974, years before the uncanny yet powerful reinforcement I received from his accumulated wisdom.

What I want to do today is to directly quote at reasonable length some of the words that Robert Greenleaf has written (taking only the most minimal liberties in paraphrasing them), and then describe the extraordinary parallelism their spirit holds with the spirit of Vanguard. I hope in this way that I can persuade you that his dreams of long ago can not only find their way into the hard reality of the world of business, but can form the basis for a corporate success story.

I'm going to touch on five areas: (1) his essay, "Building a Model Institution;" (2) the linkage between foresight and caring; (3) his reflections on the superior company and on the liberating vision; (4) a series of powerful parallel phrases; and finally, somewhat poignantly, (5) his "Memo on Growing from Small to Large." In each case, I'll then follow with examples of how directly Robert Greenleaf's wisdom has spoken to me, and has fortuitously been manifested at Vanguard.

Building a Model Institution

In August 1974, Robert Greenleaf spoke about building a model institution. Interestingly, he was speaking, not about a business, but about a woman's college affiliated with a religious order, at the celebration of its 100th anniversary. His blueprint identified the four cornerstones.

First, a goal, *a concept of a distinguished serving institution* in which all who accept its discipline are lifted up to nobler stature and greater effectiveness than they are likely to achieve on their own or with a less demanding discipline.

Second, *an understanding of leadership and followership*, since *everyone* in the institution is part leader, part follower. If an institution is to achieve as a servant, then only those who are natural servants—those who want to lift others—should be empowered to lead.

Third, an *organization structure* (or *modus operandi*) focusing on how power and authority are handled, including a discipline to help individuals accomplish not only for themselves, but for others.

Fourth, and finally, *the need for trustees*, persons in whom ultimate trust is placed, persons who stand apart from the institution with more detachment and objectivity than insiders can summon.

As it happened, Vanguard was a month away from its creation when Mr. Greenleaf spoke to this century-old institution. But our resemblance to his model is striking. Our original concept, for example, was to transform the very focus of a mutual fund business from serving two masters—something Matthew describes as, well, impossible—the fund shareholder and the owners of the funds' external manager-adviser alike. We would be the servant of the fund shareholder alone, since the mutual funds—and thus their shareholders—would own our funds' manager, and would operate at cost. In effect, our fund shareholders would become the beneficiaries of the entrepreneurial rewards that managers traditionally arrogate to themselves. While I happen to believe that this concept lifts a fund enterprise to nobler stature, the fact that no others have chosen to follow down "the road less traveled by" suggests a profound disagreement with that assessment. So be it.

But it is a fact that our concept of an institution that serves solely its own investors has provided measurably greater effectiveness. The combination of our focus on conservative equity funds, on bond and money market funds of high-quality securities within specific maturity ranges, and of stock and bond market index funds—of which we were the pioneering creators—has worked effectively. Our at-cost operation is now producing *annual* expense savings to our investors of—think of it—nearly $3 billion. Together, these successful strategies and these minimal costs have provided virtual across-the-board superiority in the long-term returns we have earned for the shareholders of the funds we serve, relative to their peer funds with similar objectives.

While I cannot in all honesty say that we began with an understanding of leadership and followership, the second Greenleaf rule for a model institution, I can say that I've spent much of my career developing similar concepts. For example, in one of my early talks to our tiny 28-person original crew, I said, "I want every one of us to treat everyone here with fairness. If you don't understand what that means, stop by my office." I constantly stressed the values that I wanted to distinguish Vanguard, above all the need to recognize that both we who serve and those whom we serve must be treated as "honest-to-God, down-to-earth human beings, with their own hopes, fears, ambitions, and financial goals."

Over the years, I have come to love and respect the term "human beings" to describe those with whom I serve and those whom we at Vanguard together serve. I even gave a talk at Harvard Business

School on how our focus on human beings enabled us to become what they there call a "service breakthrough company." I challenged the students to find the term "human beings" in any book on corporate strategy that they had read, but as far as I know, none could meet the challenge. (Surprisingly, I do not believe that I've seen that term in any of Mr. Greenleaf's vast writings, but I'm certain that he'd love it too.)

Organization structure, or modus operandi, was also integral to our new model of an investment institution. Power and authority would rest not with the managers, as is the mutual fund industry convention, but with the fund shareholders. Of necessity, to be sure, much of the power would be delegated to the managers, but the ultimate authority would be vested in the collective power of those we serve. One rule set forth in modern-day business books is, "treat your clients as if they were your owners." It is a good rule, but it is particularly easy for us to observe it: our clients *are* our owners.

It was obvious, of course, that our managers would require more direct oversight than a large mass of widely dispersed investors, most with moderate holdings in our funds, could provide. So we quickly determined that we needed truly independent trustees, who, as in Mr. Greenleaf's fourth and final requirement for a model institution, would be able to provide objectivity and detachment, and in whom the ultimate trust would be placed. Ever since, at least eight of our ten trustees have been unaffiliated with Vanguard in any way other than in the capacity of directors of our funds. In all, the Greenleaf model, described for a venerable institution, was to closely resemble a model created for a new company, with a new concept, that, as he spoke, was just coming to birth.

Linking Foresight and Caring

I now want to single out two subjects that, perhaps surprisingly, Mr. Greenleaf seemed to link: foresight and caring. He led into his subject with a few words about great leaders.

> **Edwin M. Land, founder of Polaroid, spoke of the opportunity for greatness—not genius—for the many: "within his own field (be it large or small, lofty or mundane) he will make things grow and flourish; he will grow happy helping others in his field, and to that field he will add things that would not have been added had he not come along." But greatness is not enough. Foresight**

is crucial. The lead that the leader has is his ability to foresee an event that must be dealt with before others see it so that he can act on it in his way, the right way, while the initiative is his. If he waits, he cannot be a leader—at best, he is a mediator.

Foresight is the central ethic of leadership. Foresight is the lead that the leader has. Leaders must have an armor of confidence in facing the unknown. The great leaders are those who have invented roles that were uniquely important to them as individuals, that drew heavily on their strengths and demanded little that was unnatural, and that were right for the time and place they happened to be.

Caring for persons, the more able and the less able serving each other, is the basis of leadership, the rock upon which a good society is built. In small organizations, caring is largely person to person. But now most caring is mediated through institutions—often large, complex, powerful, impersonal, not always competent, sometimes corrupt.

To build a model institution, *caring* must be the essential motive. Institutions require care, just as do individuals. And caring is an exacting and demanding business. It requires not only interest and compassion and concern; it demands self-sacrifice and wisdom and tough-mindedness and discipline. It is much more difficult to care for an institution, especially a big one, which can look cold and impersonal and seem to have an autonomy of its own.

While in 1986 I had not read the essay by Robert Greenleaf from which those paragraphs were excerpted, I had read an earlier speech which must have been the source of his inspiration. It was a speech given in 1972 by Howard W. Johnson, Chairman of the Massachusetts Institute of Technology. It inspired me profoundly, and as 1986 drew to a close, I quoted it amply in my speech to our crew. Note the similarity:

There is always a time when the longer view could have been taken and a difficult crisis ahead foreseen and dealt with while a rational approach was still possible. How do we avoid such extremes? How can sustainable growth be achieved? Only with foresight—the central ethic of leadership—for so many bad decisions are made when there are no longer good choices.

If foresight is needed to protect an institution, what are the requirements necessary to make it work? First, the sense of purpose and objective. Second, the talent to manage the

277

process for reaching new objectives. Finally, and let me surprise you by emphasizing this third need, we need people who care about the institution. A deep sense of caring for the institution is requisite for its success.

The institution must be the object of intense human care and cultivation. Even when it errs and stumbles, it must be cared for, and the burden must be borne by all who work for it, all who own it, all who are served by it, all who govern it. Every responsible person must care, and care deeply, about the institutions that touch his life.

My 1986 speech was but one of many times when I spoke of the importance of caring. Then, I reminded the crew that "only if we truly care about our organization, our partners, our associates, our clients, indeed our society as a whole, can we preserve, protect and defend our organization and the values we represent." Again, I emphasized our responsibility "to faithfully serve the honest-to-God human beings who have trusted us to offer sound investment programs, with clearly delineated risks, at fair prices. *We must never let them down.*"

Five years later, in 1991, I returned to the same theme in a talk entitled "Daring and Caring." I illustrated daring by using Lord Nelson's victory at the Battle of the Nile on August 1, 1798. That battle is part of our history (indeed at Vanguard, we're celebrating its 200th anniversary at this very moment) for Nelson's flagship was HMS *Vanguard.* Only weeks before the firm was incorporated in 1974, I had fortuitously learned of the battle, and, inspired by Nelson's remarkable triumph, chose Vanguard as our name.

At Vanguard, I reminded the crew, we dared to be different, in our unique corporate structure, in our unprecedented switch to commission-free distribution, in our decision to provide candid information to investors, and in forming the first market index fund, an idea considered so, well, stupid, that it wasn't even copied by anyone else for a full decade.

But caring quickly took center stage in my talk. I emphasized that caring must be "an article of faith," pointing out that each of those daring decisions that I had mentioned was driven by a philosophy of caring for our clients. And I reinforced the concept that caring must be also accorded to our crew, even then urging a spirit of "cooperation and mutual courtesy and respect," and reminding them that while we were so large as to require a policy manual, "it will never replace our own selves as the ultimate source of a caring attitude." Yes, a great deal of the spirit of Robert Greenleaf (and Dean Johnson, too) had found its way into our young business enterprise.

The Superior Company and the Liberating Vision

I now want to spend a few moments on Robert Greenleaf's views on the superior company and the liberating vision. Here is what he said:

> **What distinguishes a superior company from its competitors is not the dimensions that usually separate companies, such as superior technology, more astute market analysis, better financial base, etc.; it is *unconventional* thinking about its dream—what this business wants to be, how its priorities are set, and how it organizes to serve. *It has a radical philosophy and self-image.* According to the conventional business wisdom, it ought not to succeed at all. Conspicuously less successful competitors seem to say, "the ideas that the company holds ought not to work, therefore we will learn nothing from it."**
>
> **In some cases, the company's unconventional thinking about its dream is born of a liberating vision. But in our society liberating visions are rare. Why are liberating visions so rare? They are rare because a stable society requires that *a powerful liberating vision must be difficult to deliver.* Yet to have none is to seal our fate. We cannot turn back to be a wholly traditional society, comforting as it may be to contemplate it. There must be change—sometimes great change.**
>
> **That difficulty of delivery, however, is only half of the answer. The other half is that so few who have the gift for summarizing a vision, and the power to articulate it persuasively, have the urge and the courage to try. But there must be a place for servant leaders with prophetic voices of great clarity who will produce those liberating visions on which a caring, serving society depends.**

I leave to far wiser—and more objective—heads than mine the judgment about whether or not Vanguard meets the definition of a superior company. Of course, I believe it does. But I have no hesitancy in saying it is the product of unconventional thinking about what we want to be, how we set priorities, and how we organize to serve our clients. And surely our competitors—even the most successful of them—look with a sort of detached amusement and skepticism at our emergence as an industry leader. We have dared to be different, and it seems to be working just fine.

I cannot responsibly describe the ideas on which I founded Vanguard as part of a liberating vision. But I can tell you that, way back in 1951, I was writing my senior thesis on a little-known industry, which *Fortune* magazine described as "tiny but contentious" in the 1949 article that first aroused my interest in an industry about which I had never before heard. In my thesis, I sketched out my ideas of how a better industry—if not a model institution—might be built. Nearly a half-century ago, I called for a fairer shake for investors, urged lower sales commissions and management fees, cautioned against claims that mutual funds' managements could produce miracles, warned that unmanaged indexes had proved tough competition for active managers, and ended up with a ringing call for fund managers to focus, not on the peripheral diversions of the business, but on the duty to provide prudent stewardship. "The principal function of investment companies," I concluded, "is the management of their portfolios. Everything else is incidental to the performance of this function."

If all of that sounds much like Vanguard today, so be it. But it was not a dream that easily became a reality. And it was most certainly not a deterministic series of linked events. Rather it was really a long and random series of happy accidents that led from 1951 to 1981, when the essential structure of today's Vanguard was finally put in place.

But it is, I think, remarkable how the original, if crude, dream hinted at in that Princeton thesis about the need to serve a single master— our investor-owners, now more than ten million human beings in the aggregate—has to this day determined our basic corporate strategies. I've often emphasized that "strategy follows structure," a relationship that has logically led to business decisions that are shaped around our unique shareholder-owned structure. It is what makes our enterprise work. Belying the competitors to whom Greenleaf referred when he pictured them as saying "it ought not to work," putting the shareholder in the driver's seat "ought to work." And it does.

For example, as nearly all now concede, cost is a factor in shaping long-term investment returns. If a firm achieves low-cost provider status, its bond and money market funds can follow lower-risk strategies and still offer higher yields than their peers. If low-cost is the key to a successful index fund (and it obviously is), index funds can appropriately be a major focus of development. If money spent on marketing consumes shareholder assets while offering no countervailing benefit, it would seem foolish to spend much money on marketing. And all of these things are what aware investors should want. *It turns out that they do.* In the world of investing, in fact, it turns out that a superior company can be built on these strategies, all of which flow from a structure in which service to shareholders is the watchword.

Powerful Parallel Phrases

I've now touched on three broad areas of commonality between Robert Greenleaf's thinking and my own—building a model institution, foresight and caring, and the superior company and the liberating vision—as I've tried to manifest them in Vanguard's development. In this fourth section, I want to briefly describe some particularly powerful phrases that I observed in his writing that paralleled those that I have used at Vanguard forever, or so it seems. I do so because it suggests once again that his idealistic visions can in fact be successfully incorporated into a *caring, sharing, serving* business.

"Everything begins with the initiative of an individual." So reads the second sub-head in "The Leader as Servant." "The very essence of leadership" Mr. Greenleaf says—and I am confident that he was referring, not only to a sort of grand idea of corporate leadership, but to the infinite number of tasks where less sweeping forms of leadership are required if an enterprise is to succeed—is going out ahead to show the way, an attitude that is derived from more than usual openness to inspiration. Even though he knows the path is uncertain, even dangerous, a leader says: "I will go, come with me."

Almost uncannily, my words about the importance of the individual leader convey the same idea. "Even one person can make a difference" has become a Vanguard article of faith, and is in fact engraved on the Awards for Excellence that we make each quarter to individuals who have met the highest standards of service, initiative, and cooperation. And even as Mr. Greenleaf defines individual initiative as "showing the way," Vanguard's very name suggests the same idea, for the motto on the HMS *Vanguard* ship badge is "leading the way."

And then there is the matter of the dream. Greenleaf speaks of the need for a leader to state and restate the goal, using the word goal "in the special sense of the overarching purpose, the visionary concept, the dream. Not much happens without a dream. And for something great to happen, it must be a great dream. Much more than a dreamer must bring it to reality, but the dream must be there first."

And I've talked often about Vanguard's dream. In particular, my 1975 speech to the crew was entitled "The Impossible Dream." In it, I said:

The issue, it seems to me, is no longer how to make Vanguard a *bigger* company, but rather how to make Vanguard a *better* company, to provide greater convenience and enhanced investment performance, all in the name of better service for the human beings who have turned over to us the responsibility for their investment assets. A dream it may be—getting bigger only by being better—even an impossible dream, but a thrilling dream. And we must reach for it. In the marvelous musical play "The Man of La Mancha," Don Quixote puts it this way:

> *To dream the impossible dream.*
> *To fight the unbeatable foe*
> *To strive when our arms are too weary*
> *To run where the brave dare not go.*
>
> *This is our quest, to follow the star*
> *No matter how hopeless, no matter how far . . .*
>
> *And the world will be better for this*
> *That one man, scorned and covered with scars*
> *Still strove, with his last ounce of courage*
> *To reach the unreachable star.*

I don't mind at all being a bit of a dreamer, if I can share the attribute with the likes of Robert Greenleaf.

Finally, I was struck by a third powerful parallel, nautical in derivation. Mr. Greenleaf gave this advice: "No matter how difficult the challenge or how hopeless the task may seem, if you are reasonably sure of your course just keep on going!" Leaving aside the obvious similarity with the words from "The Impossible Dream" ("no matter how hopeless, no matter how far"), his words come remarkably close to my often repeated theme, "Press On Regardless," which was in fact the subject of a speech I gave to a graduating class at Vanderbilt University. But "just keep on going" is also a statement of what may well be the most universal of all the nautical themes we use—and sometimes perhaps even abuse—at Vanguard: "stay the course." It is wonderful advice for a career, superb wisdom for a project, and probably the best single piece of investment advice ever offered: "Establish a sound balance of bond funds and stock funds in your portfolio. Then, no matter what the financial markets do, *stay the course.*"

Memo on Growing from Small to Large

In about 1972, Robert Greenleaf wrote this memorandum at the request of the head of a small company that had achieved the reputation for unusual quality of products and service, which had grown rapidly to its present size, and was in the process of becoming a distinguished large institution:

The line that separates a large business from a small one might be drawn at that point where the business can no longer function well under the direction of one individual. If the company has been built largely on one person's drive, imagination, taste, and judgment, as yours seems to have been, it may be difficult to recognize when that point has been reached. The greatest risk may be that company cannot grow and keep its present quality.

I suggest that you begin to shift your personal effort *toward building an institution* in which you become more the manager of a process that gets the job done and less the *administrator of day-to-day operations*. This might be the first step toward the ultimate optimal long-term performance of a large business that is *managed* by a board of directors who act as trustees and *administered* by a team of equals who are led by a *primus inter pares*—first among equals. The result would be an institution that would have the best chance of attracting and holding in its service the large number of able people who will be required to give it strength, quality, and continuity if it is to continue to do on a large scale what you have been able to do so well on a smaller scale.

I am suggesting that a person like you who has been so successful in taking a distinguished business from a small size to large size might, at your age, find an even more exciting challenge in transforming a one-person business into an institution that has autonomy and creative drive as a collection of many able people, one that has the capacity for expansion without losing, and perhaps even enhancing, the claim to distinction it has already achieved.

To say that I found this memorandum both relevant and poignant when I first read it just two weeks ago, as I was preparing these remarks, would be quite an understatement. For what struck home to me was that, while there was much that I thought of when I decided in 1996 to relinquish my position as head of Vanguard, I had not seriously considered abandoning the traditional route of simply recommending to the directors a qualified successor to replace me. The directors agreed without hesitation, perhaps in part because my weak heart was quickly deteriorating and because of my age (I was 67 at the time), and in fairness—although they did not suggest this—perhaps because they had tired of my leadership style.

In any event, within a year I had undergone a remarkably successful heart transplantation, miraculously receiving an infusion of new energy and confidence that had to be seen to be believed. A second chance at life is not to be taken lightly! But my decision had been made, and only time will tell whether it was the correct one. But whatever the case, I have no doubt that the service-caring-ethical principles of Vanguard will remain in place for as far ahead as one can see.

In the Vanguard structure, of course, the entrepreneur is not the owner. (The stock in the company is held by the funds for *their* shareholders.) When one leaves office, then, power devolves to another. And, as Robert Greenleaf wrote:

> **In an imperfect world, some abuse of power will always be with us. In 1770, William Pitt said to the House of Commons, "unlimited power is apt to corrupt the minds of those who possess it." One hundred years later, more famously, Lord Acton (in opposing the doctrine of papal infallibility) said, "power tends to corrupt and absolute power corrupts absolutely." That corruption is reflected in arrogance. For example, the head of a large corporation, when asked what made his job attractive, listed first, before monetary reward, prestige, service, and creative accomplishment, "the opportunity to build power."**
>
> **The power-hungry person, who relishes competition and is good at it (meaning: he usually wins) will probably judge the servant leader to be weak or naive or both. But if we look past that individual to the institution which he or she serves, what makes that institution strong? I believe the strongest, most productive institution over a long period of time has the largest amount of voluntary action toward the goals of the institution. The people who staff the institution do the right things at the right time because the goals are clear and comprehensive and they know what ought to be done, and do the right thing without being instructed. It takes a strong leader to put the people who serve first, but that is the way to insure that they will deliver all that people can deliver—and to insure that the business will continue to lead in its field.**

Vanguard, in my view, has been built on an extraordinary crew—now 8,000 strong—"who know what ought to be done, and who have done the right things at the right time." And while my strong leadership may well have been described as power-driven, my drive (I think) was focused on intellectual power—to devise sensible investment policies, an efficient structure through which to offer them, and a sensible strategy for their delivery—and moral power—to make certain that both structure and strategy were founded on a sound ethical base. Those kinds of powers do not vanish when one leaves office. But other kinds of power do, including the power of the purse, the power to direct people, the power to reshape values, even the power to change what lies firmly in place. But I hope and believe that our crew and my successors will continue to hold high what we have built, its structure and strategy, and the ethical foundation that is Vanguard's rock.

Where History Comes In

Vanguard has had the marvelous opportunity to test in the real world marketplace the concept that serving is the essential ingredient of true success, and that servant-leaders and leader-servants—can successfully dedicate their careers to serving the human beings who depend upon their services. All of that may sound idealistic—it is!—but we live in an era of consumerism (in the best sense) in which business has no recourse but to make a determined effort to build a new level of trust in consumer products and services alike. In the world of finance, if we are going to make the United States a nation of investor-capitalists, we'd best give our citizens the maximum possible proportion of the fruits of investing, rather than consuming large portions of those returns with excessive costs.

The fact is that "the Vanguard way" works. Not because our principles give us some divine right to success, but because we are creating extra value for investors. And, as the numbers I presented at the outset illustrate and the growth that Vanguard is enjoying relative to our peers makes clear, investors have clearly recognized that value advantage.

Yet it is a curious fact of competitive life in the mutual fund world that, while our investment policies—most notably in index funds and in bond funds—are being copied (albeit often with little enthusiasm), our low-cost philosophy and our focus on management rather than marketing are not. But as the investing public makes known its preferences, this industry will finally change. To use a computer analogy, all mutual fund organizations have pretty much the same software—common ways to invest in securities—but the industry must adopt a new operating system—serving the fund shareholder first.

I have no way of knowing whether the coincidence of Robert Greenleaf's philosophy and my own is merely fortuitous—a happy accident, random molecules bumping together in the night—or powerful evidence of the mysterious universality of a great idea. Perhaps it is a little of each. But in the mutual fund industry the central idea of serving is being proven in the marketplace by tens of millions of investors. I've long thought that servant-leadership is on the right side of evolving corporate history. And so too, in that small but growing corner of the financial world that is the U.S. mutual fund industry, the policies and principles that Vanguard adopted a quarter-century ago—which we continue to treasure today—are on the right side of history, too.

Part IV

PERSONAL PERSPECTIVES

*I*N THIS SECTION, I offer some personal perspectives in the form of five speeches I've given to general audiences, usually in academic forums. While each speech refers at least tangentially to my investment values and my career at Vanguard, taken as a whole their focus is frankly idealistic, speaking of values that go well beyond the mundane world of finance.

"The Hedgehog and the Fox" (Chapter 21) is the lecture I gave at Princeton University in February 1999 in conjunction with receiving the Woodrow Wilson Medal for "exemplifying the spirit of Princeton in the nation's service." Using Archilochus' ancient epigram that "the fox knows many things, but the hedgehog knows one *great* thing," I contrast the pallid investment accomplishments of most of the brilliant foxes who populate the U.S. financial system—who know so very much about, well, *everything* and trade stocks with a frenzy—with the superior accomplishments of the industry's few hedgehogs, best exemplified by the index fund strategists, who know only the great value of holding a low-cost all-market stock portfolio. I also discuss the power of idealism, and applaud education that is liberal and moral alike. In the speech, I cite a *second* article from that very *Fortune* magazine of December 1949 that inspired my thesis: "The Moral History of U.S. Business," in which one early American businessman described "the enterprising man . . . [as] not merely a merchant but a man, with a mind to improve, a heart to cultivate, a character to form." To this day, I continue to strive to reach those humble goals.

The next two chapters are brief addresses, the first given when I received an Honorary LL.D. degree from the University of Delaware. Here my theme, "The Majesty of Simplicity," expounds on one of Tolstoy's maxims: "There is no greatness where there is not simplicity, goodness, and truth." The second address, perhaps surprisingly, is about the values of contemporary American society. My theme at the 115th commencement of The Haverford School in greater Philadelphia—"The Things by Which One Measures One's Life"—was based on a brief scene near the conclusion of the film *A Civil Action.* I express my concern that we have moved from Protagoras' notion, expressed 2500 years ago, that "man is the measure of all things," to a society in which, "things are the measure of the man." It's a change that appalls me, and I urged the graduates to pay no regard to "things trivial and things transitory . . . and never to forget that who you *are* is far more important than what you *have*."

Chapter 24 is the most personal of all. "Telltale Hearts" is the story of two heart transplants. One is the tragedy of a boy who dies too young, but whose death is redeemed by the nobility of his parents, who, in an alien land, unhesitatingly make the decision to donate his organs so that others may live. The other is the triumph of a life prolonged, my own story as the recipient of a heart transplant. I reflect on what that experience has meant to me, and speculate on just why it is that human beings, confronted with death, so often seem driven to carry on with their careers. Two transplants involving four lives. *Le coeur est mort, vive le coeur!*

The final speech included in this book, "Press On Regardless," given at Vanderbilt University's 1992 commencement, is also frankly idealistic—from President Coolidge, whose words gave me my title and theme; to Kipling ("triumph and disaster . . . treat those two imposters just the same"); to Gordon Gekko of the movie *Wall Street* ("Greed is good. Greed works, greed is right." I disagreed!); to John Gardner ("Learn from your failures and your successes . . . by enjoying, by loving, by bearing life's indignities with dignity . . . teach the truth by living it."); and St. Paul ("I press toward the mark")—all words by which I have tried to conduct my life. Today, almost a decade later, I continue to press on with my own mission: To help America's families invest soundly in order to secure their financial futures.

21

CHANGING THE MUTUAL FUND INDUSTRY: THE HEDGEHOG AND THE FOX

On Receiving
The Woodrow Wilson Award for Exemplifying
"Princeton in the Nation's Service"
Princeton, New Jersey
February 20, 1999

*T*HIS IS A MARVELOUS morning for me. For a mere businessman—apparently the first one—to join the distinguished roll of 42 public servants, artists, scientists, and authors who have previously been judged to represent the high standard of "Princeton in the Nation's Service," it is a signal honor.

The award citation suggests that my career as an agent of change, if not *the* agent of change, in the mutual fund industry has been in the service of the nation's 50 million fund shareholders. Whatever the case, I've done my best to meet that standard, not only for the 10 million who own Vanguard mutual funds, but also for those who own other funds. For 25 years—in a sense for 50 years—my mission has been to change the industry so that our nation's citizens—the human beings who invest in mutual funds—get a fair shake. But as awesome as is this honor, I have no intention of resting on the laurels I receive today. I still have promises to keep for fund investors and miles to go before I sleep.

I've entitled my remarks "The Hedgehog and the Fox," based on this fragment—dated to about 670 B.C.—from the writings of the Greek philosopher, Archilochus: "The fox knows many things, but the hedgehog knows one *great* thing." This ancient saying has been interpreted to describe the *philosophical* contrast between the human pursuit of many different, even contradictory, goals related by no central principle and the search for a single overarching universal condition of human existence.[1] My focus, however, will be much more modest: The contrasting conduct of the investment and business affairs of two types of financial institutions. One is the fox, that artful, sly, astute animal of the fields and the woods. The fox finds its counterpart in the financial institution that survives by knowing many things about complex markets and sophisticated marketing. The other is the hedgehog, that durable nocturnal animal that survives by curling into a ball, its sharp spines giving it almost impregnable armor. The hedgehog is represented by the financial institution that knows only one great thing: that in the long-term, investment success is based on simplicity. In the contrast between the hedgehog and the fox, we find some powerful lessons about investing that I'll use to amplify my theme.

Princeton's Vital Role

I should tell you now that I have no reluctance to cast my lot with the hedgehogs of the financial world who focus on honest stewardship and plain service. But before I turn to the investment and business philosophy for which I stand, I owe it to you, I think, to recount the story of the vital role in the development of this philosophy played a long time ago by the Princeton University family.

From the time of my matriculation in 1947—a shy young kid whose *serious* education began with two years at Blair Academy—right up to today, many Princetonians paved the way for my career. The first was Charles C. Nichols, Class of 1906, who lent me $60 to pay the General Fee required before I could enroll. (I repaid him shortly after I went to work following my graduation.) The providers of the two endowed scholarships that paid my tuition—the Class of 1918, in memory of Roy S. Leidy, a son of Nassau who tragically died at the Argonne less than a month before the Great War ended; and Mrs. Alexander Maitland, daughter of President James McCosh, in memory of her husband. The professors who did their best to educate me. My fabulous

---

1. I give special note to the extraordinary British philosopher Sir Isaiah Berlin, whose 1953 essay "The Fox and the Hedgehog" was the source of my inspiration to use this theme.

classmates in the Class of 1951, many of whom, over these past 50 years, have become good friends to this intense and determined nerd of college days. (I was not smart enough to avoid long hours of studying.) And Professor Burton G. Malkiel, Graduate School, Class of 1964, with whom I share so many investment principles, and who has both supported me and sharpened my thinking not only in professional circles, but in his two decades of service on the Vanguard Board of Directors.

I owe special gratitude to a marvelous long-time friend, a member of the Class of 1952, who now happens to rank among the University's most dedicated and effective Trustees. He befriended me when we both lived in Holder Hall during my sophomore year, and invited this insecure scholarship student to his family's home near Philadelphia. He introduced me to his young sister, then just 14 years of age. *Mirabile dictu!* Eight years later, Eve and I married and became the proud parents of six fine children (including Sandra, Class of 1990), and, so far, the grandparents of 12. Had we not attended Princeton together, I would likely have never met John J. F. Sherrerd, Class of 1952. Thank you, Jay, for all you have done to enrich my life.

A Remarkable Accident

Whatever the case, my career began with a remarkable accident that took place a half-century ago in the reading room of the newly opened Firestone Library. I had been puzzling over the choice of a topic for my senior thesis in the Department of Economics, and had determined only what I would *not* consider: Any subject on which any Princeton thesis had ever been written. There went Adam Smith, Karl Marx, and John Maynard Keynes, all in one fell swoop. I of course had no idea where to turn next. But in December 1949, I happened to open *Fortune* magazine and find, on page 116, an article entitled "Big Money in Boston." It was, of course, about the tiny, but "rapidly expanding and somewhat contentious" mutual fund industry, with "great potential significance to U.S. business." My fortuitous discovery was, at least in a parochial way, the miracle on which the career I have followed would depend, for I knew that I had found the topic for my thesis.

Read today, my thesis sounds terribly idealistic, if not callow. In its final chapter, I concluded that the infant mutual fund industry's best chance for success lay in giving the shareholders a fair shake: "Its future growth can be maximized by a reduction of sales loads and management fees"; that "the principal function of (mutual funds) is the management of their investment portfolios. Everything else is incidental"; and that serving the interests of shareholders should "be the function around which all others are satellite." Whether those simple thoughts were naive idealism, idle prattle, or a design for what Vanguard would stand for, I leave to far wiser heads. But my thesis grade did give my class standing a huge boost, and, despite a shaky sophomore year (I almost lost my scholarship, which would have ended my days at Princeton), I graduated *magna cum laude*.

Walter L. Morgan, Fellow Princetonian

I had no way of knowing that Walter L. Morgan, Class of 1920, would read my thesis. (I had sent it to a senior officer of Wellington Fund who had discussed the industry with me when I did my research.) Mr. Morgan was impressed, and when I graduated, he offered me a job. After what turned out to be an unnecessary amount of soul-searching, I accepted, and, as they say, the rest is history. Walter Morgan truly made a difference in my life. He gave me my first break, and he became my mentor. Then he entrusted me, at age 36, with the leadership of Wellington, the company he founded in 1928. But far more than that, we became close friends, establishing a mutual admiration society that endured for nearly a half a century, until his death last summer. He had just reached his 100th birthday, still bright, alert, interested *and* interesting, the oldest then-living alumnus of the Class of 1920. When I decided to dedicate my soon-to-be-published book, *Common Sense on Mutual Funds*, to him, I had an advance copy of its cover and dedication printed and framed, and gave it to him before what was to be his last birthday. It includes the phrase "fellow Princetonian," and we shared great pride in that designation. This morning, I know that in some mysterious way he's here with us, sharing this high honor with me.

Quickly after assuming my awesome new responsibility at Wellington, I impulsively made a career-threatening error. Seeking additional portfolio management talent, I merged Wellington with a Boston-based investment counsel firm in 1966. By January 1974, amidst the most ferocious bear market since 1929–1933, my new partners succeeded in firing me. But in the aftermath of the battle, I took a wild risk and formed a new company. I called it Vanguard, a name intended to suggest that its novel structure (more about that later) would one day lead the way in the mutual fund industry. It began as a tiny administrative company—just 27 young employees (crewmembers, as we have called them ever since) and me. Only after a painful, obstacle-ridden, seven-year struggle—at first opposed by the Securities and Exchange Commission—would it finally develop the form and structure that it enjoys today. But it has been built, just as my thesis suggested, on vastly reduced management fees; not merely on *reduced* sales loads, but *no* loads; by focusing on prudent management rather than aggressive marketing; and by holding the interests of shareholders paramount. If, as some accounts have it, we *do* lead the way in this industry, the path may well have been laid in a Princeton thesis written almost 50 years ago.

The Foxes—Truly a Skulk

And now to the fox and the hedgehog. In the mutual fund business today, indeed in our global financial system, the foxes hold sway, both in investment philosophy and in business philosophy. As to investment philosophy, the skulk—a large crowd of fund foxes—holds to the idea that investing is complicated and complex, so much so that to achieve investment success individual investors have no choice but to employ professional portfolio managers. Only these experts, or so it is said, can possibly steer them through a hyper-active system that constitutes the complex maze of the global financial markets. In seeking to invest your money successfully, the industry's managers present powerful credentials, including excellent education, years of experience, cunning, and even investment legerdemain; they hover over their portfolios by the hour, constantly monitoring and changing holdings, often with astonishing frequency, not only as a company's products and prospects change, but as its market price waxes and wanes. Further, some among this skulk expect to slyly sell stocks when the market is high, and buy them back when the market falls. In all, the managers add extra opportunity and accept the extra risk required in the search for superior returns. Alas, however, to the limited extent that these strategies have proven to work effectively—and for a relative handful of funds at that (of course, it would be absurd to imagine they could work for all funds as a group)—the very costs incurred by the fund managers were almost always so high as to consume any value added, even by the most cunning of the portfolio manager-foxes. Fund shareholders were left with annual returns that were generally less than 85% of the returns realized in the stock market.

The reason for this shortfall is largely fund costs. The *all-in* costs of the fund foxes now approach 3% per year on average: 1½% from management fees and expenses, often 1% or more from the costs of churning the portfolio, plus another ½%-plus annually for investors who pay sales commissions. Now, let's think long-term instead of short-term. Let's be conservative and set the total croupier's take—the amount gathered by the managers, dealers, and brokers—at 2½% per year. The *positive* impact of compound interest that magnifies long-term returns, unfortunately, also magnifies the *negative* impact of costs, so that an assumed 2½% *annual* cost consumes 20% of the investor's capital in a decade. As time goes on, costs consume 45% of capital in a quarter century, and—believe it or not—almost 70% of your capital in 50 years. *The investor, who puts up 100% of the initial capital, receives but 30% of the long-term pre-tax return.* The remaining 70% has been consumed by the financial foxes.

These numbers are more than mere mathematical abstractions. A recent chart in *Business Week* showed that since the greatest bull market in all history began in 1982, a $10,000 investment in the average equity mutual fund would have increased to *$114,000;* the same investment in the stock market (the Standard & Poor's 500 Index) would have grown to *$194,000*—a staggering $80,000 increment simply for *not* being a fox. That is the American financial system today, and that is how capital formation works in the mutual fund industry. To the extent that another investment approach can avoid, or at least minimize, the inherent pitfalls that are built into the traditional mutual fund system, that approach will hold the winning hand.

When Mr. Market Speaks, Funds Listen

Where might that approach begin? By investing for the long term. The ultimate example of long-term investing is simply buying and holding the stocks of America's businesses. Short-term speculation, its polar opposite, is buying shares—pieces of paper if you will—of hundreds of stocks listed on the nation's stock exchanges, and then feverishly trading them in the market casino. The strategy of America's most successful investor is the paradigm of long-term investing. Warren Buffett purchases the shares of a few businesses and holds them, ignoring the noise created by a man he calls "Mr. Market," who comes by and offers him a different price for the businesses in his portfolio each day. The foxy managers of the fund industry however, do precisely the opposite, trading the pieces of paper in their portfolios at turnover rates of 50% to 200% annually. Responding at each moment to the prices set by Mr. Market's madness, they pay little attention to the value of a corporation. As Columbia Law School Professor Louis Lowenstein has observed: Fund managers "exhibit a persistent emphasis on momentary stock prices. The subtleties and nuances of a particular business escape them."

To make matters worse, the feverish trading of stocks by fund managers—it *is* short-term speculation—for their fund shareholders has now spread to the shareholders themselves. Perhaps following the example set by their managers, fund investors now turn over *their own fund shares* at feverish rates, switching their funds to pick the next winner, or to time the market—fruitless pursuits, both—every three years. (In the 1950s and 1960s, the average holding period for a fund investor was 12 years.) The astonishing brevity of this period gives the lie to the industry's marquee motto: "For the long-term investor." Fund investors—the clients now acting as foxes—trade their funds just as if they were stocks, most feverishly in the marketplaces whose advertisements helped bring you the Super Bowl. These fund supermarkets constitute yet *another* series of casinos, with yet *another* set of croupiers to reduce the returns of the gamblers. Lord Keynes had it right: "When the capital development of a country becomes the by-product of a casino, the job is likely to be ill-done."

Enter the Hedgehog

Successful long-term investors like Warren Buffett are almost impossible to identify in advance, so we'll have to look to an unconventional adversary to take on the foxes and better serve the interest of fund investors. The hedgehog I have in mind, as you might imagine, is Vanguard, a firm that has tried to fill this near-vacuum since our founding in 1974. And the one great thing this hedgehog knows is an utterly simple, self-evident, overarching mathematical truth: The returns of all investors *must* equal the returns of the stock market as a whole. A return of 10% per year in the market clearly can't be parlayed into a return of an 11% for the average investor. Equally obvious conclusion: Investor returns, less the costs of investing, *must* fall short of market returns by the amount of investment expenses.

That early insight, such as it may be, reminded me of an idea that, believe it or not, also appeared in that Princeton thesis of a quarter-century earlier. Studying the record, I had concluded that "mutual funds can make no claim to superiority to the market averages." My readings in the academic journals around the time Vanguard was formed gave powerful theoretical reinforcement to that conclusion, and my careful study of mutual fund returns in the 1945–1975 period added powerful pragmatic evidence that confirmed the inability of fund managers to add value to their investors' assets. Vanguard's very first strategic decision, made in 1975, only months after we began, was obvious: To form the first market index mutual fund—an unmanaged portfolio of the 500 stocks in the Standard & Poor's 500 Index—in history. Derided for years as "Bogle's folly," it took, unimaginably, another full decade until a single competitor had the guts—or wisdom—to follow. In the words of *The Wall Street Journal*, the Vanguard Index 500 Fund has become, heaven forbid, "the industry darling."

With $80 billion of assets, our pioneering index fund is now the second-largest mutual fund in the world, well on its way to becoming the largest before the new century arrives. The decisions that followed over the years took the same direction. Following that first 500 Index Fund, we formed index funds covering our entire stock market, a wide variety of U.S. stock market sectors, international equity markets, and the bond market. We also developed stringently managed bond funds that offered investors market-like portfolios with clearly defined quality and maturity standards, entailing little trading and operating with minimal expenses. What is more, we shaped most of our managed equity funds to parallel particular investment styles, focusing on long-term horizons, relatively low portfolio turnover, and, yes again, minimal costs, achieved by negotiating fees at arm's length with external advisory firms. This hedgehog strategy remains the rock on which our investment philosophy rests.

Status Quo versus Reality

The survival of this industry, *as we know it today*, depends on the maintenance of the status quo by the foxes. Financial success for the mutual fund manager is represented far less by earning even a *market* return on the *investor's* capital than by earning a *staggering* return on the *manager's* capital. (If you don't believe that, merely compare the returns that the managers have earned on their own capital to the returns they have earned on the funds they supervise.) Were this not so, managers would not seek huge asset size for their actively managed funds, which clearly impedes the achievement of superior returns, nor spend billions on marketing shares to new investors, the cost of which is borne by existing shareholders who receive no benefit in return—except perhaps the pleasure of seeing their former portfolio manager perform on television with Don Rickles and Lily Tomlin. It goes without saying that despite the pleas in my thesis, non-management—largely marketing—functions have superseded those of management, and the interest of the managers has superseded the interest of the fund shareholders.

The foxes, nonetheless, derogate the hedgehog with criticisms, which, as far as they go, may even be valid. But they go too far. Yes, some manager-foxes inevitably beat the market by a solid margin . . . but they are impossible to identify in advance, and, once they reach the pinnacle of performance, almost never remain there. (Reversion to the mean is alive and well in the mutual fund industry!) Yes, the large-cap Standard and Poor's 500 Stock Index not only seems high— at an astonishing 29 times earnings it *is* high—but also seems significantly overvalued relative to the small- and mid-cap stocks that represent the remaining 25% of the market's $13.5 trillion value . . . but the fundamental theory of indexing is grounded in owning the *entire* stock market, and that option is available in at least a few index funds. What is more, some 75% of the $2.8 trillion of equity mutual fund assets is invested in those same 500 S&P stocks. So, for the "500" index funds and the industry as a whole, the exposure to market risk is not significantly different. Yes, interim variations in the gap between industry and index returns will surely expand and contract in the future . . . but in the long run the mutual fund industry will have to recognize the inevitability of the failure of its existing investment *modus operandi* to earn returns that are sufficient to overcome its costs, and add economic value for fund shareholders.

Investment versus Speculation

After a half-century observing this industry, I may have become too much the philosopher, maybe even too much the cynic. But it occurs to me that most mutual fund managers are barking up the wrong tree. I just can't imagine that any of those foxes in the mutual fund industry don't understand the simple arithmetic that gives the all-market index fund its powerful advantage, let alone the extra boost added by its extraordinary tax-efficiency. That I am virtually the industry's sole apostle of indexing makes the thesis easy to ignore. But even when Warren Buffett, with his unchallenged credentials, speaks—"Most investors will find that the best way to own common stocks is through an index fund that charges minimal fees . . . it is *certain* to beat the net results delivered by the great majority of professionals"—this industry fails to listen. Except, that is, for the former chairman of one giant fund complex who defends his firm against the clear truth that underlies the superiority of the index with these words: "Investors ought to recognize that mutual funds can *never* (his word) beat the index." The index fund is not merely another kind of mutual fund. It approaches investing, not as a matter of trading pieces of paper for advantage, but as a matter of owning businesses and watching them grow. *Through an all-market index fund, investors own the shares of virtually every publicly held business in the U.S., and hold them forever.* This overarching principle—the one great thing that the fund hedgehog knows—is not merely a good strategy for the long-term investor. It is a winning strategy.

Here, I am reminded of Occam's Razor, the principle that advises: When faced with a problem having multiple solutions, choose the simplest one. (This "principle of parsimony"—shaving away all complex solutions—was recently given the attention it deserves by William Safire in his Sunday *New York Times Magazine* column.) Occam's Razor is right on the mark in pointing to the solution to the seeming riddle of investment success, for index funds are the essence of simplicity. I should add that, contrary to much of what we read in the financial press, the principle that William of Occam set out in the 14th century, works—as it *must* work—in *all* financial markets. Whether in markets in which fund returns are widely divergent—small stocks or international stocks, for example—or in markets in which fund returns are narrowly spaced—bonds, for example—there is no longer any question of the power of the universal principle of low-cost indexing. It may threaten the financial interests of the fund *industry,* but it fosters the financial interests of the fund *shareholders.*

The Hedgehog as Businessman

Let me now turn to my second contrast between fox and hedgehog: From the industry's *investment* conduct, to its *business* conduct. Here the foxy strategy of entrepreneurs and promoters relies on guileful marketing, hot products, and inflated claims of performance success, while the hedgehog strategy emphasizes prudence, stewardship, and service. This strategy entails a sort of "if-you-build-it-they-will-come" approach, which works only if standards are established to assure that those who *do* come are served in a first-class fashion.

The record is clear that since managers as a group will fall short of market returns by the amount of their costs, the linchpin of the hedgehog strategy is maintaining minimal costs. *In the long run, the rewards of investing are determined by the allocation of market returns between the fund shareholders and the managers.* To help accomplish this vital goal, Vanguard has chosen a corporate structure, unique in the mutual fund industry. It is truly *mutual:* The fund shareholders *own* the management company that administers the funds. Unlike every other company in this business, we operate our enterprise on an "at-cost" basis, with each fund paying its share of corporate expenses. In turn, we hold those expenses to the bare minimum, employing a modest marketing budget and demanding stringent cost controls in every activity we undertake. We are, in a brutal but accurate word, "cheap." (It *is*, after all, our clients' money that we are spending.) The net result is savings for our investors totaling something in the range of $3 billion to $4 billion per year, a huge enhancement in shareholder returns that often makes the difference between "average" and "superior" relative to peer funds.

At the same time, our clients must be provided with an excellent level of service, distinguished not as much by efficiency and automation as by how we treat them. As I have said to our crew 1,000 times over: "Let's treat our clients as human beings—honest-to-God, down-to-earth human beings with their own hopes, fears, and financial goals." For what it is worth, at Harvard Business School we have become known as one of the two premier "service-breakthrough companies" in American business. A year ago, I was invited to reveal the secret of our success, such as it may be, to four Harvard classes. I told them that the secret was, hedgehog-like, based on a simple, unitary concept: Treating our clients as human beings—serving *them* in the same manner as we would have the honest stewards of *our* assets serve *us*.

I then asked if any of the 300 students I was addressing had ever seen the phrase "human beings" appear in a textbook on business management or corporate strategy. No heads nodded; no hands were raised. But I hope that these future leaders of American business learned something useful, if not priceless. For the hedgehog firm, Occam's razor shaves away all of the complex, and not entirely straightforward, myths that go into what is called, charitably, "modern marketing," to say nothing of shaving away all unnecessary costs. Individual human beings—no more, no less—remain the focus. Of course, our mission of service to investors requires good communications, advanced technology, and financial controls. They are conditions *necessary*, but not conditions *sufficient* to reaching our goals. Finally, the one great thing we recognize is the primacy of the individual human being.

Reinforcement . . . from a Surprising Source

You may be surprised to learn that none other than Woodrow Wilson came at his presidential mission with the same focus. He believed that productive relationships among human beings were required for serving the nation's citizenry. In 1913, he delivered his first State of the Union address in person, renewing a custom that had lapsed with John Adams more than a century earlier. Wilson did not decide to renew that custom—one that we all now take for granted—inadvertently. Right at the start of his address, he pointed out that a President must demonstrate that he is, "a person, not a mere department of Government, speaking naturally and with his own voice, that he is a human being trying to cooperate with other human beings in a common service." I could hardly have said it better.

Once the leader determines to treat those *whom* he serves as human beings, treating all of those *with* whom he serves as human beings quickly follows. In the ideal, some concept of the leader as servant and the servant as leader—each of whom can lift one another to a higher standard of moral and ethical service—can change the very nature of an enterprise. As the late Robert Greenleaf, founder of the servant-leadership movement has said, "It is not superior technology, nor more astute market analysis, nor a better financial base that distinguishes a superior company, but an unconventional thinking about its dream, how it organizes to serve . . . *a powerful liberating vision that must be difficult to deliver.*"

I am well aware that both conducting our investment strategy with the simplicity exemplified by index funds and conducting our business strategy with the simplicity of the Golden Rule are idealistic to a fault, perhaps even stupidly and naively idealistic. So be it. I for one am prepared to rise and fall on these hedgehog-like strategies, even as I am well aware that they form a mutually reinforcing set of values, the key to success for any enterprise. If the application of low cost to policies of prudent investing is key to investment success, a firm requires both a structure and an attitude that bring about low cost. So positioned, the hedgehog's spines are well-honed, his defenses ready to engage in a lifelong competition with the clever foxes of the investment profession and the wily foxes of the world of commerce, breeds that are more sophisticated and worldly-wise, and surely more brilliant, than I could ever imagine being. In this idealism, I am proud to associate myself once again with Woodrow Wilson, who said in September 1919, only days before suffering the stroke that ended his political effectiveness, "Sometimes people call me an idealist. Well, that is the way I know I'm American. America is the only idealistic nation in the world."

Liberal Education, Moral Education

When I think of the good fortune that has brought to me the extraordinary award that Princeton University bestows on me today, I give the highest order of credit to a set of strong family values and a faith in God, a fine preparation for college at Blair Academy, and the powerful reinforcement and new awakening I received through a liberal education at this remarkable place. In a recent essay in the *Princeton Alumni Weekly*, President Shapiro defined these two aims of a liberal education: "One is the importance of achieving educational objectives, a better understanding of our cultural inheritance and ourselves, a familiarity with the foundations of mathematics and science, and a clarification of what we mean by virtue . . . the other is the importance of molding a certain type of citizen." He went on to emphasize, "the search for truth and new understanding . . . and the freeing of the individual from previous ideas, the pursuit of alternative ideas, the development of the integrity and power of reason of individual goals . . . and the preparation for an independent and responsible life of choice." During my four years here, I did my best to acquire these traits.

President Shapiro also pointed to the "responsibility of a university offering a *liberal education* to provide its students with a *moral education* . . . helping them to develop values that will enrich their lives as individuals and as members of society." This aging hedgehog, looking back in hindsight through glasses that inevitably have a rosy hue, can only say that the liberal and moral education placed before me at Princeton may well have ignited some deep and unimagined spark that began to influence my life and my career in the mutual fund field. This spark, nurtured by time and experience, has erupted into some sort of flame that has permeated my ideas about the proper nature of the mutual fund. The flame will spread one day to the industry and become a blaze, one that will not be easy to extinguish. It is my prayer that my mission—my crusade, if that is not too lofty a characterization of the course of my career—will help an industry to rethink its values, and accordingly be of greater service to growing millions of American investors. Serving these new owners of American business, who are contributing to the highest values of our system of capital formation even as they strive to take personal responsibility for the security of their own financial futures, has been a marvelously worthwhile life's work.

Returning Full Circle

I now close, surprisingly enough, by returning, full circle, to where I began my remarks: Finding *Fortune*, as it were, a half-century ago. Of course, I had kept a copy of my thesis, and I obtained years ago a copy of that original mutual fund article from which so much innovation was to emerge. What is more, thanks to an enterprising Vanguard crew member, I received just weeks ago a mint-condition copy of the entire December 1949 original edition of *Fortune*. One more mystically fortuitous event occurred: the feature essay was entitled "The Moral History of U.S. Business." I have no recollection of reading it in 1949. But I read it a few weeks ago, nearly 50 years later.

As I reflect on Vanguard's two guiding principles of prudent investing and personal service, both seem to be related to the kind of moral responsibility of business expressed in the *Fortune* essay. It began by noting the non-profit motives that lie behind the labors of the American businessman: "the love of power or prestige, altruism, pugnacity, patriotism, the hope of being remembered through a product or institution." Even as I freely confess to all of these motives—life is too short to be a hypocrite—I also agree with *Fortune* on the appropriateness of the traditional tendency of American society to ask: "What are the moral credentials for the social power [the businessman] wields?" The essay begins with the example of Quaker businessman John Woolman of New Jersey, who in 1770 wrote that it is "good to advise people to take such things as were most useful, and not costly." It then cites Benjamin Franklin's favorite words—"Industry and frugality"—as "the [best] means of producing wealth and receiving virtue." Moving to 1844, the essay cites the words of William Parsons, "a merchant of probity," who described the good merchant as "an enterprising man willing to run some risks, yet not willing to risk in hazardous enterprises the property of others entrusted to his keeping, careful to indulge no extravagance and to be simple in his manner and unostentatious in his habits, not merely a merchant, but a man, with a *mind* to improve, a *heart* to cultivate, a *character* to form."

Woodrow Wilson on the Moral Impulse

As for the mind, I still strive every day—I really do!—to improve my own. As for the heart, no one—no one!—could possibly revel in the opportunity to cultivate it more than I. Tomorrow, after all, just happens to be the anniversary of the amazing grace represented by my incredibly successful heart transplant just three years ago. And as for character, whatever moral standard I may have developed, I have tried to invest my own soul and spirit in the character of the firm I founded 25 years ago. On a far grander scale than just one human life, these standards resonate—as ever, idealistically—in how we seek to manage the billions of dollars entrusted to our stewardship, and in how I pray that my company will ever see itself, putting the will and the world of a business enterprise in the service of others—in the nation's service.

Woodrow Wilson had a strong moral vision. In his inaugural speech as President of Princeton University in 1902, he demanded that the university graduate "derive his knowledge from the thoughts of the generations that have gone before him," noting that, "the ages of *strong and definite moral impulse* have been the ages of achievement." He then added, "university men ought to hold themselves bound to the upper roads of usefulness which run along the ridges, and command views of the general fields of life." His choice of those words, "the general fields of life," surely can be read as applying to mundane works of commerce—business and finance, the trades and the services—and to those Princetonians who would spend their careers honorably pursuing them.

In this sense, perhaps Woodrow Wilson is looking down on this morning's ceremony with approval, accepting with pleasure the fact that in 1999 the award that honors him will be presented to a Princetonian who, as a businessman, has spent his career in the field of finance. To an important extent, the wonderful life and the modest success I've been blessed to enjoy in an opportunity-laden career began right here, on this magnificent and tradition-bound campus. I fell in love with this place when I first arrived as a freshman member of the great Class of 1951. Now, more than 50 years after my arrival here in 1947, the honor of receiving the 43rd Woodrow Wilson Award "for the alumnus whose achievements exemplify the spirit of Princeton in the nation's service" is the ultimate reward. It will serve as a challenge to me to carry on the work I have begun.

22

THE MAJESTY OF SIMPLICITY

On Receiving
The Honorary Degree as Doctor of Laws
from the University of Delaware
Newark, Delaware
October 22, 1999

*L*ET ME FIRST express my sincere thanks for the signal honor you have just bestowed on me. I accept it with great pride, enthusiastic delight, and considerable humility. Earlier in my life, there was a point at which I actually considered becoming an attorney, and, with luck, perhaps ultimately even a respected jurist. While that dream has long since vanished, my designation by your Trustees as Doctor of Laws through the award of this Honorary LL.D. degree will be a wonderful reminder of a legal career that might have been.

Your award, interestingly enough, comes at a major milestone in Vanguard's history. Only a few weeks ago, we quietly celebrated the 25th anniversary of our founding: September 24, 1974. Since we began, our industry—driven by the great bull market in stocks and the ever-growing acceptance of the mutual fund concept—has burgeoned 150-fold in assets, from $40 billion to $6 trillion. But Vanguard's 500-fold growth in this period—from $1 billion to $500 billion—has marked us as the fastest growing firm in the entire industry.

The explanation for that success—although, to be clear, I equate neither giant size nor rapid growth with success—is not very complicated. Our defining quality, I think, is our recognition, a quarter century ago, of the majesty of simplicity. If Vanguard has dared to strive for greatness, it is because we have tried to live by Tolstoy's standard:

"There is no greatness where there is not simplicity, goodness, and truth."

Common sense investing is grounded in simplicity, but it requires faith. In the very first paragraph of the very first chapter of *Common Sense on Mutual Funds,* I write: "Investing is an act of faith. We trust our capital to corporate stewards with the faith that their efforts will generate high rates of return on our investments . . . and the faith that the long-term success of our nation's economy and financial markets alike will continue in the future."

The problem with investing, as it turns out, is not faith in our financial markets, for they have provided us with bounteous returns. Rather it is faith in our financial institutions, for the stewards of our assets have failed to capture for investors a fair share of those returns. Because of the excessive costs of participating in the markets, the principal challenge you face as an investor is to at once realize the highest proportion of the market return earned in each asset class in which you invest—stocks, bonds, cash reserves—and at the same time to recognize, *and to accept,* that your portion will be less than 100%.

Few institutions—and certainly precious few mutual funds—have offered their services at costs that are sufficiently low to enable their investors even to approach the 100% desideratum. Indeed, over the past quarter-century, fund management and marketing costs have confiscated some 40% of the stock market's cumulative profits, leaving but 60% for the human beings who, after all, put up 100% of the initial capital and took 100% of the market's risks. Such an outcome simply doesn't comport with my notion of fairness.

Since our inception, Vanguard's stock in trade has been the notion that in minimal operating costs lay the key to approaching 100% of the market's return. The unifying theme in everything we do is rock-bottom expenses. It begins with our *mutual* mutual fund structure. At the outset, we broke new ground by having the mutual fund shareholders own the funds' management company, which in turn operates on an "at-cost" basis. Just a few months later, we broke new ground again, bringing the idea of low-cost investing into crystal-clear focus by forming the first index mutual fund. In its ideal form, the index fund owns a *pro-rata* share of every security in a given market and virtually *guarantees* almost—but not quite—100% of the market return. As a result, it provides its participants with *certainty* that their returns will outpace the returns of all other investors as a group.

To explain why that proposition must be so, the analogy of the casino proves to be apt. Gamblers in the real casino play a zero-sum game until the croupier's rake descends and takes its share. It then becomes a loser's game. Investors in the stock market casino, too, play a zero-sum game in terms of beating the market, but, again, only until the croupiers' rakes descend. Then, it too becomes a loser's game. With so many croupiers raking off their shares—fund managers and marketers, investment bankers and brokers, even the Federal and state governments—investors who bet on every stock in the market, exit the casino, hold their stocks forever, and never again darken its doors, earn long-term returns that put those of the active participants in the financial markets—those who remain in the casino—as a group to shame. Yes, there are going to be some long-term winners, but they will be few, and virtually impossible to identify in advance.

In essence, investing in highly diversified portfolios focused on high-quality stocks and bonds, holding trading to a minimum, and operating at bare-bones cost proves to be the key to investment success. Today, that perspective may seem obvious. Perhaps it *always* was. One writer, determined to explain the many simple innovations we have brought to the world of investing in stocks and bonds alike, laid it to what he called my "uncanny ability to recognize the obvious"—a wonderful paradox, since the obvious ought to be something *anyone* can recognize. But however obvious, the notion that there is inevitably a gap between the returns the markets *provide* and the returns investors *receive* is gradually reshaping the way Americans invest.

Why did it take so long for the greatness of simplicity in investing to emerge? Remember what Tolstoy said: Greatness also requires "goodness and truth." While many financial firms may well have recognized just as easily as I did the mathematics of the marketplace that defines investment success by the apportionment of returns between the investors and the managers—even as between gamblers and croupiers—external fund managers had a powerful vested interest in maintaining their own extraordinarily high profitability. We alone had an internally managed structure, a structure that would provide a measurable goodness, if you will, to investors. It is putting the investor first that has given us the highest motivation, reinforced by our will and our determination, to act on such an obvious proposition and drive it to its full fruition. "The greatest good for the greatest number." Jeremy Bentham would have loved it.

Tolstoy's third element of the search for greatness—truth—also played a vital role. Our simple investment philosophy speaks for itself. In a business where marketing has become the highest priority and hyperbole the order of the day, our investment strategies are clear and uncluttered. We can not only honestly report *what* our past returns were; we can explain *why* and *how* they happened. The superiority of the index approach has been endlessly tested in academia and has not been found wanting. Indeed it is a rare MBA student today who has not been schooled in the very theory that we have made work in practice. All we had to do was keep driving the message home. At the outset, of course, it seemed counterintuitive, even ridiculous. But with the truth in our arsenal, we enthusiastically became the apostles of indexing and index-like strategies, the disciples of low cost. It's been wonderful not only to witness the investment world change, but to help it along the way. And it is the investors of America who are the winners.

Our simple investment philosophy has been a condition *necessary* to our success, but I think not a condition *sufficient*. For that condition, I turn briefly to the other main element of Vanguard's focus on service to human beings as the core of our business philosophy—"honest-to-God, down-to-earth human beings, with their own hopes, fears, and objectives." I've said it 1,000 times over. Even with 12 million shareholders, we strive to treat each one as an individual. We do the same with our burgeoning group of Vanguard crew members, now 10,000 strong, who have coped so beautifully with our astonishing growth and contributed so much to our success.

Our Award for Excellence is embossed with a phrase I've used ever since we began 25 years ago: "Even one person can make a difference." Only as the idea of treating human beings with respect, fairness, and compassion permeates our enterprise can we truly emerge as the honest stewards of our investors' assets, hard-earned and vital to their future security. Living this philosophy with those with whom we serve at Vanguard, and with those whom Vanguard serves, may sound like the Golden Rule. So be it. Such stewardship is just one more piece of evidence of the Thoreau-like simplicity that permeates our mission. "Our life is frittered away by detail. Simplify, Simplify."

As I move into the late stages of my long near-half-century career in this industry, I must admit that I don't spend a lot of time basking in the success of the investment strategies we've provided to investors, nor in the success of our enterprise, nor in dwelling on either the many challenges or the few disappointments I've encountered along the way. I look to America's future with the same idealism and hope that I've always had, and to Vanguard's future with confidence that our great warship will stay its appointed course long after I'm gone. For I believe the investment ideas and human values with which I've endowed the firm that I founded 25 years ago, those that I've sketched out today, are not only enduring, but eternal.

23

THE THINGS BY WHICH ONE
MEASURES ONE'S LIFE

Commencement Address
The Haverford School
Haverford, Pennsylvania
June 7, 1999

*I*AM PROFOUNDLY honored, if some-
what intimidated, by this opportunity to address The Haverford
School Class of 1999 at your commencement. My job, as I understand
it, is to say something important and relevant, but not speak so long as
to try your patience. I'll do my best to meet both standards.

A lot has happened in the world since my own school graduation 52
years ago (although it doesn't seem nearly that long!). But we share at
least a few similarities. Blair Academy, a boarding school in northern
New Jersey, was also an all-boys school, so commonplace then, but so
rare now. I salute Haverford for its determination to stay the course in
pursuing its 115-year mission.

After school, I too immediately went on to college, in my case
Princeton University. (It was far easier to gain admission there in 1947
than in 1999.) Supported by two scholarships and earnings from student and summer jobs, I graduated in 1951 and entered the investment business, plying the same trade that I ply to this day. A fine
education is a priceless advantage in life, and I hope you won't take for
granted your good fortune in being able to move on, almost seam-
lessly, from an outstanding preparatory school to a fine college.

As a father of two sons who are Haverford alumni and a daughter
who directs your Capital Campaign, I've come to know your school

fairly well. I learned a lot more about your school and the Class of 1999 when, in preparation for this talk, I visited with a half-dozen of you seniors a few weeks ago. I was impressed: You are considerably more mature and wise, more "together," as it were, than were we Blair graduates those many decades ago.

Shortly after Dr. Cox asked me to speak at this ceremony, my theme for today came to me. Surprisingly enough, it came in a movie theater. The film was *A Civil Action,* the story of the aftermath of deadly water pollution in a Massachusetts town. The lead character is a not entirely charming personal injury lawyer of dubious ethical standards, who at first seeks to earn millions for himself by winning millions for the families of the victims. But as the case develops, he finds himself getting involved with the families, and the search for right and justice begins to consume him. By standing up for principle, he risks failure. Alas, he goes down in flames, and the film's final sequence finds him in personal bankruptcy court.

There, the judge finds it hard to believe that the only assets owned by this successful and once-wealthy litigator are $14 and a portable radio. Incredulous, she asks, "Where are the things by which one measures one's life?" *Where are the things by which one measures one's life.* But he has no "things." He has stood up for the worthy cause of children who have died and families who have been devastated. He has put his career on the line, and he has lost. Should we measure him by what he *has,* or by who he *is?*

It seems rather out of character for Hollywood to deal with how we measure our lives. But the question remains: What are the things by which we should measure our lives? For my part, I urge you never to let "things" as such—the material possessions you may come to accumulate—become the measure of your lives. It is an easy trap to fall into during these days of such material abundance in America—or at least in the privileged part of America that we see—with grander homes, bigger stores, more powerful cars, smarter phones, more exotic rock concerts, more sophisticated toys for children and more elaborate toys for grown-ups, a cornucopia of "things" almost beyond measure. Two thousand five hundred years ago, the Greek philosopher Protagoras told us that "man is the measure of all things." Today, I fear, we are becoming a society in which "things are the measure of the man."

But such a measure is superficial and, finally, self-defeating. The world that you enter has far too many calls on its limited resources to expend them on things trivial and things transitory. There are literally billions of human beings out there, all over the globe, who cry out for support and for salvation, for security and for compassion, for education and for opportunity. But virtually all of you seniors are able to take for granted those intangible "things." They carry a value that far surpasses so many tangible things whose nature is, finally, inconsequential.

If you are surprised that a Hollywood film would be concerned with the things by which one measures one's life, you may be even more surprised that a businessman—particularly one in the investment arena, where greed seems the order of the day—would choose that as his commencement theme. But I've spent my career trying to build a different and better kind of financial enterprise. Our goal is to serve—in our case, to serve investors "in the most honest, efficient and economical way possible," the idealistic words I wrote in my senior thesis at Princeton nearly a half-century ago. Our philosophy centers on simple principles of investing and on simple principles of fair-dealing with the human beings we serve as stewards. While those ideas have stood the test of time, you should know that I've experienced failure along the way. Paradoxically, however, getting fired 25 years ago proved to be the break, as it were, that led to my founding of The Vanguard Group. Life is filled with surprises.

As the company's creator, I've been called an entrepreneur. I'm not so sure, but if entrepreneurship includes "the will to conquer, the impulse to fight, to succeed for the sake, *not of the fruits of success, but for the sake of success itself*"—the economist Joseph Schumpeter's standard—perhaps I am. For my goal in forming Vanguard was never to build an empire nor to amass staggering personal wealth. While the assets we manage now approach the half-trillion mark and our crew numbers nearly 10,000, those boxcar numbers are, if you will, "things" that have little meaning to me. The things that do matter to me are how well we serve the human beings who are our investors, the opportunities we give to our crew, and our name and reputation.

I didn't build the firm by myself. *No man makes his mark by himself alone.* Your lives and mine have been shaped by chance, by breaks, and by mentors, to say nothing of the innate advantages of simply living in the United States of America. Our lives have also been shaped by the blessings of caring families, home environments that would be the envy of something like 99% of the world's population, and the superb preparation of our minds and values by extraordinary teachers who have quite literally dedicated their lives to the education of young men. These are just a few of the truly meaningful "things" by which we ought to credit the remarkable start in life that we have enjoyed. We have the solemn obligation to repay that debt by serving the common good.

Even for you who are so incredibly well prepared for college, however, the road of life will rarely be smooth. So remember Ecclesiastes' warning that "the race is not to the swift, nor the battle to the strong, neither yet bread to the wise, nor yet riches to men of understanding, nor yet favor to men of skill, but time and chance happeneth to them all." You happen to be among the swifter, stronger, and wiser, the more understanding, and more skilled of this world—yes, you are— but never forget that, despite these blessings, the battle is neverending. You too are apt to experience failure along the way. When it comes, have the courage to press on. But never forget that who you are is far more important than what you have. It is up to you, finally, to decide just what kinds of "things" you will seek as the measure of your own lives.

My sense is that you of the Class of 1999 will make the right choices. To get to where you are on this commencement morning, you have worked hard. And you have played the game fair and square. In one of the finest secondary schools in the nation, you have stayed the course, and have won your first major battle. The value of your accomplishment far surpasses the value of the material things by which only fools measure their lives. Having earned the Haverford School diploma you receive this morning, you can accept it proudly as one wonderful measure of your own worth.

24

TELLTALE HEARTS

The Nicholas Green Scholarship Fund
The Investment Company Institute
Washington, D.C.
May 17, 2000

I CAN'T THINK OF a more apt title
than "Telltale Hearts" for my talk today. For I will indeed tell you a
tale of two hearts. Both of them continue their unremitting beat, as
regular as the seconds that tick away on your watch (if a bit faster), but
both of them are also—behold a miracle!—"thumping away like
native drums" in human beings with whom they had not yet been
united just six years ago. One is the tale of a heart given by a young
American boy. The other is the tale of a heart received by an aging
businessman.

Fitting as the title is, I confess that I borrowed it from a "Talk of the
Town" piece I read in *The New Yorker* only a week ago, perhaps
inspired by Edgar Allan Poe. Hearts have been in the news, and that
brief essay (which included the wonderful metaphor about native
drums that I quoted at the outset) talked about the heart of the
Dauphin of France—Louis XVII, had he been crowned—and the fos-
silized four-chambered heart of a dinosaur, recently discovered in
South Dakota. "If the Dauphin's heart ends one legend," the essay
noted, "the dinosaur's amazingly modern heart feeds another . . . yet
within these two hearts beats one story, for the truly odd thing is that
we *care* so much. . . . We want a heart to be a heart," Adam Gopnik's
essay continues, "the final thumping vault of our deep, permanent
incurable folk vitalism, the summer house of the particular spirit. *Le
coeur est mort, vive le coeur!*" The heart is dead, long live the heart!

Telltale Heart #1

But I want to tell you the tales of two other hearts, those I mentioned at the outset. The first tale is of young Nicholas Green, an extraordinarily gifted seven-year-old American boy who was murdered by thugs on a highway in Italy five and one-half years ago. It was a brutal tragedy, redeemed only by a gesture of extraordinary grace by his parents; an act of love—under circumstances to which, I fear, few of the rest of us could rise—so sweeping in its nobility as to defy our own humdrum, self-centered imaginations.

A few weeks ago, I read again *The Nicholas Effect,* the beautifully written story of young Nicholas' life and death, and the role of his organs in the rebirth of seven Italian people. I felt the same overpowering sense of tragedy and triumph, of sadness and hope that I felt when I read it a year ago, a gift from Reg Green, the author and Nicholas' father. I couldn't avoid tears as Reg recounted the story of his happy family vacation, hiking in the Alps, then on to Southern Italy. His son is a seven-year-old boy thrilled by the stories of classical "heroes risking their lives for the common good . . . and puzzled by the cheap tricks of gods who know better"; an imaginative boy who dressed up and emulated the swashbuckling deeds of Robin Hood; a typical boy who liked spaghetti and Parmesan cheese, but wouldn't eat his crusts; a sensitive boy who on his last night of life told his father, "when I was in the water, some sea splashed in my face. When I licked it off, it tasted really good."

And then tragedy. On the autostrada near the Italian coast, late at night, the two children asleep in the back of the car, evil strikes. A car draws next to the Greens, malevolent men screaming at them to pull over. Petrified and having no other sensible choice, Reg increases speed. Explosions blow out the car's windows. The Greens speed away. The outlaws' headlights gradually disappear. All is well. Fright subsides, and the Greens are mightily relieved.

But when they stop, little Nicholas, in the back seat, is not moving. The police are called. An ambulance comes. The boy is taken to the hospital, but only after Reg puts in his hand the little shred of sheepskin Nicholas takes to bed with him. The next day, "the small shoots of hope wither away." The bullet has lodged at the base of his brain. Another day of hoping for a miracle, and then, "I have bad news. We can find no sign of brain activity." Nicholas Green has died.

And now the triumph. A few moments later, either Reg or Maggie Green—they can't remember which—says, "Now that he's gone, shouldn't we give his organs?" And the other says "yes." In his book, Reg tells us that, "it was the least difficult decision we have ever had to make; the boy we know was not in that body any more." The triumph begins with seven organ transplants—the heart to a 15-year-old Italian boy who had spent half his life in a hospital, the liver to a 19-year old Sicilian girl in her final coma, the kidneys to a girl 14 and a boy 7, previously ruled by dialysis machines. Pancreas cells to a Roman, and corneas for two Sicilians, restoring their sight. Seven human beings, some given an enriched life, the others given that miracle of miracles, a second chance at life.

The Nicholas Effect

And then the triumph soars. The whole world is electrified by the story of this tragedy, of American grace in a foreign land, and of the miracle of organ transplantation. Newspapers, magazines, radio, television, all cover the story and inspire an awakening of the staggering need for organ donors. This awakening becomes known as "the Nicholas Effect," as around the globe millions become aware of transplants and the monumental good that the families of those who die can bestow on those anxiously hoping to escape death, and to live healthier, happier, more productive lives. The largest hospital in Italy is now named the Nicholas Green Hospital. "Grazie, Nicholas," indeed. Pope John Paul II blesses the main bell for the Children's Bell Tower erected in Nicholas' memory in Bodega Bay, California, the Green's hometown. *And the world is a better place.*

Reg Green speaks: "Transplantation is a leap of the human spirit that transcends mere numbers. Death we know has a necessary purpose, replacing the old and infirm with fresh life. But in its clumsy way death gathers up spring flowers too. Transplantation meant that we were no longer at the mercy of this arbitrariness. We had a say in the outcome."

Yes, Reg and Maggie, you did. And I claim the high privilege of saluting you in a way that few other mortals can. For I received my own second chance at life four years and three months ago, when the heart of a 26-year-old man was transplanted into my chest. It is simply impossible for me not to liken the heart that departed the broken body of a young Nicholas Green in October 1995 with the heart that was implanted in the damaged body of aging John Bogle on February 21, 1996.

Telltale Heart #2

The link is more than merely the timing. Reg Green has been a mutual fund industry colleague of mine since the 1970s. He tells part of my story in his book. After saying some generous words about my reputation, he writes:

> **Jack Bogle, chairman of the Vanguard Group, wore a pacemaker when I first met him in the 1970s and played tennis with the punishing energy he brought to everything. "That's going to kill him," I thought. But no, he went on increasing in influence, fathering index mutual funds and conducting his crusade against anything he thought smacked of laxity. To him, the fiduciary responsibility in handling other people's money is an almost sacred trust.**
>
> **More than twenty years passed and at last even his battling heart was ready to give up. He was saved by one of those five thousand families in this country who, with no idea what the results will be, make their gift to the world. I wrote to him to say I couldn't think of a better result of transplantation than that it could save a man of his ethical and intellectual stature. His reply was typical: generous praise for donors, a sense of hope for the world, and a copy of his latest speech castigating mutual fund fees that he felt were too high.**

I'll comment later on those three elements that Reg sensed in my reply: Praise for donors, hope for the world, and continuing my mutual fund mission. But first I'll tell the tale of my heart. I was born with a rare genetic heart disease called right ventricular displaysia, which first manifested itself in 1960 when, playing tennis at age 30, I suffered what was then believed to be a standard heart attack. Six weeks in a local hospital, but an elusive recovery. Periodic bouts of ventricular arrhythmia, normally entailing a late-night mad rush to the hospital, became more frequent, and I was warned that my life might be short. In 1967 I went off to the Cleveland Clinic for treatment. The doctors there decided that a pacemaker—then brand-new, and large!—would relieve my symptoms. The operation very nearly terminated my existence, and when I returned home the arrhythmia's continued to interrupt my life.

I sought the finest cardiologist in the nation, and in Boston found Dr. Bernard Lown, one of the world's truly great physicians, skilled, yes, but a superb humanist, too. Without his care, I doubt I'd be alive today. While he was confident that the initial diagnosis was wrong and the pacemaker unnecessary, he could not identify the disease, and put me on a heavy dose of anti-arrhythmia drugs. While my problems continued, they did not appear life-threatening, and he agreed to allow me to continue my active business career. I had become head of Wellington Management Company in 1967, and also served as ICI chairman in 1969–71, an extremely active participant in the fund industry. He also allowed me to return, after a seven-year absence, to tennis and squash.

The arrhythmias continued, albeit with less frequency, and on each occasion I'd be off to Boston for two or three weeks in the hospital, where I tried new drug protocols, took scores of stress tests on the treadmill, and determined to press on and let nothing disturb my pace. (Parenthetically, in 1974, amidst all this activity, I was fired by Wellington, but before the year was out had founded Vanguard.) Even a cardiac arrest on the squash court in 1980—when my opponent saved my life by pounding on my chest—couldn't slow me down. But I did begin to carry a portable defibrillator around with me for protection. Inevitably, however, time took its toll. More cardiac arrests, one in a school auditorium in 1986 (I was revived by two doctors doing CPR); another in a railroad station in 1988 (I think my tumble to a hard floor jarred my heart into starting), forced me to slow and then cease my athletic endeavors, and by 1992, it was clear that only a heart transplant would keep me alive.

Still on Watch

Within a year, I could barely climb the stairs, and I was placed on Status B on the waiting list for a transplant. But you have to be Status A to get top priority. Good news (in a sense): My condition deteriorated! I was placed on Status A in the summer of 1995, and was admitted to Philadelphia's Hahnemann Hospital on October 17, 1995. Just the day before, an optimistic omen: I received in the mail a wristwatch from a devoted shareholder in California. On the dial were printed our Vanguard logo, my name, and a phrase that was an indication I was still looking out for our shareholders: "Still on Watch." It was also an outrageous pun: "Still on *Watch*." Confident that it would be my rabbit's foot, I put the watch on my wrist, where, having proved itself, it remains to this day. (Yes, I knew about the $50 limit on gifts. So I checked the catalog for the price. It was $14. Talk about value!)

Shortly before I was admitted, only the left half of my heart was beating. Conscious both of my duty to our shareholders and the possibility that a new heart might not arrive in time, I turned my chief executive responsibilities over to my successor, with his and the Board's agreement that I'd remain as Chairman. The long wait began, and I was placed on life-prolonging drugs for the duration, carrying my bag of intravenous fluid with me on a pole whenever I walked around the floor. My guardian angels—the physicians and nurses at the hospital, led by Dr. Susan Brozena—kept me alive, as day after day we waited. There is no favoritism in the transplant arena. (I've described it as "democratic as a traffic jam.") We are all, in essence, date-stamped in priority. A healthy heart—usually the survivor of a violent accident that leaves its owner brain dead—arrives sporadically, two months of drought, then two hearts in three days, and so on.

Unlike nearly all of those who watched and waited with me, I worked at my Vanguard duties each day, usually starting at about 10:30 A.M. after the doctors' rounds were over. Our Annual Report season is long—August through January fiscal years—and I wrote, as was my career-long practice, each one. Daily visits from my wonderful wife, usually around 5:30 to 7:30 P.M., broke the pace. When she'd leave, I'd go back to work until 10 P.M., read the papers until 10:45, then get a sleeping pill, tackle *The New York Times* crossword puzzle, and fall into a fitful sleep about 11:00, but only after reading the 23rd Psalm and saying a prayer which always ended, "not *my* will but *Thy* will be done."

"You Have a New Heart"

The doctors and nurses thought I was daft, but the time passed with reasonable ease. At last, after 128 days in the hospital, I was awakened at about 2 A.M. on February 21. My new heart had arrived! I called my family with the good news, tried to finish what was my final Annual Report, was prepped for the operation, and, as is the custom, was given a rousing send-off by the others awaiting transplant as I was rolled out to the elevator. The next thing I remember is waking up in what seemed to be blackness, doctors hovering over me. I was frightened that something had gone wrong, and then heard the most wonderful words imaginable: "Congratulations. You have a new heart. And it is young and strong."

After some terribly difficult times during the year that followed (none enough to slow the busy pace of life to which I had returned),

I've had a truly remarkable recovery. I've had 32 heart biopsies, all marked "zero" in my body's effort to reject the priceless heart I'd received—the approximate equivalent of a pitcher with a perfect game about to start the 33rd inning. The only match required in a heart transplant is blood type (I'm an "O," which means the longest wait), but my donor's body chemistry must have been quite similar to mine—a special break, since it enabled me to quickly cease use of the meanest anti-rejection drug of the bunch—prednisone. I still pop almost 20 pills a day (down from 55), but they're all pretty benign.

It turns out too that older recipients are less likely to experience problems because our rejection mechanisms aren't as powerful as those of the young. That fact has allayed, to a small degree, my fear that I was not as deserving as a younger person with a long life ahead. My recovery has also been enhanced, I think, by my willingness—my eagerness, really—to adhere to a rigorous, virtually fat-free, salt-free, anything-you-truly-enjoy-free diet, and my unalloyed delight at being able to exercise to, well, my heart's content. My wife and I do lots of walking and some biking; we climb an occasional (if small) mountain in the Adirondacks; and I'm back hoisting the sails of my ancient 15-foot O'Day Javelin, *Blue Chip*, and sailing her around Lake Placid. And, yes, I'm back playing squash, which poses absolutely no heart risk whatsoever. In short, I've got it made!

Almost everyone I meet tells me how well I look, and I always respond that, "I couldn't possibly look as well as I feel." Telephone callers seem surprised at the power of my voice. Of all the compliments, however, my favorite took place a year after the great day, when I was standing outside a lecture room at Princeton, waiting for an alumni seminar to begin, my name badge on my jacket, but without my class numerals. An alumnus walked by, turned, looked at me, and said, "Oh, John Bogle. How's your *father* doing after his heart transplant." Go ahead, make my day!

Continuing My Mutual Fund Mission

Now, *how* I should use the truly incredible energy and enthusiasm I enjoy in my new lease on life is an issue that perplexes me. Through Vanguard's Bogle Financial Markets Research Center, I've simply stepped over the boundary, as it were, between Greece and Rome, where each ancient god had the same name—then Zeus, now Jupiter. I'm carrying on my quarter-century-long mission of doing my best to ensure that all 80 million mutual fund investors get a fair shake, though so far my progress has not been notable. I'm traveling, largely around the U.S., writing incessantly, speaking to groups frequently, and working a business day that I honestly think is surpassed by few of my Vanguard colleagues.

My second chance at life has also given me the opportunity to write another best-seller, *Common Sense on Mutual Funds*. And this September McGraw-Hill will publish my third book. It will be the first volume of their new series *Great Ideas in Finance*, entitled *John Bogle on Investing: The First 50 Years*. Why 50 years? Because it includes my Princeton senior thesis on the mutual fund industry that I began to write in December 1949 and completed in April 1951, published at last. Even back then, as you'll see, I was calling on this industry to operate in "the most efficient, economical, and honest way possible." The more things change, the more they remain the same, I guess.

I can't really explain the dauntless, indefatigable attitude I've had through all those 40 years of physical challenge, nor my failure to fall into the slough of despond, nor my passion to "press on, regardless"— the classic family phrase that is the title of the last chapter of my new book. But an article that I read in *The New York Times* a few weeks ago may explain it:

> **When confronted with a life-threatening disease, most people want to do precisely what they were doing before that awful day when the doctor gave them the news . . . some collapse under the pressure, but most want to be the way they were. George Bernard Shaw called it a life force—what you experience as a human being, a determination to get back into life, to be a part of life.**

And yet today I have doubts. Why have I been so blessed? "Why me," I ask, a question I'd never asked during the dark days. Is continuing my mission my best and highest use? Is that what the Lord expects of me? Have I outlived my use to the company I created and into which I've put my heart and soul over all those years? Am I being fair to my family—my wife, my six children, my 12 grandchildren? But my "press-on" attitude is so strong that while these questions trouble my mind, usually in the wee hours of the morning, they quickly pass away, and I'm back to my old self. In fact, I have but a single post-transplant regret: Despite the miracle that has given me a second chance at life that has to be seen to be believed, I fear that I am pretty much the same deeply flawed human being I've always been. But, by golly, I'm determined to be better!

Gratitude to the Donors

You'll recall that Reg saw in my letter to him not only my determination to continue my mutual fund mission, but my generous praise for donors. How could I have not expressed my gratitude to Reg? Who is really to say that the donor of *my* heart wasn't part of the Nicholas Effect, inspired by the Greens' nobility to sign a donor option card? And of course I also expressed my gratitude to the family of my donor, who proved to be a young man, only 26 years of age. (This information was kept quite secret. I learned it by happenstance when I met the recipient of my donor's liver—now a sort of cousin of mine, I guess—whose wife made the linkage when she read a news article about my transplant on the same date as his.)

It's difficult to write a letter like that. Indeed it took me until Thanksgiving 1996—a thoroughly appropriate, if belated, day—to put down the words. "Thank you for the love and human kindness you displayed," I wrote in part, "by allowing the heart of your loved one to continue to beat in the body of another human being . . . it is a medical miracle, but a spiritual miracle as well, for I am renewed in body and in spirit." My note was never answered. It might have been that the family was too heartbroken to respond, or they decided not to reveal themselves, or could not read English, or perhaps there were no remaining family members. But I hope that, if there were, I gave them a moment of solace and peace.

I've also spoken to groups of donor families, surely the hardest audiences I've ever had to face. In 1998, as the "heart speaker" along with the recipients of other organs, I said, in part:

We are unlikely to know the age, or sex, or race, or nationality, or religion of the person you have loved and lost, nor will you know those things about us. But we all can know, finally, that while the world in its ignorance magnifies those superficial attributes of who we are, none of those things truly matter.

What matters is that we live the best lives that we can while God gives us life, and act with human kindness always, even when a life is over. That you have done, in an act of giving that is the noblest deed a family could ever do.

Shocked and grief-stricken in an alien land, yet unhesitantly donating young Nicholas' organs, Reg and Maggie Green are the apotheoses of that nobility.

To donate a loved one's heart is not an easy decision, even under circumstances when you might think it would be. At one meeting of donor families at which I spoke, I met a man with three ribbons on his lapel—two green, one gold. He'd received two organs, and had lost a family member whose organs were donated. It turned out that he had received *two* heart transplants, five years apart. A year later, his son died in an automobile accident. But the decision to allow his son's heart to be donated, he told me, "was the hardest decision I've ever had to make." I could only say, "God bless you."

A Sense of Hope for the World

Reg's final words about my letter to him mentioned my sense of hope for the world. How could one *not* feel hope for the world in the majestic union of human nobility and miraculous scientific advance that transports the human heart from a body that has failed to a body that, absent the heart, will soon itself fail. In my hope for the world, I can only call your attention to the subtitle of *The Nicholas Effect*: "A Boy's Gift to the World."

We celebrate and reaffirm his gift today. Through the Nicholas Green Scholarship Fund, each year we enable two or three young American students, gifted and promising and interested in international travel, even as was young Nicholas, to study abroad. As one of its judges, I've read, I suppose, the résumés of two dozen young people, and each one impressed me as extraordinarily worthy. It is our progeny who are our hope for a better world, and I urge each one of you and the fund groups you represent to make a gift to this fund in the same generous and noble spirit demonstrated nearly six years ago by our colleague of 30 years, Reg Green, and his wife, Maggie. Reg was born in Great Britain, but he exemplifies the American spirit of generosity to others, first noted by Alexis de Tocqueville nearly 200 years ago, as well as any human being I've ever known.

Now, the two telltale hearts have told their two tales. We can go back to our own material worlds and ordinary existences. But I hope that these tales will inspire you in the listening as they have me in the telling—the tales of the heart that Nicholas Green donated, and the heart that John Bogle received. Carry that inspiration to the world out there! *Le coeur est mort, vive le coeur!*

25

PRESS ON REGARDLESS

Commencement Address
The Owen School of Management,
Vanderbilt University
Nashville, Tennessee
May 8, 1992

I IMAGINE THAT it is a rare uncle who has served as the inspiration for a commencement address, but that is nonetheless the case today. My late uncle, Clifton Armstrong Hipkins, was a model citizen, an integrity-laden investment banker, and, most relevant to my theme today, a dedicated sailor. I shall never forget the message captured in the name of his old New England lobsterboat, "Press On Regardless." And that is the message that I shall urge on you today: press on, regardless.

One of my avocations is lexicography. I love to study the derivation of words and phrases, and a highlight of my life was my contribution to one of William Safire's "On Language" columns in *The New York Times* a few years ago. But I have been unable to discover a precise provenance for "Press On Regardless." However, Calvin Coolidge—a taciturn Vermonter who seems to have wasted fewer words than any American President in the 20th century, perhaps because he engaged in the rapidly disappearing art of writing his own speeches—surely made a major contribution:

> **Nothing in the world can take the place of persistence. Talent will not; nothing is more common than unsuccessful men with talent. Genius will not; unrewarded genius is almost a proverb. Education will not; the world is full of educated derelicts. Per-**

sistence and determination alone are omnipotent. The slogan "Press on" has solved, and always will solve, the problems of the human race.

Adding "regardless" is simply a reminder that we must press on under *all* circumstances. While it is commonplace to assume that it means something like "regardless of stormy seas, failure, or even disaster," I suggest that it also means "regardless of smooth sailing, success, or even triumph." Kipling reminded us of both in his wonderful poem, *If*:

> *If you can dream, and not make dreams your master,*
> *If you can think, and not make thoughts your aim,*
> *If you can meet both Triumph and Disaster,*
> *And treat those two imposters just the same.*

So the challenge is to persevere in times thick and times thin alike. Let me illustrate my point with some examples of large, successful American firms that ignored this advice, and an example of a small, faltering firm that heeded it. Then I shall conclude with some advice to you on your own careers as you begin them at this rite of passage that we properly call *commencement*.

Corporate America

Somewhere along the way, Corporate America—the nation's driving force and the envy of the civilized world during most of the 20th century—lost sight of the need to "press on" during its period of triumph. The list of leading American enterprises that have fallen on parlous times of late, or even vanished from the scene, reads like a who's who of our preeminent corporations of only a few decades ago. Consider these three companies that have tumbled from the pinnacle of success:

- IBM—Once America's quintessential growth stock (it rose by 90 *times* during the 1950s and 1960s), the market price of its common stock today is less than it was in 1971. It was "blind-sided" by U.S. competition, as it lost its flexibility and capacity for innovation.
- Citicorp—The largest bank in the world as recently as 1985, it now ranks number 21. The risk in its real estate loan portfolio came home to roost, as did its muscle-bound management style.

- General Motors—It failed to treat product quality and global competition with determination. Fully one-third of GM's market share has evaporated, and last year's losses totaled an incredible $4.5 *billion.* (At long last, the Board of Directors revolted. To say the least, this is unusual in American business!)

These examples of the failure to press on in the face of success are not isolated. Consider American Express (unwise diversification), Travelers Insurance (unsound real estate investments), and Macy's (excessive leverage). At least these enterprises have survived. Many of yesterday's blue chips have not been so fortunate, and PanAmerican World Airways, Time Incorporated, The Pennsylvania Railroad, National Steel, and RCA are all, as it were, history. It almost seems as though "nothing fails like success."

If there is a common thread in all of this, it is that too many corporations complacently fail to press on at the time of their greatest triumph. Too often, they relax and lose sight of their mission; they fail to deal with change, fail to realize that competition lurks around every corner, fail to adjust to the challenges of managing a large organization. Together, these failures are changing the establishments of American business into its dinosaurs.

I acknowledge, of course, that these examples have been selected to make my point. Nonetheless, it must also be noted that, in its entirety, Corporate America is failing in its mission. The operating earnings of America's 500 largest companies have grown at a compound annual rate of but 3% since 1984; or, adjusted for inflation of 3.6% and translated into constant 1984 dollars, a "growth" rate that is negative. If these figures don't indicate the need for a new generation of American management, I am not sure what would! Surely opportunities are rife to solve the problems that plague American business today, if only the generation you represent will press on, with persistence and determination.

The Vanguard Saga

Let me now turn, in this second section of my remarks, from the macrobusiness of American industry to the microbusiness of a single firm. In stark contrast to the failure of many leading American corporations to press on in the face of success, this small firm *did* press on. Facing failure, it *had* to do so. I am speaking of The Vanguard Group (though

I shall not again identify it), and of myself (though I shall use "he" rather than "I"). Please forgive me for this personal note, but there is no firm that I know better.

The saga begins early in 1974. He was fired (with enthusiasm!) from his job as chief executive of a large mutual fund firm. Out of that heartbreaking upheaval, he founded and named a brand-new firm. It began by operating the business-side activities (administration, accounting, etc.) of his former firm, and within a few years, the portfolio management activities for many of the funds. Thus did a narrowly focused administrative enterprise quickly become a full-fledged mutual fund complex.

He was also "fired with enthusiasm" to make the new enterprise a success. But it was to take a long time and a lot of frustration. Each and every month from January 1974 to January 1978—four long years— more money was withdrawn from the mutual funds than was added. With this unremitting capital outflow, totaling more than $500 million, it was only through the grace of an improving stock market that the funds' assets, $2 billion at the beginning of the period, totaled $1.8 billion at the end. Success—or at least its putative proxy, growth—then followed. It was soon to become the fastest growing firm in the mutual fund industry.

Its growth resulted largely from three distressingly simple ideas: (1) that, in the long run, investors would seek out the highest sustainable returns, and that such returns would most likely be achieved by the firm with the lowest operating cost structure; (2) that, in a world of increasing financial knowledge, self-motivated investors would seek these returns directly, without demanding the help (or paying the cost) of a sales representative; and (3) that, as the industry blossomed from its common-stock-fund-only base into a more complex asset base, which included bond funds and money market funds as well, investors would demand, in their interaction with the mutual fund organization that they chose, the highest quality of service.

There is a old axiom that says: "treat the customer as an owner." The firm's secret—such as it may be—was to go one step further: "treat the client as an owner . . . *by making him an owner.*" The firm was organized as the first *mutual* mutual fund complex, in which the fund shareholders actually own the management organization. As owners, they receive the truly awesome profits that are generated even by mediocre managements in these halcyon days when the mutual fund industry and the financial markets are burgeoning to all-time high levels. Confidence in this unique concept of mutuality, even after years of reversal and frustration, gave the firm the ability to press on.

A "Hot Tip" on Stocks

My final example of persistence and determination arises from the request, perhaps whimsical, that I give you some "hot tips" on stocks. Paradoxically, the hottest tip that I can give you, *mirabile dictu*, is to eschew hot tips, by using index funds as the core of your own personal investment programs. (Essentially, an index fund holds *all* of the stocks in the stock market.) The magic of indexing, if such it be, is that it virtually eliminates the usual expenses of investing, such as portfolio transaction costs and investment advisory fees.

In a nutshell, active investors *in the aggregate* and index funds alike earn identical *gross* returns, but index funds, by reason of their substantial cost advantage, earn higher *net* returns. The likely outcome is that those who adopt an indexing strategy should earn higher net returns than about seven out of every ten active investors here today. (One of the problems with supporting this thesis, of course, is that the seven will be silent about their lack of success, but the remaining three—who beat the index by virtue of skill, or perhaps luck—will be outspoken in their condemnation of indexing as a failed investment strategy.)

Our firm started the first index fund in the mutual fund industry back in 1976, partly to see if theory could be translated into practice. By proving that it could indeed match the market, the index fund was an artistic success; however, investors, in droves, ignored it, and it was a commercial failure. But, again, the firm knew that the notion was sound. With unshaken determination, unaffected by early failure in the marketplace, it stayed the course. With assets of $5 billion, the index fund is now America's sixth largest equity fund. "Press on, regardless" indeed!

Begun with a firing, inaugurated with failure, but sticking to a few commonsense principles, our microbusiness story ends on a note of triumph. With $83 billion of assets today, the firm is the third largest mutual fund complex in the world. But, as in history, a new chapter always follows. And this firm's main challenge today is to press on *despite* its success, to avoid becoming just another corporate dinosaur. Does the firm have the determination to keep its competitive edge? Can it avoid the mediocrity of maturity and the boredom of bureaucracy that often go hand in hand with massive growth? Will its sense of urgency persist? It will be fascinating to observe how the answers to these questions unfold in the chapter that lies ahead.

Advice to the MBA Graduate

In the tradition of the occasion, let me conclude with some advice to the MBA graduate. I was not favored with the priceless kind of business education that you have received here at Vanderbilt's fine Owen School of Management. (Full disclosure, however, compels me to acknowledge that my son graduated from the Owen School in 1983, and gained here at Vanderbilt an education that has been a major factor in his success as partner in a small, computer-intensive investment advisory firm.) But I do bring a lifetime of observations about myriad aspects of the world of business and finance.

From all of this experience, I could write a book (and perhaps I will . . . but not this morning!). What I would like to reiterate in these concluding remarks is the notion that persistence and determination are indeed the keys to success. Of course you need more than that: education, hard work, and dedication come quickly to mind. Working effectively with others—partners, superiors, and subordinates alike— must be a given. These are all *necessary* conditions for your success but not *sufficient* conditions, in and of themselves. It is your determination that will be the *sine qua non*.

So, let me offer my final words on just two subjects: integrity and learning. On the first of these, directly put, if you cannot pursue your career with integrity, go back and start all over again. Whatever the spotty record of the 1980s, corporate ethics are back in style, and our new world is properly intolerant of greed, shortcuts, rip-offs, perquisites, and less-than-candid disclosure. This intolerance applies to business at large, to education, to government, indeed to all American institutions. Good! And, as an incurable optimist, I'll wager that our national ethic is going to get stronger with each tomorrow.

A few years ago, one of the best-known Wall Street arbitrageurs gave a commencement speech at a respected university. His words were repeated in the film *Wall Street,* and I quote them to you here:

The point is, ladies and gentlemen, greed is good. Greed works, greed is right. Greed clarifies, cuts through, and captures the essence of the evolutionary spirit. Greed for life, money, love, knowledge has marked the upward surge of mankind—greed will save that malfunctioning corporation called the U.S.A.

My respect for you new Owen graduates and your families demands that I not express the barnyard expletive that would otherwise be my response to this tomfoolery. So, let me just observe that the speaker, finally convicted for securities fraud, spent several years in a Federal penitentiary. The point is, ladies and gentlemen, greed is *out*. Integrity is in. And, if you seek success and fulfillment, please accept my advice to hold yourselves to the highest moral standards. It will be "good business," but it will be good for your souls as well.

One's own words on a given subject, it seems, have often been said so much better by another. Thus it is with my words on the subject of *learning*. For, as far as I am concerned, the legendary John Gardner did my work for me when he gave the commencement address a year ago at Stanford University's centennial:

Learn all your life. Learn from your failures, from your successes, learn by taking risks, by suffering, by enjoying, by loving, by bearing life's indignities with dignity. Learn that self-pity and resentment are the most toxic of drugs. Learn that the world loves talent but pays off on character.

Self-knowledge isn't enough. You build meaning into your life through your commitments—whether to your religion, to your conception of an ethical order, to your loved ones, to your life work, to your community. . . . Make the world better . . . by the gift of kindness or courage or loyalty or integrity. Teach the truth by living it.

The test for this nation is whether in all the confusion and clash of interests, all the distracting conflicts and cross purposes, all the temptations to self-indulgence and self-exoneration, we have the strength of purpose, the guts, the conviction, the spiritual staying power to build a future worthy of our past. You can help.

And indeed you can help, each and every one of you. If that doesn't say it all, surely St. Paul does in his letter to Philippians:

This one thing I do, forgetting those things which are behind, and reaching forth unto those things which are before . . . I press toward the mark.

So, press!
Press on!
Press on, regardless!
Press on regardless!

Part V

THE PRINCETON
THESIS

As I RE-READ MY thesis "The Economic Role of the Investment Company," from cover to cover, three things struck me. First, it wasn't too bad! While the quality of the writing was hardly first-rate, it seemed quite serviceable and comprehensible, especially considering that I was a not-particularly-mature young man but 21 years of age, and that it was my first major writing project. The organization seemed about right too, and the research—in a field where data were scarce—remarkably complete.* I'm not sure that I would place the thesis in the high honors category, but I surely reveled in that outcome all those years ago.

In retrospect, I wish that I had done more research on the extent of the mutual fund industry's success in serving investors, and, in particular, that I had evaluated fund investment performance more comprehensively. First, I accepted at face value the industry's claim that, as cited in my thesis, "the attainment of objectives is proof of good management," and ignored the perhaps inevitable vagueness of most funds' goals. (It's difficult to refute a claim, as made by one fund that I cited in the thesis, of having provided "reasonable dividends, profits without undue speculation, and conservation of capital," worthy as those objectives are.) But the kind of comparative data we take for granted today were then almost three decades away. I did present some data comparing the returns of a few funds with the Standard & Poor's (then) 90-Stock Average, and found those funds' records satisfactory. But I nonetheless concluded that "*funds can make no claim to superiority over the market averages.*" I leave to wiser heads the judgment of whether that was a harbinger of my founding, a quarter-century later, of the first market index mutual fund, modeled on the (by then) S&P 500 Stock Index.

Second, I was surprised by my high hopes for the growth of this then embryonic industry. Just *what* was the Securities and Exchange Commission thinking when it called the growth of this tiny $2.5 billion industry, "the most important single development in the financial history of the United States during the last 50 years," as quoted at the start of my thesis? In fact, the industry was

---

* I should note that my original hand-typed text and charts proved difficult to reproduce and were replaced by the more elegant version that you see here.

almost irrelevant in 1950, dwarfed by the $63 billion life insurance industry, the $58 billion in U.S. savings bonds, and the $56 billion in bank and savings deposits. Further, mutual funds then owned but 1% of the shares of America's corporations, even as I urged the industry not to "refrain from exerting its influence . . . on corporate policy." In fact, my thesis applauded the SEC's desire that funds serve "the useful role of representative of the great number of inarticulate and ineffective individual investors." But to no avail. While funds now own some 24% of all U.S. corporate shares, they remain to this day largely passive investors.

It goes almost without saying that I could not have even imagined the coming increase in aggregate stock, bond, and money market fund assets to $6.5 *trillion,* representing a 50-year compound annual growth rate of 17% in an economy growing, in nominal terms, at only one-third that rate. Nor did I imagine the change in the financial markets that lay ahead: Since I wrote my thesis, the aggregate value of U.S. stocks has increased from $75 billion in 1950 to $17 *trillion* today, a similar, if slightly lower, growth rate than that of mutual fund assets. Further, the investment character of the industry has changed. Equity mutual funds were *income* producers in 1950, and, as I duly noted that in my thesis, stocks were then yielding 6.63%, corporate bonds 2.96%, and prime commercial paper 1.48%. Today, the spread has been turned upside down and it is bonds that produce income. Stocks presently yield 1.1%, bonds 7.5%, and prime commercial paper 6.2%. Clearly, the investment climate is different—at least for the moment.

Most important of all, a third aspect of my thesis delighted me. On page after page, my youthful idealism speaks out, calling over and over again for the primacy of the interests of the mutual fund shareholder. At the very opening of my thesis, I get right to the point: Mutual funds must not "in any way subordinate the interests of their shareholders to their other economic roles. *Their prime responsibility must always be to their shareholders*" (italics added). Shortly thereafter, "there is some indication that costs are too high," and concluding, "future industry growth can be maximized by concentration on a reduction of sales charges and management fees." (As it happened, fees have actually soared to far higher levels. Again, so much for my advice!) Still later, "fund influence on corporate policy . . . should always be in the best interest of shareholders, not the special interests" of the fund's managers. Yet today the passive governance policies of most funds hardly serve their shareholders.

My conclusion powerfully reaffirms the ideals I hold to this day: Mutual funds should *serve*—"the needs of both individual and institutional investors . . . serve them in the most efficient, honest, and economical way possible. . . . Providing advantages to the investor . . . is the function around which all others are satellite. . . . *The principal function of investment companies is the management of their investment portfolios. Everything else is incidental. . . .* Other roles must be discarded if they interfere in any way with the interests of the investors." And the very last sentence of my thesis sets forth the optimum economic role of mutual funds: "To contribute to the growth of the economy, and to enable individual as well as institutional investors to have a share in this growth."

In the light of 50 years in this industry, I would add to that ringing peroration but a single word: "fair." Now, far more than in 1949, when I began to write my thesis, mutual fund investors deserve not only a *share*, but a *fair share* of the returns generated in the financial markets. Not only a fair *share*, but a fair *shake!*

PRINCETON THESIS

*Dedicated to
my mother and my two brothers,
whose sacrifices
made my education possible.*

THE ECONOMIC ROLE
OF THE
INVESTMENT
COMPANY

by

John C. Bogle

Submitted to Princeton University
Department of Economics and Social Institutions
In Partial Fulfillment of the Requirements for the A. B. Degree

April 10, 1951

TABLE OF CONTENTS

LIST OF TABLES

PREFACE

The writing of this thesis has been at once a source of both despair and pleasure for the author. It has been a despair primarily because of the lack of a single previous authoritative sourcebook of information on the open-end investment company, with Wiesenberger's book being perhaps the sole exception.[1] But it has been a pleasure to write for two reasons: the natural pleasure of synthesizing diverse fragments of information into a comprehensive whole, and the perhaps vain hope that this thesis may fill the gap of ignorance with respect to the economic role of the investment company.

There has been an overflow of information for the first chapter, the advantages supplied to the individual investor by the investment company. But mixed with this information have been over-zealous and unsubstantiated claims, so the difficulty was primarily that of separating the wheat from the chaff. For the other four chapters, however, available information was meager, insubstantial, and incomplete, so the primary direction of the exposition was to make the best use of what was available and attempt to organize it in a significant fashion. Typical of the vacuum of sources for those chapters is the letter received by the author in February 1951 from the National Association of Investment Companies, which stated in part:

The use of investment in mutual funds by pension and trust funds is increasing . . . but we have no complete data

---

1. Wiesenberger, Arthur, *Investment Companies, 1950.* 336 p.

on this point. . . . Most investment companies invest . . . in outstanding or seasoned securities, and they do not generally provide new equity capital. . . . Investment companies are not designed, and it is not their purpose to stabilize the securities market. . . . The exercise of control or influence over the (corporate) management is an exception rather than a rule.

Writing *The Economic Role of the Investment Company* would have been impossible without the aid of men far more experienced than the author, and he would like to take this opportunity to thank them for their assistance, as sources of inspiration and confidence, as well as information. First, three executives whom he had the privilege of interviewing: Mr. Joseph E. Welch, Executive Vice-President of the Wellington Fund, Mr. L. Sherman Adams, Trustee of the Massachusetts Investors Trust, and Mr. John McG. Dalenz, Vice President of Calvin Bullock; second, three securities salesmen who very kindly gave up their valuable time to talk with the author: Mr. Harold S. Schifreen, of Newberger & Co., Mr. William S. Ketcham, of Hornblower & Weeks, and Mr. Richard L. Hogoboom, of Kidder, Peabody & Co. Also, Mr. John M. Sheffey, executive secretary of the National Association of Investment Companies, who supplied a large volume of statistics, and Mr. Clifton A. Hipkins, the author's uncle and a member of Braun, Bosworth & Co., who was particularly helpful in arranging a most profitable interview. Finally, and perhaps most important, Mr. Philip W. Bell, of the Department of Economics and Social Institutions, Princeton University, the author's adviser, who in his excellent and greatly appreciated efforts to assist in removing basic errors and to steer the author along the proper course has probably learned as much about the investment company as has the author himself.

John C. Bogle
Princeton, N. J.
April 10, 1951

INTRODUCTION

THE ALMOST FABULOUS growth of the open-end investment company has been termed "the most important single development in the financial history of the United States during the last 50 years" by the Securities and Exchange Commission.[1] From 1924, when the first two open-end companies were organized, the industry has grown spectacularly to a thriving group of over 100 companies. Total assets, but $140 million in 1929 and $64 million during the Depression two years later, had risen to $370 million in 1937.[2] In 1940, when the great expansion of investment companies began, assets were about $450 million, and by the end of 1950 they had reached the tremendous total of $2.5 billion, a ten-year growth of almost 500%. (Table I.)

The open-end investment company is but one type of investment company, which is a financial institution whose sole business is the investment in securities of the money entrusted to it. The size of the open-end segment as well as its differentiating aspects are such that it can validly be considered a distinct branch of business, that is, an industry. This thesis will mention open-end investment companies by other names, including "mutual funds," "investment trusts," and simply "investment companies." Its particular differentiating features are two: the continual offering (at net asset value plus a commission) of new

---

1. Quoted by Troutman, William V., "Open-End Investment Fund Shares," *Commercial and Financial Chronicle*, CLXVI (October 30, 1947), p. 1749.
2. Securities and Exchange Commission, *Investment Trusts and Investment Companies* (Part 2), p. 33.

349

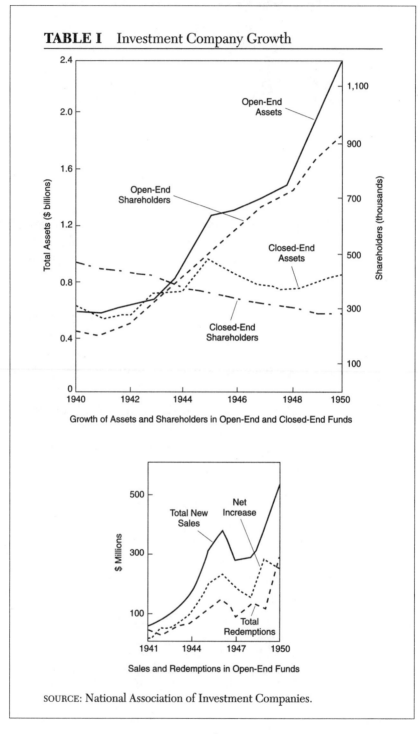

TABLE I   Investment Company Growth

Growth of Assets and Shareholders in Open-End and Closed-End Funds

Sales and Redemptions in Open-End Funds

SOURCE: National Association of Investment Companies.

shares for sale and therefore unlimited capitalization, and the readiness to redeem shares at net asset value. The other form of investment company is the closed-end type, with a fixed number of shares outstanding, which are bought and sold at prices based on supply and demand and therefore may not approximate the actual share value. The closed-end type was always the larger of the two until 1944, when total open-end assets exceeded closed-end assets for the first time. The open-end assets have always been greater since then and now are some three times as great as those of closed-end companies. It will be noted that neither holding companies nor insurance companies qualify as investment companies by the above definition.

The historical development of the investment company is popularly supposed to begin with the *Societe Generale de Belgique*, organized by King William I of Belgium in 1822. Closer to the modern concept of the investment company, however, was Robert Fleming & Co., organized in Scotland in 1873 for the purpose of making diversified investments in American business as the result of firsthand investigation, with due regard for protection of principal and continuous income. In America, the inception of the closed-end company was in 1893, when the Boston Personal Property Trust was founded.

The development of the open-end investment company began in the United States in 1924. The distinguishing features of this type, mentioned above, have made it particularly advantageous: the continual offering means great expansion is possible for each firm, and the redeemability feature leads to a very high degree of management responsibility. Its growth was slow at first, largely because of the tremendous demand for the closed-end company shares which skyrocketed in the speculative ascendancy of the market in the 1927–1929 period. When the market fell, the public reaction to the frequently ill-managed investment trusts of this type was the fixed trust, which assembled a group of securities in a portfolio that could not be altered. The popularity of the fixed trust ebbed by 1932, since it was clear that the lack of management was at best a poor substitute for bad management. That same year marks the beginning of the rise of the open-end company.

Without going into unnecessary detail, the author cites the following reasons for this rise: First, the "business sense" of professional securities distributors, who saw, in 1932, that closed-end shares were being discounted by securities dealers. They turned to the open-end company with its high sales commissions, the opportunity to profit from the continuous distribution of shares, and the sales appeal in the form of redeemability at net asset value, single class of stock, and limited management discretion. At the present, also, these factors are operative in the growth of the investment company industry. Second, the basic integrity of the open-end management. The open-end group was remarkably free from abuse, while the other investment trusts were in many cases characterized by self-dealing, complex capital structures, subordination of investors' interests to those of the management, and the outright looting of assets, as well as being used for controlling other corporations and for dumping unmarketable securities. Third, the Investment Company Act of 1940. This act helped to restore in large part public confidence in the investment company group as a whole, which had justifiably been lacking since the Depression. A comprehensive study by the Securities and Exchange Commission revealed the above-cited abuses, which were remedied in the 1940 legislation. Although the Act did substantially little in the open-end field other than require by law many of the practices the mutual funds had already been following, it had intrinsic value since it reestablished public confidence. Fourth, the Internal Revenue Act of 1936, Supplement Q of which gave investment companies tax exemptions from those dividends, from portfolio securities, which were distributed to the investment company shareholders, thereby virtually requiring the disbursement of all income received by the fund. Fifth, the insecurity psychology in the nation, which has led to a desire to minimize risk. The mutual fund does this by a combination of skilled management and diversification. Sixth, and perhaps most important, is the fact that the American economy has shifted from a society of the very rich and the very poor to one in which there is a very high proportion of middle-income citizens.[3] They can make best use of the professional investment management of the mutual fund and the small dollar-unit cost of its shares. In short, the investment company is a middle-income medium of investment, and the United States has become a middle-income society.

To generalize, the open-end investment companies have applied the trustee principles of investment to their investors' funds and successfully weathered the stormiest period of American economic history, surviving a major depression, a tremendous stock market collapse, a World War, and years of social experiment by the Federal Government.

The subject of this thesis is the economic role of the investment company. Of necessity, there are many aspects included which are highly hypothetical and may be of limited validity at the present time. Many men in the industry are reluctant to point out its potential economic role primarily because of the small size of investment company assets with respect to other financial institutions in the nation. Life insurance companies have some $63 billion in assets; there are over $58 billion of United States savings bonds outstanding; and bank time deposits total $56 billion.[4] The $2.5 billion of assets under mutual fund supervision is likely to look small by comparison. But the growth of those three great financial institutions is in turn dwarfed by recent mutual fund growth: since 1945, investment company assets have increased by 100%, but life insurance assets have risen by only 40%, savings bonds by 30%, and time deposits by but 25%. It is upon the continuance of such investment company growth, approximately 20% each year, that much of the validity of this thesis must rely. It will treat first the ultimate basis of success for the investment company, the fulfillment of its role of giving advantages to the individual investor, and then proceed with an examination of its potential success in providing profitable investment for small trust and pension funds. Having examined the sources of investment company assets, the work will then examine their economic use: as a source

---

3. *Cf. infra,* Table XVI.
4. *Federal Reserve Bulletin,* XXXVII (February, 1951), p. 167 *passim.*

of equity capital, as an influence in corporate management, and incidentally as a stabilizing factor on the securities exchanges. These functions were chosen as those for which there is a need in the society. The investment companies can fill this need by staying in their present sphere, and not in any way subordinating the interests of their shareholders to their other economic roles. Their prime responsibility must always be to their shareholders.

Table II shows the relationships among all of the aspects of the investment company's role in the economy, by showing how it facilitates the flow of savings into investment.

TABLE II Mutual Funds and the Relationship Between Savings and Investment

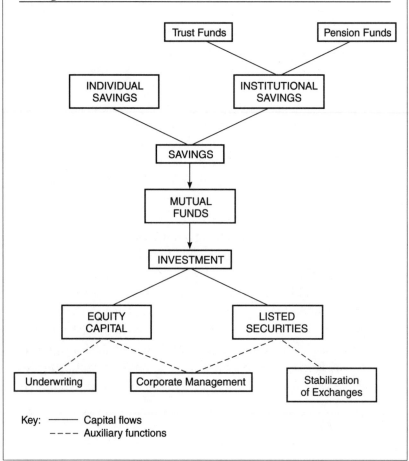

Chapter

I

ADVANTAGES TO THE
INDIVIDUAL INVESTOR

THAT THE INVESTMENT com-
pany has fulfilled its functions to the individual investor appears
manifest. The very fact that the number of shareholders has tre-
bled in the last ten years seems to indicate that they have found
it a suitable means to accomplish their investment ends.[1] It will
be the place of this chapter to show what advantages the investment company gives the investor, using particular examples
wherever practicable.

Several things must be made clear, however. First, investment
companies have generally tried to encourage the purchase of
their shares by investors, not savers. Many funds point to the
need for adequate cash reserves, insurance, and perhaps additional savings or government bonds before placing the remainder in a mutual fund. This chapter, then, will be oriented toward
those individual investors who can afford investment, which by
its very nature entails a certain amount of risk.

Second, the funds can make no claim to superiority over the
market averages, which are in a sense investment trusts with fixed
portfolios; e.g., the stocks composing the particular "average."
They state, rather, that their performance must be judged against
what the individual could have done at the same cost over the
same period, with the same objectives as has a given fund.

---

1. Author's computation from figures given by the National Association of
   Investment Companies.

Third, it is evident that the open-end investment company cannot attain perfect fulfillment of all the objectives stated below, but makes available the most adequate combination of facilities for the individual investor; that is, it offers the package with the greatest total amount of management, diversification, income, liquidity, and dollar appreciation. There will be no claim in this thesis that the management of the investor's capital will produce better results than that of an investment counsel who handles large accounts individually; that the diversification will be sounder than that of insurance companies under legal list requirements; that the income will be as stable as that of government bonds or as high as that from a given common stock; that the liquidity will be as great as that given by a savings bank; nor that the share will appreciate in value with the cost of living as a closed-end leverage share does. The only claim will be that the investment company offers the best combination of these facilities to the individual investor.

In offering to the investor a greater degree of diversification and more expert management than he could otherwise obtain, investment companies present a wide variety of fund types with diversified objectives, from which the investor may choose. He may pick the balanced fund, which attempts to plan its portfolio with regard to current conditions, especially by shifting its ratio of "aggressive" common stocks and "defensive" bonds; or the common stock fund, which maintains a largely fully invested position with a view toward selecting seasoned issues; or the bond fund, which maintains a portfolio solely of bonds. If the investor prefers to exercise a greater degree of management, he may choose the specialty fund, of which there are two types: the industry type, in which a share is backed by a diversified list of issues in an industry of the investor's choice; and the objective type, in which the investor picks his objective and participates in a diversified list of stocks most likely to fulfill it. Thus, the mutual fund offers the investor a wide variety of shares from which to choose, to suit his objectives of either capital appreciation, capital preservation, or reasonable income, or varying combinations of each.

The advantages of management, diversification, income, liquidity, and inflation hedging which the funds provide will be discussed in separate sections. However, the investment companies perform several additional minor functions which may be mentioned here: their portfolio shares are held by a custodian—usually a bank—and are thus safe from damage or loss (but not depreciation in value, as the recent Securities and Exchange Commission Statement of Policy indicated[2]); the dividends are quarterly, not scattered and small, and the investor need not be concerned with proxies, warrants, and stock splits; and finally, there is convenience in income tax returns, with the investment company required to send a year-end statement of the taxability of dividends. This chapter will now proceed with an analysis of the degree of success the funds have attained in providing the more important advantages to the investor.

Management

... the judicious selection of securities, based on extensive research and systematic plan, in order to accomplish the objectives of investment ...

The individual investor in most cases has neither the time nor the knowledge to manage his own investment account. This lacking is made clear in the oft-quoted statement by the late Louis D. Brandeis, Associate Justice of the United States Supreme Court:[3]

> **... the number of securities on the market is very large. For the small investor to make an intelligent selection from these—indeed, to pass an intelligent judgment on a single one—is ordinarily impossible. He lacks the ability, the facilities, the training, and the time essential to a proper investigation. Unless his purchase is to be little better than a gamble, he needs the advice of an expert, who, combining special knowledge with judgment, has the facilities and incentive to make a thorough investigation.**

2. *Cf. infra*, p. 386.
3. Quoted in *Trusts and Estates*, LXXXVIII (August, 1949), p. 495.

The mutual fund supplies the investor with this expert management, at relatively low cost, with its objectives stated so that the
investor can carefully determine which fund best suits his needs.
Besides these advantages, the management usually has sufficient
cash position to "average-down" in a period of market recession,[4]
and is therefore able to take advantage of prevailing low prices.
The individual investor usually lacks the capital to do this.

The duties incumbent upon management may be roughly classified as follows: determining secular as well as short-term trends in
economic and market fluctuations, allocating their funds with
regard to both industries and companies in those industries, and
ascertaining which securities are priced such as to be purchased for
the portfolio and sold from it. The duties with regard to the distribution of income are severely limited by the Internal Revenue Act
of 1936, which virtually requires that income be distributed in toto
to the shareholders. A good example of management in action is the
work of the Wellington Fund after the Korean War began in June,
1950.[5] Although the balance between common stock (about 60%),
preferred stock, and bonds changed only slightly, the management
was alert to any possible economic trends, taking into consideration
all possible developments. Expecting potential high taxes to cut
heavily into expected profits from their "growth" shares, these
types were disposed of in many cases; shares of Aluminium Co. of
America, Kennecott Copper, and Atlantic Refining were sold at a
realized profit; and issues such as General Electric and Detroit Edi-
son were sold, since they seemed to the management to be priced
"out-of-line" with other issues of similar quality in their respective
industries. Purchases included Goodyear Tire, Bethlehem Steel,
and Southern Pacific, all expected to fare well in a semi-war economy; Westinghouse, Standard Oil of California, and Standard
Brands, likely to do well in either war or peace; and American Can,
American Tobacco, and National Cash Register, the prices of which
were seemingly low enough to discount expected tax increases.

---

4. That is, has sufficient cash in order to buy shares at the low market prices
   and therefore lower the average price of the shares in the portfolio.
5. "Trusts Adjust to Semiwar," *Business Week* (September 16, 1950), p. 115.

Investment company management is usually steered by a Board of Directors or a Board of Trustees, composed largely of the company officers, established businessmen, directors of corporations, accountants, lawyers, bankers, and members of stock exchanges. The Boards do not suffer by comparison with the director lists of any large corporation, and include a Trustee of the Committee for Economic Development, the treasurer of American Telephone and Telegraph, an ex-governor of West Virginia, president of the Wilson Line, and an associate dean of the Graduate School of Business Administration of Harvard University.[6] In accordance with the Investment Company Act of 1940, the Board of Directors may not be radically changed without stockholder consent; a majority of the directors may not be affiliated with investment bankers or the investment company's regular brokers, and must be independent of the company's sales-distribution organization; and 40% of the board may not be investment advisers or officers of the company.[7] These provisions give positive protection against control of fund investment policy by sales groups, brokerage concerns, and investment banking houses.

The cost of management is usually stated as a percentage of net asset value per share, computed quarterly in most cases. It ranges from $\frac{1}{2}$ of 1% to 1% of total assets, and is stated even as a daily figure ($\frac{1}{730}$ of 1% of average daily net assets) in order to give the investor the impression of an extremely low cost. Nevertheless, there is some indication that the cost of management is too high: first, the fees come to from 5% to 15% when computed as a percentage of income; and second, there are costs additional to the management fee, such as custodian and stock transfer fees, mailing and printing, clerical salaries, administrative and legal fees, and state and local taxes, which usually amount to from 20% to 50% of total expenses, the remainder being composed of

---

6. The directors of today are presumably more cautious than was Charles F. Kettering, vice president of General Motors Corp., who invested $260,000 during the late 'twenties in an investment trust of which he was a director, and subsequently realized but $20,000.

7. Respectively, sections 16(a), 10(b), and 10(a).

the management fee. However, the careful investor can ascertain these percentages for himself by investigating the prospectus, and then make his investment on the basis of his findings.

Evaluation of Management Success

Investors must expect the value of their investment company shares to rise and fall with the market, although the average open-end fund is likely to dampen the amplitude of any market fluctuation. Management can scarcely be expected to buy so that the fund can stay ahead of the market when the very securities that it buys are a part of that market. However, the investment company should not saddle its investors with a greater loss than the fall in portfolio values. The closed-end companies did this in many cases after the 1929 crash, since their shares were purchased at a premium and sold at a discount during the Depression. Open-end shares may not be bought or sold in this way, however, and their comparative superiority can be clearly seen in relative performances in the 1929–1936 period: in 193 closed-end management companies, the average per share asset value declined by 35.3%, while in 49 open-end funds, the value increased by 6.7%.[8]

Since management performance must be related to the stated investment objectives of the fund,[9] the evaluation of the open-end investment company cannot rest on industry-wide statistics, but rather must rest on specific analyses of given funds. Five such analyses will be presented below. In each case, the three prime aspects of performance—market value of shares, dividend payments, and capital gains disbursements—will be examined with regard to the individual fund's statement of objectives, and, where necessary to the logical development, additional aspects will be examined.[10]

---

8. Securities and Exchange Commission, *Investment Trusts and Investment Companies* (Part 2), p. 508.
9. Basic investment policies must be stated to the SEC (Securities and Exchange Commission), after which they may be changed only with shareholder consent, in accordance with section 13(a) of the Investment Company Act.
10. *Cf. infra*, p. 369, for a further discussion of dividend income and capital gain disbursements.

Wellington Fund states its objectives as ". . . to pay reasonable dividends, to secure profits without undue speculation, and to conserve principal."[11] Its record reveals a 3.8% dividend rate over the past sixteen years, during which it also made security profit distributions averaging 2.6% each year. The net asset value has fluctuated only slightly over one-half as much as the Dow-Jones 30-stock Industrial Average in the last decade.[12] Fund principal has been conserved quite remarkably, as revealed by the net asset value per share variation: the high was $24.58 in 1929 (the year the fund was organized) and the low was $11.50 in 1932. A share purchased at any year-end in the fund's history would have a greater value at the present, except for purchases in 1929, 1936, and 1945, all of which were peak market years. Assuming all dividends were reinvested, the share value increased by 100% in the 1934–1949 period, compared with an 83% increase in the Standard & Poor 90-Stock Average.

"The primary objective . . ." of the United Income Fund ". . . is the production of a regular and satisfactory rate of income."[13] This relatively young fund (organized in 1941) has paid an annual income, including that from capital gains, of from 7.02% to 9.84%, averaging 8.3% each year. Although only 5.5% was paid from dividend income, the security profits distributions apparently have not impaired the capital, since assets have increased during the fund's history from $9.12 in 1941 to $9.74 in 1949.

"To provide for shareholders the most favorable income that is consistent with . . . prevailing business conditions, dividend and interest rates, and long term preservation of capital," is the policy of Investors Mutual Inc.[14] Income averaged 6.3% per share each year, of which 2.4% was from security profit distributions. With regard to capital preservation, a share worth $9.50 in

---

11. Wellington Fund, *Prospectus* (April 14, 1950), p. 2. Other figures from their sales literature.
12. Wiesenberger, Arthur, *op. cit.*, p. 113. All future "fluctuation" figures also from this source.
13. United Funds Inc., *Prospectus,* April 14, 1950, p. 2.
14. Investors Mutual Inc., *Prospectus,* October 15, 1949, p. 1.

1940 was worth $12.34 at the 1949 year-end. Only the shares of 1945 and 1946 would have brought the investor a capital loss if he had sold them at the end of 1949. While the Standard & Poor average rose 138% in the 1940–1949 period, Investors Mutual asset value per share increased by 127%.

The Eaton & Howard Balanced Fund favors a regular and satisfactory rate of return and reasonable protection of capital, with any appreciation directed toward long-term growth. In only six of its nineteen years of existence did the per share value decline, indicating reasonable capital protection. The fund's disinterest in capital gains is born out by the fact that only $1.9062 per share has been distributed from capital gains during the firm's history, in which the net asset value per share has risen from $15.25 (in 1932) to $27.14 (in 1949). Dividend income averaged 4.4% each year, and the fund exceeded the rise in the Standard & Poor average by 28% in the 1937–1949 period.[15]

A unique chance for the analysis of fund objectives is possible in the case of the Keystone Common Stock Funds, each of which has a different objective; S-1 consists of high-grade "blue-chip" common stocks; S-2 is the income fund, oriented toward a generous rate of return; S-3 is speculative, stressing capital growth; and S-4 is low-priced and includes fast-moving common shares. The figures in Table III seem to substantiate the fulfillment of objectives by management.

---

15. Eaton & Howard Balanced Fund, *Semi-Annual Report,* June 30, 1950.

TABLE III   Comparison of Keystone Common Stock Funds

	S-1	S-2	S-3	S-4
Net asset value—1940	$23.71	$12.17	$ 8.97	$3.45
Net asset value—1945	$29.24	$17.45	$14.32	$5.99
Net asset value—1950	$31.59	$16.66	$16.24	$6.54
Average Income:				
From capital gains	2.1%	1.2%	1.7%	6.0%
From dividends	4.9%	7.3%	6.4%	5.1%
Capital increase; 1940–50	39%	37%	81%	90%
Value fluctuation	30%	35%	53%	65%

SOURCE: The Keystone Co.

The five preceding analyses indicate clearly a high degree of achievement of investment objectives by the sample mutual funds. They seem to have "out-performed the market" with regard to their objectives, and a careful investor who investigates the fund before he buys its shares is apparently justified in assuming a fairly satisfactory performance once he makes his choice, since the attainment of objectives is proof of good management.

Diversification

... the distribution of investments among different issues of securities in order to decrease the risk on any one investment ...

Closely connected with the concept of management of the investors' funds is the idea of diversification, which is said to minimize the risk of any single commitment and contribute to the stability and continuity of income. Investors must realize, however, that with a decrease in the chance of a net loss by the spreading of risks, there is also a limitation on the effect of a windfall gain. This aspect of a limit to profit as well as to loss is naturally one rarely stressed by investment companies. Investors must also realize that diversification cannot protect against cyclical market declines.

Diversification is tied to management by the fact that it must be informed and intelligent, not merely wide; it must be managed rather than random. Most funds do use sound judgment in diversifying their portfolios, and the criticism that the funds merely "buy the averages" is seen as invalid, since a survey by the writer of twenty funds indicated that each had an average of but eight of the thirty widely known stocks comprising the Dow-Jones Industrial Average. The fallacy of merely wide diversification is clearly indicated by the stock market crash of 1929. Although closed-end leverage companies averaged 87 issues in their portfolios, and closed-end non-leverage companies averaged 60.2 issues, their capital decline was far more severe than that of the open-end companies, which averaged only 46.8 issues.[16] The latter were virtually required to buy sound, sea-

---

16. Securities and Exchange Commission, *op. cit.*, p. 546.

TABLE IV Leading Issues Which Declined
in Value in 1949

STOCK	DECLINE
American Telephone & Telegraph	−3¼
Electric Storage Battery	−9¾
Gulf Oil Co.	−4%
Standard Oil of N.J.	−5%

SOURCE: Wiesenberger, *op. cit.*, p. 162.

soned, marketable issues, primarily because they had to be able
to liquidate parts of their portfolios on demand for redemptions
by shareholders.

A few examples of why the individual needs diversification
may be made. First, he cannot properly invest in a single stock
without risk, as shown by the examples in Table IV of "blue-chip"
stocks which declined in value in 1949, a year when the averages
rose about 10%.

Even over longer periods, a single investment offers a very
great risk. In the 1939–1949 period, when the Standard & Poor
90-Stock Average rose 110% (assuming all dividends reinvested),
the major issues listed in Table V declined.

With the indication that selection of individual securities is at
best an extremely risky proposition, it seems pertinent to indicate the requirements for diversification in the fund portfolio.
First, the Investment Company Act requires that

TABLE V Issues Which Declined in the 1939–1949 Decade

	PERCENTAGE DECLINE IN MARKET VALUE	LOSS INCLUDING DIVIDENDS PAID
Air Reduction	−65%	−38%
International Nickel	−50%	−13%
N.Y. Central Railroad	−46%	−18%
United Aircraft	−38%	+25%
Allis Chalmers	−31%	+4%
Continental Can	−15%	+21%

SOURCE: Wellington Fund sales material; computations by the author.

at least 75 percentum of the value of its total assets is represented by cash and cash items, government securities, securities of other investment companies, and other securities
limited in respect of any one issuer to an amount not greater
in value than 5 percentum of the value of the total assets of
such management company and to not more than 10 percentum of the outstanding voting securities of such issuer.[17]

Moreover, the investment company is not allowed to change
its basic policy statement (i.e., from a diversified to a non-
diversified company) without the consent of a majority of its
stockholders.

In the second place, many funds impose upon themselves
greater restrictions as to the amount and quality of diversification through restrictions in their charters. The following examples are typical:

1. To hold no more than 10% of any company's stock.
2. To invest no more than 5% of assets in any company.
   (These two restrictions in effect make the government requirements effective for the entire portfolio.)
3. To limit borrowing to 10% of assets.
4. To limit underwriting to 5% of assets.
5. To invest not more than 2% of assets in securities of an issuer that has been in operation for less than three years.
6. Not to invest in securities of other investment trusts.
7. Not to hold more than 5% of assets in securities not listed
   on the New York Stock Exchange or on the over-the-
   counter markets.

A few examples of diversification in various investment companies indicate how wide it is (Tables VI and VII).

Naturally, the investor has to pay a price for diversification. In
the open-end company it is the load, or sales charge, on the purchase of each share.[18] There has been much criticism of the large

---

17. Section 5(b)(1).
18. There is ordinarily no charge in redeeming the share.

TABLE VI   Diversification by Industry in Selected Funds

FUND	NUMBER OF INDUSTRIES	LARGEST	(% OF ASSETS)		SMALLEST
Affiliated	19	Petroleum	19.1	1.1	Rubber
American Business Shares	10	Automobile	9.7	1.7	Machinery
Broad St. Investment	22	Building	15.6	.7	Publishing
Knickerbocker	13	Steel	11.0	2.2	Petroleum
Scudder, Stevens & Clark	25	Retail	4.8	1.0	Amusement

SOURCE: Recent prospectuses of indicated funds.

size of the load, which usually runs from 6% to 9% of the net asset value per share, depending on the fund. Although, strictly speaking, the load is the cost of distribution, since the fund itself never receives any part of it, it may be considered as the cost of diversification for two reasons: first, because the test of cost is the value (i.e., the portfolio shares) obtained for a price, and secondly, because the load is a commission paid in buying an investment company share, just as a brokerage commission must be paid in the purchase of shares of listed stock, of which the portfolio is composed. Although it is more favorable to compare the load with any dealer commission—since both are the costs of bringing the service to the consumer—it seems closer to reality to compare it with the costs incurred in actually duplicating the purchase of the investments in the portfolio which the investment company share represents.

The funds claim that, for the individual, commissions and other buying and selling costs in obtaining diversification would

TABLE VII   Diversification by Issues in Selected Funds

FUND	NUMBER OF ISSUES	LARGEST HOLDING		SMALLEST HOLDING	
Boston Fund	101	1.9%	Cities Service	.22%	Sharpe&Dohme
Selected Industries	180	5.2%	Union Securities	.02%	Marine Midland
Putnam Fund	126	1.6%	Gulf Oil	.2%	Allied Stores

SOURCE: Recent prospectuses of indicated funds.

exceed the cost of the mutual fund shares. To buy but one share of each of the securities in the Dow-Jones 30-Stock average would cost $1,800.81. The commission charges on the purchase and the resale of each share would amount to 11.16% of this purchase price.[19] This example indicates the importance of the "round-trip" feature of the sales load, which means essentially that the investor is paying both the buying and the selling commissions at the same time.

Also, a random survey made by the writer compared the spread between investment company bid and asked prices and the bid and asked prices of a variety of over-the-counter industrial stocks, which proved the average cost to be about one-quarter point less on the former than on the latter (Table VIII).

The load payment, as mentioned before, does not go to the fund itself. An eight-dollar commission would be distributed in approximately the following fashion: $2.00 to the dealer, $3.50 to the salesman, and $2.50 to the sponsor, or principal underwriter, who pays for the sales literature and wholesaling. This peculiar

19. Wellington Fund sales brochure, *Cost vs. Value,* p. 3.

TABLE VIII Relation between Over-the-Counter "Spreads" and Investment Company Sales Loads

	Asked Price	
Bid Price	INDUSTRIAL	INVESTMENT CO.
4	5	4⅜
6⅜	7⅜	7
10¾	11¾	11⅝
14¾	16¼	15⅞
17½	19	19
20½	22	22
23½	25	25¾
26	28	28⅜
31	35	33½
38½	40½	41⅜
60½	64½	63

SOURCE: Author's random selection from prices quoted in Philadelphia *Inquirer* financial section, December 28, 1950.

situation, whereby the fund does not profit directly from the sale of its securities, means that a fall in the cost of a share (through a reduced load) will not lead to a rise in the amount of shares demanded: a lower load is likely to mean decreased sales, since it entails a lower profit for the salesman, who in turn can divert his effort to the sale of another fund, since there are a great variety of similar fund shares available. Merrill Griswold, chairman of Massachusetts Investors Trust's Board of Trustees, presented the implications of a lowered load when he told the Securities and Exchange Commission, at the 1939 public examination of MIT:

> **If we had at that time (1932) reduced our sales load to 5¾ (it was then 8¼), I don't think anybody would have sold any of our shares to anybody.**[20]

On the shares of some investment companies there is either a very small sales charge or none at all, when the sponsor is an investment counsel firm rather than a distributing firm which supports an extensive marketing system. Examples of the former are the Loomis-Sayles funds (no selling charge, 2% redemption fee) which were organized by the investment counsel firm of the same name; and Scudder, Stevens & Clark Fund, Inc. (1% to buy and 1% to sell). Neither of these funds have distributors (or principal underwriters). An example of the distributing firm type with a large marketing organization is Vance, Sanders & Co., a firm "underwriting" the shares of MIT (8.1% load), Massachusetts Investors Second Fund (8.1%), Boston Fund (8.1%), and Bond Fund of Boston (2.96%). A survey made at the end of 1936 by the SEC indicated that 78% of the open-end companies were sponsored by securities distributors, the remainder by investment counsel.[21] At the present, the percentage is probably weighted even more heavily in favor of the former.

The sales charge is often graded down for larger investments. For example, the Fidelity Fund has a basic load of 7.5% of the offering price, with reductions as follows:[22]

---

20. SEC, *op. cit.* (Part 3), p. 811.
21. *Ibid.,* p. 804.
22. *Prospectus,* April 18, 1950, p. 9.

5%: $25,000–50,000
4%: $50,000–100,000
3%: $100,000–200,000
2%: $200,000 and above

All things taken into consideration, it would seem that the load is perhaps too high. Although it is justified in a purely economic sense since the public is willing to pay that price for shares, and in a social sense since it keeps the small investor from speculative "switching," an eventual reduction in sales loads would doubtless increase the number of holders of investment company shares, at the same time increasing the distributors total revenue by the higher sales volume.

Income

. . . the recurrent money payments proceeding from the disbursements of the institutions in which funds are invested . . .

With the fall in interest rates and bond yields the reasonable and regular dividends provided by investment companies are extremely important to the individual investor. So far as is known, no mutual fund with income as its objective has ever passed a dividend from investment income. Although there is no guarantee of continuous future return, it seems logical to assert that dividends will be forthcoming as long as American industry continues to make profits, since it is the return on the portfolio of the investment company which provides it with cash for its disbursements.

That "the" interest rate has undergone a drastic decline in the last twenty years can be clearly seen by comparing different rates in 1929 and 1949 (Tables IX and X). Commercial loan rates declined from 5.83% to 2.62%, short-term prime commercial paper fell from 5.85% to 1.48%,[23] and Moody's Corporate Bond

23. Bureau of Census, *Historical Statistics of the United States: 1789–1945,* p. 278, and *Statistical Abstract of the United States—1950,* p. 952.

TABLE IX   Interest Rate Decline

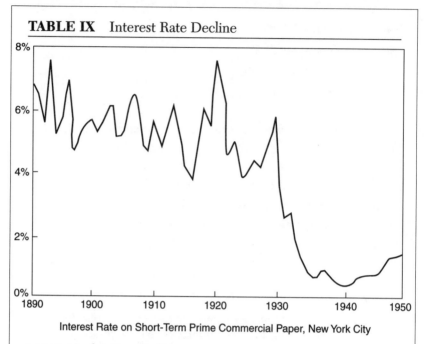

Interest Rate on Short-Term Prime Commercial Paper, New York City

SOURCE: *Moody's Manual of Investments.*

Average yield dropped from 5.21% to 2.96%.[24] Over the same period, Moody's 200-common stock yield rose from 3.41% to 6.63%.[25] The mutual fund reflects this high common stock yield, paying out an average of 4.5% in dividends from income in 1949. Over the last decade, while the Moody average was 5.36%, the funds averaged something over 4%.

The increasing divergence of stock dividends and bond interest rates is probably a substantial reason for the growth of the investment company. The Depression and the great capital losses to investors which resulted from it caused a greater desire for safety of principal, but gradually confidence in stocks (and especially in a diversified group of them) returned, and during the same period bond rates fell. The combination of high income and safe principal thus shifted in favor of the common stock element. In spite of the fact that many funds urge that part of the

24. Porter, John S. (editor-in-chief), *Moody's Manual of Investments, Indus-trial Securities,* p. a17.
25. *Ibid.,* p. a20.

TABLE X Stock Yields and Bond Yields

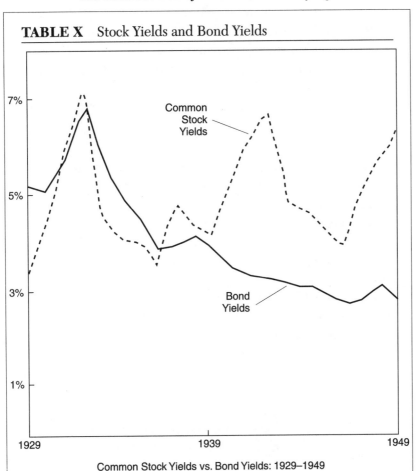

Common Stock Yields vs. Bond Yields: 1929–1949

SOURCE: *Statistical Abstract of the United States.*

investor's capital should be devoted to bonds, after he has cash reserves and insurance needs filled, it seems doubtful that this advice has been widely followed.

Proof of the relative regularity of investment company dividends can be seen from an analysis of three companies. Boston Fund, Fidelity Fund, and MIT averaged 4.3% in dividends from income over the past ten years, and never missed a quarterly dividend (Table XI).

There is a virtual legal requirement for the investment company to pay out its income in dividends, for to qualify (and thus gain tax exemptions) under the Internal Revenue Code, Supple-

TABLE XI Investment Company Dividends from Income: Selected Funds Over a Five-Year Period

FUND	1944	1945	1946	1947	1948
Boston	$0.64	$0.70	$0.71	$0.82	$0.79
Fidelity	0.71	0.65	0.91	1.07	1.50
MIT	0.96	1.01	1.10	1.23	1.40

ment Q, the investment company must distribute as taxable dividends not less than 90% of its net income, exclusive of capital gains, for any taxable year. If it complies with this requirement, it pays no tax on the amount so distributed. This supplement prevents what would otherwise be triple taxation, with the government receiving a tax on corporate earnings, on the dividends from those earnings distributed to investment companies, and on the amount mutual fund stockholders get from their dividends.

Capital gains distributions present a problem to the investor as well as to the investment company. They are derived from net profits realized from securities transactions, and generally occur in periods of rising stock prices. For this reason, most companies encourage their reinvestment, and thus hope to prevent this reduction of working assets. The encouragement usually consists in the elimination of the loading charge when dividends are reinvested. Examples of this policy are evident in the Keystone prospectus, which says that capital gains distributions ". . . may be reinvested in additional shares of the fund at net asset value at the time of reinvestment," which must be within thirty days after the date of payment.[26] MIT says in its 1950 prospectus that they should ". . . be regarded by the shareholders as distributions of principal and not as income . . ."[27] and that ". . . shareholders will be offered the opportunity to reinvest the cash so distributed in shares of the trust at net asset value."[28]

Supplement Q virtually forces the distribution of capital gains income, since there is no tax on it if it is distributed; otherwise

---

26. *General Prospectus*, February 10, 1950, p. 7.
27. *Prospectus*, February 24, 1950, p. 4.
28. *Ibid.*, p. 8.

the mutual fund must pay 25% on long-term gains and 38% on short-term gains. Capital, therefore, cannot be built up as a cushion against future capital losses or as a dividend-equalizing reserve account. In 1936, an investment trust called Mayflower Associates, Inc., liquidated and distributed its assets to its shareholders, claiming that under the Internal Revenue Act it could not continue its policy of concentration on growth (in the mining and petroleum industries) rather than the distribution of high dividends.

The instability of capital gains dividends can be seen by a survey of the three companies in Table XI whose dividends from income were shown as quite regular (Table XII).

This instability has been in many cases disregarded by the funds in their sales literature, in which dividends were often quoted as the total of securities profit distributions and income distributions, thereby showing an abnormally high rate of return. It is clear that in a declining market, the capital gains portion would certainly decrease if not disappear entirely, so the practice seems misleading to the investor. The SEC Statement of Policy of August 11, 1950, took account of this when it declared that it is ". . . misleading . . . to combine into any one amount distributions from net investment income and distributions from any other source."[29]

One advantage of capital gains dividends that has been exploited in a few cases by specialty funds has been the fact that the investor need only pay capital gains taxes on security profit distributions, thus cutting his tax roughly 50%. Growth and

---

29. SEC, *Statement of Policy*, p. 2.

TABLE XII Investment Company Capital Gains Disbursements: Selected Funds over a Five-Year Period

FUND	1945	1946	1947	1948	1949
Boston	—	$0.90	$1.50	$0.50	—
Fidelity	$1.10	$0.83	$0.38	—	$0.15
MIT	$0.50	$0.70	—	—	—

SOURCE: Recent prospectuses.

speculative funds have therefore been made available to the investor whose taxable position is such that capital gains are more valuable than regular dividend income.

Liquidity

. . . the quality of being convertible into cash at a price approximating the value of the investment . . .

Liquidity of shares, or their redeemability by the fund at approximately net asset value, serves a dual advantage for the investor.[30] First, it makes it possible for him to receive the fair value of his share on demand, and second—a corollary of this advantage— the management must be sensitive to his desires and is thus responsible directly to him. Although redeemability is the unique feature of the open-end company, the Investment Company Act of 1940 made it statutory, giving the investor the privilege of redeeming shares at a price approximating net asset value within seven days, except when the New York Stock Exchange is closed under extraordinary conditions or SEC declares an emergency to exist, during which it is impracticable either for the investment company to dispose of its securities or for it to fairly determine the net value of its assets.[31]

The redemption feature establishes a continual market for the fund shares. Incidentally, there was no interference with the redeemability right in the market breaks of 1929, 1937, and 1946; and the New York Stock Exchange has been closed only once in the twenty-five years that the mutuals have been in business. In practice, there has never been any appreciable waiting period between the time shares are tendered for redemption and the fund's payment of cash to the shareholder.

There are two factors which can relieve the company of the necessity of liquidating its portfolio securities to meet a run on redemptions, both of which are provided for in the Investment Company Act. First, section 18(f) allows bank borrowing

---

30. In many cases the fund authorizes the principal underwriter to act as agent in the repurchase of shares.
31. Section 22(e).

". . . provided that . . . there is an asset coverage of at least 300 percentum"; thus the funds may borrow to meet current (and temporary) negative net sales. Second, the issuer is allowed, under section 2(a)(31), to compensate the holder with "approximately his proportionate share of the issuer's current net assets," rather than, ". . . the cash equivalent thereof." This provision has not been used, however, and some funds limit their redemption payments to cash value alone.

In practice, redemptions have proved to be a relatively fixed percentage of total assets, so with greater size, the investment company must increase its sales in order to gain the same amount of net sales (Table XIII).

During economic crises, sales and distribution efforts have to be increased in order to offset high redemptions by the jittery public. These increased efforts were clearly shown in the 1927–1936 period, when only in two quarters did redemptions exceed sales. Incorporated Investors had 889,801 shares outstanding in September, 1929, and between then and December, 1932 had 785,898 shares redeemed; yet on the latter date, due to increased sales, it had 1,158,030 shares outstanding.[32] Similarly, MIT had 298,687 shares in 1929; it redeemed 235,016 of them during the next three years, and yet had nearly one million shares outstanding in 1932.[33]

---

32. SEC, *op. cit.*, p. 807.
33. *Ibid.*, p. 808.

TABLE XIII Relationship of Fund Redemptions to Total Fund Assets

YEAR	PERCENT	YEAR	PERCENT
1941	11.2%	1946	10.9%
1942	6.2%	1947	6.2%
1943	7.8%	1948	8.5%
1944	7.9%	1949	5.4%
1945	8.5%	1950	11.1%

SOURCE: National Association of Investment Companies figures; computations by the author.

A recent example of redemptions in time of crisis came in June, 1950, when 64 of the largest funds repurchased 91% as many shares as they sold in the last week of that month.[34] Although this short period is out-of-line with earlier ratios, which averaged close to 40% in the 1945–1950 period, a close analysis of the figures reveals an interesting situation: in the second and third quarters of 1950 (which surround the week ending June 30) when the ratio of redemptions to sales for the industry was 60%, the ratio for common stock funds and balanced funds was 45%, while the ratio for bond and specialty funds was 103% (e. g., redemptions exceeded sales). Since bond funds comprise only a small percentage of this group, the high redemptions during crisis indicate dissatisfaction with their own choice of industry or of objective by the investors; conversely, the 45% figure for the common and balanced funds seems to indicate continuing satisfaction, if not with management, at least with diversification.[35]

Besides the advantages of redeemability *per se* to the investor, the concept has three very important implications; first, a major portion of the portfolio must be composed of highly seasoned securities of ascertainable market value; the holding of this type of security, the writer submits, is one of the reasons the open-end fund survived the Depression so much better than its closed-end counterpart. Second, the redeemability feature prevents the use of senior securities, since redemptions could destroy the equity behind such securities. The investor, therefore, is never in danger of having his interests subordinated by the use of preferential capital.[36] Third, the threat of withdrawal means that management must continually provide satisfactory performance, at the risk of having to liquidate its portfolio and go out of business.

Individual fund redemption policies vary considerably. The certificate of incorporation of Investors Mutual Inc. gives regis-

---

34. "How Did Trusts Make Out?" *Business Week,* July 29, 1950, p. 52.
35. Author's computations from National Association of Investment Companies figures.
36. Section 18(f) of the Investment Company Act makes it illegal for open-end investment companies to issue senior securities, thus incorporating this provision into law.

tered shareholders the right to require the company to redeem shares at asset value on the business day following the day of surrender of the certificate. No more than a seven day wait is allowed unless there is an (SEC) emergency. The directors are allowed to deduct from asset value ". . . an amount equal to brokerage commissions, transfer taxes and charges . . . if any, which would be payable on the sale of all of the securities in the portfolio,"[37] in the case where issuance of new shares is discontinued. Wellington Fund reserves the right in computing liquidation value to deduct brokers' and other costs which would be payable if it were necessary to liquidate fund assets, a deduction estimated at 10¢ (about ½ of 1%) per share in March, 1950. The charter of Affiliated Fund provides that the company be obligated to sell securities in order to obtain funds to effect redemptions; that is, they have elected not to take advantage of the borrowing provision of the Investment Company Act. Axe-Houghton Fund may redeem shares in kind with stockholder consent in an emergency, the Board of Directors having the power to select and value the particular investments used in these payments.

Hedge Against Inflation

. . . to safeguard the purchasing power of capital by investing it in things which advance, in both price and yield, as the cost-of-living advances . . .

It seems a basic economic truth that the most likely investment to appreciate in value and in return as the purchasing power of the dollar falls is an investment in common stocks. Although the correlation between stock value and price level is by no means perfect, common stocks offer the investor far greater purchasing power protection than do bonds or savings accounts. It is logical to assume, therefore, that the investment companies, varying with the market and having portfolios composed largely of common stocks, will also provide the investor with a "hedge" against the rising prices of consumer goods. Tables XIV and XV seem to

---

37. *Prospectus,* October 15, 1949, p. 4.

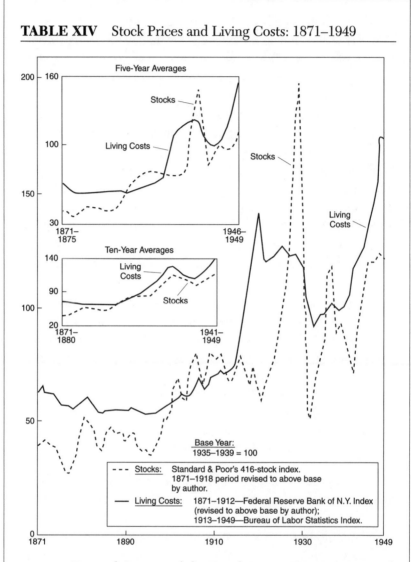

TABLE XIV   Stock Prices and Living Costs: 1871–1949

SOURCES: *Historical Statistics of the United States: 1789–1945; Statistical Abstract of the United States: 1950.*

indicate the validity of these assertions, and it is on their pictorial evidence rather than on verbose assertions that the author's case must rest.

Professor Sumner Slichter, professor of economics at Harvard University, has said that an investment counsel who advises his

TABLE XV   Stock Yields and Living Costs: 1929–1949

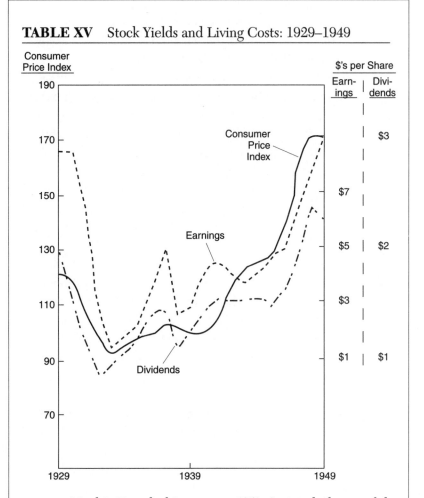

SOURCES: *Moody's Manual of Investments, 1950; Statistical Abstract of the United States: 1950.*

client to place his funds in savings banks, postal savings, or government securities "is assuming a very heavy responsibility," asserting that properly selected stocks should prove to be a reasonable protection against the rising cost of living.[38] In his opinion, unless the government issues savings bonds payable in a

---

38. Quoted by Long, Henry A., "Mutual Funds Mature," *Trusts and Estates,* LXXXIX (September, 1950), p. 606.

fixed amount of purchasing power rather than in fixed dollar amounts, the well-managed mutual fund is the best answer to the problem of inflation for the small investor.

Certainly the mutual fund offers a better hedge against purchasing power decline than would bank deposits or bonds, which are fixed in dollar rates. The value of common stocks, in a survey by Emerson W. Axe, was shown to yield an average of $2.80 for each dollar invested during twenty-year periods from 1858 to 1948, under a plan of dollar-cost-averaging which required the investment of $1,000 each quarter in a common stock average.[39] This procedure enables the investor to spread his investment over time, and the close correlation of the ten-year chart shows that it eliminates the periodic fluctuations of both living costs and securities prices.[40] In the worst period (1918–1938), the amount realized was $164,181 on an initial investment of $80,951 (plus reinvested dividends of $56,112). The best was 1908–1928, after which $347,474 was realized from an initial investment of $81,015 and reinvested dividends of $87,896. These amounts are comparable with $99,594, the realized amount from $4,000 invested annually for twenty years in a savings bank, at current rates.

Some funds specifically attempt to procure common stocks which will provide a hedge against inflation. Bullock's Dividend Shares, for example, claims that 67.6% of the shares in its portfolio provide this characteristic in an exceptional degree.[41] Inflation hedge stocks are

> **namely, the common stocks of those companies producing basic raw materials, as well as others which can be expected to experience an increase in dollar income sufficient to offset the decline in the purchasing power of the dollar.[42]**

---

39. Axe, Emerson W., "The Record of Equity Investment," *Trusts and Estates*, LXXXIX (August, 1950), p. 508.
40. *Cf. supra*, Table XIV.
41. Dividend Shares, *Today's Tests for Common Stock Investment*, p. 1.
42. *Loc. cit.*

They include all stocks whose 1940–1950 net earnings per share have increased in an amount exceeding the rise in the cost of living.

On the basis of limited information, then, it appears valid to assert that both income from the principal of an investment company share will tend to keep pace with the cost of living; at any rate it will do so better than fixed-income investments. It must be noted, moreover, that the last thirty-five years have been years of extremely unstable price levels, as a result particularly of price control during the first and second World Wars, and extremely unstable securities, particularly in the decade surrounding the 1929 crash.

Fund Sales Policies

With these advantages for the small investor, the fund has left the traditional marketing area for securities to tap wealth in other parts of the country. The North Atlantic seaboard, which supplies some 69% of the volume of trading on the New York Stock Exchange, bought but 31% of the one billion dollars worth of fund shares sold in the 1946–1948 period.[43] A study made by the National Association of Securities Dealers showed only three states with less than 1,000 mutual fund shareholders—Delaware, Nevada, and Wyoming—the top seven states being California, New York, Missouri, Michigan, Massachusetts, Illinois, and Pennsylvania. However, the states with the highest ratio of fund investors to total population were New Hampshire and Maine, with New York ranking twenty-sixth and Pennsylvania thirty-second.

Besides going to largely new geographic areas, the funds are taking advantage of the new distribution of the national income in the United States: only 32% of the population now earn less than $3,000 each year, compared with 85% in 1937; 51% earn from

---

43. National Association of Securities Dealers figures quoted by Dorsey Richardson, *Speech to Investment Bankers' Association,* December 6, 1949 (mimeo.), p. 4.

$3,000 to $7,500, compared to 7% in 1937.[44] The distribution of the income has gravitated considerably toward the hypothetical "line of equal distribution," with the highest percentiles having moved one-half the way to perfect equality since 1937. (See Table XVI.) In addition to this new distribution of wealth, there is a new total wealth in the economy: since 1937, savings have increased

---

44. Investment Companies Committee, *Report to Investment Bankers Association of America* (1949), p. 1. (mimeo.)

TABLE XVI   Income Distribution

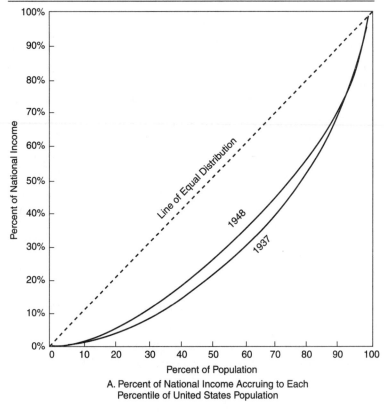

A. Percent of National Income Accruing to Each
Percentile of United States Population

SOURCES for A: 1937—*Economic Almanac* 1948—*Statistical Abstract of the United States: 1950.*

TABLE XVI   Income Distribution

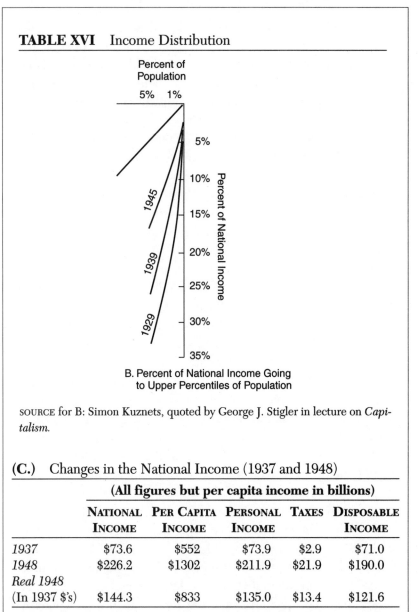

B. Percent of National Income Going
to Upper Percentiles of Population

SOURCE for B: Simon Kuznets, quoted by George J. Stigler in lecture on *Capitalism.*

(C.)   Changes in the National Income (1937 and 1948)

	(All figures but per capita income in billions)			
	NATIONAL INCOME	**PER CAPITA INCOME**	**PERSONAL INCOME**	**TAXES**	**DISPOSABLE INCOME**
1937	$73.6	$552	$73.9	$2.9	$71.0
1948	$226.2	$1302	$211.9	$21.9	$190.0
Real 1948 (In 1937 $'s)	$144.3	$833	$135.0	$13.4	$121.6

SOURCE for C: *Statistical Abstract of the United States: 1950;* "Real" computations by the author.

by $20 billion, disposable income by $120 billion, and liquid assets in individual hands by $107 billion.[45] The investment companies are trying to reach this new wealth. There are three general ways in which the attempt is being made: sales and distribution policies, periodic payment plans, and advertising.

In addition to the sales forces of the distributors of mutual funds, there are some 4,000 over-the-counter dealers who handle mutuals. Estimates of sales forces are unavailable, but a very high average might be indicated in the case of Investors Diversified Services, which is said to have 1,700 salesmen in the United States and Canada. The number of investment houses which handle investment company shares has increased, during the last ten years, from only a handful to over 500, possibly to take advantage of the small dollar-unit transactions through mutual fund shares. The funds can bring new investors to Wall Street more easily than the New York Stock Exchange can, since commissions there are too low to permit high advertising, canvassing, and distribution expenses. Wall Street ought to be grateful to the funds for their merchandising, since "investment companies are the best customers for common stocks that the market has today."[46] Certainly one reason for the success of the sales and distribution expansion of the investment companies are the advantages it gives to the dealer and salesman, the former of whom likes the high commission, the constant supply of shares, and the fact that he does not need to tie up any capital; and the latter of whom appreciates the publicly announced price of the shares, the generous commission, and the variety of literature and fund facts available.

Periodic payment plans have been increasing in recent years, and are oriented toward small investors who are able to invest only small amounts of money at one time. The plans are in most cases "non-contractural"[47] and a large West Coast firm is reported to be opening some 400 new accounts each month

---

45. Investment Companies Committee, *op. cit.*, p. 1.
46. Mindell, Joseph, "Wall Street Doesn't Sell Stocks," *Fortune*, XL (April, 1949), p. 79.
47. They involve no penalty for discontinuance of the payment plan.

under the plan. One example—perhaps the most lenient one—of the periodic payment plan is the Multiple Purchase Plan of the Commonwealth Investment Company, which requires only $50 as an initial payment, the only other requirement being that the shareholder's future payments be greater than $25. The payments may be made at any time and increased or decreased without prior notice, giving the investor complete flexibility of investment. Promotional literature, however, urges him to authorize the automatic reinvestment of all of his dividends and distributions. The Axe Investment Plan demands a $200 down payment and at least $200 invested each year; MIT's Cumulative Investment Program requires $250 down, with future payments greater than $50; and the requirements of the National (Securities) Investment Program are $250 initially and $25 each month. In these days of installment buying and easy credit, the investment companies are capitalizing on psychology to increase the numbers of their investors.

With regard to advertising, the funds (and their distributors) have incurred large expense by the publication of elaborate brochures and sales literature. This expense is paid for, in effect, by the shareholders, through the medium of the sales load. Examples of the type of literature—generally more promotional than informative—can be seen from the titles of several pamphlets: "A Personal Investment Account for the Professional Man," "A Plan for Tomorrow for the Woman of Today," "Dollars at Work in American Industry," "The Investor's Hour of Decision," and "What can a Mutual Investment Fund do for me?" All mediums—radio, television, newspaper—are used for advertising, with the importance of the latter having been increased in recent years due to a more liberal interpretation by the SEC of the Securities Act of 1933, which in part restricted the advertising of new issues of securities (under which investment companies are classified because of their unlimited capitalization) to "tombstone" advertisements. However, by the summer of 1950, the advertising became too zealous and in many cases too misleading, so on August 11, 1950, the SEC issued a Statement of Policy, written with the cooperation of the NASD and several fund executives. Its restrictions indicate where many of the malfeasances of the investment company advertising lie, so some of its major provisions will be listed below. The Statement of Policy makes it "materially misleading" for sales literature:

1. to imply assurance of stable, continuous, dependable, or liberal return.
2. to imply preservation of capital without indicating the market risks inherent in investment.
3. to refer to government regulation without stating that it does not involve supervision of management investment policies.
4. to imply redemption value will exceed cost.
5. to imply shares are generally selected by fiduciaries.
6. to compare performance with market averages without indicating that the period was selected.
7. to make extravagant claims with respect to management competency.

It is clear that the correction of advertising abuses will in the long run be beneficial to the industry as a whole, since investors that are misled, even unintentionally, will certainly not be satisfied "consumers" and buy more fund shares.

Insofar as providing advantages to the individual investor, then, the investment company has fulfilled its economic role. The soundness of management, the careful diversification, the liberal income, the share liquidity, and the hedge against inflation all combine to make the investment company share the most proper investment for the middle-income investor.

Chapter

II

AS A REPOSITORY FOR TRUST AND PENSION FUNDS

ALTHOUGH THE mutual fund's potentialities in the field of institutional investment have not been realized to their optimum, it has been reticence on the part of the fiduciaries and restriction by state law which have in many cases limited the potential, rather than any specific inadequacies on the part of the investment companies themselves. There has been limited use of investment company shares by institutions, however, and recent trade estimates place institutional holders as owners of some 7% of all mutual fund shares.

The basic problem for institutional investors is to provide a reasonable income for their beneficiaries without sacrificing the security of principal. In past years, this has been accomplished largely with the use of high-grade corporate and government bonds, which were expected to provide the most efficient accomplishment of these objectives. However, such has not proved to be the case. Over a span of the past twenty-five years, two factors have decreased the attractiveness of bonds: the yield has fallen from 5% to 2.5%;[1] and the purchasing power of the dollar has fallen to $0.75. The percentage yield to the institutional investor's beneficiaries, therefore, is decreased by 50%, and that decrease is accentuated by an additional 25% in real terms, because of the inflation of consumer goods prices.

Fortunately for the institutional investor, however, he can avoid the horns of this dilemma. For while bond yields have

---

1. Moody's Aaa bonds. *Cf. supra* Table X.

TABLE XVII   Institutional Investors in Selected Funds

	MASS. INVES- TORS	EATON & HOWARD	KEY- STONE FUNDS	BOSTON FUND	AMERICAN BUSINESS SHARES
Fiduciaries					
Individual	2,115	603	1,151	364	324
Banks	1,807	98		94	100
Non-Profit Groups					
Religious	301	151	138	79	41
Hospitals	199	61	8	46	28
Libraries	56	23	10	—	—
Educational	122	51	30	17	53
Charities	93	—	60	—	—
Other	—	58	73	16	—
Other Institutions					
Insurance Cos.	67	27[e]	12	15	—
Clubs, lodges	109	35	52	45	—
Investment Cos.	44	—	—	—	—
Pension funds	46	17[e]	15	14	—
Other	436	50[e]	310	62	76
Total Inst'l. Inv'rs.	5,395	1,174	1,859	751	622
Percentage of:					
Total share- holders	7%	10%	4%	6%	2%
Total shares held (e-estimated)	14%	20%	8%	10%	—

SOURCE: Prospectuses and sales literature.

fallen, common stock yields have risen from 4.3% to 6.6%, an increase some 10% greater than the cost-of-living rise.[2] However, many institutions have been reluctant to purchase common stocks, partially due to legal limitations and partially due to a fear

---

2. Porter, *op. cit.*, p. a20.

of losing principal. For the small and medium-sized institutions, particularly, the investment company can allay these fears; it provides diversification to protect principal against risk, skilled management and reasonable income, and a tendency for both value and yield to keep pace with the cost of living.

These advantages are just like those which the mutual fund offers to individual investors, and it is clear that the institutional investor is merely the fiduciary for a single individual or group of individuals. This chapter will not, therefore, cite the particular advantages of investment in mutual funds, but rather stress the development of their use by institutions. From the many types of institutional investors, two will be examined here: trust funds, because of their present importance as investment company shareholders (they comprise about one-half the total of institutional holders); and pension funds, because of their growing importance in the economy.

Trust Funds

Fiduciaries cannot be put in a vacuum and set apart from other investors. They too must scan the turbulent horizon of our financial and industrial life and do the best they can.[3]

This statement indicates the growing realization of the need for trustees to have widened powers of investment if they are to fulfill the spirit and purpose of the trust. In recent years, it has become increasingly difficult for them to efficiently administer estates through the use of bonds alone. It appears clear, however, that a certain proportion (possibly from 10% to 50%) of common stocks in the trust fund will provide a reasonable and adequate income without sacrificing long-term safety of principal. In fact, it seems impossible for today's trustee to discharge that joint duty, with taxation and living costs as they are, unless some common stock investment is undertaken. Table XVIII illustrates the

---

3. Stevenson, Alec B., *Investment Company Shares*, p. 48. Quoted from court decision on *Carwithen's Estate* 327 Pa. 490, 495, 194A. 743 (1937).

TABLE XVIII   Income from a $100,000 Trust Fund Invested in Corporate Bonds (Selected Years)

	1929	1939	1949
Percentage yield	4.92%	3.28%	2.77%
Income	$4,920	$3,280	$2,770
Income after taxes	$4,613	$3,012	$2,253
Income in 1929 dollars	$4,613	$3,720	$1,630

SOURCE: Ayer, Hazen H., "Protect Purchasing Power?" *Trusts and Estates,* LXXXIX (April, 1950), p. 258.

terrific toll of income taken by falling yields, rising taxation, and declining purchasing power.

For the individual trust funds and small bank trust departments, investment companies can provide this common stock investment either as a supplement to corporate and government bonds (as in common stock funds) or as a supplement to only government bonds (as in balanced funds). Trustee use of investment company shares is limited by two factors: the investment caliber of the mutual funds and the legal limitations on trustee investment.

That the first factor should be a limiting one seems impractical: it is clear that a carefully selected mutual fund share is of high investment caliber. The ever-widening use of investment company shares by individuals, who are the ultimate beneficiaries of any trust, indicates the satisfactory performance of mutual funds. They are widely diversified, thus yielding relative stability of price and income; they give "automatic" supervision and research to their own portfolios; and they also give mechanical advantages to trustees, such as simplified taxation, custodianship, and less cumbersome record-keeping. It is certain that if the trustee undertakes careful examination of open-end company objective, policy, past history, and portfolio, he can find a fund that suits the interests of his trust. He can choose from the balanced, the common stock, and the specialty funds, selecting a policy of capital preservation or income, or one oriented in accordance with ". . . an individual's portfolio representing his entire long-term investment program."[4] The prime concern seems to be that principal may not be conserved if common stocks are used. However, a diversified list of common stocks—similar to those of any investment company portfolio—does not fluctuate over long periods, if a system of dollar-cost-averaging is used. Proof of this assertion is furnished by Emerson W. Axe, whose study of common stock investment indicated that a quarterly investment of $1,000 in various twenty-year periods always yielded a value greater than its price (Table XIX).[5]

Legal limitations make the institutional investor's position with regard to investment company shares highly complex. Investment in mutual fund shares is complicated by a diversity of state laws and ramified by a variety of judicial decisions. Only two cases of trustee use of investment company shares are clear: it is not allowed when the state provides a legal list from which investments must be chosen, if not specifically provided for in the trust instrument; and it is allowed where specifically permitted by state law or by the trust instrument. In between these two poles, however, there lies a sea of uncertainty. In large part the dilemma is based on two widely separated groups of state laws. One is the "Legal List" type, in which trust investment is regulated by a list of legal investments and trustees are virtually forbidden to purchase equity shares or investment company shares in the absence of specific provision in the testament; the list, which is the same for trusts as for banks and insurance companies, is generally restricted to government and municipal bonds and railroad and public utility bonds which meet prescribed earning requirements. The second type is the "Prudent Man" type, in which the trustee may make those investments which a prudent man of intelligence and discretion would employ in his own affairs, with adequate regard for income and safety of principal. There are some 23 Prudent Man States at the present, listed in Table XX.

---

4. Scudder, Stevens & Clark Fund, *Prospectus,* October 3, 1949, p. 3.
5. Axe, *op. cit.,* p. 508. *Cf. supra,* p. 380.

TABLE XIX   Stock Costs and Stock Values

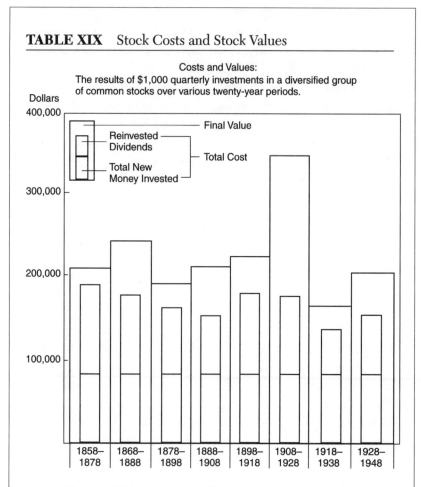

Costs and Values:
The results of $1,000 quarterly investments in a diversified group of common stocks over various twenty-year periods.

SOURCE: Emerson W. Axe in *Trusts and Estates,* August, 1950.

The two types of rules evidence a long evolution of legal decisions spreading over more than a century. A Massachusetts judge in the case of *Harvard College v. Amory* in 1830 declared that the only test of trust investment was the practice of prudent men, while 39 years later a New York state court declared that classes of securities may be declared unfit for trust investment, in *King v. Talbot.* There has been an increasing trend toward the Prudent Man Rule in recent years, with thirteen states having instituted the rule since 1943. The reason for this trend seems to

TABLE XX   States Using the Prudent Man Rule

California	Kentucky	Missouri	Oregon
Connecticut	Maine	Nevada	Rhode Island
Delaware	Maryland	*New Hampshire	Texas
Idaho	Massachusetts	*New York	Vermont
Illinois	Michigan	North Carolina	Washington
Kansas	Minnesota	Oklahoma	

*With respect to a limited percentage of the assets of the trust.

be the fact that legal lists were predicated on 5% or 6% yields from high-grade bonds, and such yields are no longer forthcoming. The actual importance to investment companies of the liberality of the Prudent Man Rule seems clear from the fact that of the fourteen states with the highest ratio of investment company shareholders to total population, thirteen make use of the Prudent Man Rule.[6]

Recent legal developments have gone far to clarify the trustee's position in investing in mutual fund shares. With regard to the only significant limitation—that of delegation of authority—particular progress has been made. This question looms as important to the trustee, since he is not allowed to delegate to others those powers incident to duties he ought reasonably be expected to perform himself. The question turns on whether or not the trustee has abandoned to the investment company the selection of investments for the trust and the control of the trust; that is, has made an unwarranted delegation of his power. The important case developing the delegation concept with respect to the mutual fund was *Marshall v. Frazier*,[7] in which the court said that the trustee had in effect delegated his management duties as trustee when he purchased stock in Quarterly Income Shares, Inc., an open-end fund. Later decisions in other states, however, have taken the opposite view. In 1948, sixteen Massachusetts Probate Judges agreed that a fellow judge was correct when he ruled that investment in mutual fund securities did not

---

6. Survey by the author based on NASD study. *Cf. supra,* p. 381.
7. 159 Ore. 491, 80P. (2nd) 42, 81P (2nd) 132 (1938).

constitute a delegation of authority on the part of the trustee that would warrant objection on that point alone. Moreover, they reserved the right to apply the Prudent Man Rule in the use of investment company shares as well as in all other securities. In 1949, the Court of Appeals of the Eighth Judicial District of Ohio upheld a probate court decision in the William D. Rees case, to the effect that the purchase of investment company shares is not an improper delegation of authority and power by the trustee. The testament had allowed the trustee to use his own judgment, unhampered by the legal list, and the court ruled that the power to invest in stocks gives the trustee the power to invest in an investment company. With regard to the state Model Prudent Man Statute,[8] the District Court of Oklahoma County, Oklahoma stated, in 1949, that trustee investment in mutual funds was a discharge of his discretionary power in the sense required by law.

In addition to judicial developments, there have been numerous recent legislative developments. The first state to specifically make open-end investment company shares legal trust investments was Nebraska, in 1945. Besides limiting the mutual funds for legal investment to those fulfilling certain requirements, the Nebraska act restricted the maximum investment by fiduciaries to 20% of a single account. New Hampshire in 1949 authorized trustees to use the Prudent Man Rule with regard to 50% of the assets of the trust, and specifically allowed them to use the shares of qualified investment companies. Shortly after the passage of that law, the State allowed its savings banks to invest up to 5% of their deposits in mutual fund securities, provided that the fund was more than ten years old, had more than $10 million in assets, had paid annual dividends from income for ten consecutive years, and had a loading charge not in excess of 7.5% of net asset value. Even more recently, the New York State Legislature passed a bill allowing the application of the Prudent Man Rule to 35% of the assets of its strict trusts. The implications of this bill may be widespread, since $13 billion of all the trust funds in the United States

---

8. Sec 161, Title 60 Okla. Statutes Cumulative Supplement 1949.

(just over one-third of the total) are in New York, and that state is the virtual founder of the Legal List Rule, often called the New York Rule, in fact. The reasons given for the passage of the bill were the fact that bond principal safety was not as high as anticipated, with some $800 million worth of par value bonds on the legal list having been defaulted in the 1928–1940 period; that bond income had fallen sharply; and that legal list bonds frequently sold at a premium due to eligibility for trust requirements, thereby decreasing the percentage yield even further.[9]

With the legal doors opening to allow trust fund investment in mutual fund shares, there are still deterrents, however. A survey of probate attorneys and trust officers by Scudder, Stevens & Clark Fund in 1949 revealed that of the 66% who did not use investment company shares, one-third had no objections to their use in trust administration. The remainder gave the following reasons as the major ones in deterring them from the use of mutuals:

1. Load   28.5%
2. Delegation   26.5%
3. Management fee   21.8%
4. Unfamiliarity   12.9%
5. Indifference   10.3%

However, 68% of those answering favored specific statutory authorization to use investment company shares in their state. Scudder, Stevens & Clark Fund drew the following conclusions with regard to its survey, only a few of the questions of which are listed above: more certain judicial precedent or clearer language in will and trust instrument would increase the use of investment company shares; the fiduciaries are interested in them particularly for the diversification of the common stock portion of small trusts; corporate trustees with limited research facilities need the investment company type of vehicle; and favorable legislation would yield wider acceptance of investment company shares.

---

9. "N. Y. State Trust Law," *Business Week*, March 11, 1950, p. 111.

The greatest use of mutual funds would certainly seem to come from small trust institutions and individual fiduciaries. These groups usually can ill-afford the cost of managing and diversifying minimal accounts, especially since administrative expense is proportionately higher, the smaller the account. A majority of trusts do in fact have less than $50,000 in assets, with 73.5% of all trusts producing annual incomes of less than $3,000 per year, and 54% yielding less than $1,200 annually.[10] 85% of bank trust departments have assets of less than $5 million, with two-thirds having less than $1 million.[11] Therefore the income accruing to beneficiaries through these small fiduciary groups seems too small to enable the latter to furnish an adequate staff for proper equity investment. Small trust departments and fiduciaries are the two groups which must comprise the bulk of institutional investment in mutual fund shares: they can make optimum use of the low management costs, the diversification of portfolio, and the relative adequacy of income. To cultivate these accounts, investment companies have in many cases made use of a proportionately decreased load as the size of the investment increases.[12]

The use of investment company shares by fiduciaries seems destined to increase in the future. As the mutual funds gradually grow in stature and through performance prove themselves, and with the widened tendency for liberality in state use of an enlightened prudent man rule, the limit to small trust investment in investment company shares is set only by the need for the strictest conservation of principal.

Retirement Plans

One of the most significant facets in the trend toward security in the American economy today is the widespread increase in retirement plans, which now number over 13,000, compared with 1,300 in 1942.[13] The significance of the mutual fund in

10. Wiesenberger, *op. cit.,* p. 63.
11. *Loc. cit.*
12. *Cf. supra,* p. 368.
13. Wellington Fund, *The Mutual Fund in Retirement Plans* (Brochure published in September, 1950), p. 1.

this area lies both in the profit-sharing plan, where the annual cost is in direct relation to the profits of the company, and in the pension plan, where the annual cost is relatively fixed. In many cases, the two are combined, with the latter offering a floor of minimum payments, the former adding benefits as earnings increase. The investment company can be of particular service to the many retirement plans in use by medium and small business, because of its provision of skilled management not ordinarily available to non-professional pension trustees and the wide diversification of both equity securities and bonds in its portfolio. In addition, the performance records and policies are available, and retirement plan trustees may judge them empirically.

Besides general applicability to retirement plans, mutual funds are particularly applicable from the union point of view, as evidenced by the following quotation:

> **Naturally, the manner in which union money can be made available to industry through Mutual Fund investments needs to be investigated and worked out in detail. But, generally speaking, there is little question that Mutual Funds are tailor-made for labor treasuries faced with the problem of investing their growing resources at substantial returns while safeguarding the interests of the membership. They are particularly desirable media from the union point of view because of their independence in choosing appropriate investments and their freedom from any obligation to industrial management.[14]**

As with trust funds, the primary problem of pension funds is inflation. The fixed yields of the present day are predicated on the constant value of the dollar, which has proved to be wholly inconstant during the past decade. Retirement funds, then, cannot expect dollar security in the future, and for this reason some use of equity investment by them seems necessary. The growing importance of this type of investment indicates that the mutual funds will far surpass their recent total of 184 employee-benefit

---

14. Lipsett, Alexander S., *Labor's Partnership in Industrial Enterprise,* p. 16.

plan investors, whose shares total over $4 million in value.[15] The second problem of pension funds, also like that of trust funds, is falling bond yields, with the days of high interest rates probably gone forever. Still a third problem confronts retirement plans, the actuarial phenomenon of longer life. Pension benefits have to be paid over a longer period of time, with a man of 40 now being expected to live to the age of 73 years, compared with 71 years in 1937 and 68 years in 1868.[16] Thus pension funds have to cope not only with lower real revenues, but also with increasing costs.

Types of pension plans vary widely. In mid-1946, some 9,370 qualified plans listed by the Department of Internal Revenue were distributed as shown in Table XXI.

Most companies, it can be seen, have insurance or annuity contracts; however, the larger companies favor the trust fund type, since their employment is large enough that they may make actuarial computations accurately. This type is flexible, with investment policy controlled by the trust agreement: investment company shares could be used in cases which do not restrict the fund to legal lists or government bonds, and where the pension fund is not large enough to finance its own diversification and

---

15. Cates, Dudley F., "Mutual Fund Investment," *Trusts and Estates,* LXXXIX (May, 1950), p. 329. Figures for 22 funds with 75% of the industry's assets.
16. Wellington Fund, *Fundamentals of Retirement Plans,* p. 5.

TABLE XXI Types of Retirement Plans

FUNDING METHOD	NUMBER OF PLANS	EMPLOYEES COVERED	AVERAGE NO. OF EMPLOYEES PER PLAN
Individual Policy Insured	44%	6%	49
Group Annuity	16%	24%	602
Trust Fund Pension	7%	52%	2,900
Combination	6%	8%	496
Profit-sharing	27%	10%	146

SOURCE: Wellington Fund.

management. More suitable for the small companies which lack large capital and dependable earnings, and are therefore unable to guarantee an annual deposit in the fund, are the profit-sharing plans. The company pays the trustee a given percentage of profits (with a ceiling limit) each year. Mutual fund shares in this case form a particularly good method of supervision of capital, diversification against risk, and reasonable income.

That the attractions of common stocks now outweigh the risks of holding them can be seen by an examination of the results of a $120,000 annual payment into three mediums over a twenty-year period (Table XXII). It should be noted that the common stock segment investment began when the market was at 248; it was at only 200 when the investment ended, and had fluctuated widely over the period. Yet the common stock investment evinced a gain roughly fourfold as great as the other methods.

Retirement funds are ideally suited for the process of dollar-cost-averaging. This plan requires the purchase of a given dollar-amount of stock at given intervals, regardless of cost. Thus, more shares are gained for the same price when the market is low. If the long-term trend of the market is upwards, the average cost will remain below the average price, regardless of fluctuation. The investment company shares may be purchased by the retire-

TABLE XXII   Returns from Investment in Three Media: December 31, 1929–December 31, 1949

	DOW-JONES AVERAGE	INSURANCE ANNUITY	GOVERNMENT BONDS
Amount invested	$2,400,000	$2,400,000	$2,400,000
Income return	$1,593,375	$874,500	$708,258
Rate of return	5.06%	3.15%	2.65%
Fund value: 12/31/49	$5,323,874	$3,274,500	$3,108,258
Rate of return	7.72%	3.15%	2.65%
Value plus reinvested dividends	$6,769,177	$3,502,376	$3,251,824
Rate of return	9.86%	3.81%	3.08%
Net gain	182%	46%	35%

SOURCE: Wiesenberger, *Investment Companies-1950*, p. 56.

ment fund at, for example, quarterly intervals, thereby solving the problem of timing for the fund. The problem of selection is also virtually eliminated by the diversification of portfolio shares by investment companies.

Certainly the ideal solution to the retirement fund problems is a combination of stocks and bonds. Wellington Fund has suggested the following portfolio as ideal: for safety, 37.5% government bonds and 12.5% corporate bonds, and for income, 20% preferred stocks and 30% common stocks. This portfolio is said to provide an average yield of some 3.76% at current rates. This yield, as well as any capital gains, is tax-free for those pension plans qualified with the United States Treasury Department, so common stock investment is proportionately more valuable for them than for either trust funds or individual investors. The higher yield is estimated to reduce pension costs about 30%, because of the 1.25% increase in income over that which bonds would offer.[17]

The lack of restrictive limitations on retirement plan investment indicates a considerable use of mutual fund shares in the future, probably in combination with some bond investment. Particularly for the pension plans and profit-sharing plans of small companies, the solution to the problem of prudent investment—stability of principal with reasonable income at low cost—is the investment company.

---

17. Wellington Fund, *op. cit.,* p. 5.

Chapter

III

AS A SOURCE OF EQUITY CAPITAL

THE FUNCTIONS that the investment company has fulfilled for the individual investor and small institution has been indicated. However, there are additional functions which the companies should fulfill, since, as well as providing the investors with a safe and profitable investment, it is possible for mutual funds to put the capital thus gained to economic use. By and large, however, such has not been the case. One clear and present use for some of the investment company capital, the author submits, is in the field of venture capital. This need was clearly stated in the SEC report to Congress in 1942:

> **It is manifest that if investment companies persist in engaging only in the activity merely of buying and selling outstanding seasoned securities, these organizations at most will perform only a most limited function and will not play the vital and important role that may be possible by virtue of their control of such large pools of funds. The traditional policy of many such companies of investing substantially all of their funds in market leaders, although performing some functions for investors desiring to invest in common stocks, does not realize the real contribution which these organizations can make to the national economy. With the need for capital for industry, particularly small industries and new ventures, and with the difficulties of these industries in obtaining the capital required for their development of expansion, the failure of investment companies to play a more important part in these financing activities creates serious doubts as to their effec-**

tiveness and significance in the economic advancement of the country.[1]

It will be the purpose of this chapter to examine the need for venture capital in the economy, the agencies capable of fulfilling the need and the limitations of each, the two major instances of investment company participation in the venture field, and the future of the investment company in the venture field.

The Need for Equity Capital

A growing economy needs a high level of capital expenditure by business. This requirement has always been met in the United States economy through three principal channels: retained earnings, borrowing and the sale of fixed-payment obligations, and the sale of shares of ownership. In recent years, however, there have been two serious dislocations in the equity capital market, in which shares of ownership are sold: an irregularly large amount of debt financing by large business firms; and a shortage of funds available to small business. Both of these instances indicate the lack of equity capital.

Statistical evidence of this lacking is evident. While stock issues amounted to 50% of new corporate financing in 1929, they were only 12% in 1946, 10.5% in 1947, and 8.1% in 1948.[2] In the 1939–1948 period, manufacturers' debt rose 138%, while stockholders' equity rose but 76%.[3] Open-market issue contributions to the capital expenditure of business declined from $1.5 billion per year in the 1925–1929 period to $.5 billion in both 1936 and 1937.[4] With regard to small business needs, from 1935 to 1939 only $52 million of the $185 million worth of issues of less than $1 million each were sold, with 36% of the 670 issuers selling none at all.[5]

Probable reasons for the shortage of equity capital include the decline in bond interest rates, partially because of the United

---

1. SEC, *op. cit.*, (Part 4), p. 375.
2. Subcommittee on Investment of the Joint Committee on the Economic Report, *Volume and Stability of Private Investment*, p. 9.
3. "Are Stockholders Necessary?" *Business Week*, March 18, 1950, p. 118.
4. SEC, *op. cit.*, p. 340.
5. *Ibid.*, p. 344.

States Treasury Department policy of keeping interest rates on government bonds low; and the taxation policies of the New Deal and Fair Deal, which have redistributed, in part, the national income to persons unaccustomed to investing funds,[6] who place them in institutional hands rather than in equities. The great attractiveness of the bond form of finance springs also from the facts that bond charges are deductible before taxation, and bonds may be privately placed with institutional investors, thus saving time and expense.

There are objections to the financing of companies by retained earnings and bonds, however. With regard to the former, the company is allowed to expand without economic justification, in some cases, since the capital market does not determine the amount of funds allocated to the firm. Industry has recently been retaining a proportionately greater share of its earnings, distributing 66% of earnings to stockholders in 1929, 75% in 1939, and but 40% in the 1946–1948 period.[7] Retained earnings, in fact, accounted for one-half of corporation investment in 1948.[8] Secondly, of course, retained earnings are of no consequence to new companies; and thirdly, they are an irregular and unstable source of capital. The objections to fixed-obligation finance are the financial rigidities and the economic concentration caused thereby, and the fact that fixed charges may cause new businesses to fail before they have sufficient opportunity to succeed. Moreover, there must be an adequate base of equity capital for the senior securities; the $14.8 billion of new corporate debt in the 1946–1948 period therefore appears grossly inadequate with respect to only $3.6 billion of new stock.[9] Equity finance, on the other hand, lacks these disadvantages: the company expansion is determined in large part by the public, to whom the new shares

6. A 1950 Survey of Consumer Finances showed that only 10% of those earning less than $7,500 per year held common stocks. *Investment Dealers Digest*, XVII (March 5, 1951), p. 46.
7. Sulzbach, Dr. Walter, "Decline of Equity Finance," *Barron's*, XXX (March 20, 1950), p. 9.
8. Subcommittee on Investment, *op. cit.*, p. 10.
9. United States Bureau of the Census, *Statistical Abstract of the United States: 1950*, p. 425.

must be sold; dividends are payable only when earned, giving flexibility. Moreover, common stocks give the investing public an opportunity to participate in the economic growth of industry.

A great amount of liquid wealth, then, is concentrating in the hands of institutional investors, who put the money, by and large, in high-grade bonds. Of $168 billion of savings in 1948, $12 billion was in savings and loan associations, $50 billion in life insurance, $19 billion is mutual savings banks, $35 billion in commercial banks, $3 billion in postal savings, and $49 billion in United States savings bonds.[10] Thus promising enterprises, technical innovations, and advanced methods face failure for the want of adequate financial backing. The economic system needs ventures of this nature if it is to remain dynamic, maintaining full employment and high levels of production. But the inherent risks in the developing of new enterprises and the revamping of old ones have meant that the institutional investors have shied away, although they have the financial resources to furnish the capital and diversify the risks. These institutions therefore ought to reexamine ". . . their traditional policies in the light of contemporary needs and circumstances."[11]

Fulfilling the Need for Equity Capital

Four groups of investors are capable of alleviating the need for equity capital: individual investors, insurance companies, government organizations, and investment companies. It is clear that the responsibility for the supply of venture capital is not confined to any single group, but probably a share ought to devolve on each, in relation to its capacity.

First, individual investors. The wealthy investors, who must gain a fair share of the credit for the capital expansion of the economy up to about 1930, have by and large been unable to fill that need any longer. The high taxes they must pay on incomes have meant they are not disposed to make venture investments. An example of the force of taxation is shown by the Subcommit-

---

10. *Ibid.*, p. 401.
11. Subcommittee on Investment, *op. cit.*, p. 8.

tee on Investment in its report to Congress. Table XXIII shows that the motive to invest is greatly diminished. That the capacity to invest of top-bracket income earners is also diminished is indicated in Table XXIV.

The result of this high rate of taxation is also revealed in the Committee report, which notes that upper-income investors have turned to state and municipal tax-exempt securities: on June 30, 1949, individuals (presumably those in upper-income brackets) held 43% of the state and municipal bonds outstanding.[12] The only way in which the large investor could be persuaded to risk more of his capital would be by a reduction, if not of over-all income taxation, at least of double taxation on securities income. This reduction seems totally impossible at the present.

---

12. *Ibid.*, p. 30.

TABLE XXIII   Return on Investment for Varying Incomes

Annual income	$10,000	$50,000	$200,000
Amount invested	$10,000	$10,000	$10,000
Corp. profit: 10%	$1,000	$1,000	$1,000
Corporate tax	$380	$380	$380
Distrib. dividends	$620	$620	$620
Income tax	$205	$409	$508
% of income tax	33%	66%	82%
Income after tax	$415	$211	$112
% Return on investment	4.15%	2.11%	1.12%

SOURCE: Subcommittee on Investment, *op. cit.*, p. 30.

TABLE XXIV   Effects of Taxation and Inflation on Incomes of More Than $25,000 Per Year

	1929	1949
Number of returns	111,000	174,000
Income subject to tax	$8.6 billion	$9.5 billion
Total income after tax	$7.6 billion	$4.8 billion
Average income after tax	$68,239	$27,623
Average income in 1929 $'s	$68,239	$19,787

SOURCE: *Sales Management*, February 11, 1950, p. 69.

As the high-income people have lost, so the low-income people have gained, with 65% of the 1948 national income going to those earning less than $10,000 per year.[13] But they cannot be expected to venture their minimal savings directly. Although indirect venture investment may be possible in the future, at the present the

> ... savings of the little people are not being channeled into new ventures because the system by which that flow could be directed has not been established.[14]

However, two members of the Subcommittee on Investment believed that

> ... some method should be developed by which the savings of private investors could be channeled into investment trusts or investment companies (which would invest in many different enterprises and thus) spread the risk so that no individual investor would suffer the entire loss of his capital through the failure of some one investment.[15]

This problem will be examined below.

The provision of equity capital by life insurance companies is a perplexing problem. The enormous size of their assets—at $57.3 billion in 1949 and growing at the rate of $3 billion each year[16]—indicates their potential effect on the equity field, but as yet their contribution has been negligible. Their purchases of bond issues through the medium of private placement, however, are tremendous, and they are said to have absorbed most of the recent debt securities. Yet because of conservative investment policy based on strict legal requirements, less than ½ of 1% of the assets of life insurance companies are invested in common stock equities.[17] Even this small amount is probably invested in the stock of established large corporations. In order that life insurance companies

---

13. *Ibid.*, p. 12.
14. *Ibid.*, p. 2.
15. *Ibid.*, p. 34. The two members are Senator R. A. Taft (Ohio) and Representative C. A. Herter (Massachusetts).
16. *Ibid.*, p. 6.
17. *Ibid.*, p. 12.

provide additional equity capital, there would have to be a great change in state laws followed by a corresponding change in the ultraconservative financial policy of insurance companies. The most that can be anticipated along this line would be provision for investing up to 5% in common stocks.

The role of the government in providing equity capital to industry is a nebulous and potentially dangerous one. The Subcommittee on Investment makes recommendations to the effect that the Reconstruction Finance Corporation be broadened so that it can answer the specific needs of small business and provide longer maturities for business loans. Other recommendations concern government insurance of small business loans and stock equities and cooperative business loan organizations of the Federal Housing Administration type. Although the recommendations, if followed, would doubtless increase the capital available to small business, there are the usual difficulties inherent in any government-sponsored finance.[18] The Committee recognized this fact, saying that the government was not only ill-adapted but almost adversely equipped to try to handle investment.

The government does not have the know-how required to make a venture enterprise succeed and lacks the fortitude to say "no" or to liquidate, especially at times when . . . such decisions might be fraught with administrative or political difficulties.[19]

Another potential source of equity capital is the closed-end investment company. Suffice it to say that although the fact that closed-end shares are non-redeemable makes that industry more able to provide equity capital than its open-end counterpart, its assets have been shrinking in recent years, thus impairing its ultimate potential. In addition, it often has fixed obligations, which might be difficult to fulfill were a large proportion of venture investment made. However, the closed-end company may be put

---

18. These difficulties have been brought into particularly sharp focus by the recent Senate Banking subcommittee's revealing investigation of influence in the RFC.

19. Subcommittee on Investment, *op. cit.*, p. 26.

to economic use in conjunction with the open-end company. This combination will be examined below.

Mutual Funds and Equity Capital

Investment companies are a likely source of equity capital for a number of reasons: first, because their portfolios are composed largely (80%–90%) of common stocks, which have been indicated as the most economically sound method for the provision of risk capital; second, because they have the business ability, research facilities, financial resources, and trained personnel to investigate venture projects; third, because their degree of diversification is such that the risk of any single venture commitment would be minimal; and fourth, because they have a growing amount of capital and an apparently increasing importance in the economy.

However, certain limitations have in the past militated against the participation of investment companies in the venture field. Although the Investment Company Act refrains from any influence on mutual fund investment policy, it does have certain restrictive elements: section 12(c) limits the amount of underwriting commitments; section 12(d) states that a mutual fund may not hold more than 3% of another (venture) investment company's outstanding voting stock; and section 10(a) sets the above-mentioned limits on 75% of the portfolio: no more than 5% of assets may be placed in any one corporation, nor may more than 10% of any issuer's voting stock be held, the significance of these limits being that the investment company would usually invest in a risk company with a view toward some influence in order to perform managerial service during the young and inexperienced years of the new firm. Although the importance of these restrictions is not great, there is a very important restriction instituted at the state level: numerous states have "blue-sky" requirements which make it unlawful for investment companies to buy stock in corporations of less than three years existence. Recently Ohio, New Hampshire, and Minnesota modified this provision, making it inapplicable to 5% of a fund's assets. The National Association of Securities Commissioners, at their 1945 convention, unanimously passed a resolution favoring this modification in all states.

More important than legal requirements are the self-imposed portfolio regulations of many funds, which restrict underwriting, investment in companies of less than three years existence, the purchase of more than 10% of the outstanding stock of any company, and the purchase of unlisted shares. In addition to these restrictions, there is a general feeling that risk investment is against the best interests of the shareholders, and in many cases shareholders are led to expect that investment will be made only in seasoned securities. Co-existent with this idea is the thought that the investment company does its service to the venture market by channeling the funds of its holders into the listed securities markets. The market for seasoned equities is in this way kept "healthy," and therefore provides a good "climate" for the issue of new securities. Although this is a valid concept, it is a very negative one, and is but an insubstantial reason for abstaining from the venture capital field.

The redemption feature, however, is a very significant reason for staying out of the equity field. The difficulty of valuation of unseasoned securities, particularly unlisted ones, and the consequent difficulty of liquidating them, save at great sacrifice, mean that the investment company can hold at most a small percentage of risk capital. The system of daily asset-value pricing also means that only a small percentage of assets may be placed in securities of unascertainable market value, if the listed price is to be a fair indication of the portfolio worth.

Finally, the taxation of open-end companies militates against their holding of more than a small amount of risk capital. The virtual necessity of distributing capital gains when they are realized would sharply reduce the working capital of an investment company selling its venture shares when the issue becomes seasoned.[20]

For these reasons, the past experience of the open-end investment company has been largely outside the scope of the venture capital field. Figures available for the 1927–1937 period indicate

---

20. *Cf. supra*, p. 373.

that less than 1% of the industry's assets were placed in new securities.[21] Although the mutual funds did purchase 4,567 new issues, 2,245 were purchased via the exercise of rights and options, thus making the 1% figure even less significant.[22]

Many of the above-cited reasons may be minimized or eliminated, however, and in two instances, the investment company has entered the equity market: once in the case of American Research & Development Corporation, a closed-end venture company which sold its shares to numerous open-end companies; and more recently in the case of Affiliated Gas Equipment Company, which executed a private placement of a new issue of its common stock with open-end companies as participants.

American Research and Development Corporation

This unique venture into the equity field was formed in June 1946 by a group of public figures, including Ralph Flanders, United States Senator from Vermont, Karl T. Compton, Chairman of Massachusetts Institute of Technology, and Merrill Griswold, Chairman of Massachusetts Investors Trust. The policy of American Research and Development[23] is to engage in the furnishing of venture capital to industry, financing development enterprises, and purchasing securities for which no ready market is in existence, and to use its funds for scientific research, engineering, industrial economics, or business research, while keeping its investments in any one company to less than 10% of its capital.

The main purpose of AR&D is to free some of the great amounts of institutional savings for use in the venture market, and it therefore invited numerous investment companies, life insurance companies, closed-end companies, and universities to participate. Included in its present list of shareholders are the following institutions, which hold some 40% of AR&D's 177,000 shares outstanding:

---

21. SEC, *op. cit.*, p. 350.
22. *Loc. cit.*
23. Hereinafter referred to as AR&D.

Massachusetts Investors Trust (14,615 shares)

Consolidated Investment Trust (2,000)

Investors Mutual (8,000)

Massachusetts Investors Second Fund (6,000)

John Hancock Mutual Life Insurance Co. (10,000)

Home Insurance Co.

Massachusetts Institute of Technology

University of Pennsylvania

University of Rochester

Rice Institute

Adams Express

American International Corporation

To form the Corporation, several legal manipulations were required. First and most important was the exemption granted by the SEC (commensurate with its power under section 6(c) of the Investment Company Act) from section 12(e), which allows an investment company to hold more than 3% of the voting stock of another investment company formed for the purpose of providing risk capital to industry only if all of the latter's securities are issued to registered investment companies.[24] The SEC waived this requirement with the agreement that a minimum of $1,500,000 of the AR&D financing would come from institutional investors. The remainder of section 12(e), requiring a limit of one class of stock in the venture company, a limit of 5% of any investment company's assets in said venture company, and a maximum of $100 million capitalization all had to be complied with. Secondly, since no capital had then been subscribed, the SEC exempted the Corporation from section 14(a), which requires a minimum initial net worth of $10,000.

---

24. This section is itself an exception to 12(d)(1), which requires that no investment company hold more than 3% of the outstanding voting securities of another investment company.

It seems likely that section 12(e) was written solely to provide for investment in the venture capital field, since by its very wording it speaks of corporations engaged

in the business of underwriting, furnishing capital to industry, financing promotional enterprises, and purchasing securities of issuers for which no ready market is in existence.

The statement of David Schenker, counsel to the investment trust study by the SEC, also indicates that such was the case. In a preliminary hearing in 1940, he said that since open-end companies must be in a liquid condition in order to redeem shares, the demand for which cannot be anticipated, the closed-end form is likely as a possibility for larger open-end companies joining

together to create a substantial pool of venture capital by participation in the type of company for which this bill (the Investment Company Act of 1940) provides.[25]

The activities of AR&D are said to be four:

finding new projects, analyzing those projects, setting up and assisting in the operation of affiliates, and obtaining more capital for the (AR&D) Corporation.[26]

Its main interest has been investment in companies expected to have a sales volume of from $500,000 to $2 million per year, and development of commercially practicable processes and products with the prospect of ultimate profit. The Corporation attempts to provide two of the members of its Board of Directors on the board of each affiliate, in order to give management advice as well as to manifest some control. AR&D in many cases has a controlling stock interest, as well as holding notes, debentures, and preferred shares.

Due to the risk inherent in all venture enterprises, the AR&D has diversified its ventures to a high degree, with regard to loca-

---

25. SEC, *American Research & Development Corporation*, File #812-440, p. 9. (mimeo.)
26. *Fourth Annual Report: 1949*, p. 6.

tion and process as well as to company. Examples of the nineteen companies in which it holds stock at the present are listed in Table XXV.

At the end of 1949, six of the projects were making money, four were breaking even, two were losing money, and seven were still in the development stage (Table XXV(a)).

Thus, the American Research and Development Corporation seems to be a step in the right direction. Though far from spectacular as yet, its assets are increasing and its deficit is shrinking. If more companies of its nature are formed, the investment company industry will be well on its way as an important factor in the growth of the economy.

TABLE XXV   Selected Investments of AR&D

NAME	PROCESS-PRODUCT	LOCATION	% OF AR&D ASSETS
Specialty Products	Vapor degreasing	Cleveland	4.1%
High Voltage Eng'g.	Generators	Cambridge	6.5%
Tracerlab	Radioactivity	Boston	7.7%
Baird Associates	Spectrochemicals	Cambridge	9.5%
Jet-Heet	Heating units	Englewood, N.J.	7.5%
Snyder Chemical	Adhesive resins	Bethel, Conn.	3.3%
Colter Corp.	Frozen shrimp	Palacios, Tex.	11.3%
Carlon Products	Plastics	Cleveland	5.8%
Island Packers	Tuna canning	American Samoa	0.9%

SOURCE: *Fifth Annual Report: 1950.*

TABLE XXV(a)   Year-End Assets and Annual Net Losses of AR&D

	1946	1947	1948	1949	1950
Total assets (million)	$3.4	$3.6	$3.3	$4.3	$4.7
Net loss (thousand)	$37	$55	$44	$38	$18

SOURCE: *Fifth Annual Report: 1950.*

Affiliated Gas Equipment Company

Just as the American Research and Development Corporation represents the entry of the mutual fund into the market for new equities, so Affiliated Gas Equipment Company represents its unprecedented entry into the field of additional equity capital for established business. The underwriting of a $2,130,000 issue of common stock for this large producer of dwelling heating units was done under the organization of Reynolds & Co., a brokerage concern, which sold the issue of 200,000 shares at $10.65 to six open-end companies, including Investors Mutual, Investors Stock Fund, Fundamental Investors, Investors Management Fund, National Investors, and Bullock Fund, between December 31, 1949 and March 8, 1950.

There were numerous complaints with regard to the divulgence of this information by Reynolds & Co., since it was both a violation of client anonimity and caused securities dealers to complain to the participating funds that they were usurping the former's function, that of placing new shares on the market. Although some of the funds have their own retailing organizations, others rely largely on securities dealers to retail their shares. The dealers' criticism, therefore, is likely to deter future transactions of this nature, for the investment companies cannot afford to lose this valuable contact with the investing public.

The underwriting was in many ways reminiscent of the private placement of bonds with insurance companies, since it eliminated the expense and waiting period of an SEC registration for a public offering. It may indicate a growing willingness of investment companies to take economic responsibilities, as they do in Great Britain, and a new policy of fund appraisal of the needs of established companies for new money through securities issues. On the other hand, and perhaps more likely, it may indicate merely a desire to purchase large blocks of securities "off-the-board" at a price lower than the market.

The proceeds of the stock issue, which increased the common stock outstanding of Affiliated by some 20%, were to be used, along with a simultaneous $1.1 million bond flotation, to provide the $19 million firm with a new plant at Indianapolis, equipment for the plant, and additional working capital. The effect of the announcement of the stock and bond flotation and the expansion was to send the stock value, which was 11¼ on March 3 and 12¼ on March 9, to 13¼ on March 18.

Judgment of the unprecedented private placement of stocks with investment companies must be witheld pending further developments. For the present, however, it seems to be a financial function that the investment company will fulfill only to a limited extent and will not and cannot threaten the existence of the investment banker and the securities dealer.

Future of the Investment Company in the Equity Field

Economic policy should recognize that the bulk of saving will come from people in the middle income brackets who are rightly more concerned with the safety of their investment than with gains that involve high risks. This calls for financial institutions that transfer these savings into venture capital. Study should be made of the experience of nationwide or local investment companies which can extend venture capital with diversification of risks. The possibilities of developing other types of organizations which would effectively channel private savings into venturesome fields of investment and the extent to which the government can promote them require thorough exploration.[27]

The increase of the equity capital function seems certain to increase in future years, especially as the size of the investment company industry increases. But to open the door for expansion, certain legal revisions may be helpful. Without going into unnecessary detail, it may be said that the most important are a revision of tax policy, first so that research and development company shareholders may be treated as if they were direct owners of the portfolio securities in which their funds are

---

27. *Economic Report of the President* (1949), p. 65.

placed (e. g., get the same provisions regulated investment company shareholders receive); and second, in order to allow investment companies a given percentage (perhaps 25%) of realized capital gains which may be retained without being fully taxable. Amendment to the Investment Company Act of 1940 is also recommended, to specifically allow the investment of perhaps 5% of a company's assets in companies of less than three years existence, including new ventures and underwritings. Finally, the inter-investment company shareholding regulation ought to be made applicable when 50% of the shares of a venture company are sold to other investment companies, rather than 100%, as the law now stands. It seems clear that these changes would in no way damage the interests of the shareholder, as set forth in Chapter I of this work, if any fund policy of venture investment is stated in the prospectus, with percentage limits noted, so that it would be entirely clear to the investor.

However, there is considerable question that the funds will invest in venture issues even if the door is opened for such investment. They must be guided, it is clear, by the profit motive and not by any altruistic motive of social need. Although carefully selected and diversified ventures would seem certain to provide a large yield over the long run, the investing public is apt to shy away from this type of investment. The justification for this assertion may be seen in an examination of two funds under the same management, that of Calvin Bullock. Dividend Shares has a policy of placing

major emphasis on relatively high income through broadly diversified investment primarily in common stocks.[28]

This relatively conservative fund is Bullock's bread-winner, with total assets of $79.7 million. Calvin Bullock management also supervises a "growth" fund, Bullock Fund, whose policy is

to place major emphasis on growth characteristics and possibility of appreciation . . . (and on) companies not so

---

28. Dividend Shares, *Prospectus*, August 28, 1950, p. 1.

well-known which appear to have considerably better-than-average growth or cyclical possibilities.[29]

The public's choice between the two fund policies is reflected in the difference between the total assets of the two: Bullock Fund has a total of $6.9 million, only 9% of the magnitude of Dividend Shares. Therefore, before the funds can go far into the venture field, they must have some sign of public approbation.

In conclusion, the author will outline three possible means of providing equity capital through the investment company medium, consistent with the legal changes advocated above. First, in the additional finance of established companies, it seems that private placement in a joint underwriting operation is satisfactory. Each company could provide a small percentage of its assets in the participation (the Affiliated Gas placement entailed less than 1% of each company's assets) and it is clear that the research organizations of the funds would not be over extended in analyzing the issuing company. Second, in new finance, there are two methods open: the mutual funds could form additional closed-end companies on the order of AR&D, investing limited amounts of their assets in such companies (.01% of MIT's assets provided 10% of AR&D's capital), as seems to be within the specific intent of the law; or the mutual funds could form an amalgamated contributory research group, perhaps under the jurisdiction of the National Association of Investment Companies, with the technical and economic skill requisite to the study of new undertakings, and then individual funds could buy into ventures on the basis of information so furnished. A trained group of this nature could do a valuable job in investigating projects, which is said to require

knowledge of the present, understanding of the past and of what goes on in a particular field, of competitive problems, trends and evolutions in technique, design, production, marketing, and customer habits.[30]

---

29. Bullock Fund, *Prospectus,* October, 1949, p. 1.
30. Ford, Horace S. (Treasurer of AR&D), *Statement before Subcommittee on Investment of Joint Committee on the Economic Report,* December 12, 1949, p. 2. (mimeo.)

Third, there may be possible a combination of the additional finance and venture finance functions in a Venture Capital Fund (similar to a specialty fund), the redeemability feature being maintained by a requirement that the management may value its risk capital holdings at a nominal sum, to prevent their sale in redemption runs. This is the only way in which a venture fund could be an open-end fund, but as indicated above, there is no reason that a group of mutual funds could not sponsor a closed-end company.

The investment company, therefore, may prove to be of economic use in supplying venture capital to new business and in providing additional capital to established firms. As long as any policy of this nature is made clear to the fund's investors, there can be little objection to the policy, particularly if investors support the objective by purchasing shares in such funds.

IV

AS AN INFLUENCE ON CORPORATE MANAGEMENT

ALTHOUGH IT IS manifest that the open-end investment company can never exercise control over a corporation the shares of which it holds in its portfolio, there is no reason it should refrain from exerting its influence, where deemed necessary, on corporate policy. The SEC, in its 1940 report to Congress, called on investment companies to serve

> **... the useful role of representatives of the great number of inarticulate and ineffective individual investors in industrial corporations in which investment companies are also interested.[1]**

Since they possess not only a greater knowledge of finance and management than the average stockholder, but also the financial means to make their influence effective, the mutual funds seem destined to fulfill this crucial segment of their economic role.

Control of corporations is impossible in the mutual fund field, since the Investment Company Act restricts fund holdings to ten percentum of any company's outstanding voting stock, with regard to 75% of the investment company's total assets, and control is presumed to exist when "any person (or company) . . . owns beneficially . . . more than 25% of the voting securities of a company."[2] Most funds, due to conservative financial policy and, in some

---

1. SEC, *op. cit.*, p. 371.
2. Section 2(a)(9). Control is defined as the ability ". . . to exercise a controlling influence over the management or policies."

cases, state laws, make the 10% limit applicable to the entirety of their assets, not merely 75%. Examples of funds with this type of policy are Axe-Houghton, Affiliated, Boston, Bullock, Dividend, Fidelity, Investors Mutual, Lexington, MIT, Putnam, and Wellington. The John H. Lewis Fund restricts its investments to 5% of the outstanding securities of any one corporation. But while control is impossible, influence is not, and it may be exerted primarily through the exercise of share proxy votes. Although the traditional practice of most funds has been to vote their proxies in favor of the management, their potential influence lies in a reversal of this policy when objection is deemed necessary.

The influence of the investment company is obviously proportional to the strength of its holdings of a company's shares in its portfolio. This total only in rare cases exceeds 5%, in spite of the broader provisions of the charters and the law. For example, the largest trust, Massachusetts Investors, held more than 5% of the outstanding securities of but one concern, the American Research and Development Corporation, the nature of which seems to require that a greater influence be possible.[3] The fifth and sixth largest funds, Wellington and Dividend Shares, reported no holdings of more than 5%. A recent survey by the National Association of Investment Companies revealed "... the almost complete absence of control by investment companies of the corporations in which they invest."[4] Of 68 open-end companies with 90% of the industry's assets, none held more than 25% of the voting power of an issue, and only $13 million (less than 1%) of assets represented more than 5% of any corporation's voting power.[5] Although it is clearly impossible to generalize, perhaps a typical example of fund influence might be Dividend Shares, which holds an average of ¼ of 1% of the outstanding stock of the issuers of its portfolio shares.[6] Its twelve largest percentage holdings are listed in Table XXVI.

---

3. *Cf. supra*, pp. 410–413.
4. Stires, Hardwick, *Statement before Subcommittee on Investment*, p. 4. (mimeo.)
5. *Loc. cit.*
6. Author's computation from *Prospectus*, April 30, 1950.

TABLE XXVI   Companies in Which Dividend Shares Has the Greatest Potential Influence.

NAME	SHARES IN PORTFOLIO	OUTSTANDING SHARES	PERCENT IN PORTFOLIO
Mueller Brass Co.	25,000	531,000	4.7%
Louisville Gas & Electric	25,000	1,170,000	2.1%
National Gypsum Co.	40,000	2,112,000	1.9%
Shamrock Oil Corp.	24,000	1,346,000	1.8%
General Telephone Corp.	20,000	1,196,000	1.7%
Sharpe & Dohme, Inc.	18,500	1,080,000	1.7%
General Portland Cement	15,000	1,037,000	1.5%
Cleveland-Graphite Bronze	10,000	667,000	1.5%
Illinois Power Co.	32,500	2,196,000	1.5%
Flintkote Co.	17,200	1,260,000	1.4%
American Brake Shoe Co.	14,400	996,000	1.4%
Cincinnati Gas & Electric	34,000	2,991,000	1.2%

SOURCE: *Prospectus,* April 30, 1950, and *Fitch Stock Summary,* July 1, 1950. Computations by the author.

The conclusion that few mutual funds hold appreciable blocks of any company's stock is also indicated by a study of the "Favorite Fifty" stocks held by 100 open-end and 58 closed-end companies. Although the study does not include blocks of stock held for control or a similar purpose and stocks held by less than fifteen companies, it is significant in that it gives some indication of the way in which the largest issues are divided among invest-ment companies as well as indicating the percent of stock held by the entire industry (Table XXVII).

There is a tendency for the influence of the funds in corporate management to grow greater as assets increase, since these increases are not paralleled by corresponding increases in the number of issues in the portfolio. It has been estimated that in the period when investment company assets rose 100%, the number of securities issues held by them rose but 16%.[7] Several random surveys by the author indicated that this estimate is a

---

7. "The Trend to Trusts," *Forbes,* LXIII (June 15, 1949), p. 12.

TABLE XXVII First Ten Stocks in Dollar Value Held by Investment Companies

STOCK	VALUE HELD BY INV. COS. ($MILLION)	NUMBER OF INV. COS. HOLDING	SHARES HELD (THOUSAND)	PERCENT OF OUTSTANDING STOCK HELD
International Paper	43.8	52	826	9.29
Continental Oil	38.9	69	414	8.58
Amerada Petroleum	37.8	24	233	14.80
Gulf Oil	37.5	67	458	4.03
Texas Company	29.1	54	355	2.57
Kennecott Copper	27.2	63	363	3.36
Standard Oil (N.J.)	26.7	58	290	0.96
Goodrich Tire	24.5	43	198	14.95
Standard Oil (Calif.)	23.7	42	258	1.80
General Electric	23.3	68	467	1.62

SOURCE: Aigeltinger & Co.

reliable indication of the true phenomenon. Table XXVIII shows the ten-year increases in assets and issues for three companies, while Table XXIX explores the record of MIT over five-year periods.

The primary reason for the increasing amount of assets invested in a single issue is not the desire for increased influence in corporate policy, but rather a fear of over-diversification; that is, having a greater number of issues than the firm can adequately supervise. The limit the industry seems to set is approximately 150 issues, so as assets increase, the total number of shares from a given issue, rather than the securities of a new issue, will absorb the additional capital. The classic example of

TABLE XXVIII Relation of Increases of Assets to Increases in Issues

	Number of Issues		Total Assets ($millions)		Percentage Increase	
FUND	1940	1949	1940	1949	ISSUES	ASSETS
MIT	136	135	108	278	–½%	160%
Wellington	139	183	6	105	32%	1750%
Dividend	94	113	46	70	20%	52%

SOURCE: Prospectuses figures, author's computations.

TABLE XXIX Relation of Asset Increases to Issue Increases: Massachusetts Investors Trust

			Percentage Increase	
YEAR	TOTAL ASSETS ($MILLIONS)	TOTAL ISSUES	ASSETS	ISSUES
1949	278	135	30%	–5.6%
1945	214	143	98%	5.1%
1940	108	136	64%	27.0%
1935	66	107	230%	–21.0%
1930	20	135	150%	0.7%
1928	8	134		
Increases: 1928–1949			3375%	0.7%

SOURCE: Figures from annual reports and prospectuses, computations by the author.

over-diversification seems to be the Scotch investment company which held over 1,000 different issues, and was obliged to examine some of them no more often than every three months. The American investment companies have never approached this figure, and it is unlikely that they ever will.

The potential influence of the investment company can be clearly seen from an analysis of various funds' holdings in the 200 largest nonfinancial corporations in 1937, the only survey available (Table XXX). While the average fund holding was but 1.1%, the average holding of the largest holders, not including the investment companies, was only 2.3%. It must be indicated, as is obvious, that the corporations were selected, and represented

TABLE XXX   Mutual Funds and Corporate Management

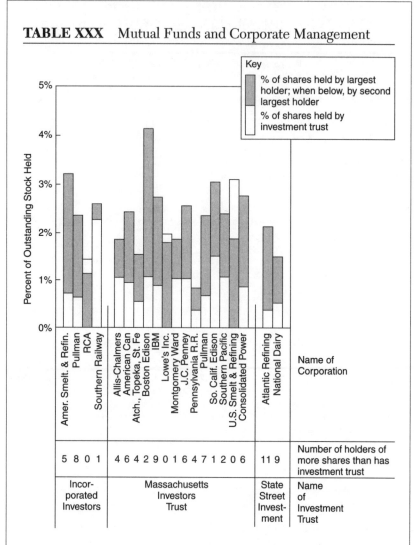

SOURCE: *Survey of Shareholdings in 1710 Corporations with Securities Listed on a National Securities Exchange.* The corporations selected from this book are all of those in which the investment company voting power was significant. The survey was made in 1937.

only those in which the investment company had potential influence by virtue of its large shareholdings.

In spite of their potential influence, the investment company has often been reluctant to manifest criticism of the corporation by voting its share proxies against the management. This widely held opinion takes the view that if the management of the corporation is incapable or the policy misdirected, the shares should be sold, without calling public attention to the investment company's attitude. Although this policy is in many ways advisable, it presents an enigma when a given corporation follows a policy to which the fund management objects, yet continues to pay 10% dividends. It seems incongruous to sell the shares paying the best yield in a given industry merely because they could be yielding more.

However, numerous funds follow the opposite policy, that of keeping the shares while opposing the management. MIT's Griswold has said:

> **Investment companies are . . . in a position to work intelligently with corporate managements on plans for mergers, recapitalizations, and other corporate changes. They can point out objections to such plans and suggest changes necessary to assure fair treatment of all stockholders. As intelligent and unbiased stock holders, investment companies can also come to the defense of business organizations and their managements against unwarranted attacks by others.[8]**

Funds with similar attitudes feel that the responsibility for using stock rights and proxies must be discriminate, and used in what the mutual fund management believes to be the best interests of its shareholders.

Examples of Influence in Corporate Management

Examples of the influence of the investment company in corporate management are scarce, first because it is exerted only in rare cases, and second because the publication or recording of

---

8. Quoted in *Harvard Business Review*, XXVII (November, 1949), p. 740.

the examples is also unique. There are, however, three instances which indicate the diversity of investment company policies toward management, as well as the success with which they have met.

The Montgomery Ward & Co. incident provides an excellent example of the diversity of investment company policy. The dissatisfaction of the investment companies was based largely on their disapproval of the personnel policies of the chairman of the company's board, Sewell Avery. In 1948 and 1949, Avery had caused the resignation or dismissal of five vice-presidents, five directors, and President W. H. Norton. For many years, the business world had made humorous allusion to the "Ward Alumni Association," because the company had lost three presidents, as well as nineteen vice-presidents, since 1931, when Avery became chairman. Due to his dictatorial methods, the board of directors, which was fifteen in August, 1948, numbered only nine in March 1949. The apparent cause of this turnover of top management was authority demanded by Avery, not only in financial matters, his own sphere, but in the spheres of personnel and merchandising. Although the directors limited his power in the latter in May, 1949, they restored it in June of the same year, when many of the resignations took place, due in large part to the enmity of the top-management personnel to Avery's iron hand over all the details of company operation. Two courses were open to the investment companies that disapproved of Avery's policies: they could vote their proxies against the reelection of Avery to the Board at the stockholders meeting in April, or they could dispose of their holdings in Montgomery Ward.

Massachusetts Investors Trust and Wellington Fund took the former course. MIT voted its 104,000 shares (1.6% of the Montgomery Ward common stock outstanding) for three nominees other than Avery, while Wellington voted its 8,000 shares for one of those three nominees. Avery, however, was reelected, getting the most votes of the four unopposed nominees. In 1950, MIT witheld its Ward proxies, rather than voting against the management, in order to show its lack of confidence. Merrill Griswold said that Avery's

... dictatorial methods are bound to be destructive to the morale of the personnel (and that he) would not be surprised if many other stockholders did not send in their proxies.[9]

He hoped that the witholding of enough proxies would make the other directors see the light. Wellington Fund justified its action as follows:

Our purpose in voting against Mr. Avery was to register a strong protest against the exceedingly high turnover of the management personnel . . . We did not expect that our vote which was, of course, not a controlling amount of stock, would remove Mr. Avery from office. We were gratified, however, that our effort along with that of MIT, focused national attention on the Montgomery Ward situation. We believe our votes have had a good effect.[10]

Other funds took an opposed view, however, notably those under Calvin Bullock management, saying that if they had not approved of the present management, they would have liquidated their Montgomery Ward stock. The Bullock group, including Dividend Shares, Nation-Wide Securities, Bullock Fund, Canadian Investment Fund, and Carriers & General Corporation (a closed-end trust), held a total of 24,000 Ward shares at the beginning of 1949. At the annual meeting, these were voted in favor of the management, which subsequently thanked the Bullock firm for its support. However, the vote was not one of confidence, apparently, but rather the fulfillment of the given Bullock policy: the firm either votes for the management or sells the shares. Apparently, they did not approve of Avery's policies, for they did sell their shares shortly afterward, and the five Bullock funds listed no Montgomery Ward holdings whatsoever at the 1949 year-end.[11]

---

9. "Investment Trust Guns Again for Sewell Avery," *Business Week,* April 15, 1950, p. 103.

10. Welch, Joseph E., (Executive Vice-President of Wellington Fund), letter to the author, February 26, 1951.

11. Late in 1950, they are reported to have repurchased Montgomery Ward shares, perhaps either due to management improvement, or at a price low enough to discount the undesirable attributes of the management.

The Curtiss-Wright Corporation's proposed merger with the Atlas Corporation (a closed-end fund) indicated the strength of the open-end investment company in influencing corporate management. On March 18, 1940, the proposal was announced, and its fulfillment was considered a foregone conclusion.[12] The proposed merger, as approved by the directorates of both corporations, would have Atlas transfer $36,500,000 in general market securities to Curtiss-Wright in exchange for the latter's stock, thus giving the aircraft company additional working capital. $25,000,000 of Atlas' assets (the approximate remainder) would be invested in a "special situations" company, with the Atlas shareholders owning a proportional number of shares in both concerns. In addition, measures were proposed by which the capital structures of both corporations would be simplified.

Two investment companies, however, did not approve of the plan. MIT, owner of 21,700 Class A shares, and Supervised Shares,[13] owner of 4,000 (these two amounts represented approximately 2.2% of the Class A stock outstanding), asserted their reasons in a letter to the Curtiss-Wright Corporation on April 15, 1940. They said, in part, ". . . we do not feel that the Board of Directors has acted in the best interests of Curtiss-Wright Corp. and of its stockholders in voting for the merger with the Atlas Corp.,"[14] indicating not only that the Curtiss-Wright Corporation did not need additional permanent financing, but that if it were to issue new securities, present stockholders should have pre-emption on them. They listed specific reasons for their opposition to the merger, the most important of which were:

1. **The company does not need $37,000,000 of additional capital and can finance its operations adequately with its present cash position and earnings.**

---

12. The *Wall St. Journal* headlined "Atlas, Curtiss Merge." CXXVI (March 19, 1940), p. 1.

13. Supervised Shares was at that time under the management of MIT, and has since become the Massachusetts Investors Second Fund.

14. *Moody's Industrials—1939–1940*, XI (April 17, 1940), p. 1245.

2. The Curtiss-Wright Corp. gives securities worth $47,679,796 in exchange for the $37,000,000 of additional capital, a cost of $8,600,000 which is deemed excessive and unwarranted.

3. The Atlas Corp. common stockholders are in effect allowed to purchase Curtiss-Wright common stock at a price of 7½, compared to a market price of 10½. This right, if given any-one, should be given to the Curtiss-Wright stockholders.

4. (6) The Curtiss-Wright common stock capitalization is expanded from 7,429,000 shares to at least 10,418,000 shares and the earnings in the common are diluted.[15]

In addition, the two mutual funds requested that a copy of their resolution be included in the official proxy notice.

On May 10, 1940, the presidents of the two corporations, G. W. Vaughan (Curtiss) and F. B. Odlum (Atlas), announced that the proposed merger would not take place, since it seemed apparent that the requisite two-thirds majority of the holders of the out-standing stock would not support the plan. The two most impor-tant reasons for its abandonment even before the proxies were dispatched to the shareholders were the dissention in the Curtiss-Wright management and the announced objections of MIT and Supervised Shares. The strength of the influence of the two funds is clear in this case: they gave the proposal deserved publicity, which apparently led the directors to believe that the shareholders would disapprove of the plan; in addition, they gave impetus to the dissention in the directorate, which did not exist when the pro-posal was originally presented and passed. L. Sherwin Adams, a trustee of MIT, had told the directors of Curtiss-Wright, "In our opinion, we're the only friends you've got, in opposing this merger," and they later thanked him for his advice.[16]

However, it is not in all cases that mutual fund influence meets with such notable success in dealing with corporate man-

---

15. *Ibid.,* p. 1245.
16. Adams, L. Sherman, telephone conversation with the author, February 27, 1951.

agement. MIT has witheld its proxies from a large oil company, the name of which it did not divulge, for some ten years. The firm maintains an "over-strong" financial position which has led MIT to lose confidence in the prudence of the management. The oil firm has held from $20 million to $38 million in current liquid assets (primarily cash) for a number of years, and in spite of the urging of the Trust has failed to put this money to productive use.[17]

In conclusion, then, although the investment company can never control a corporation, it seems clear that it can exert influence on corporate policy, often in a decisive manner. This influence, quite naturally, should always be in the best interests of the investment company shareholders, and dedicated not toward the special interests of the investment company directorate but rather toward improvement of either the value or the yield of the fund's portfolio.

---

17. This description seems to fit the Mid-Continent Petroleum Corporation. If that is the corporation in question, MIT's shares are over 2% of the total, and cash represents some 25% of total assets. The apparent justification for holding the issue would seem to be the generous return, which approximated 8% in 1949.

Chapter

V

AS A STABILIZING FACTOR ON THE SECURITIES EXCHANGES

 ${A}$ S THE INVESTMENT compa-
nies have an increasingly great value of portfolio securities, their
influence on the securities markets is bound to increase.
Although at this time, their influence is minimal, if their growth
of expansion continues at the present rate, they will of necessity
exert some influence in the future. It is the contention of this
chapter that the potential effect will be a beneficent one that will
contribute not to greater fluctuation, but rather to stabilization.

The economic danger of a widely fluctuating securities market
is in the implications it has for investment. Since prospective yields
on investment are uncertain, the more uncertain is the market the
greater will be the danger of uneconomic investment, and the
greater the chance of loss to the investor, who is said to increase
investment as the rate of interest rises. The very instability of the
market, in fact, is likely to be a deterrent to equity investment.

The primary reasons for fluctuation in the market, according
to Lord Keynes, are four:[1]

1. The increase in equity owned by persons who have no special knowledge of their particular investment has decreased their accurate valuation of such investment.
2. Short-term fluctuation in business activity has an excessive
   influence on the market with respect to its actual importance.

---

1. Keynes, John M., *General Theory of Employment, Interest and Money*, p.
153 *passim*. Paraphrased by the author.

3. The conventional valuation of stocks is based on the mass psychology of a large number of ignorant individuals, so factors entirely independent of the security's prospective yield may change this valuation violently.

4. Even professionals and experts in the securities business cannot offset the mass opinion, so they try to forsee changes in the public valuation.

The market is therefore a ". . . battle of wits to anticipate the basis of conventional valuation a few months hence rather than the prospective yield of an investment over a long term of years."[2]

The peculiar characteristic of the investment companies which can remove this precariousness from the market, or at least alleviate it, is their interest in enterprise—"forecasting the prospective yield of an asset"—rather than speculation—"the activity of forecasting the psychology of the market."[3] They supply the market with a demand for securities that is steady, sophisticated, enlightened, and analytic, a demand that is based essentially on the performance of a corporation rather than the public appraisal of the value of a share, that is, its price. An example of this policy is clearly seen in the case of the American Telephone and Telegraph Company, the traditional "choice of the public" in recent years. This stock was held only in exceptional cases by the mutual funds, and its decline of 15% in the last decade (during which the Dow-Jones Industrial Average rose 33%) in a sense vindicates their policy. The funds, then, in general tend to shift the conventional basis of valuation from short-term appreciation to long-term yield. In fact, investment companies specifically controvert the four bases of fluctuation presented by Keynes:

1. Equity is owned, in an increasing amount, by institutions having specialized knowledge of their investments, which are therefore capable of an accurate valuation of them.

---

2. *Ibid.*, p. 155.
3. *Ibid.*, p. 158.

2. The short-term fluctuations in business activity are apt to influence the market only slightly, since investment companies tend to discount factors such as those when making their initial purchase.

3. The conventional valuation, as pointed out above, is based on yield, not on the psychology of ignorant individuals.

4. As the size of investment companies increases, they may restore a sophisticated demand to the market, trying to forsee changes in corporate policy rather than in individual valuation.

The way in which the investment trusts may offset the interest "in discovering what average opinion expects average opinion (of a share's worth) to be"[4] is by selling shares as the market rises and buying them as it falls. The amplitude of the cycle wave is thus decreased. It is clear that as the value of the portfolio rises, the investment company management may at any time sell issues the value of which appear to have reached their peak. The buying of shares as the market value falls, however, is somewhat more complicated: the company, if it has sufficient "cash position",[5] may utilize this both to reduce the average cost of a particular issue by the additional purchase of shares at lower cost levels, and to buy new issues at "sacrifice" prices. That the investment companies do in fact maintain a sufficient cash position can be clearly seen by figures from random samples of 1949 cash positions of both balanced and common stock funds (Table XXXI).

A particular, specific plan for the sale of securities in the upswing and their purchase in the downswing is the formula timing plan, developed in large part by Keystone Custodian Funds, Inc., of Boston. This plan is based on the movement of the Dow-Jones Industrial Average, which has fluctuated within a normal long-term channel which rose at the rate of something over 3% per year.[6] This channel is divided into seven smaller zones, and as

---

4. *Ibid.*, p. 159.
5. Including readily saleable government bonds as well as cash.
6. This is the approximate rate ascribed to the growth of the economy, also.

TABLE XXXI Cash Positions of Selected Mutual Funds

NAME	TOTAL CASH	% OF TOTAL ASSETS
Balanced Funds		
Am. Business Shs.	$6,300,000	19.4%
Axe-Houghton	$200,000	6.3%
Wellington	$21,000,000	20.5%
Boston	$7,000,000	14.9%
Common Stock Funds		
MIT	$7,700,000	2.8%
Dividend Shares	$6,100,000	8.7%
Inc. Investors	$5,300,000	7.3%
State Street	$18,000,000	26.1%

SOURCE: Recent prospectuses.

the Average moves through them, the investor varies his stock-bond (aggressive-defensive) ratio in the following proportions:

ZONE	DOW-JONES RANGE	% BONDS	% STOCKS
1.	—139	10	90
2.	140–159	20	80
3.	160–183	35	65
4.	184–210	50	50
5.	211–242	65	35
6.	243–277	80	20
7.	278—	90	10

Usually the rebalancing is done quarterly, or at more frequent intervals. Thus, in pessimistic times, when stock prices are low, investment is required, and when prices are high and the market is optimistic, profit-taking is mandatory. Both of these actions shorten the amplitude of market fluctuation. The formula plan was developed by Keystone principally for the use of its investors, who are urged to shift between their common stock and bond funds (at reduced sales loads) as the market fluctuates. However, many other funds use variants of this plan, in most cases more flexible, to determine the composition of their own portfolios. An example of the inflexible type is the First Mutual Trust Fund, which uses the National Formula Plan, based on

Standard & Poor's 365-stock industrial average, evincing a capital growth of 3.73% annually. The Fund rigidly maintains the percentage ratios called for by the particular market level.

The tendency of the funds to buy in a downswing of the market was clearly manifested recently in the Korean Crisis. After the war broke out in June, 1950, the market took its sharpest drop since 1940; the Dow-Jones Average fell 31 points from its high of 228 in June, and $8 billion was erased from the value of shares listed on the New York Stock Exchange.[7] Yet while many individuals were engaged in panic selling, the investment companies were buying hundreds of thousands of shares at prices far below their peaks. During the first week of the downturn, 64 of the open-end companies, with some 95% of the industry's assets, had bought $13,822,000 worth of securities, while selling but $6,228,000 of their holdings.[8] Indications are that this trend continued as the market fell. This illustration is exemplary of the diametrically opposed tendencies of the professional investor and the amateur individual investor.

The fact that the funds tend to stabilize the market is open to the criticism that the market would fluctuate only slightly in any event, since the speculation is limited by SEC supervision and margin requirements. It is certainly true that SEC restrictions on borrowing by members, brokers, and dealers, its prohibition of manipulation of security prices, and its regulation of stop-loss orders and short sales do prevent speculation. It is true, moreover, that the margin requirements imposed by the Federal Reserve Board will limit speculation.[9] However, these requirements, it seems clear, will only prevent a recurrence of the boom-bust monstrosity of 1929–1932, when the Dow-Jones Average fell from 381.17 to 41.22. Despite present requirements, the 1918–1927 decade is closely similar to 1940–1949 with regard to market fluctuation, as seen from only a cursory analysis of the

7. Porter, Sylvia, "Stock Experts Keep Buying," Philadelphia *Inquirer*, July 26, 1950, p. 25.
8. Porter, *op. cit.*, p. 25.
9. The margin was, in fact, raised from 50% to 75% on January 16, 1951, to halt the galloping pace of the highly inflated market.

averages: they varied from 64 to 200 in the former period, and from 93 to 212 in the latter, fluctuating intermittently in a similar manner. Thus, although legal requirements will tend to prevent the great swings of the cycle, the fund type of investment may limit, to a certain extent, the more minor fluctuations.

The present influence of the mutual funds on securities exchanges can be seen from the percentage of its share transactions on the securities exchanges of the economy. To simplify the discussion, the relation of fund purchases and sales to the total volume of sales on the New York Stock Exchange will be considered, since the funds do some 90% of their transactions there and over 85% of the nation's securities transactions are made there. The open-end companies transacted only 2.5% of the total business on the "Big Board" in 1940, but in 1949 this figure had risen to 8.4% (Table XXXII). In 1940, the total assets of the funds were less than 1% of the market value of all shares listed on the New York Stock Exchange, while in 1949, they represented slightly under 3% (see Table XXXII).

As they grow, the funds will certainly increase their importance on the exchanges. With the trend toward sale in rising markets and purchase in falling markets, and valuation in terms of performance rather than speculation, the market should certainly be stabilized. It must be clear, however, that the funds are stabilizing the securities exchanges not through altruistic interest or specific intent, but rather in an indirect fashion through their desire to provide their investors with a reasonable income, since their success in fulfilling their investors' objectives is the life-blood of investment companies. Yield, therefore, must prevail over speculation.

Nevertheless, investment company growth will have to be great before the influence on securities exchanges will be appreciable. In 1929, when total assets of all investment trusts were some 8% of the value of all listed securities on the New York Stock Exchange, the ". . . investment trusts had little to do either with emphasizing or alleviating the market break."[10] At this time,

---

10. Thomas, Walter F., *The Investment Trusts and the Market Break*, p. 23.

TABLE XXXII   Fund Transactions on the New York Stock Exchange

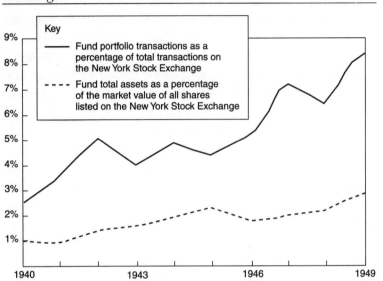

Key

——— Fund portfolio transactions as a percentage of total transactions on the New York Stock Exchange

- - - - Fund total assets as a percentage of the market value of all shares listed on the New York Stock Exchange

SOURCES: Figures from *Economic Almanac* and National Association of Investment Companies; computation by author.

the ratio of investment company assets to total value of listed securities is only one-half of the 1929 figure.

There have been several claims that the funds influence the market in an adverse way. Three principal arguments along this line are as follows: that by removing a large number of shares from market "circulation," the funds have caused small transactions to have large effects on prices; that a run on redemptions of fund shares will cause the market to collapse when portfolio securities are necessarily redeemed; and that the funds will cause the market to fall when they sell large blocks of their holdings of particular securities as a part of their normal transactions.

The first argument is the so-called "thinness" argument; e.g., that the market is made thinner by the fact that the trusts take stocks out of it. One of its advocates is Leslie Gould, financial editor of the New York *Journal-American,* who claims that the market is such that the sale of 300 shares of a security could cause its market price to drop three points.[11] He sees the fund purchases of seasoned shares rather than untried issues as drying up the market, and tending to destroy its function of liquidity, since the individual buyer or seller will by his own demand or supply change the price of the very security in which he deals. This argument, on careful analysis, is seen to be fallacious, because the funds do not remove the shares from the market, but rather are continually buying and selling them. In truth, the turnover of their portfolio shares is greater than that of securities listed on the New York Stock Exchange: total *combined* purchases and sales by the funds (excluding purchases representing investment of new capital) as a percentage of year-end portfolio values are 41%, whereas the ratio of the dollar volume of transactions to the year-end market value of shares listed on the Stock Exchange is only 17%. These percentages are averages of the past nine years (see Table XXXIII), during which the Exchange has considerably slackened its turnover, said to be 119% in 1929.[12]

The fact that the turnover is consistently higher for investment companies than for the Exchange as a whole means that the funds are not thinning the market, but—if anything—requiring a greater volume of transactions to cause a given price change.

A run on fund redemptions is unlikely to occur, and has in fact seen redemptions exceed sales in quarterly periods only in very rare cases.[13] However, it is argued that, if such occurs, the investment company would have to "dump" a portion of its large volume of portfolio securities on the market, thereby causing a decline, or accentuating one already extant. Again, this argument is based on feeble ground. The funds do not have to sell portfolio securities, in the first place, for they are permitted to borrow to meet redemptions so long as their asset coverage is

---

11. Gould, Leslie, "Investment Trusts as Market 'Thinners,' " *Commercial and Financial Chronicle*, CLXX (September 1, 1949), p. 851.

12. Mindell, *op. cit.*, p. 79.

13. *Cf. supra*, p. 375.

TABLE XXXIII   Turnover of Mutual
Fund Portfolios and New York Stock
Exchange Shares

YEAR	FUNDS	NYSE
1949	42%	12%
1948	41%	15%
1947	35%	14%
1946	55%	21%
1945	42%	24%
1944	41%	17%
1943	47%	20%
1942	41%	10%
1941	31%	13%

SOURCE: National Association of Investment
Companies figures and *Economic Almanac-
1950*, p. 83. All computations by the author.

greater than 300% of the loan. Secondly, if their redemptions are
in the midst of a general market collapse, they are allowed, if the
SEC declares an emergency, to halt redemptions during such
emergency. And thirdly, the power of their distribution networks
has been sufficient, in the past, to sell enough new shares to offset even the highest volume of redemptions.

The final argument is one that claims the funds will exercise
an unstabilizing influence on the securities markets since their
normal sales and purchases of shares will reach such ponderous
proportions as to cause great fluctuations on the market. As yet,
this has positively not proved to be the case. When the portfolio
lot is of such size that its transaction on the floor will bring inadequate bids or offerings, the investment company uses a "secondary offering" procedure, in which large blocks of stock are
traded off-the-board at special commissions to brokers, much in
the manner of an underwriting. Transactions of this nature were
but 4% of total portfolio transactions in 1948.[14] Massachusetts
Investors Trust has only used this method six times in recent
years, and, according to its Chairman, Merrill Griswold, all of its

---

14. Figures by the National Association of Investment Companies.

stock save one or two minor exceptions could be liquidated at a price close to current market value. In addition to the secondary offering procedure, an issue may be slowly liquidated by selling small units at intervals through different brokers.

Evidence, therefore, indicates that the investment company must stabilize rather than unstabilize the market, as its assets approach a size such that influence on it is appreciable. Once this magnitude is reached, it will militate against Lord Keynes' dismal and socialistic conclusions, in which "a substantial government transfer tax on all transactions . . ." is introduced ". . . to [mitigate] the predominance of speculation over enterprise,"[15] and the "State, which is in a position to calculate the marginal efficiency of capital goods on long views and on the basis of general social advantage . . ." assumes ". . . an even greater responsibility for directly organizing investment."[16] The investment companies will never control the market, since their tendencies are frequently counteracting one another; they will, however, keep the market dynamic by their portfolio turnover, as they base their supply of and demand for shares on enterprise, not speculation. Continuance of their present rate of growth will mean, in short, that enterprise in investment will cease to be ". . . a mere bubble in a whirlpool of speculation."[17]

---

15. Keynes, *op. cit.*, p. 160.
16. *Ibid.*, p. 164.
17. *Ibid.*, p. 159.

CONCLUSION

As ... the principles of diversification on which these (investment) companies operate is a sound one, the only probable causes for loss of public confidence would be gross mismanagement or, more likely ... , misunderstanding on the part of the public as to the nature of equity investment as such, and consequent expectation of miracles from investment company management.[1]

THE TREMENDOUS growth potentiality of the investment company, in conclusion, rests on its ability to serve the needs of both individual and institutional investors. It can do this best by stating its objectives explicitly, so that a minimum of investor misconception as to the fundamentals of equity will exist. The investment company industry must prepare for its next hurdle, which is likely to come from a serious decline in the securities market, by making it clear that its shares are not panaceas for all the ills of investment. That the market will fluctuate is certain, and merely because it has experienced a general upward trend in the decade of the investment company's greatest growth may have made many investors fail to realize that the share value, like the market, is liable to decline.

To further serve the interests of investors, and thereby increase its own size, the investment company may institute new types of shares in the future. There is need for a venture

---

1. Richardson, Dorsey, *Address before National Association of Securities Administrators,* October 9, 1950, p. 6. (mimeo.)

capital fund, as well as funds composed of tax-exempt securities, funds with the securities of industries in given geographic areas, and special investment companies to serve the specific needs of pension and trust funds by placing a higher percentage of government and corporate bonds in the portfolio. Aside from serving investors by increasing the breadth of its activities, the investment company must continue to serve them as it has in the past, with management operating in the most efficient, honest, and economical way possible. By this high-grade operation, the investment companies in the future can sell their shares to the non-investors of the present, thereby increasing the percentage of securities holders above the 8% of the population which hold them today. The investment company has grown up to now by concentrating its sales power on the prospering stratum of the economy; perhaps its future growth can be maximized by concentration on a reduction of sales loads and management fees.

The fact that the investment company may serve economic roles other than providing advantages to the investor should in no way be construed to imply that that is not the function around which all others are satellite. It seems clear that through investment in equity capital, through influence on corporate management, and through stabilizing the securities exchanges, the mutual funds are serving to the fullest advantage of their shareholders. If other roles arise in the future, they must be cautiously analyzed, and discarded if they interfere in any way with the interests of the investors. As it was stated in the *Harvard Law Review:*

> **It is important to bear in mind that the principal function of investment companies . . . is the management of their investment portfolios. Everything else is incidental to the performance of this function.**[2]

---

2. Motley, Warren, *et al.,* "Federal Regulation of Investment Companies since 1940," *Harvard Law Review,* LXIII (July, 1950), p. 1142.

Mutual funds, then, are not designed to replace bonds, the banks, and insurance companies, but rather to supplement their stability with a more adequate income. The investment company can realize its optimum economic role by the exercise of its dual function: to contribute to the growth of the economy, and to enable individual as well as institutional investors to have a share in this growth.

❀

f i n i s

❀

BIBLIOGRAPHY

Books

Conference Board, *Economic Almanac for 1950* (New York: The National Industrial Conference Board, 1950). 663 p.

Economic Statistics Bureau, *The Handbook of Basic Economic Statistics: 1950 Edition* (Volume IV, number I) (Washington: Economic Statistics Bureau, 1950). 246 p.

Educational Conference on Investment Companies (Boston: Vance, Sanders & Co., 1945). 76 p.

Fainsod, Merle, and Lincoln Gordon, *Government and American Economy* (New York: W. W. Norton & Co., 1941), pp. 400–460.

Flynn, John T., *Investment Trusts Gone Wrong!* (New York: New Republic, Inc., 1930). 276 p.

Fowler, John F. Jr., *American Investment Trusts* (New York: Harper & Bros., 1928). 415 p.

Goldsmith, Raymond W., and Rexford C. Parmelee, *The Distribution of Ownership in the 200 Largest Nonfinancial Corporations* (Temporary National Economic Committee Monograph No. 29) (Washington: Government Printing Office, 1940). 1557 p.

Granby, Helene, *Survey of Shareholdings in 1710 Corporations with Securities Listed on a National Securities Exchange* (Washington: Government Printing Office, 1941). 258 p.

Harwood, Edward C., and Robert L. Blair, *Investment Trusts and Funds from the Investor's Point of View* (Cambridge: The Hampshire Press, Inc., 1940). 102 p.

Investment Trusts and Investment Companies: Hearings S 3580, (Parts 1–4) (Washington: Government Printing Office, 1940). 1131 p.

Kaplan, Abraham D. H., *Small Business: Its Place and Problems* (New York: McGraw-Hill Book Co., 1948). 279 p.

445

Keynes, John M., *General Theory of Employment, Interest and Money* (New York: Harcourt, Brace & Co, 1935). 403 p.

Lipsett, Alexander S., *Labor's Partnership in Industrial Enterprise* (New York: Floyd L. Carlisle, Inc., 1950). 19 p.

Porter, John S. (Editor-in-Chief), *Moody's Manual of Investments, 1950: Investment Trusts et al,* (New York: Moody's Investors Service, 1950). 1528 p.

Porter, John S. (Editor-in-chief), *Moody's Manual of Investments, 1950: Industrial Securities* (New York: Moody's Investors Service, 1950). 3016 p.

Securities and Exchange Commission, *Investment Trusts and Investment Companies* (Washington: Government Printing Office). Part 1. 158 p. (1939) Part 2. 937 p. (1940) Part 3. 2804 p. (1941) Parts 4 & 5. 384 p. (1942).

Stevenson, Alec B., *Investment Company Shares* (New York: Fiduciary Publishers, Inc., 1947). 52 p.

Stevenson, Alec B., "Investment Trusts and Investment Companies," *Fundamentals of Investment Banking* (New York: Prentice Hall, Inc., 1949), pp. 698–732.

Subcommittee on Investment of Joint Committee on Economic Report, *Volume and Stability of Private Investment* (Washington: Government Printing Office, 1950). 32 p.

United States Bureau of the Census, *Historical Statistics of the United States: 1789–1945* (Washington: Government Printing Office, 1949). 353 p.

United States Bureau of the Census, *Statistical Abstract of the United States: 1950* (71st Edition) (Washington: Government Printing Office, 1950). 1040 p.

Wiesenberger, Arthur, *Investment Companies—1950* (New York: Arthur Wiesenberger & Co., 1950). 336 p.

Senior Theses

(Submitted to the Princeton University Department of Economics and Social Institutions in partial fulfillment of the requirements for the A. B. degree.)

Adams, Edmund M., *Investment Company Act of 1940* (1946).

Ashmun, John B., *Investment Trust and Investment Company Development* (1945).

Thomas, Walter F., *Investment Trusts and the Market Break* (1931).

Periodicals

Barron's

Bleiberg, Robert M., "New Kind of Company Finances Venture," XXIX (February 21, 1949), p. 5.

Johnston, Paul A., "Investors' Own Standards Key to Mutual Fund Choice," XXXI (January 1, 1951), p. 17.

Sulzbach, Dr. Walter, "Decline of Equity Finance," XXX (March 20, 1950), p. 9.

Business Week

"Investment Dilemma," July 11, 1936, p. 47

"Taxes Oust Investment Trust," November 28, 1936, p. 22.

"Regulated Trusts," November 9, 1940, pp. 53–55.

"Gauging Investment Trusts," July 16, 1949, pp. 70–71.

"Trust Sales," February 18, 1950, pp. 96–98.

"N. Y. State Trust Law," March 11, 1950, p. 111.

"Are Stockholders Necessary?" March 18, 1950, p. 118–121.

"Investment Trust Guns Again for Sewell Avery," April 15, 1950, p. 103.

"How Did Trusts Make Out," July 29, 1950, p. 52.

"Trusts Adjust to Semiwar," September 16, 1950, p. 115.

Commercial and Financial Chronicle

Dalenz, John McG., "Investment in Mutual Funds," CLXXIII (February 15, 1951), p. 725.

Gould, Leslie, "Mutual Funds as Market 'Thinners,' " CLXX (September 1, 1949), p. 851.

Troutman, William V., "Open-end Investment Funds," CLXVI (October 30, 1947), p. 1749.

Wiesenberger, Arthur, "The Far-Reaching Implications of the Investment Company Idea," CLXIX (February 17, 1949), p. 767.

Whitehead, Louis H., "Economic Role of the Investment Company," CLXIX (March 10, 1949), p. 1077.

Fortune

"Big Money in Boston," XL (December, 1949), pp. 116–121.

Mindell, Joseph, "Wall St. Doesn't Sell Stocks," XL (April, 1949), pp. 79–80.

Trusts and Estates

Axe, Emerson W., "Record of Equity Investment for Trust and Pension Funds," LXXXIX (August, 1950), pp. 508–510.

Ayer, Hazen H., "Protect Purchasing Power," LXXXIX (April, 1950), pp. 258–259.

Cates, Dudley F., "Pensions and Mutual Fund Investment," LXXXIX (May, 1950), pp. 329–330.

Kurtz, Cornelius, "Field for Pension Plans," LXXXIX (April, 1950), pp. 266–268.

Long, Henry A., "Canadian Investment Companies," LXXXIX (September, 1950), pp. 590–591.

Long, Henry A., "Mutual Funds Mature," LXXXIX (September, 1950), pp. 606–607.

Murray, Roger F., "Common Stocks in Trusts," LXXXIX (December, 1950), pp. 829–830.

Putney, William B., "Mutual Funds Make Small Trusts Possible," LXXXIX (December, 1950), pp. 836–840.

Stevenson, Alec B., "Investment Company Shares," LXXXIX (April, 1950), pp. 228–230.

United States Investor

"Investment Company Shares for Trustees," LIX (February 7, 1948), p. 216.

"Investment Trusts for Trustees," LX (April 23, 1949), p. 664.

"Investment Trusts for Savings Banks," LX (May 28, 1949), p. 1053.

"Investment Companies as 'Legals,' " LX (June 4, 1949), p. 1068.

"Investment Companies," LX (June 25, 1949), p. 1278.

"Investment Shares," LX (September 1, 1949), p. 1680.

"The Case of Investment Trusts," LX (November 5, 1949), p. 2230.

"The Case of Investment Companies," LX (December 3, 1949), p. 2485.

Miscellaneous

Cabot, Paul C., "The Investment Trust," *Atlantic Monthly,* CXLIII (March, 1929), pp. 401–408.

Carter, William D., "Mutual Investment Funds," *Harvard Business Review,* XXVII (November, 1949), pp. 715–740.

Gaston, Frank, "Investment Companies, a Neglected Source of Equity Capital," *Conference Board Business Record,* VI (November-December, 1949), pp. 458–462.

"How to Keep a Buck," *Time,* LIV (July 11, 1949), pp. 84–86.

Motley, Warren, Charles Jackson Jr., and John Barnard Jr., "Federal Regulation of Investment Companies Since 1940," *Harvard Law Review,* LXIII (July, 1950), pp. 1134–1156.

Ruml, Beardsley, "The Little Capitalists Get Together," *Colliers*, CXXV (January 21, 1950), pp. 26–27.

Slichter, Sumner H., "Enterprise in Post-War America," *National Association of Investment Companies Membership Forum* (January 25, 1943), pp. 9–24.

"The Trend to Trusts," *Forbes*, LXIII (June 15, 1949), pp. 11–13.

INDEX

455

About the Author

John C. Bogle is the founder and former chief executive of The Vanguard Group, the world's largest no-load mutual fund company, with more than $500 billion in assets owned by 12 million shareholders. In 1999, *Fortune* named Mr. Bogle one of the four financial giants of the 20th century, and Princeton University, his alma mater, awarded him its coveted Woodrow Wilson Award. His first book, *Bogle on Mutual Funds*, has sold over a quarter-million copies in hardcover and paperback.